Annual Review
of
Political Science

VOLUME 2

Edited by

SAMUEL LONG
Empire State Poll

ABLEX PUBLISHING CORPORATION
NORWOOD, NEW JERSEY

JAI
A7
vol 2

Printed in the United States of America.

ISBN: 0-89391-401-0

ISSN: 0748-8599

Ablex Publishing Corporation
355 Chestnut Street
Norwood, New Jersey 07648

Contents

Introduction

The primary objective of the ANNUAL REVIEW OF POLITICAL SCIENCE is to provide comprehensive literature reviews which assess major empirical and theoretical advances in political science, written by experts in the various subdivisions of the discipline. The authors included in this volume of the series have amply met this goal.

The ANNUAL REVIEW OF POLITICAL SCIENCE is prepared with two types of readers in mind. The first, generally familiar with a specific subject area, wishes to remain up-to-date by reading of new developments in the field. The second, unfamiliar with a specific subject area, wishes a general overview and suggested topics which might be pursued in greater depth elsewhere. The authors of the chapters which follow should satisfy both types of readers.

The next volume of the ANNUAL REVIEW OF POLITICAL SCIENCE will be comprised of chapters written by the following authors:

Richard Boris. Empirical Political Theory.
Carole Barner-Barry. Political Psychology.
William Gore. Administrative Behavior.
Douglas Lackey. Ethics and Logic of Nuclear Deterrence.
Stuart Nagel. Public Policy Analysis.
Richard Pious. The Presidency.
Roland Pennock. Normative Democratic Theory.
Herbert Reid. The Decline of Liberal Political Theory.
Leroy Rieselbach. Legislative Behavior.
Harmon Zeigler. Comparative Interest Group Behavior.

I thank the authors of this volume for their cooperation and patience.

Our editorial board, composed of Karl Deutsch, Seymour Martin Lipset, and Nelson Polsby, provided great encouragement and support.

The Empire State Poll furnished financial backing for this enterprise.

Samuel Long
Empire State Poll
New York City
March 1987

Economic Socialization*

Barrie G. Stacey

Department of Psychology, University of Canterbury
Christchurch, New Zealand

I. INTRODUCTION

This chapter surveys the field of economic socialization. The research and the theoretical contributions pertaining to economic socialization will be covered, with an emphasis upon the current state of the field. No attempt will be made to provide an exhaustive bibliography. Unpublished material will be largely ignored. But little selectivity is involved, as most published studies will feature in the survey. The work directly related to race or ethnic socialization and to occupational socialization will not be reviewed. Both of these topics have substantial literatures of their own. The authors of these literatures have not been concerned with the findings from published research on economic socialization.

One striking aspect of the literature on economic socialization is an emphasis by empirical researchers on preadult socialization; an emphasis that does not stem from the view that significant socialization experiences occur only in early life. Such researchers have been particularly concerned with money, possessions, property, income, consumer behavior, inequality, social differentiation, and related economic matters from a developmental per-

*I should like to thank Ken Strongman (Canterbury University) for helpful comments on every section of this review. Comments on various sections of the review by Roger Katz (University of the Pacific) and Cynthia Stohl (Purdue University) are gratefully acknowledged. A correspondence with Paul Webley (Exeter University) also proved helpful.

spective. They have also been concerned with the processes and agents of economic socialization. The recent trend in the social sciences stressing an approach to socialization that covers the entire life span does not apply to the study of economic socialization, where the emphasis has been upon childhood and early adolescence. Yet it is obvious that individuals cannot prepare fully in the preadult years for their economic lives as adults, including the predictable responsibilities and strains of life-cycle and family changes, in a world economic system undergoing radical technological, demographic, economic, and other changes.

Economic socialization has not been clearly demarcated as a field of study. It has been variously described as socialization into the business life of society, economics, economic relations, the economic system, and the economic life of society. It has also been described as the deliberate inculcation of economic information, values, attitudes, and practices to foster acceptance of the prevailing economic order by dominant classes or forces, that is, largely a process of massive indoctrination. But in general, economic socialization appears usually to be regarded as all the economic aspects of socialization whether productive of conventionality, unconventionality, deviancy, or rebellion. Socialization refers to the developmental processes, at every stage of the life cycle, whereby each person acquires the knowledge, skills, values, attitudes, and dispositions that enable her or him to function as a more or less effective, though not inevitably compliant, member of society. Adult socialization refers to socialization occurring after the completion of school education.

Economic socialization is not an established, well-explored field of study comparable to political socialization. The books and review papers dealing with "political socialization" are not matched by equivalent publications dealing with "economic socialization" though, of course, these features of human development and life are not separate and distinct. The social scientists who have argued that preadult political socialization is an important source of stability in the American and a number of other political systems have not been concerned with the economic aspects of socialization (Cummings & Taebel, 1978; Niemi & Sobieszek, 1977; Stacey, 1978). Miliband (1969) criticized much of the discussion of political socialization because it does not take account of the operation of the economic system and the socializing influence of powerful economic forces in society. He emphasized the economic features of "the process of legitimation" in Western capitalist nations; that is, the legitimation of the capitalist social order. Presumably the same emphasis would be warranted for socialization in socialist and Islamic nations. Miliband's criticism holds substantially to the present day, though political and economic themes have been intermingled or examined in some socialization studies (e.g., Connell, 1977; Cummings & Taebel, 1978;

Furth, 1978; Jahoda & Wordenbagch, 1982a; Stacey, 1978; Stern & Searing, 1976; Torney, Oppenheim & Farnen, 1975).

The origins of work on economic socialization are diverse. Throughout the century a number of theorists have posited an instinct of acquisition in a variety of forms, most recently sociobiological forms. The notion of innate determinants of acquisitiveness has long been attractive to some people, including some social scientists. Many economists assume that a desire to acquire, to possess, to gain privately, to have and to hold possessions, is an inherent human trait. During this century acquisitive and possessive behaviors have been observed by specialists as features of child development, and sometimes explained by instinctual drives. James, Freud, Isaacs, and Fromm, for example, considered acquisitiveness in childhood in their work (Loewental, 1976; Monte, 1977). Psychoanalysts have argued that acquiring, taking, collecting, possessive, hoarding types of behavior in young and old stem from the experiences of early childhood. They have also argued that acquisition and possession are means of coping with anxiety and personal problems, adapting to social demands, satisfying power and status needs, and controlling relations between people. The usual criticisms leveled at psychoanalytic work have been leveled at these arguments. Beaglehole (1932) critically analyzed a great deal of biological, psychological, and anthropological material dealing with property, possessiveness, and human nature. He rejected any instinctual explanation of acquisitiveness.

In the post-1945 period, empirical and experimental studies of economic socialization among the young were occasionally published, with the rate of publication increasing in the late 1970s (e.g., Danziger, 1958; Furnham, 1982; Miller & Horn, 1955; Moessinger, 1975; Strauss, 1952; Sutton, 1962; Winocur & Siegal, 1982). In the 1970s a number of sizeable empirical research projects were initiated. Lita Furby carried out a series of investigations dealing with possessions, their function and meaning throughout the life cycle, with an emphasis upon the preadult years (Furby, 1976, 1978a, 1978b, 1978c, 1979, 1980a, 1980b). Hans Furth explored the development of children's understanding of society, emphasizing the role of money in this development (Furth, Baur, & Smith, 1976; Furth, 1978; Furth, 1980). Gustav Jahoda explored the construction of economic reality by children, including the development of ideas about economic institutions (Jahoda, 1979, 1981, 1983a; Jahoda & Woerdenbagch, 1982b). Earlier he had studied the childhood development of the perception of social differences (Jahoda, 1959). Anna Berti and Anna Bombi conducted a series of investigations dealing with Italian children's ideas about money, the circulation of manufactured goods, banking, and the means of production and their owners (Berti, 1981; Berti & Bombi, 1981; Berti, Bombi, & Lis, 1982). A major cross-national study of the political education of young people dealt with their perceptions of welfare agencies, labor or trade unions, large business organizations and some economic issues (Torney et al., 1975).

Much of the theoretical stimulation for these empirical and experimental studies came from the cognitive-developmental, structuralist theory of Jean Piaget, though Piaget was much more concerned with the young person's construction of the physical than the social world (Piaget, 1972; Piaget, 1974). He emphasized the individual's own activity in her or his construction of knowledge about the world, and the dynamic relationship between the individual and the external world. Cognition grows out of behavior and involves a set of structures that are periodically reconstructed as the individual continuously interacts with her or his world. For Piaget, the development of intelligence involves changes in the content and modes of reasoning through an invariant sequence of stages, each stage reflecting an underlying structure of thought which determines reactions to situations, events and problems.

Berger and Luckmann's (1967) phenomenological analysis of the social construction of reality was another theoretical influence on researchers. In their account of "primary socialization," they treat the child as a relatively passive organism adapting to the world, though they refer to the interplay between subjective human actions and society as objective reality. This part of their analysis has been relatively uninfluential, probably because of its speculative nature and the impact of Piaget's theory, which is based upon an enormous amount of empirical and experimental research. But their emphasis upon the social construction of reality has been influential. This applies particularly to the reproduction of everyday social knowledge in each new generation: an essential part of upbringing and education or, more generally, of socialization. Such everyday knowledge takes in economic concepts, perceptions, meanings, practices, skills, rules, law, values, and legitimations. At the very lowest level of socialization every person needs to be able to handle personal finance and to live within the rules and legal limits of society. Berger and Luckmann's (1967) analysis requires that the language, perceptions, actions, and interpretations of the layperson, child, adolescent, or adult, be taken seriously. This requirement does not sit easily with those who believe attention should be focused on the laws, theoretical axioms, models, and methods of economists or the realities constructed by social scientists and intellectuals.

Marxists and American neo-Marxists have presented descriptive accounts of economic socialization, being particularly concerned with the ideological legitimacy of the capitalist social order and the practical needs of the capitalist class. They have stressed the hegemony exercised by this class in capitalist society, including the transmission of its ideas to the subordinate classes (Connell, 1977; Miliband, 1969; Sarup, 1978). Miliband (1969) argues that the capitalist system by its very existence, must socialize persons within dominant and subordinate classes alike to the conditions of the system. Economic and political socialization is generated by the operation of the economy as a natural mode of production, and is enhanced by other agents of socialization including the family, educational system, mass media, churches and religion, political parties, and state. In a polemical work, Bowles and Gintis (1976) assert that there is a direct correspondence between the social relations of production and the social relations of education. The public or state educational system is basically a means of training the young in the interest of producing a docile adult population subordinate to the capitalist class, subordinate occupationally, economically, and politically. Levin (1974) and Rosenblum (1975) deal with education and socialization in a similar way. Connell (1977) described the Australian ruling class, the pattern of hegemony in Australia, and the development of class consciousness among young Australians. Cummings and Taebel (1978) reported a modest survey of American school pupils to test the neo-Marxist argument "that economic socialization functions primarily as a mechanism not only to legitimate the corporate order but also the general structure of inequality in American life" (p. 200).

Two other areas of research have produced information about economic socialization: first, developmental studies dealing with class, status, and social differences, and second, consumer socialization, with the former being of importance and the latter of modest significance to the present time. Stern and Searing (1976) reported an empirical study of the stratification beliefs of English and American adolescents and examined adolescent uses of stratification beliefs and knowledge. The perception of social differences and inequalities by children and adolescents was reviewed from two different perspectives by Stacey (1978, 1982). The consumer socialization of infants, children, and adolescents has generated a certain amount of research, discussion, and contention. The main concern of researchers has been the selling of products to the young, including the role of mass marketing and advertising (e.g., Churchill & Moschis, 1979; Moore & Moschis, 1983; Stephens & Stutts, 1982; Ward, Wackman, & Wartella, 1977). There has also been some interest in the consumer education of the young (e.g., Langrehr, 1979; Stampfl, Moschis, & Lawton, 1978). Kassarjian (1982) has provided a short review of consumer socialization in his account of consumer psychology. Roberts and Bachen (1981) briefly reviewed research dealing with the reactions of the young to advertising. Stampfl (1978) presented a descriptive account of the consumer life cycle.

The research pertaining to economic socialization will be examined in the following sections of this review, including the research referred to in the introduction. Money, personal possessions, consumer socialization, and economic inequalities will be dealt with. Developmental trends in the preadult years will be summarized. Adult economic socialization will be briefly discussed. More psychological detail on money, possessions, social differentiation and inequality, and socioeconomic understanding can be found in

Stacey (1982). But to begin with, the major theoretical approaches to economic socialization will be briefly discussed.

II. THEORETICAL APPROACHES

The theoretical approaches to economic socialization are varied and not too far advanced. While theoretical matters are dealt with explicitly in some publications, in others they are presented incidentally or implicitly. Theoretical treatment of economic socialization (or some feature of it) may be subsidiary to another concern: for example, the legitimation of the state and social order, the contribution of ruling class hegemony to the maintenance of the political and economic system, the development of class consciousness, or cognitive socialization. There is substantial theoretical variation in conceptions of what constitutes economic reality, economic socialization, the socializee's contribution to the process, the causal factors considered to be of greatest importance, and the role of ideology in the process.

The background to some of the theoretical discussion and research about economic socialization has been provided by Berger and Luckmann's (1967) analysis of knowledge in everyday life within the context of a view of society as a dialectic process between objective and subjective reality (see, e.g., Burris, 1982; Furth, 1978; Jahoda, 1979; Loewental, 1976; Sarup, 1978; Stacey, 1982; Taylor, 1982). In their discussion of society as subjective reality, Berger and Luckmann outline a speculative general account of the internalization of reality that is clearly inadequate for their purposes, that does not attempt to come to terms with the body of developmental research findings available to them.

The major theoretical work of Bowles and Gintis (1976) has made a marked impact. From their Marxist perspective, and emphasizing experiences within the family and educational system that legitimate the social relations of production and prepare the young to be future workers on the various levels of the occupational hierarchy, they describe the processes through which the young develop ideas about, and are initiated into, economic life. However, the book has been criticized because of oversimplification, empirical weakness, lapses into excessively mechanical causal reasoning, and lack of realism (Gintis & Bowles, 1980; Heyns, 1978; Sarup, 1978; Taylor, 1982). Recently, the radical constructivist approach advocated by Furth (1978, 1980) has begun to influence researchers (Berti & Bombi, 1981; Furnham, 1982; Hong Kwang & Stacey, 1981; Jahoda, 1981; Stacey, 1982; Winocur & Siegal, 1982).

In the constructivist approach to development, the individual, over time, constructs successive versions of the political, economic, and social world—representations that are more like models or blueprints than copies. The individual may encounter, or offer, views of economic reality in words, pictures, logical propositions, play, dreams, or other forms. Representations of reality that strike people as being "right" are those that seem to reflect significant aspects of their own experience. Their constructs of the world continue to change, no version or reality being inevitably entrenched. Furth (1978) argues that the growth of societal understanding is best conceptualized as a continuing process of the individual constructing, exploring, and testing theories and practices in connection with personal experiences. He regards childhood socialization not primarily as the impact of the political, economic, and social system on the child, but as the child's construction of her or his political, economic, and social world. He defines what is constructed and developed within the child as the form or framework and what is provided from the outside world as particular content. Further, he emphasizes an understanding of money and its functions in society as a prerequisite to mature social development. Furth's radical constructivism is the most important development of Piaget's theory with reference to economic socialization.

There are many versions of economic reality, reflecting different political, economic, and religious outlooks, potentially available to children, adolescents, and adults. The ways in which people come to understand, to reason about, and to behave in their economic world are determined in part by political, economic, and social forces; their immediate situation; economic constraints; and culture. Children, adolescents, and adults alike must generate strategies for coping with a changing economic situation of great complexity, having many conflicting interests and numerous constraining features (Bronfenbrenner, 1979; Coles, 1977; Rockwell & Elder, 1982). Different views are held by social scientists about the nature of economic reality, and where scientific explanations of economic reality, including its comprehension by social scientists, are to be found. However, three views or positions are particularly important: (a) the positivist or absolutist; (b) the phenomenological or relativist; and (c) the Marxist. All three positions are evident in theoretical writing about economic socialization.

In the positivist or absolutist position, it is assumed that economic reality is located "out there," with its own independent, objective character divorced from the mass of people with their personal concepts, notions and interpretations of economic reality. The forces of the economic world are seen to be acting continuously on the individual from the environment, making the individual what he or she is. In the phenomenological or relativist position, economic reality is whatever is constructed as a result of human experiences and practices; largely through language, awareness, interpretation, and effort in search of meaning. Obviously, economic reality is socially constructed because of the various ways in which people conceive of their economic world, its institutions, and their own and other people's economic activities. The objective appearance of economic reality, it absolute quality, is merely indicative of human interpretation, intention, and activity, as people invest the world with meanings. The Marxist position is that economic reality is an outcome of the activities engaged in by people, particularly productive and creative activities. Knowledge of economic reality is mediated through the construction of concepts one uses to think about it, concepts which often reflect only limited aspects of reality. In this position there is a sharp distinction between actual or objective economic relations (of which people are often fully or partly unconscious) and those surface relationships of the economic order that people observe. Economic relations tend to generate a smoke-screen of misleading appearances: they are seen to be relations between things not people.

It is assumed in positivist theory that the individual is shaped or molded by what is imposed upon her or him during the formative years; that is, an individual is made social in a rather predictable way by society, through its institutions and members, including parents and teachers. Thus the active role of the child, adolescent, and young adult in her or his own socialization, with its potential for autonomous development, is played down. Youthful ability to resist and subvert would-be molders and controllers of the young is ignored. Behaviorism is a major expression of positivist theory in the study of human development, but it has not been significant in the study of economic socialization, probably in part because of the powerful influence of Piaget's theory. However, theorists of varying complexion who insist upon the massive socializing pressure of the political, economic, and social order tend to emphasize a passive, amenable model of the young in their work, and to end with an oversocialized adult. This applies to Marxists as well as to other theorists, and is particularly evident in Bowles and Gintis (1976). The issue of the socializee's contribution to socialization is of significance to the contentious debate over several hegemony or dominant ideology theses (see, e.g., Berger & Luckmann, 1967; Chamberlain, 1983; Connell, 1977; Kluegel & Smith, 1981; Rootes, 1981; Sarup, 1978). This debate is concerned with matters such as political cohesion and stability, the ideological instrumentalism of the ruling class or dominant classes, their need for legitimacy, the socialization of the working class into the dominant view of reality (false consciousness), and the political containment of the working class.

Phenomenological theorists suggest that one of the persistent problems of the older adult sections of society is their need to win the allegiance of the young to their versions of the politcal, economic, and social reality in order to ensure that their "world," which gives meaning to their lives, survives in future generations. They also suggest that the versions of reality constructed by the young cannot be exactly those of older generations, and that they may differ considerably. Phenomenologists emphasize the cognitive activity of the young in constructing their reality, with data being supplied by the senses and language the means of construction. Berger and Luckmann (1967) asserted that identity, society, and reality are crystallized in the young with the internalization of language. It is held by phenomenologists that individuals and social groups construct their reality and make sense of it partly through ongoing negotiations with others in the family, neighborhood, school, and so on, in a particular culture that is actualized in social relationships with dominant schemes of description and interpretation being used by most people. Phenomenologists tend not to be concerned with the material bases of reality (Frank, 1979; Sarup, 1978). Political, economic, and social reality is equated with what is commonly taken as valid of society, which in practice tends to be the status quo. Esland (1973) claimed that "the apparent absoluteness and objectivity which we impute to the world is one of the most pervasive features of human existence" (p. 9). Phenomenologists have been criticized for being excessively mentalistic, too given to intellectual relativism, too concerned with the subjective, and underestimating the significance of ideology in their work.

Marxists give far more weight to the material bases of society and culture in their treatment of ontogenetic development. Materialist psychology, Luria (1976) wrote, "assumes that human action changes the environment so that mental life is a product of continually new activities manifest in social practice," (p. 9). It is through activity (including language learning, object and tool use, play and study) that a young person's consciousness is formed. Language is central to development, not only in relating activity to thought, but in rendering thought conventionally logical and in creating new meanings and interpretations of reality which react back onto language. Through language, the individual appropriates other people's experience, including their economic experience, in a generalized form. At the same time, individuals and social groups do not necessarily accept passively the personal, cultural and political, economic, and social influences acting upon them. Rather, some influences are embraced or accepted, the pressures of others are modified either deliberately or unconsciously, and some are resisted or rebelled against. Thus, through the mediation of social relations and societal institutions, consciousness and behavior are affected by the economic order. Yet through human activity, consciousness makes some impact on the external circumstances that are acting upon it. As Baumrind (1978) states, "Humans are not mere products of circumstances and upbringing but develop as a result of their own activity and in contending with their circumstances" (p. 62).

Marxists stress the importance of dominant ideology and linguistic stereotypes in the transmission of class-based assumptions about political and economic realities to young and old alike. What unifies diverse, even contradictory, dominant ideas and themes, for Marxists, is a belief in the sanctity of capitalist property and an apparently nonclass view of life and society. But economic changes, difficulties, conflicts, and crises lead to the development of language and ideology encapsulating working class interests (and possibilities) and challenging the interests of the ruling class. Marxist arguments about dominant ideology or hegemony have been subjected to empirical and theoretical criticism (see e.g., Chamberlain, 1983; Rootes, 1981). Marxists have also been criticized for giving too much stress to the significance of economic factors in their treatment of socialization. Further it is recognized that there is a functionalist undercurrent to some Marxist analyses at least (Gintis & Bowles, 1980; Sarup, 1978).

Furby (1978c, 1980a) has presented a motivational–developmental theory of possession in the Western capitalist type of society. Her central concerns are the meaning (or subjective nature) of possessions and the motivational determinants of possession among people of different age. Other concerns are, first, the personal functions of possessions at various stages of the life cycle, and second, people's views about and judgments of the unequal distribution of possessions. In this theory there is an emphasis upon the following as important variables in acquisitive and possessive behavior: (a) the owner's use, and right to control use, of her or his possessions; (b) positive affect for what is possessed; (c) the relationship of possessions to the owner's ability to produce effects in the environment, that is, to experience causal efficacy and personal control (effectance motivation). In formulating her theory, Furby draws upon concepts and ideas presented in other theories, including psychoanalysis. This is the most significant, if indirect, use of psychoanalysis in the study of economic socialization. To date, Furby's theory has had little impact. However, it could be extended to connect possessions-related behavior directly to political behavior from a life-span perspective. It could also prove useful with reference to some of the issues in the debate over economic well-being and political behavior (Feldman, 1982).

III. MONEY

One feature of economic socialization, namely money, has received a fair amount of attention from researchers with reference to the preadult years. Studies have been explicitly focused on money and its sources, buying and selling, riches, poverty, debt, payment for work, prices, banking, and economic relations (for example, Berti & Bombi, 1981; Burris, 1982; Fox, 1978; Furnham, 1982; Furth, 1980; Hong Kwang & Stacey, 1981; Jahoda, 1981; Marshall & Magruder, 1960; Miller & Horn, 1955). Researchers have employed observation, interviewing, the questionnaire, role playing, and the experiment to obtain developmental data about money. Piaget's structuralism has become the main theoretical influence on researchers, with functionalism and phenomenology being other evident theoretical influences. Given that Marx argued the need for money is the true need produced by the capitalist system, it is surprising that Marxists have had very little to say about money from a developmental perspective. Research results have been highly consistent across researchers in different countries, but not totally consistent across cultures (Jahoda, 1983b; Ng, 1982). Ng (1982) has presented limited evidence that the rate of economic development is unusually fast among young Chinese in Hong Kong; and interpreted it as reflecting the impact of Hong Kong's socioeconomic conditions.

Young children completely lack monetary understanding. Around 4 to 6 years, children associate money with buying and become interested in economic settings such as shops and stores. At a simple level, they gain experience of economic activities, including buying, owning, bartering, and giving, and they make some use of economic themes in their play. They have a providential view of life and believe money comes from various sources; for example, shops, banks, "just having it," rich people, the Queen (in Britain), and God. Between 6 and 8 years, monetary concepts are grasped and the purchasing power of money becomes appreciated. Between 7 and 9, most children begin to comprehend the numerical value of money and the impersonal monetary aspects of vendor–purchaser transactions. The idea of easy adult access to money starts to decay, and paid employment is likely to be seen as a source of money as well as government, welfare or social service agencies, and banks. Between 8 and 11 children recognize that money is needed to buy goods, but they are confused about the links between producer and seller. By later childhood, 9 to 12 years, the young have developed a none-too-coherent, rudimentary representation of economic life, which includes notions of cheating and dishonesty. They are able to connect isolated economic events, and to create simple systems of economic ideas, with (a) producing, selling, buying, and money, and (b) work, bosses, employees, and money being important systems. Some achieve the concept of profit and become aware of profit motivation, a necessary but not sufficient condition for understanding bank operations (Jahoda, 1981; Ng, 1982, 1983).

Children of 12 and 13 have a more sophisticated understanding of money and monetary transactions in which personal financial activities and impersonal economic practices, rules, and customs are separated. They recognize differences in earnings due to training and talent, see the existence of constraints on economic choices, and understand the meaning of payment for results in employment. At 14 and 15 years, teenagers can give near-adult conventional explanations of economic behavior and events. They have integrated much information into a more coherent and more complex representation of economic life that includes a variety of economic actors — owners, bosses and managers, workers, the unemployed, criminals, and others. They are aware of their own family's position in the social structure and have formed definite views about economic inequalities. In general, the early- to mid-teens do not appear to be an age of economic radicalism. However, economic hardship or disaster in the family may promote radicalism. Further, children in poor and oppressed social groups can become aware of poverty, discrimination, and group conflict at an early age (Coles, 1977; Niemi & Sobieszek, 1977; Stacey, 1978).

Children and teenagers have direct experience of money and its use in shops, stores, school, entertainment, recreation, and holiday places. In commercial settings that are publicly visible, the young also observe people at work and gain knowledge of work roles and activities. The same applies to certain government services. The young have some direct experience of the use of money at school, and there they also observe teaching and nonteaching staff at work. They will almost certainly encounter fund-raising at school and in the local community. Marshall and Magruder (1960) explored the relationships between parental money education practices and children's knowledge and use of money among 7 to 12-year-old Americans. They found that children's knowledge of money is directly related, first, to the extent of their experience with money and its use and, second, to parental effectiveness in handling the family income. Miller and Horn (1955) investigated the reactions of over 1000 American children and teenagers to 20 actual court cases of debt. They found that though the young believe, on the whole, there is a moral obligation to pay debts, about one-third of their judgments did not coincide with those of the courts. They also found boys to be more sympathetic to debtors than girls, and the young in the lower socio-economic strata to be more sympathetic than those in the higher strata.

Initially, at the beginnings of awareness, children are confused with regard to work and employment, ownership, and management; the occupational hierarchy; and the payment of staff in shops, schools, buses, and other workplaces. But by 7 or 8 most realize employment is a source of money, that people work for money, and then realize quickly that some work is paid and some is not paid. The basis of the wage system is comprehended during the 6 to 10 age period. By 10 to 13 years, children can differentiate ownership from management of a concern, and describe a line of command from owner to manager to worker. In later childhood, the young develop ideas about an occupational scale or hierarchy, economic stratification beyond a simple rich–poor dichotomy, and a political order or hierarchy with bosses and subordinates (Berti, 1981; Berti et al., 1982; Connell, 1977; Stacey, 1978).

The bank is largely remote from the direct experience of most youngsters, as well as being complex and impersonal in its economic activities. But they are aware of the bank from an early age, partly as a result of the presentation of banks, banking, and bank robberies on television (Connell, 1977; Furth, 1980; Jahoda, 1981; Jahoda & Woerdenbagch, 1982b; Ng, 1982; Sutton, 1962). Further, the incomplete conceptual separation of the personal sphere (in which interpersonal economic transactions are carried out) and societal sphere (wherein impersonal economic activities occur) constitutes a source of difficulty for young persons who try to understand economic matters including banking, finance and credit. Many children see the bank not as a trading enterprise, but as a form of public service which helps people with their money problems. The cognitive tasks involved in the development of thinking about banking and finance include apprehending that the bank employs money deposited and does not just keep it safe, making sense of the concept of interest, resolving the imbalance between personal versus market economic relationships, realizing that the bank operates so as to make a profit, and resolving the uncertainties, problems, and conflicts encountered in coming to understand the working of the bank and other financial concerns. It appears that a majority of 13- to 16-year-olds have a rather low level of financial knowledge and financial reasoning ability. It also appears that the rate of development of the manual working-class young tends to lag behind that of the young higher in the social structure. We do not know whether a spurt in the development of financial capacity occurs in early adulthood, or whether many people grow up to be citizens whose skills in personal finance and understanding of financial institutions remain severely limited.

The research findings of Berti and Bombi (1981), Burris (1982), Furth (1978, 1980), and Hong Kwang and Stacey (1981), among others, indicate that there are some general cognitive trends in the preadult development of thinking about money and economic matters. These are (a) a shift from confusing socioeconomic and natural phenomena to differentiating them; (b) the decline of childish realism based upon perception of the immediate external aspects of things (for example, the size of a coin or the authority of a uniform or a bank keeping safe the actual money deposited) and therewith the growing recognition of conventionality and social norms in economic matters; (c) the moderation of tendencies to project personal characteristics onto society; (d) the progressive understanding of individual and role differences; (3) declining reliance on rules, orders, imperatives, and coercion and increasing use of internalized principles, conventions, norms, and notions of mutual agreement and mutual benefit in interpreting economic behavior; and (f) a shift from conceiving the economic world in narrow individualistic terms to awareness of the complexities of economic life involving government, taxes, economic institutions, and policy issues. It appears that these developments tend to occur relatively slowly among the working-class young.

The research findings concerning money support interpretations of economic socialization as a dynamic process of interaction between the individual and society, wherein the young person actively engages in a constructive process rather than just passively absorbing what is communicated by older generations. The findings show, first, incremental growth in knowledge with age and, second, the existence of qualitative stages in the development of a youngster's representations of money and economic life. Successive transformations advance the young person toward adult levels of functioning and improve the economic skills of that person. There exists considerable variation in economic development among the young in any age category. Evidence of class differences in economic socialization suggests that external socioeconomic conditions can have a significant impact, as does Ng's (1982) cross-cultural evidence from Hong Kong and Jahoda's (1983b) evidence from Africa. To date, sex differences have not been shown to be of particular significance.

IV. PERSONAL POSSESSIONS

Private ownership is obviously of enormous importance in society, including individual ownership and collective ownership within the family. Personal possessions, their acquisition and use, are involved in a great deal of activity throughout life. Abundance of money and possessions, including income-producing possessions, is of crucial importance to the lives of the very rich and their offspring (Coles, 1977; Stacey, 1978). But it has been argued from a number of perspectives that possessions and possessiveness play an important role in ontogenetic development in all social strata (Furby, 1978c, 1980a; Loewental, 1976; Stacey, 1982). If this is so, it may well be relevant to the debate on economic self-interest and political behavior (Feldman, 1982).

Babies, infants, and children are provided with food, toys, and other objects. It has been suggested that the infant's experience with such items is the starting point for socialization of acquisition and possession (Fox, 1978; Furby, 1980a; Loewental, 1976; Stacey, 1982; Stampfl et al., 1978). Psychoanalysts emphasize the relationship between food and possession in this socialization. Infants learn and express possessive relations early in their language development. They are deliberately taught the distinctions between their possessions and those of others, and rules of behavior relating to possessions. They are also taught not to damage or destroy possessions. The young gain direct experience of receiving, sharing, giving, lending, buying, bartering, and the settling of disputes. Quite early in life they become aware of the use of possessions in interpersonal relations, with control being a prominent feature of their use. They hear proverbs, tales, and stories in which there are references to money and possessions. They observe the acquisition and use of possessions frequently portrayed in the mass media and are constantly exposed to advertisements promoting the acquisition of possessions. Misbehavior with possessions may lead to criticism, ridicule, or punishment. This probably encourages a greater involvement by children with their own possessions, with what they control as "mine". Burris's (1982) study suggests a stage progression in the child's understanding of property rights from modes of reasoning based exclusively on externally imposed imperatives to modes which reflect a greater degree of empathy and reciprocity, culminating in awareness of "universalistic principles which define the rights of property as a coherent system of obligations and expectations" (p. 317).

Behaviorists regard the young as being molded by society via the rearing and educational practices of parents, teachers, and others, who through rewards and punishments reinforce particular beliefs, values, attitudes, and behaviors relating to acquisition and possession. Socialization takes place through the interaction of the person and the various individual and institutional socializing agents. Child and adult alike are continuously presented with models of acquisition, ownership and possessive behavior by people in their immediate environment and by people presented in the mass media, including celebrities of all kinds. Models of salience to young observers will stimulate some observational learning and imitation. Behaviorists argue for the importance of the active acquisition of possessions (and the possibilities it creates); that is, the importance of the strength of aquisitive behavior and its relation to contingencies of reinforcement.

Functionalists treat socialization as operating to promote considerable uniformity among different classes and races in their conceptions of possession and of the nature of the class system. The functions served by such uniformity are to encourage the stability of the socioeconomic system and to justify for members of society the unequal distribution of incomes and possessions. This justification may be linked to the notion that the way to progress is to make the economy more productive, hence providing more possessions to distribute.

In a series of studies Furby explored the socialization of possession among small samples of Americans and Israelis whose ages ranged from 5 to 50 years (Furby, 1978c, 1979, 1980a, 1980b). She was concerned with the nature of possession throughout the life span in Western societies. She reported some age-specific and developmental findings, and also presented a theoretical formulation about the origins and functions of possession which would be valid in the differing circumstances to be found in various countries. Socialization of possession, for Furby, is a very important feature of political socialization in countries where the purpose of government is to protect private property and the capitalist social order.

Furby (1980a) suggests that the origins of possessive behavior "are not very dependent upon particular experiences, but rather are the result of universal motivational characteristics of young children in interaction with equally universal structural characteristics of their surrounding environments" (p. 39). She argues that the possible universal desire to experience causal efficacy leads to the individual to attempt to control objects and people and to produce effects in the environment, from infancy onwards. It is not possessions or quantity of possessions as such, but rather personal efficacy in the environment that is the critical factor; hence possessions that can

be used to attain efficacy are the important ones. Active acquisition of possessions increases an individual's sense of competence and decreases her or
his dependence on others. It also represents elements of causal efficacy and
control within the environment. Further, Furby argues that since a person's
concept of self is partially defined by that which he or she controls, possessions are a constituent of the self concept and are experienced as an extension
of the self. Given that certain possessions are widely valued in society, then
the status of an individual is enhanced by such possessions. They can generate joy, pleasure, pride, and other positive affects in their owner. They can
imply, proclaim or be used to demonstrate their owner's accomplishment,
status or power. In brief, Furby's theoretical formulation asserts that command over certain possessions makes for causal efficacy within (and control
over aspects of) the environment, status, power, and positive affect for possessions, while allowing for positive self-evaluation and public esteem. Her
formulation could easily be related to a variety of self-interest and collective-
interest hypotheses and theories in politics.

Coles (1977) has described the socialization of those born into rich, important American families. These financially privileged youngsters grow up sur-
rounded by abundant property, money, and other possessions. They learn
how to accept, to hold on to, and use massive family resources; to appreciate
that they have much and will have more; to take for granted enormous inequalities, injustice, poverty, and discrimination; to be highly self-conscious,
family-conscious, and class-conscious; to become sensitive to political and
economic perils to the rich. They develop great expectations of what is in
store for them and their kind, with their lives so different from the lives of ordinary people. Their families value privacy and live in seclusion, yet regularly
travel world wide. These youngsters have to learn how to deal with family
employees of varying occupational status and other people of lower social
status, including their educators. Politeness, grace, good manners, and correct behavior are of great importance to them in daily life and, at times, symbols of class power. Before high school, according to Coles, these youngsters
"get to appreciate who has what power and why in their family domain"
(p. 533). Parental power in the family domain is visibly in line with parental
power outside that domain. In this social milieu, news about parents, relatives, friends, and neighbors is encountered in the mass media by the young.

In coming to terms, however adequately or inadequately, with money,
ownership, possessions, property rights, and so on, the young person is confronting the distribution of economic power in her or his society, with its sex-
ual, racial, and other characteristics. The economic concepts, beliefs, values,
and attitudes developed by the young are of political significance, not least to
the rich and powerful. These economic entitites can become the means of apprehending the political, economic, and social world. For Western nations,
the scattered empirical evidence suggests that, during the teen years, the

young in general become more positively oriented towards private ownership and economic inequality. During the same period, commitment to personal concerns, goals and well-being tends to intensify among the young. It is possible that the private acquisition of possessions, or an ever-increasing quantity of possessions, is widely believed to be an effective way of pursuing such private interests. Furby's formulation would imply that merely acquiring possessions without increasing ability to produce effects in the environment may not improve personal well-being, or may even be associated with a deterioration of well-being. On the basis of limited survey evidence, Cummings and Taebel (1978) suggested that teenage Americans typically see socialism and communism as being in direct opposition to personal success and fulfilment. Connell (1977) stresses the political importance of the young learning a prudential respect for authority and private property. He argues that a crucial feature of the defense of capitalism is the prevention of widespread adoption of an oppositional world-view and alternative values. The multinational study of civic education indicates that evaluation of large business organizations tends to become more negative during the high school years in Western countries, including the United States (Torney et al., 1975).

Possessions are significant to family relations (and family life), peer relations, other interpersonal and social relations, and many features of human development. By the mid-teens, young people are aware of the highly favorable evaluation of expensive possessions, property, and riches in society at large. During the advance in comprehension of property rights with age, the young come to link these rights with the rationality of the economic system and its attendant economic stratification. Before adulthood is reached, the young are clearly aware of money and possessions as the basis for varying styles of life and as instruments for exerting influence and control (even dominance) in human affairs. They associate power, and the distribution of power between social groups, with economic factors. They relate income and possessions to occupational status and property ownership. Finally, they are establishing connections between money, possessions, the occupational hierarchy, class system, and party politics.

V. CONSUMER SOCIALIZATION

As currently used, the term consumer socialization refers to the acquisition by children and adolescents of consumer related knowledge, beliefs, values, attitudes, and behaviors. Consumer education is part of the larger process of consumer socialization. The generally accepted aims of consumer education are the promotion of consumer knowledge and skills, including the ability to appraise sales promotion devices, among the young. It is sometimes maintained that "successful" consumer education will reduce the need for consumer protection agencies and the regulation of business in the market place, because "educated" consumers will be able to deal with the market themselves. It is commonly assumed that preadult consumer socialization is of great importance in shaping adult consumer behavior (Churchill & Moschis, 1979; Langrehr, 1979; Mayer & Belk, 1982; Moore & Moschis, 1983; Stampfl et al., 1978). Moore and Moschis (1983) posit the anticipatory socialization of adult consumer values, attitudes, information, skills, and roles during the preadult years and draw a parallel with the description of anticipatory political socialization by Hess and Torney (1967). The main theoretical influences on consumer socialization research have been the cognitive developmental and behaviorist (social learning) theories.

To date, the study of consumer socialization has been dominated by Americans with a background in marketing, advertising, and business. They have been primarily concerned with children and adolescents as (a) consumers who spend money and aquire possessions in their own right; (b) family members who exert some influence on family consumer expenditure; (c) segments of the total population in the economy; and (d) future adult consumers whose development can be influenced by commercial forces, particularly advertising. They have produced a fragmented body of information, primarily relevant to the selling of products and services. Television advertising has been a topic of particular interest to those researchers, and a subject of controversy.

Concern has been growing among advertisers and their critics over the influence of television advertising on the young and on family relationships, though this concern arises from different reasons (Churchill & Moschis, 1979; Gunter, 1981; Kassarjian, 1982; Peck, 1979; Stephens & Stutts, 1982). In the ensuing ferment, arguments about the extent to which commercial interests should be allowed to exploit the kindergarten, primary school, and adolescent markets and to influence the development of the young, have been prominent. Sexism, racism, and ageism in television advertising are contentious issues that have been related to these arguments.

The responses of the young to television advertisements have been studied by a variety of research techniques (Gunter, 1981; Kassarjian, 1982; Peck, 1979; Roberts & Bachen, 1981; Stephens & Stutts, 1982). Research has shown that purposive viewing begins as early as 2 or 3 years. The amount of viewing generally increases during childhood and declines somewhat during the teens. American youngsters are likely to see more than 20,000 television advertisements every year. The ability to understand the presentation, nature, and purpose of advertising, as distinct from adjacent program material, is not acquired until late childhood or adolescence. Among infants and children there is much confusion of advertising and program material, and of celebrities who appear in advertisements and programs. According to some media analysts, this gives advertisers an unfair advantage over the young. The empirical evidence indicates that children and adolescents are influenced as consumers by advertising, and that advertising tends to foster positive attitudes towards advertised products. Though trust in advertising declines with increasing age during the school years, advertising has an impact on teenagers (Churchill & Moschis, 1979; Moore & Moschis, 1983). Television advertising is a force for consumer materialism in society and repeatedly promotes claims that problems and troubles can be easily dealt with by the purchase of household goods, pills, cosmetics, tranquilizers, and so forth. However, factors such as parental influences, cognitive ability, education, socioeconomic status, and peer influences, mediate the responses of the young to advertising.

The varied evidence available shows that consumer socialization begins in the preschool period and, in terms of conventional notions of consumer behavior, proceeds rapidly during childhood and adolescence. Money; posessions; the concept of price, buying and selling; consumer information, attitudes, and stereotypes are fundamental to this process. On the basis of American and British research, Mayer and Belk (1982) conclude "before even leaving elementary school, children have largely learned the consumer stereotypes used by adults" (p. 316).

It appears that purposive training in consumer skills occurs infrequently in the family and school classroom (Churchill & Moschis, 1979; Fox, 1978; Moore & Moschis, 1983; Moschis & Moore, 1978; Ward et al., 1977). The young acquire most of their consumer information and skills informally, partly by drawing upon experiences with parents, peers, and the mass media. Parents discuss with their offspring various facets of consumption and advertisements presented by the mass media, and they may attempt to communicate notions of "good" money management, consumer purchasing, use of credit, and planning for future needs. Their own consumer behavior is observed by offspring, and some of their own decisions or actions may be discussed within the family. Parents provide their young with opportunities for consumption by giving them money. However, simply giving the young money does not lead to greater consumer competence, rather it is the range of experiences with money that counts. Undoubtedly, there is great variation in the skills of personal finance and consumer behavior taught or conveyed to the young. By the time children enter school they have had direct experience, at a simple level, of a wide variety of consumer activities (Fox, 1978; Stampfl, 1978). This experience is increased during the school years, yet consumer education typically does not improve the competence of those so educated (Fox, 1978; Langrehr, 1979). Some primary school children are forced by circumstances to begin developing economic survival skills. Advancing age during the teen years relates positively to strength of consumer materialism, that is to an orientation stressing acquisition of money and possessions for personal happiness. It has been suggested that the mass media directly influence acquisition of the expressive or conspicuous aspects of consumption by teenagers; aspects that provide the means for teenagers to express personal characteristics and status (Churchill & Moschis, 1979; Moore & Moschis, 1983).

Theoretical speculations and research findings point to a positive relationship between socioeconomic status and consumer skills acquisition (Churchill & Moschis, 1979; Coles, 1977; Mayer & Belk, 1982; Moschis & Moore, 1978; Moore & Moschis, 1983; Ward et al., 1977). Acquisition of consumer skills and consumption stereotypes tends to be more rapid, particularly for males, among the young in the higher social strata; where there is a relatively strong emphasis on money, possessions, and social status. The young in higher, as compared with middle and lower, income families tend to have a wider range of experiences with money, including the saving and possibly investment of money. Their parents use more sources of information in consumer decision making, and are more likely to monitor their children's consumer activities in order to steer them towards appropriate social values and norms. During adolescence, the young in the higher strata are more likely to use reality-oriented rather than fantasy-oriented consumer material in the mass media. Social differences in economic self-defense, against those who wish to exploit others or against the problems wrought by economic change, have not been studied in the developmental context. It has been argued that the upper or ruling class partially inhibits radicalism in the working class by encouraging its adolescents and adult members to consume goods that merely symbolize achievement, attractiveness, and status, while plunging many of them into debt because they use commercial loans to purchase the goods (Connell, 1977; Mayer & Belk, 1982). Motor vehicles are especially important here, and so are mass entertainment products, clothes and fashions, sex-appeal products, and certain household goods. This argument is in accord with Furby's (1978c) theoretical formulation which links acquisition, possession, the production of effects in the environment and personal well-being.

VI. ECONOMIC INEQUALITIES

Developmental studies dealing with class, stratification, occupational status, social differences, and poverty have produced information about the perception, understanding, and experience of economic inequalities in the preadult years (e.g., Baxter 1976; Furnham, 1982; Gurney, 1981; Stacey, 1982; Stern & Searing, 1976). Some studies have dealt specifically with socioeconomic inequalities (Baldus & Tribe, 1978; Furby, 1979; Jahoda, 1959; Leahy, 1981, 1983; Siegal, 1981; Stacey, 1978; Winocur & Siegal, 1982). Though investigators have relied heavily upon the interview and the questionnaire to obtain information, observational and quasi-experimental studies have also been reported. Such experimental work has shown that children, particularly young children, are aware of socioeconomic differences and ine-qualities they may not be able to express in words but can indicate non-verbally, which is a limitation on verbal communication not appreciated by some investigators. All the major theoretical approaches to economic sociali-zation are evident in these developmental studies dealing directly or indirectly with economic inequalities.

By the time children are 3 to 6 years old, they can understand that people are located in different social groups or categories: for example, according to race, sex, language, religion (e.g., Northern Ireland). As early as 5 or 6 chil-dren can perceive socioeconomic differences associated with housing or ac-commodation, residential area, cars and clothes. During the primary school period, children's understanding of socioeconomic differences and inequali-ties develops rapidly. At the same time, they come to accept the inequalities of occupational status and income, and the conventional reasons used to le-gitimate them (Baxter, 1976; Connell, 1977; Jahoda, 1959; Lauer, 1974; Simmons & Rosenberg, 1971; Stacey, 1978). By early adolescence, the occu-pational perceptions of the young are very similar to those of adults. Dra-matic contrasts of money and possessions are important in the socioeco-nomic thinking of children from 5 to 8; for example, contrasts between wealth and poverty, large fashionable residence and slum, bright new car and old shabby car, riches and rags. Between 8 and 12 children learn a good deal about the concrete economic details of the social structure and occupational hierarchy. They are able to perceive socioeconomic differences in their own community and in the wider society, and to comprehend that some sorts of people do not interact on equal terms with others. In the early- and mid-teens, information and notions about education, employment, income, pos-sessions, and life styles are integrated to form the types of ideas, beliefs, and images found among adults.

Investigators have consistently reported a marked change in beliefs, atti-tudes, and feelings about economic inequalities, about rich and poor people, and about the distribution of incomes and possessions during childhood and adolescence (Baldus & Tribe, 1978; Connell, 1977; Cummings & Taebel, 1978; Furby, 1979; Leahy, 1981; Siegal, 1981; Stacey, 1982; Winocur & Siegal, 1983). These investigators have worked in several countries, using various research techniques, drawing upon samples whose ages cover the pe-riod from 4/5 to 18 years. Their studies show that young children (say 8 and under) tend to take economic inequalities, when they are recognized, for granted. Of all age groups, they are most likely to regard observable inequali-ties as unfortunate, and to be sympathethic to the poor. By contrast, 16- to 18-year-olds predominantly believe that economic inequalities in general are justified, and that people are responsible for their own economic position. Some hold with the functionalist principle that inequality motivates people to work and compete, which, in turn, benefits society. Siegal's small-scale studies suggest that concern for the economic needs of families declines with age (Siegal, 1981; Winocur & Siegal, 1983). As they get older, young people offer an increasing number of explanations for social inequalities, with perceptions of the skill and effort involved in different occupations becoming increasingly important and the most common justification for a positive evaluation of inequality. It appears that during the teen years economic outcome becomes a more important determinant of economic judgment. This possibly contributes to the conventional view — that economic reward should be appropriate to occupational effort — often carrying the implication that economic reward is proportionate to effort. Referring to the beliefs of American and British adolescents, Stern and Searing (1976) use the phrase "individual effort reaps its reward, or at least . . . those rewarded deserve their gains" (p. 197). They were surprised to find over a third of their American adolescent subjects favoring the "economic leveling" of wealth, but this may have been partly the result of using a vague abstract question in their survey (which produced an unusual result out of accord with other published findings).

Developmental studies of beliefs about the rich and poor consistently show a prevailing positive view of the rich and negative view of the poor, with an accompanying tendency to credit the rich and blame the poor (Baldus & Tribe, 1978; Furth, Baur, & Smith, 1976; Coles, 1977; Connell, 1977; Furby, 1979; Furnham, 1982; Leahy, 1981; Stern & Searing, 1976). The individualistic view that rich and poor alike receive their just deserts is less widely accepted in the lower than the higher socioeconomic strata. Older children and teenagers in the lower strata more frequently attribute poverty and unemployment to the economic system, the government, employer policies, and other nonindividualistic factors. From early childhood, with increasing age there is an increasing tendency for the young to conceive rich and poor people as not only differing in their economic characteristics, but also as being very different kinds of people. Rich people are typically described by children and teenagers in attractive physical, personality, and behavioral terms, with their money and possessions contributing to their attractiveness. Poor people, however, are described in terms of unattractive appearance, personality flaws, and behavioral deficits including laziness, poor work performance, and lack of money management skills.

A general developmental trend, which is marked during the second decade of life, is for the young to become less sympathetic towards the poor with increasing age and to come to believe in the legitimacy of extremes in economic inequality as natural in society. This trend is most intense in the higher socioeconomic strata and least intense in the lower strata. Coles (1977) has shown that American "children of privilege" have to learn to renounce their compassion for those less fortunate than the rich, their sense of unfairness in life, their curiosity about injustice and its origins, and their interest in the lives of their socioeconomic inferiors. They have to become incurious about many inequalities and to accept the inevitability of extreme inequalities. Very often, domestic employees serve as object lessons for the teaching of ideas about race, class, and inequality. Coles (1977) states that in "some privileged homes the children learn the specifics of race and class more explicitly and pointedly than any other American children do" (p. 533).

Developmental studies of class and stratification have produced further information about the young and socioeconomic inequalities (Connell, 1977; Stern & Searing, 1976; Stacey, 1978). During childhood and adolescence, working-class youngsters tend to lag behind those in the higher strata in the development of class and stratification awareness. The young who are economically most disadvantaged are less aware of the characteristics of the social structure than their counterparts who are economically better placed. The more personally ambitious among teenagers tend to be more aware of class and stratification phenomena. But for most young people outside the upper socioeconomic strata, class does not seem to be a salient criterion for defining or judging the self. Older children and teenagers display a definite tendency to place themselves somewhat higher in the social structure than their family situation warrants. This tendency to upward self-placement results in many working-class youngsters assigning themselves to the middle class. Teenagers in the lower socioeconomic strata display surprisingly little feeling of being seriously deprived, and tend to be unrealistically optimistic about their own futures while being aware of socioeconomic differences in life chances. Teenagers in the higher strata tend to be most supportive of existing class divisions in society. Connell (1977) asserts that money is the most important agency of socialization to class relations and that money "in a property-based economic order takes on the character of a thing, independent of men and women and capable of controlling them" (p. 187). Stern and Searing (1976) argue that detailed stratification knowledge serves three functions for adolescents. It can help adolescents to: (a) locate themselves and others in the social order, (b) interpret and evaluate the social order, and (c) cope with personal problems. Their data suggest that adolescent upward mobility aspirations intensify alertness to stratification.

These developmental studies of class and stratification have produced evidence that not all is economic acceptance and acquiescence among the young, especially teenagers. The young are vulnerable to feelings of discomfort and unease, even of inferiority, in the presence of people from different socioeconomic backgrounds. They readily perceive segregation, snobbery, and privilege and may react against any of them. The peer groups they create are usually socioeconomically homogeneous groups. Investigators have reported the young expressing critical, radical, and intensely anticapitalist beliefs, attitudes, and preferences, and antibourgeois sentiments, and economic ideas, and ideological notions that compete with orthodox capitalist ones. They have also reported behavioral radicalism: for example, cooperative work organizations, communal living, and countercultural activities. Coles (1977) found some questioning of the economic status quo among the members of his sample of privileged youth. Stern and Searing (1976) draw a parallel between declining support for political institutions during adolescence and the growth of dissatisfaction with the stratification system during adolescence. One could also draw a parallel between the abstract economic and abstract political radicalism of middle-class teenagers (Stern & Searing, 1976; Stacey, 1978). However, in the various samples that have featured in these studies, criticism of and dissatisfaction with capitalism and economic inequality in general has appeared with far less frequency than satisfaction with or acceptance of prevailing economic arrangements. Further, outside the upper socioeconomic strata there is an exceedingly marked tendency for older children and teenagers not to have strong feelings about class, not to develop a sense of common class interests, and not to believe themselves and their families caught up in any kind of class conflict. Referring to Australia, Connell (1977) stated that the young "develop a detailed interpretation of class without a firm consciousness of class membership" (p. 150).

Awareness of the behavioral correlates of socioeconomic position develops in later childhood and adolescence. Teenagers come to relate party politics to social stratification (Connell, 1977; Stacey, 1978). In Britain, most high-school students can relate occupational status to voting behavior, and by age 15 they are aware that trade unions are associated with the Labour Party and private business with the Conservative Party. Similar relationships are comprehended by the young in Australia, and probably many other countries. However, teenage awareness of relationships between occupational status, class, and party politics does not mean there is awareness of the interplay between economic interests and party politics, particularly in the working class. Nor does it mean the beginnings of an economic polarization among the young (being generated by class differences in their experience of economic and political life). The party preferences of teenagers tend to be weak, and there is a large potential for malleability in their views of politics and political parties (Stacey, 1978). There is probably considerable potential for malleability in their views of economic matters, class, and stratification. The quantity and kind of material conveyed by the mass media to children and adolescents, the heavy use of the mass media by the young, the role of peer groups, and youthful reactions to economic and political events will influence how the young emerge as adult actors.

VII. PREADULT ECONOMIC SOCIALIZATION

It appears that the origins of economic socialization lie in early possessive behavior, language development, differentiation of self from others, and the development of self-concepts. Conflicts and misbehavior involving possessions arouse adult training of the young in the control and use of possessions. Early in the child's experience with relatives, family friends, age-mates, and others, possessions and possessive behavior acquire social characteristics stemming from ownership and power over possession, and from possessions reflecting favorably on owners. In her theoretical formulation, Furby (1978c; 1980a) proposes that (a) both the meaning of and the motivation for acquiring possessions in their many forms are related to self-concepts, effectance motivation, and personal competence from early childhood onwards and (b) possessions are continuously important in interpersonal and social relations, including peer relations. Around 4 to 6 years, children begin to gain monetary understanding, partly through the experience of buying. When children enter school, notwithstanding their many limitations of immaturity and lack of experience, they have developed some understanding of economic behavior as well as economic attitudes and ideas and have been exposed for some time to the economic images presented by television. As an agent of socialization, the school serves only to make a contribution along with parents, other relatives, the mass media, peers, and the economy itself. Niemi and Sobieszek's (1977) conclusion that the role of the school in political socialization is overshadowed by other socializing agents applies to economic socialization.

With increasing age and expanding experience, children and adolescents gradually come to understand some of the main characteristics of self, other people, the economy, and society in which they all live. They come to distinguish between the personal and societal features of life, and to construct increasingly realistic "working models" of economic affairs. Their growing comprehension of money, finance, and banking are part of their increasing understanding of economic life as they encounter it. Grasping the notion of profit is a necessary but insufficient condition for much economic understanding, including banking. Acquisition of consumer skills contributes to increasingly effective personal functioning in the economy. The claim that the mass media have a major impact on consumer spending patterns and hence on economic socialization is no more than a claim at present. Anticipatory economic socialization, which prepares people for roles that may occur in the future, takes place during the preadult years. The desire of the young to become fully part of adult society encourages the extension of their understanding of self, others, social behavior, and of the political, economic, and social world.

Comprehending the basic functions of money, the principal ways of acquiring money, payment for goods and services, borrowing, saving, taxation, getting financial skills, and gaining knowledge of ownership, property, and other possessions are a part of children's and adolescents' social development. Several researchers have stressed the contribution of the activities of the young to their own economic socialization, including the ways they deal with uncertainties, contradictions, and conflict. We have seen that Furth (1978, 1980) stresses an understanding of money and its functions as a critical prerequisite for social development. He argues that, firstly, money is a neutral means of exchange for all goods and services and, secondly, the money economy has been the main instrument through which the sphere of personal behavior has been separated from the societal sphere of impersonal economic transactions, though these two regions of social life constantly interact and influence each other. On the basis of many research reports, Furth claims that the young are the principal authors of their own minds or intellects, and that the ideas, images, and theories they construct about their world are a result of their developing cognitive capacity. However, their environment is indispensable to such social development, because it provides the content for their constructions and representations of the political, economic, and social world. It follows that what is provided for the young by their environment varies between social classes, cultures, and nations.

Beginning in early childhood with crude simple notions of the differences between riches and poverty, youthful understanding of economic inequalities progresses continuously during later childhood and adolescence. Evaluation of inequalities changes with advancing age. By the mid-teens young people tend to evaluate general economic inequalities, riches, and rich people positively, and poverty, unemployment, and poor people negatively. They also tend to value economic individualism and personal concerns of a materialistic kind highly. By this age there is widespread acceptance of the economic order. These tendencies are most marked in the higher socioeconomic strata. Available empirical findings have been interpreted as supporting the argument that economic socialization in Western countries effectively produces in the young a favorable view of capitalism and the general structure of inequality in society. However, future research based on large representative and purposive samples may well uncover among the young, especially the working-class young, more variation in economic beliefs, attitudes, and ideas, less acceptance of the legitimacy of the economic order, and a greater diversity of negative and critical evaluations of existing inequalities than is evident in the current literature. Further, we do not know how the young react to major economic events in society, and whether their reactions are similar to those of adults (MacKuen, 1983).

Though the young develop detailed class and stratification schemes during the teens, usually they do not acquire strong feelings of class membership or interpret their own economic interests in class terms. Connell (1977) concluded that the young are "subjectively classless in a class society, informed and ignorant at the same time" (p. 151). Class consciousness appears to be most prevalent in the upper socioeconomic strata, especially among those who have attended reputable fee-charging schools. Class consciousness can be stimulated by certain economic events or situations: for example, among the young who expect to meet socioeconomic obstacles and among those in families who experience financial upheaval. But by the mid-teens there are social differences in political attitudes, beliefs about democracy, political party preferences, and evaluations of political leaders (Stacey, 1978). With advancing age, youth's beliefs, attitudes, ideas, and images about politics, socioeconomic differences, and inequalities undergo developmental transformations and approach the "maturity" of adults. These trends in preadult economic socialization have been observed in contemporary Western capitalist societies and cannot be taken as necessarily applying to other societies (e.g., China, Saudi Arabia) and other historical periods.

VIII. ADULT ECONOMIC SOCIALIZATION

The view that socialization of basic beliefs, values, attitudes, and behaviors is essentially completed in the preadult years has not been influential in the study of economic socialization, unlike political socialization (Niemi & Sobieszek, 1977). It has been widely accepted that the economic experience of the young is severely limited though important. With adulthood comes much more direct experience of the labor market, taxation, insurance, financial institutions, rent, mortgages, major consumer purchases, household expenses, and other features of economic life, including its marginal and illegal features. It has been widely accepted that significant economic socialization takes place during the adult years, particularly in association with life-cycle changes in occupational, marital, and family roles. On the basis of an examination of the empirical literature Stampfl (1978), for example, suggested there are at least 13 stages in the consumer life cycle, which are associated with the family cycle. It is further accepted that there are major differences between socialization occurring in adulthood and that occurring in earlier years (Mortimer & Simmons, 1978). Nonetheless, adults as well as the young are exposed to socialization agents such as political parties, private business, the mass media, and the economic system.

It is not known how extensive developmental change in economic beliefs, values, attitudes, and behaviors is beyond late adolescence. Evidence from the fields of political and occupational socialization indicates a considerable degree of developmental change for many people during the adult years (Mortimer & Simmons, 1978; Niemi & Sobieszek, 1977; Stacey, 1978). This may well apply to the economic aspects of life. Adults tend to change in response to altered circumstances, which are likely to occur during the adult life cycle. It has been suggested that there is a spurt in economic development on entry into the world of employment, another spurt associated with setting up a home, and economic adjustments stemming from retirement. An unknown minority of the population will reach high levels of economic functioning and apply their skills to personal, community, and national economic affairs. However, it has been suggested that a sizeable proportion of any national adult population has no more than a rudimentary grasp of economic concepts, the skills of personal finance, financial institutions and economic policy issues, and that these people are handicapped in their capacity to deal with a whole range of personal and public economic affairs, though they regularly handle money. It is assumed that such handicapped people are concentrated in the lower socioeconomic strata. There are also marginal and negative sides to economic socialization: for example, gambling, tax avoidance, tax evasion, bribery, financial manipulation, frauds, and "fiddles" of various kinds. Substantial empirical data in these matters do not exist.

In his treatment of the hegemonic situation in Australia, Connell (1977) relates consumption, debt, and the subordination of the working class in society to social development in the late teens and twenties. He argues that the economic system sets up pressures on older adolescents and young adults, first, to buy the expensive products of the "pop industries" and cars; second, after setting up home, to fill it with appliances and other domestic items; and third, to move to suburbia if possible. This results in a load of debt that fastens a couple into the system with the woman subordinate to the man and both at the mercy of the labor market. The status differences between cars, homes, and residential areas segments the working class and inhibits the formation of working-class consciousness. Anticommunism and racism are used to sustain threat images to "our way of life" with its flow of consumer goods and freedom for private enterprise. Connell sees the working class manacled by consumer stereotypes and debt rather than bought off by affluence. There is now substantial empirical evidence that money and material goods do little to promote life satisfactions and increase happiness, though economic deprivation and unemployment promote life dissatisfactions and unhappiness (Andrews & Withey, 1976; Kammann, 1983; Lane, 1978; Shin & Snyder, 1983). This research outcome contradicts entrenched economic beliefs and will not easily gain serious consideration. But in an examination of the effects of the market economy, Lane (1978) concludes that its participants are discouraged not only in the effective pursuit of happiness but also the maximization of gratification and, that such an economy tends to create doubt about the larger purposes of life and a sense of futility. Furby's (1978c) developmental theory of possessions might usefully be brought to bear on such quality-of-life issues.

Mortimer and Simmons (1978) show that the need for adult socialization depends partly on complex interactions of life-cycle effects on the individual, generational effects that have a lasting impact on a particular age cohort, and macrosocietal changes that cut across generations and the life cycle (period effects). Life's progression changes individual characteristics and role expectations. A significant consequence of such change may be the gaining of economic coping strategies, particularly to deal with new problems and situations. In the economic socialization literature one can find speculative

comments about economic generations, for example, the "Depression generation" or the "post-war generation," but no hard data, though the political
generations literature could be interpreted from an economic perspective
(Niemi & Sobieszek, 1977; Stacey, 1978). Period effects have not been examined in the economic socialization literature. It seems reasonable to assume
they may exist. For example, in the United States, the recent economic depression may have produced a general decline in economic trust comparable
to the decline in political trust during the 1960s and into the 1970s (Lane,
1978; Niemi & Sobieszek, 1977). Unraveling the relative impact of life-cycle,
generational, and period effects in the economic domain will undoubtedly
prove to be a complex matter, as Niemi and Sobieszek (1977) concluded
about the political domain.

This review of the literature on economic socialization published by early
1983, reveals a gross imbalance in the concern of researchers with the
preadult and adult years. The study of the preadult years seems to have been
gaining momentum in the recent past, but not the study of the adult years.
There is an obvious need to investigate the interaction of economic socialization with decision making about higher education, vocational training, occupational choice, marriage, and parenthood during late adolescence and early
adulthood. There is a further obvious need to investigate economic change
during the adult stages of life. Sex differences in economic socialization may
prove more significant among adults than the young. We know little about
the impact of background socioeconomic variables on economic socialization, though they appear to be influential. Attention needs to be given to the
interaction of economic socialization with changing economic circumstances, which will lead to the subject of economic adaption to external pressures. The question of whether the economic socialization of any age cohort
has consequences for society at large as it passes through its life cycle is important. The linkages between economic socialization and specific role requirements through life's stages should be explored. More integration of empirical, experimental, and theoretical work is needed. I have pointed to
salient parallels between economic and political socialization. Integration of
these two fields of study would probably benefit both.

REFERENCES

Andrews, F., & Withey, S.B. (1976). *Social indicators of well-being.* New York: Plenum Press.
Baldus, B., & Tribe, V. (1978). The development of perceptions and evaluations of social
inequality among public school children. *Canadian Review of Sociology and Anthro-
pology, 15,* 50–60.
Baumrind, D. (1978). A dialectical materialist's perspective on knowing social reality. In W.
Damon (Ed.), *Moral development.* San Francisco: Jossey Bass.
Baxter, E.H. (1976). Children's and adolescents' perceptions of occupational prestige. *Canadian
Review of Sociology and Anthropology, 13,* 229–238.

Beaglehole, E. (1932). *Property: A study in social psychology*. New York: Macmillan.

Berger, P.M., & Luckmann, T. (1967). *The social construction of reality*. London: Allen Lane.

Berti, A.E. (1981). The "boss": its conceptual development in children. *Italian Journal of Psychology, 8,* 111–119.

Berti, A.E., & Bombi, A.S. (1981). The development of the concept of money and its value: a longitudinal study. *Child Development, 52,* 1179–1182.

Berti, A.E., Bombi, A.S., & Lis, A. (1982). The child's conceptions about means of production and their owners. *European Journal of Social Psychology, 12,* 221–239.

Bowles, S., & Gintis, H. (1976). *Schooling in capitalist America*. New York: Basic Books.

Bronfenbrenner, U. (1979). *The ecology of human development*. Cambridge: Harvard University Press.

Burris, V. (1982). The child's conception of economic relations; a study of cognitive socialization. *Sociology Focus, 4,* 307–325.

Chamberlain, C. (1983). *Class consciousness in Australia*. Sydney: Allen and Unwin.

Churchill, G.A., & Moschis, G.P.. (1979). Television and interpersonal influences on adolescent consumer learning. *Journal of Consumer Research, 6,* 23–34.

Coles, R. (1977). *Children of crisis*, (Vol. 5). Boston: Little Brown.

Connell, R.W. (1977). *Ruling class, ruling culture*. Melbourne: Cambridge University Press.

Cummings, S., & Taebel, D. (1978). The economic socialization of children: a neo-Marxist analysis. *Social Problems, 26,* 198–210.

Danziger, K. (1958). Children's earliest conceptions of economic relationships (Australia). *Journal of Social Psychology, 47,* 231–240.

Esland, G. (1973). *Language and social reality*. Milton Keynes, UK: Open University Press.

Feldman, S. (1982). Economic self-interest and political behavior. *American Journal of Political Science, 26,* 446–466.

Fox, K.F.A. (1978). What children bring to school: the beginnings of economic education. *Social Education, 42,* 478–481.

Frank, A.W. (1979). Reality construction in interaction. *Annual Review of Sociology, 5,* 167–191.

Furby, L. (1976). The socialization of possession and ownership among children in three cultural groups: Israeli kibbutz, Israeli city, and American. In S. Modgil & C. Modgil (Eds.), *Piagetian research: compilation and commentary, volume 8*. Windsor, UK: NFER Publishing Co.

Furby, L. (1978a). Possession in humans: an exploratory study of its meaning and motivation. *Social Behavior and Personality, 6,* 49–65.

Furby, L. (1978b). Sharing: decisions and moral judgments about letting others use one's possessions. *Psychological Reports, 43,* 595–609.

Furby, L. (1978c). Possessions: toward a theory of their meaning and function throughout the life cycle. In P.B. Baltes (Ed.), *Life span development and behavior* (Vol. 1). New York: Academic Press.

Furby, L. (1979). Inequalities in personal possessions: explanations for and judgments about unequal distribution. *Human Development, 22,* 180–202.

Furby, L. (1980a). The origins and development of early possessive behavior. *Political Psychology, 2,* 30–42.

Furby, L. (1980b). Collective possession and ownership: a study of its judged feasibility and desirability. *Social Behavior and Personality, 8,* 165–184.

Furnham, A. (1982). The perception of poverty among adolescents. *Journal of Adolescence, 5,* 135–147.

Furth, H.G. (1978). Young children's understanding of society. In H. McGurk (Ed.), *Issues in childhood social development*. London: Methuen.

Furth, H.G. (1980). *The world of grown-ups: children's conceptions of society*. New York: Elsevier.

Furth, H.G., Baur, M., & Smith, J.E. (1976). Children's conception of social institutions: a Piagetian framework. *Human Development, 19,* 351-374.

Gintis, H., & Bowles, S. (1980). Contradiction and reproduction in educational theory. In L. Barton, R. Meighan & S. Walker (Eds.), *Schooling, ideology and the curriculum.* Lewes, UK: Falmer Press.

Gunter, B. (1981). Scheduling television advertisements to protect young viewers. *Bulletin of the British Psychological Society, 34,* 271-274.

Gurney, R.M. (1981). Leaving school, facing unemployment, and making attributions about the causes of unemployment. *Journal of Vocational Behavior, 18,* 79-91.

Hess, R.D., & Torney, J.V. (1967). *The development of political attitudes in children.* Chicago: Aldine.

Heyns, B. (1978). Review essay: schooling in capitalist America. *American Journal of Sociology, 83,* 999-1006.

Hong Kwang, R.T., & Stacey, B.G. (1981). The understanding of socio-economic concepts in Malaysian Chinese school children. *Child Study Journal, 11,* 33-49.

Jahoda, G. (1959). Development of the perception of social differences in children from 6 to 10. *British Journal of Psychology, 50,* 159-175.

Jahoda, G. (1979). The construction of economic reality by some Glaswegian children. *European Journal of Social Psychology, 9,* 115-127.

Jahoda, G. (1981). The development of thinking about economic institutions: the bank. *Cahiers de Psychologie Cognitive, 1,* 55-73.

Jahoda, G. (1983a) Levels of social and logico-mathematical thinking: their nature and inter-relations. In W. Doise & J. Palmonari (Eds.), *Social interaction in individual development.* Cambridge: Cambridge University Press.

Jahoda, G. (1983b). European 'lag' in the development of an economic concept: a study in Zimbabwe. *British Journal of Developmental Psychology, 1,* 113-120.

Jahoda, G., & Woerdenbagch, A. (1982a). Awareness of supra-national groupings among Dutch and Scottish children and adolescents. *European Journal of Political Research, 10,* 305-312.

Jahoda, G., & Woerdenbagch, A. (1982b). The development of ideas about an economic institution: a cross-national replication. *British Journal of Social Psychology, 21,* 337-338.

Kammann, R. (1983). Objective circumstances, life satisfactions, and sense of well-being: consistencies over time and place. *New Zealand Journal of Psychology, 12,* 14-22.

Kassarjian, H.H. (1982). Consumer psychology. *Annual Review of Psychology, 33,* 619-649.

Kluegel, J.R., & Smith, E.R. (1981). Beliefs about stratification. *Annual Review of Sociology, 7,* 29-56.

Lane, R.E. (1978). Autonomy, felicity, futility: the effects of the market economy on political personality. *Journal of Politics, 40,* 2-24.

Langrehr, F.W. (1979). Consumer education: does it change students' competencies and attitudes? *Journal of Consumer Affairs, 13,* 41-53.

Lauer, R.H. (1974). Socialization into inequality: children's perception of occupational status. *Sociology and Social Research, 58,* 176-183.

Leahy, R.L. (1981). The development of the conception of economic inequality. I. Descriptions and comparisons of rich and poor people. *Child Development, 52,* 523-532.

Leahy, R.L. (1983). The development of the conception of economic inequality. II. Explanations, justifications, and conceptions of social mobility and social change. *Developmental Psychology, 19,* 111-125.

Levin, H.M. (1974). Educational reform and social change. *Journal of Applied Behavioral Science, 10,* 304-319.

Loewental, K. (1976). Property. *European Journal of Social Psychology, 6,* 343-351.

Luria, A.R. (1976). *Cognitive development: its cultural and social foundations.* Cambridge: Harvard University Press.

MacKuen, M.B. (1983). Political drama, economic conditions, and the dynamics of Presidential popularity. *American Journal of Political Science, 27,* 165-192.

Marshall, H.R., & Magruder, L. (1960). Relations between parent money education practices and children's knowledge and use of money. *Child Development, 31,* 253-284.

Mayer, R.N., & Belk, R. (1982). Acquisition of consumption stereotypes by children. *Journal of Consumer Affairs, 16,* 307-321.

Miliband, R. (1969). *The state in capitalist society.* London: Weidenfeld and Nicolson.

Miller, L.N., & Horn, T.D. (1955). Children's concepts regarding debt. *Elementary School Journal, 55,* 406-412.

Moessinger, P. (1975). Developmental study of fair division of property. *Eurpoean Journal of Social Psychology, 5,* 385-394.

Monte, C. (1977). *Beneath the mask.* New York: Holt, Rinehart and Winston.

Moore, R. L., & Moschis, G.P. (1983). Role of mass media and family in development of consumption norms. *Journalism Quarterly, 60,* 67-73.

Mortimer, J.T., & Simmons, R.G. (1978). Adult socialization. *Annual Review of Sociology, 4,* 421-454.

Moschis, G.P., & Moore, R.L. (1978). The analysis of the acquisition of some consumer competencies among adolescents. *Journal of Consumer Affairs, 12,* 277-290.

Ng, S.H. (1982). Children's socio-economic cognitions of the bank and shop profit: a Hong Kong study. Department of Psychology, University of Otago, Dunedin, New Zealand.

Ng, S.H. (1983), Children's ideas about bank and shop profit: developmental stages and the influence of cognitive contrasts and conflict. *Journal of Economic Psychology, 4,* 209-221.

Niemi, R.G., & Sobieszek, B.I. (1977). Political socialization. *Annual Review of Sociology, 3,* 209-233.

Peck, J. (1979). Children's television advertising: an analysis. *Australian Journal of Social Issues, 14,* 64-76.

Piaget, J. (1972). Intellectual evolution from adolescence to adulthood. *Human Development, 15,* 1-12.

Piaget, J. (1974). *The child and reality.* London: Muller.

Roberts, D.F., & Bachen, C.M. (1981). Mass communication effects. *Annual Review of Psychology, 32,* 307-356.

Rockwell, R.C., & Elder, G.H. (1982). Economic deprivation and problem behavior: childhood and adolescence in the Great Depression. *Human Development, 25,* 57-64.

Rootes, C.A. (1981). The dominant ideology thesis and its critics. *Sociology, 15,* 436-444.

Rosenblum, S. (1975). Education against freedom. *Social Praxis, 3,* 243-260.

Sarup, M. (1978). *Marxism and education.* London: Routledge and Kegan Paul. 1978.

Shin, D.C., & Snyder, W. (1983). Economic growth, quality of life, and development policy. *Comparative Political Studies, 16,* 195-213.

Siegal, M. (1981). Children's perceptions of adult economic needs. *Child Development, 52,* 379-383.

Simmons, R.G., & Rosenberg, M. (1971). Functions of children's perceptions of the stratification system. *American Sociological Review, 36,* 235-249.

Stacey, B.G. (1978). *Political socialization in Western society.* London: Edward Arnold.

Stacey, B.G. (1982). Economic socialization in the preadult years. *British Journal of Social Psychology, 21,* 159-173.

Stampfl, R.W. (1978). The consumer life cycle. *Journal of Consumer Affairs, 12,* 209-219.

Stampfl, R.W., Moschis, G., & Lawton, J.T. (1978). Consumer education and the preschool child. *Journal of Consumer Affairs, 12,* 12-29.

Stephens, N., & Stutts, M.A. (1982). Preschoolers' ability to distinguish between television programming and commercials. *Journal of Advertising, 11,* 16-25.

Stern, A.J., & Searing, D.D. (1976). The stratification beliefs of English and American adolescents. *British Journal of Political Science, 6,* 177-201.

Strauss, A.L. (1952). The development and transformation of monetary meaning in the child. *American Sociological Review, 17,* 275-284.

Sutton, R.S. (1962). Behavior in the attainment of economic concepts. *Journal of Psychology, 53,* 37-46.

Taylor, S. (1982). Schooling and social reproduction. *Australian Journal of Education, 26,* 144-154.

Torney, J.V., Oppenheim, A.N., & Farnen, R.F. (1975). *Civic education in ten countries.* New York: Wiley.

Ward, S., Wackman, D.B., & Wartella, E. (1977). *How children learn to buy.* Beverly Hills, CA: Sage.

Winocur, S., & Siegal, M. (1982). Adolescents' judgments of economic arrangements. *International Journal of Behavioral Development, 5,* 357-365.

2

Generational Politics*

Richard G. Braungart

Department of Sociology
Syracuse University

Margaret M. Braungart

General Studies, CHRP
SUNY, Upstate Medical Center
Syracuse, New York

---

*This paper originally was presented at the Sixth Annual Scientific Meeting of the International Society of Political Psychology, St. Catherine's College, Oxford University, Oxford, England, July 19–22, 1983. It was published previously in *Micropolitics 3* (1983), 349–415, and is reproduced here with the permission of Crane, Russak & Company, Inc.

I. INTRODUCTION

One of the most fundamental categories of human history is that of a generation. The word "generation" is rooted in the Greek word *genos* and reflected in the verb *genesthai,* which means "to come into existence" (Nash, 1978). The placement of birth not only separates offspring from their parents but locates individuals in the historical process with others born around the same time. "The truest community to which one can belong," wrote Wohl (1979) "is that defined by age and experience." We share with those born around the same period in time a similarity in both life-cycle development and historical experiences. The entrance of successive age groups into society has been a constant feature of human history, but each group has "come into existence" within a particular historical and political setting, which provides an important reference point for generational identification — the Spanish Generation of '98, the Generation of 1914, the 1960s Protest Generation (Eisenstadt, 1956; Esler, 1974, 1982; Feuer, 1969; Rintala, 1968; Wohl, 1979).

Generations are made not born; they represent a unique force beyond chronological age-group identification. A generation shares not only age-group membership — based on life cycle (maturational or developmental changes that occur with age) and cohort position (demographic factors associated with birth placement in history) — but a sense of social consciousness and participation in the historical process. That is to say, while an age group represents a distinct social category "in itself," a generation acts as a social group "for itself" (Jansen, 1975; Mannheim, 1952; Marias, 1968, 1970; Ortega y Gasset, 1962). This distinction between age group and generation has not always been made clear. When societal change is rapid, with age groups maturing under different sets of historical circumstances, an age group may form its own views of society and politics, at variance with older and younger age groups. An age group is transformed into a generation when its members are aware of their uniqueness, feel a sense of solidarity, and join together to become an active force for social and political change.

Politics, which has often provided the focus of generational divisiveness and conflict, involves the struggle for power in society, as groups compete over material and ideals. At times, the struggle over politics and the state has been between generations, as young "foxes" compete with older "lions" for political power and control. From the Age of Revolution in the early nineteenth century to the global political turbulence of the 1960s, youthful militants periodically have revolted against the politics of their elders. Political struggles, of course, may be based on social divisions other than purely generational — social class, ethnicity, or other status groupings. And generations may draw sides in arenas other than the political one — such as social, cultural, scientific, or intellectual (Esler, 1982; Feuer, 1974; Marias, 1970;

Spitzer, 1973). The focus of this essay, however, is on ways in which generational forces interact with politics.

The relationship between generations and politics partly involves the common frame of reference that develops as a generation takes form. Because of its unique social and psychological experiences, a generation consciously perceives itself as holding a distinct set of political attitudes. At odds with other age groups or generations in society, a generation may mobilize to change the direction of politics. When the purposes and activities of a generation are directed toward extraordinary political change, we have what has been called a "political generation" (Heberle, 1951; Rintala, 1968, 1979).

A number of political generations have emerged during various times in recent world history: the nineteenth century Young Europe movements in Germany, France, Italy, Austria, and Russia; the *fin de siècle* political generations in Germany, India, Turkey, Bosnia, China, Mexico, and Latin America; during the 1930s depression years throughout Europe and the United States, along with nationalist movements in India and China; and in the 1960s on an unprecedented global scale (Braungart, 1982a). Political generations characteristically break with the past and mobilize against the ruling status quo and other age groups in society in their attempt to redirect the course of politics. Historically, the thrust of political–generational conflict has come from the young, and during times of heightened intergenerational activity, competing intragenerational units have emerged on the political left and right.

Despite past and present interest, the relationship between generations and politics has not been fully explored. The most explicit link between generations and politics is found in the discussions of political generations, which grew out of the theoretical literature on "the problem of generations" first outlined in the nineteenth century, and focused for the most part on the various political movements that erupted along generational lines (Heberle, 1951; Rintala, 1968, 1979). The field of generational politics, however, represents more than just the study of political–generational movements. Crucial to the development of a political generation are the shared attitudes and behavior that exist within an age group that provide the necessary foundation for a political movement to take place. Other aspects of generational politics involve the examination of the relationship between age (life cycle and cohort) and political attitudes and behavior. Much of the literature devoted to this topic generally has been concerned with the period of youth as a stage in the life cycle when political attitudes begin to form, the various historical and social influences that shape the direction of political attitudes and behavior, and the identification of age groups that share a highly similar set of political attitudes — suggesting, of course, the possibility of a political generation in the making.

Generational politics involves both the study of age as it relates to the development of political attitudes and behavior, as well as the dynamic formation of political generations. Of concern in the study of generational politics are the influences of life cycle and cohort placement on political outlooks, the extent of political solidarity and diversity between and within age groups and generations, and the mobilization of shared political attitudes into political–generational movements. The interplay between generations and politics has much to do with political stability and change in society — a process that has intrigued scholars since the days of the ancient Greeks.

The purpose of this essay is to outline and examine the broad area of generational politics: its theoretical traditions, empirical contributions, and conceptual and methodological issues. Section II summarizes the theoretical foundations of generational politics. In Section III the relationship between age group and the formation of political attitudes and behavior is examined; the focus here is on the role of life-cycle and cohort factors in promoting age-group differences in politics, as well as on other forces that enhance the likelihood of age-group political agreement — period effects (solidifying events and experiences to which all age groups respond in a similar way), intra-age-group variation in politics, and the political socialization efforts of adults to inculcate political values and behavior in the young. Section IV describes the dynamics of a political generation: the historical circumstances associated with its development, the mobilization and activation of a political generation into a genuine force for political change, and the emergence of generation units or subgroups competing for power. Finally, in Section V, some of the conceptual and methodological issues involved in research on generational politics are discussed.

II. GENERATIONAL POLITICS

The interest and concern with generations goes back to antiquity. Early recognition of the "generation gap" was evident in the inscription on a 4,000-year-old-tablet from the Biblical city of Ur which read: "Our civilization is doomed if the unheard-of actions of our younger generation are allowed to continue" (Lauer, 1977, p. 176). The ancient Greeks were among the first to clarify differences in the life cycle and their implications for generational relations and behavior, explicitly recognizing that generational rhythms have much to do with stability and change in politics and society. To the Greeks, youth was a time of great energy, action, impulsiveness, hubris, and heroic self-sacrifice — themes that were well documented in the classic Greek tragedies. Older age, on the other hand, was viewed as a time for contemplation and counsel, due in part to "grievous" weakened limbs, with the impetuousness of youth requiring the steady hand of their elders (Nash, 1978).

The relations between the generations are typically unharmonious, as Plato and Aristotle observed, often having dramatic political and social consequences. Plato identified generational strife as a significant force for change, while Aristotle noted that political revolutions are not only due to the conflict between rich and poor, but to the struggle between fathers and sons. One of the first generational–political analysis was offered by Herodotus, who wrote that generational awareness was so strong after the Persian Wars that it seemed to be the first principle of historical thought (Feuer, 1969; Marias, 1970).

A. Early Generational Theorists

In the nineteenth century, the discussion of generations as a force for social and political change began to take a more scientific and theoretical form. The French positivists, who led the discussion, divided the life span into distinct ages that act as conditioning forces for human experiences. One of the foremost goals of the positivists was to discover the law of historical development, which was viewed as rooted in the human life cycle (Jansen, 1975). In 1839, Auguste Comte noted that the duration of human life plays an important part in social evolution, as one generation gives way to another. John Stuart Mill took the idea of the generation a step further, arguing that the "principle phenomena" of society differ, with the generation most clearly marking these changes. A generation, to Mill, was a time when a new group of individuals reaches maturity and influences the character of social and political institutions. A more explicit connection between generations and politics was made by the Italian historian and politician, Giuseppe Ferrari, who, in his examination of political history, observed that the political picture changes approximately every 30 years and is decidedly influenced by the generation. According to Ferrari's laws of political succession, "Generations . . . are in turn preparatory, revolutionary, reactionary, and conciliatory" (Marias, 1968, pp. 88–89). This four-phase cycle of history repeats itself, with generations defined largely in terms of their political function.

Opposing the positivists, the romantic-historical movement developed in Germany. While the positivists argued in favor of an unilinear concept of progress based on the succession of generations, the romantic-historical school claimed that progress is not unilinear, although it is influenced heavily by generations. Rather than emphasizing life-cycle development, the romantic-historical approach stressed the qualitative content of historical experiences as the conditioning force for generations (Jansen, 1975). It was out of this movement that the notion of generations was given its first major theoretical formulation, beginning in the 1860s with the German cultural historian Wilhelm Dilthey.

Observing that many of the great romanticists were born in a single decade, Dilthey characterized generations as a relationship of "contemporaneity" between individuals, and emphasized the importance of generational placement, along with the significant influence of cultural and social forces on the thinking of the young. A generation, according to Dilthey, "is consti-tuted of a restricted circle of individuals who are bound together into a ho-mogeneous whole by their dependence on the same great events and transfor-mations that appeared in their age of [maximum] receptivity, despite the variety of other subsequent factors" (Schorske, 1978, p. 121). Thus began the concept of a "social generation," defined in terms of historical differences and social change. A social generation differs from older and younger age groups and is both strongly influenced by institutional, intellectual, and so-cial change, as well as itself contributing to the direction of further societal transformations and changes (Esler, 1982; Jansen, 1975; Marias, 1968).

The concept of social generations begun by Dilthey gained support in the 1920s. Francois Mentré's doctoral dissertation *Les Générations sociales* (1920) at the Sorbonne defined a generation as "a collective state of mind embodied in a group of human beings, which extends over a period of time comparable to the duration of a genealogical generation." Emphasizing so-cial unity, the mysterious "tie that binds" is a generational one, which pro-duces a community of creative activity in a number of different fields. Mem-bers of a generation share a common outlook and at times have been known to duplicate insights and discoveries (Esler, 1974, p. 4). In his dissertation, Mentré distinguished between familial generations and social generations. Familial generations are continuous — born every day with the succession of grandfathers, fathers, and sons. The key to the study of social generations is the development of "sentiments and beliefs." But Mentré rejected the notion that social generations are determined by the course of political events, since political events merely reflect "spiritual transformations" or "a quiet labor of minds that gives birth to a new ideal of human activity" — most receptive within the minds and hearts of young people. Intellectual life, he maintained, develops through opposition, ultimately derived from the struggle between fathers and sons. Mentré assumed that generations possess a regular rhythm, concluding they last about 30 years, since that is roughly the duration of a man's effective social action. Discontinuity between the generations is the rule and continuity the exception. The struggle of one generation with an-other is more violent and thus more evident at some times than at others. Mentré's dissertation did not have a favorable reception and, for the most part, was ignored (Esler, 1974, 1982).

More widely known are the discussions of generations offered by the Spanish philosopher and social critic José Ortega y Gasset in *The Modern Theme* (1961) and *Man and Crisis* (1962). Each generation goes through the rhythmic evolutionary development of youth (ages 15–30), young manhood (ages 30–45), culminating in the ascension to power and domination of soci-ety (ages 45–60). Ortega argued that "age . . . is not a date, but a 'zone of dates'; and it is not only in those born in the same year who are the same age in life and in history, but those who are born within a zone of dates" (Ortega y

Gasset, 1962, p. 47). Like Mentré, Ortega claimed it is less historical events that mold a generation than intellectual thought. Economic and political change, after all, depend upon changes in ideas, taste, and mores. A generation represents a new integration, having its own unity of "vital style" among coevals and its own sense of destiny and "vital trajectory" (Ortega y Gasset, 1974).

Life for each generation partly is rooted in the previous generation (institutions, ideas, values), and the liberation of the creative genius inherent in the generation concerned. Interaction between two age groups of masters and new initiates is especially important, Ortega claimed. When they agree on fundamentals, they reinforce each other, providing a sense of harmony and purpose — which Ortega termed an "age of accumulation." When they disagree, an age of polemics and rebellion results — termed an "age of elimination" — a period that belongs to the young (Ortega y Gasset, 1962).

Around the same time as Ortega, the Hungarian-born sociologist Karl Mannheim outlined "The Problem of Generations" in his famous essay published in 1928. Mannheim's special interest was identifying the classes or subgroups in society that shape one's world view. Mannheim (1952, p. 291), in fact, likened belonging to a generation to that of belonging to a social class, in that both endow the individuals sharing in them with a "common location" in the social and historical process, thereby limiting them to a specific range of potential experiences and predisposing them for a certain "characteristic mode of thought" and type of "historically relevant action." Mannheim (1952, p. 292) defined a generation as "a particular kind of identity of location, embracing related 'age groups' embedded in a historical-social process," but he suggested that biological generations are not necessarily sociological generations until the shared historical experiences produce similar perceptions and understanding of reality. A "concrete nexus" is needed to constitute a generation as an actuality, and this nexus is a sense of "participation in the common destiny" shared by a historical and social unit (Mannheim, 1952, p. 303).

What is important, Mannheim insisted, is the process of social change that sets one generation apart from the next. The more rapid the sociocultural change, the greater the chances that the various generational groups will react by producing their own generational style, but how often a new generational style appears depends on the "trigger action" of the social and cultural process (Mannheim, 1952). Social and cultural change accelerates the "stratification of experience" of each successive generation. During periods of rapid social and historical transformation, attitudes take on new meaning and quickly become differentiated from traditional patterns of experience. As these newly emerging patterns of experience consolidate, they form fresh impulses and cores for generational configuration, which result in unique generational styles. Mannheim offered the qualification that periods characterized by war, natural catastrophe, and total political mobilization rarely develop generational differentiation due to the leveling of values resulting from fear and/or national solidarity. But, during times of relative security and protracted institutional growth, the quicker the tempo of social and cultural change, the higher the probability that successive generations will develop their own outlooks (Braungart, 1974).

Mannheim, like others, considered youth to be a critical stage for the development of political and social attitudes. Each generation, as it comes of age, experiences a fresh contact with traditional values and principles, and when social change is rapid, traditional ways may appear outdated. The fresh contact of youth—at a time when they are beginning to reflect on problematic issues and are dramatically aware of the process of destabilization—provides a revitalization process for society. Mannheim observed that although the romantic-conservative and liberal-rationalist youth belonged to the same actual generation, they embraced different ideologies. These different subgroups within the same generation he termed "generation units," or those groups within the same generation that "work up the material of their common experience in different ways" (Mannheim, 1952, p. 304). Within a generation there can exist any number of pro- or antagonistic generation units competing with one another, who exert pressure on their members to conform to partisan points of view. Mannheim's discussion of generation units represented one of his most important contributions to generation theory.

These early generational theorists viewed generations as more than the biological succession of age groups. The essence of a generation is social, a sharing of attitudes and viewpoints that links together members of the same age group. Youth and young adulthood are considered a formative stage in the life cycle for the development of social awareness and attitudes toward self and society. What gives shape to these youthful, emerging attitudes are the prevailing social, economic, cultural, and political circumstances and intellectual thought that characterize society as its younger members come of age. When change is rapid, young people born around the same time in history often have a different set of historical experiences than their elders and consequently develop their own distinctive style and response to society and politics.

B. Contemporary Generational Theorists

The early generational theorists addressed the concept of a social generation, bounded by age-group membership and historical placement, which may become a genuine force for social change. Beginning in the 1950s, the idea of a social generation was extended to political generations. Although contemporary political–generational theorists drew heavily from the early generational forebearers, they tended to emphasize different aspects of the relationship between generations and politics. That is, while some pointed to the key role of historical factors, others gave more focus to life-cycle forces, or the structure of society itself in influencing age-group political similarities and differences and the rise of generational-based political movements.

In his book *Social Movements*, Rudolf Heberle (1951) noted that changes in political ideas appear to be closely associated with the rhythm in the change of generations. Strongly influenced by Mannheim, Heberle adapted the basic concept of a social generation to the political generation. Certain experiences that occur during the formative period of youth (approximately ages 20–30) have a decisive impact on the development of the individual's political philosophy and attitudes. A generation is comprised of contemporaries who, because of their similar age and experiences, have more in common and are more likely to associate with each other than with older and younger generations. Heberle used the example of the Nazi movement in Germany, which was led by those born between 1885–1900 who were between the ages of 18–33 when World War I ended. It was the experiences of the war and the postwar aftermath that had a decided effect on the formation of these young Germans' political outlooks. And, although they supported various political parties after the war, their thinking differed markedly from the prewar generation. Torn apart by political factionalism, many of the World War I youth generation became high susceptible to Nazi appeals.

Intergenerational political relations are often problematic, according to Heberle, because the ruling generation already has been through its formative period. Yet, they see the issues of the day in light of their earlier experiences and often in ways quite different from the younger generation. In keeping with Mannheim, Heberle observed that political differences may well exist not only between generations (largely as a function of rapid social change) but within generations (based on different subdivisions, such as social class and occupation).

Around the time Heberle discussed political generations, Samuel Eisenstadt (1956, 1963) examined generations and politics by focusing on age groups in the social structure, specifically addressing the issue why young people are such likely candidates for political and social movement activity in modern societies. The reason youth movements arise during certain historical periods but not others has to do with the cultural and social conditions of a society. According to Eisenstadt, it is a universal fact that age serves as a basis for defining the social and cultural characteristics of humans, as well as their interrelations, roles, and activities. In primitive and traditional societies, the personal, temporal transition of youth is linked to society—most fully expressed in the formal *rites de passage*. However, the breakdown of tradition and onset of modernization, industrialization, urbanization, and secularization disrupts the family and changes the "mutual evaluation" of the generations. In modern or modernizing societies, the connections between youth and society are weakened; consequently, young people must search for new self-identification, often expressed in ideological conflict with the older members of society.

Eisenstadt (1963) argued that modernization and the national trends of the nineteenth and twentieth centuries have fostered the rise of a youth culture and youth organizations. For example, most of the nationalistic movements in the Middle East, Africa, and Asia were comprised of young people who rebelled against their elders and the traditional familistic setting. At the same time, a youth consciousness and ideology emerged that intensified the nationalistic movement to "rejuvenate" the country. Thus, in modernizing societies, young people's social and political identities have been connected closely with new symbols of collective solidarity and sociopolitical change.

Another contemporary political–generation theorist, Marvin Rintala (1968, 1979), emphasized the key role of historical factors in influencing generational mentality and the formalization of an active or decisive political generation in history. According to Rintala's definition, a political generation is a group of individuals who have undergone the same basic historical experiences during their formative years (ages 17–25). When these experiences are qualitatively different from those of previous generations, communication between the generations becomes problematic. Once formed, the political ideas developed during youth tend to endure throughout the life course. It is Rintala's thesis that the boundaries and size of a political generation are not determined as much by age as they are by the given historical event(s), with the uniqueness of the event(s) affecting the extent of difficulty in intergenerational communication. Those whose formative experiences are essentially different are not members of the same generation, despite their coexistence in time.

Rintala (1979) supported Mannheim's notion of generation units as a force for active political change. As an example, events associated with World War I transformed the nature of European society and created a decisive political generation throughout Europe among those who were in their formative stage of development during the war years. Although the young Europeans of 1914–1918 were influenced strongly by their war experiences, not all reacted to those experiences in the same way, resulting in three distinct generation units: those who never recovered from the war and retreated from politics; those who entered politics determined to prevent any future war; and those that "never left the battlefield" and engaged in politics to continue the war by other means.

While Rintala emphasized historical events in the formation of a political generation, Lewis Feuer (1969) focused on psychodynamics and life-cycle factors as the underlying sources of intergenerational conflict and political change. In attempting to explain student political unrest in the 1960s, Feuer generally ignored concrete historical causes such as the Vietnam war and civil rights, asserting that student movements are rarely materialistic but are derived from deep unconscious sources in the conflict of generations. They are born of vague, undefined emotions in search of some issue or cause to attach themselves. Youth movements arise from a breakdown in the "generational equilibrium." Always present is a disillusionment with, and rejection of, the values of the older generation, along with the conviction that the youthful generation has a "generational mission" to fulfill where the older members of society have failed. In the dynamics of the formation of a political generation, the younger generation deauthorizes the older generation and directs its own members to seize the political initiative.

What is mentioned in the political–generation theories, but not fully discussed, are the cohesive political attitudes within an age group that provide the foundation for a political generation to develop. The relationship between age and political orientations has not gone unnoticed, however, and has received considerable attention in the literature of life-span development and political socialization (Baltes & Schaie, 1973; Bengtson & Cutler, 1976; Cutler, 1974, 1977; Elder, 1980; Goulet & Baltes, 1970; Renshon, 1977; Riley & Foner, 1968). Widespread interest in the so-called "generation gap" during the 1960s encouraged sociologists, political scientists, and developmental psychologists to take a closer look at age differences in politics, the development of political attitudes and behavior as a function of age, and whether political orientations remain relatively stable or tend to change with advancing age. The association between age and politics is pertinent to the study of generational politics and needs to be linked more directly to understanding political generations.

The study of the relationship between age and politics represents what Bengtson and Cutler (1976) term "generational analysis," the goal of which is to apply a "comparative framework" to the problem of age groups, and succession and change in the sociopolitical system. Political attitudes and behavior are seen as a function of temporal placement, involving the life-cycle stage of maturational development (life time), the demographic and historical cohort experiences based on time of birth (historical time), and the social structure and age patterning of experiences in a sociocultural structure (social time). Considerable effort has been devoted to clarifying and developing a framework for generational analysis. This framework, when applied to the study of generational politics, suggests a number of different comparisons for the relationship between age and politics: (a) between age groups, or intergenerational politics; (b) within age groups, or intragenerational politics; (c) within families, or lineage politics; and (d) within the individual, or intraindividual politics (Cutler, 1977; Elder, 1980; Jennings & Niemi, 1981; Nesselroade, 1977; Riley & Foner, 1968). Much of the discussion of age-based politics has revolved around the young; however, the more recent concern with gerontology has spurred an interest in the political orientations of older age groups. It has been argued that elderly citizens, who are increasing in numbers with better health and education, may become as politically active in the future as were young people in the 1960s (Bengtson & Cutler, 1976; Pratt, 1976; Rose, 1965).

The contemporary discussions of age groups, generations, and politics provide theoretical focus, in addition to a framework for analyzing age-group similarities and differences in politics. The thrust of the recent discussion suggests that the natural inclination of young people is to view society and politics from a fresh perspective and to disagree with their elders over a number of issues, including politics. These youthful inclinations are exacerbated in modern and modernizing societies, when the young and the old have been conditioned by different sets of historical circumstances. The older members of rapidly changing societies tend to cling to the political views learned in their youth, often failing to understand the attitudes and behavior of the young—a situation that facilitates the likelihood of generational misunderstanding and conflict over politics. Disagreement over politics, however, occurs not only between generations (intergenerational), but within generations (intragenerational). Although young people may fervently criticize the politics of their elders, they also may support and reject a variety of political viewpoints within their own ranks (ranging from extreme left-wing, to moderate and conventional, to far right-wing).

Generational politics, as a field of investigation, involves both the study of age-group similarities and differences in politics, as well as the formation of generation-based political movements. The extent to which age has any effect on the development of political attitudes and behavior has been debated, but most of the political–generation theories posit that when political attitudes divide along age-group lines a political generation may be taking form. The next section of this essay outlines the dimensions involved in investigating age-group similarities and differences in politics, followed by an analysis of political generations. Undertaking research in generational politics involves a number of considerations, and the final section of the essay points to some of the conceptual and methodological problems that arise.

III.   AGE AND THE FORMATION OF POLITICAL ATTITUDES AND BEHAVIOR

Numerous researchers have attempted to identify areas of age-group agreement and disagreement over politics. Once age-group political differences are evident, however, the next issue is to determine whether they are due to life-cycle effects or to cohort effects. Differences in life-cycle and cohort placement tend to promote political disagreement and misunderstanding among the age groups; at the same time, consideration needs to be given to forces that minimize political differences on the basis of age, such as period effects, age-group heterogeneity, and the political socialization efforts of parents and adults.

A.   Life-Cycle Politics

According to the life-cycle argument, since the various age groups are in different stages of maturation or development — each stage with its own physiological changes, socioemotional concerns, roles, needs, and pursuits — young, middle-aged, and older adults are not likely to perceive and respond to the political situation in a similar way. The assumption of the life-cycle model is that as individuals mature into subsequent stages of the life cycle, their needs, roles, and emotional outlooks change. Briefly, some of the characteristics of the three major stages of the adult life cycle have been described as follows. Youth and young adulthood represent a time of peak energy, heightened cognitive processing, and the attempt to define the self and the relationship between the self and society (Erikson, 1968; Keniston, 1977; Piaget, 1967). Middle age is characterized by increased decision making and power, expanded social networks, and a drop-off in vitality (Borland, 1978; Lowenthal & Chiriboga, 1977; Valiant, 1977). Older adulthood frequently involves greater physical and health problems, role loss, greater cautiousness, and introspection (Botwinick, 1978; Huyck & Hoyer, 1982). As Conger (1971) expressed it, young people need ways to consume energy, are concerned about where they are going, are impatient, impulsive, and imperious, tending to worry most about themselves. Adults look for ways to conserve energy, are concerned about where they have been, tend to be tempered and cautious, and worry more about their children.

These life-cycle changes that occur with age may in turn alter the individual's political outlook. For example, it has been argued that the natural slow-downs of advancing age promote political conservatism among older persons (Hudson & Binstock, 1976). Also, the tendency for middle-aged and older adults to be politically conservative is facilitated by the roles they are expected to perform in society. Adults act as the conservers of tradition, whose job is to transmit the cultural and political heritage to the younger members of society. Young people, however, have a fresh contact with society that furnishes, partially at least, their impelling basis for generational conflict and social and political change.

The stage of youth is of special concern to those interested in life-cycle politics. Certain cognitive changes develop during youth that provide the foundation for the formation of political and social attitudes. Qualitatively different ways of thinking occur as the young person becomes better able to reason abstractly, to see alternatives and hypothesize, to be more future-oriented, and to evaluate and criticize (Keniston, 1977; Piaget & Inhelder, 1969). And, in general, much of the political research confirms that the stage of youth involves a new political awareness, along with the ability to comprehend and evaluate political issues (Gallatin, 1980). For example, Adelson's (1975) study of American and European adolescents indicated that during the stage of youth, political evaluations became less simplistic, as well as more cynical, pessimistic, and pragmatic.

In addition to the cognitive changes that enable the young person to develop a better grasp of politics, important social-emotional changes occur during adolescence and youth that enhance the likelihood of tension and political conflict between the age groups. One of the major tasks for individual growth and maturity during the stage of youth is the movement away from parents and towards increased self-sufficiency. Youthful striving for both security and independence may be expressed in intergenerational turmoil over politics, as well as in other types of behavior — countercultural styles, delinquency, and escapist pursuits.

Freud, of course, saw the purpose of this drive for independence as necessary to gain "genital primacy" and the "definitive completion of the process of nonincestuous object finding" (Spiegel, 1951, p. 380). According to this argument:

> Detachment from the incestuous object brings the "problem of generation" into the foreground and gives it its psychological explanation. The emotional detachment results, at least for a time, in rejection, resentment, and hostility toward parents and other authority . . . . (Muuss, 1968, p. 40)

Admittedly, Freud did not pay much attention to political factors or history in his psychoanalytic theory, but he provided the foundation for subsequent explanations of generational animus and youth rebellion.

One offshoot of the Freudian psychodynamic perspective of life-cycle development is Erikson's psychosocial concept of identity formation in adolescence, which he viewed as "essentially a generational issue." The older generation provides "those forceful ideas which must antecede identity formation in the next generation — if only so that youth can rebel against a well-defined set of older values" (Erikson, 1968, p. 30). Developing ego strength is a key to healthy personality, and Erikson strongly emphasized the importance of the interaction between the individual and the community. Youth is a time of crucial contact with society, a major task of which is to define the relationship between self and society. At the core of youth's "most passionate and most erratic striving" is fidelity — a search for something and somebody to be true, which arises "only in the interplay of a life stage with the individuals and the social forces of a true community" (Erikson, 1968, p. 235). In the process of "decentering" (the developmental tendency to gradually concentrate or center less on the self and become more objective in dealing with the external world), young people become increasingly aware of the larger society — beyond self, family, and friends — and more concerned with their potential place in the world. The youthful search for fidelity, self-identity, and the relationship between self and society can be expressed in a number of ways, according to Erikson (1968, p. 243), such as "being on the go," vigorous work, absorbing sports and dance, or through participation "in the movements of the day."

The historical situation and the structure of the society have a lot to do with how youth go through the developmental process. For example, Bettelheim (1963) argued that modern technological societies make young people's integration into society difficult and exacerbate the probability of intergenerational conflict. In traditional societies, the energy and physical strength of the young are needed by the adult society, but in modern societies, the old and the young no longer require each other. Self-identification and self-realization among the young often depend on adults allowing people to come into their own. In modern societies, young people have turned from being an economic asset to a liability, with an extended period of dependency — becoming more expensive to clothe, feed, and educate. Kept on the margins of society, young people use the one power resource they have, which is "to be the accuser and judge of the parents' success or failure as parents" (Bettelheim, 1963, p. 75). Young people, expected to create a new but "not yet delineated society," find themselves "rebels without a cause" (Bettelheim, 1963, p. 75). Youth are happiest, Bettelheim maintained, when they feel they are striving to reach the goals set, but not yet realized by the adult generation. In this way, young people prove to themselves that they are gaining in their own maturity.

Several political consequences follow from the life-cycle interpretation. First, age groups are likely to interpret political event in different ways, given their divergent psychosocial and biological orientations. In particular, young people, with their new political awareness, high idealism, and desire for independence may disagree with the current social and political conditions soon to be bequeathed to them by their elders, and press for change. As the conservers of tradition, the middle-aged and older members of society are less idealistic and more cautious. With their peak power and strong developmental stake in society, adult age groups are better integrated into the mainstream and more supportive of the status quo (Bengtson & Cutler, 1976; Martin, Bengtson, & Acock, 1974).

Second, inherrent in the life-cycle view of politics is the likelihood of generational conflict. Whether the source of conflict is psychosexual or psychosocial, such conflict is assumed to be universal. For example, youth unrest in the 1960s was explained by some observers as the result of youthful strivings for personal independence and the need to belong, fulfilling deep emotional needs, and a way of undoing past disappointments and conflicts (Duncan, 1980; Feuer, 1969; Hendin, 1975; Murphy, 1974). From this perspective historical causes tend to be treated as secondary, with youthful political protest seen as growing out of unconscious psychological conflicts as one generation confronts the next.

A third political consequence that may follow from a life-cycle explanation suggests that young people change their political views over time, as they age and assume greater social responsibilities. Once the young person takes his or her place in society and begins to meet the demands of work and family, political outlooks are predicted to change. Specifically, political alienation lessens, while political conservatism and voter participation increase (Milbrath & Goel, 1977). In answer to the question, "where have all the 1960s activists gone," it was reported that they joined the the establishment and settled into society. As one former 1960s activist was quoted as saying, "You can't make a revolution if you have to make a living" (Goldman & Lubenow, 1977). Certainly some of the radicals appeared to have changed in their adult years. Rennie Davis (cofounder of Students for a Democratic Society and member of the Chicago Seven) by the late 1970s was married, had children, and sold life insurance for a time with the John Hancock Insurance Company. Eldridge Cleaver (author of the provocative *Soul on Ice,* who was involved in shoot-outs with police in Oakland and escaped to Cuba, Algiers, and Paris) became homesick and turned himself over to authorities in the 1970s. Cleaver then joined the lecture circuit—sometimes with former Watergate felon and born-again Christian Charles Colson—telling about his religious experiences and was involved in designing slacks and marketing men's clothing (Braungart & Braungart, 1980).

Empirical evidence supporting a shift to conservatism with advancing age has been provided by political surveys that have compared age differences in liberal versus conservative or Republican versus Democratic Party support. Most studies report that young people are much more likely to endorse liberal and Democratic political positions, whereas middle-aged and older people have a higher proportion of conservatives and Republicans within their ranks—a consistent pattern for more than three decades of research (Abramson, 1983; Hendricks & Hendricks, 1977; Hudson & Binstock, 1976; Lipset, 1981).

It is the assumption of life-cycle politics that much of the political disagreement between age groups is an outgrowth of the natural maturational struggles and stresses inherent in the aging processes, with political divisiveness one possible outcome or symptom of intergenerational conflict. There are, however, several problems with the life-cycle interpretation of generational politics. To begin with, since youthful strivings for identity and independence are part of the growing-up process—with young people perhaps needing to directly confront adults and parents in order to gain personal autonomy—why are not youth unrest and rebellion a constant feature of political life? Why were young people of the 1930s and 1960s so politically active, whereas youth in the 1950s or late 1970s appeared politically quiescent or apathetic? Next, just because young people respond in a more politically liberal fashion than their elders, are these attitudes and behavior necessarily attributable to life-cycle differences in development?

B. Cohort Politics

The cohort perspective offers a slightly different explanation for the relationship between age and politics. Both the life-cycle and cohort interpretations emphasize the importance of youth and young adulthood as a time in life when political attitudes and behavior begin to crystallize. However, the life-cycle or maturational view focuses on inherent developmental processes and changes that occur within the individual, while the cohort approach stresses the political events and historical setting as young people come of age in society.

The socialization experiences of a cohort are initiated at birth. Each cohort has a distinctive demographic composition and character, particularly its size, and as Ryder (1965, p. 845) explained: "Any extraordinary size deviation is likely to leave an imprint on the cohort as well as on the society." Moller (1972, p. 232) attributed many modern youth revolutions to the rapid demographic growth in sheer numbers of young people, maintaining that "the greater the proportion of young people, the greater the likelihood of cultural and political change." Each cohort grows up with a specific set of age norms, experiences, and opportunities that help condition its way of thinking and influence the nature and direction of its political attitudes and behavior.

Social and political events may have different effects on the various age cohorts, depending on each cohort's relative stage in life-cycle development. Major historical events such as war, economic depression, immigration, new or revolutionary intellectual thought, and technological innovation, have a strong impact on most members of society, but especially on the attitudes and behavior of the young. Dramatic events, such as war and economic depression, interrupt the stage of youth at a critical time in social development. Elder (1974) described the effect of the 1930s depression on adolescents, many of whom had to abandon adolescent pursuits to take on family responsibilities, delaying their own education and marriage. Such experiences during youth tended to have a lasting impact on later adult orientations and behavior. Employing a cohort interpretation of politics, Loewenberg (1974) attributed the rise of Nazism in Germany to the specific historical experiences of the relatively large cohort of children who grew up during the World War I and postwar years. According to Loewenberg, having fathers off fighting in a war who later returned in defeat, the hunger and deprivation endured during the war, the collapse of imperial Germany and political authority, and postwar unemployment made this cohort of young Germans receptive to the bitter and simple-minded Nazi solutions. This was a cohort, Loewenberg observed that was

> . . . seeking restitution of a lost childhood. . . . What the youth cohort wanted was a fantasy of warmth, closeness, security, power, and love. What they recreated was a repetition of their own childhoods. (1974, p. 105)

Ortega stressed that cohorts are defined by a zone of dates, making it possible for two persons born within several years of each other to be part of separate cohorts or generations. A few years difference in birth can have a dramatic effect on the mentalities of cohorts. As the writer J.B. Priestly described: those born soon after 1904 and grew up in pre-World War I Europe knew that the world was a cruel and dangerous place, but those born prior to 1904 became aware of a jagged crack in history, with one world ending in 1914 and another beginning in 1919 (Rintala, 1979). Society is comprised of a series of age cohorts that are born, raised, come of age, and mature under a particular set of historical circumstances. When social change is intense and rapid, the mentality of youthful cohorts may be very different from other cohorts.

The key assumption of the cohort perspective is that the political and social attitudes that crystallize during youth and young adulthood do not change appreciably as individuals mature. As Chief Justice Bushe remarked in 1831, "I have read over a pamphlet which I wrote in 1791 when in my twenty-fifth year . . . yet at the end of forty years, I abide by most of the principles that I then maintained" (Rintala, 1979, p. 18). The political attitudes that are developed early in life provide, as Mannheim (1952) said, the formative principles by which subsequent political events are interpreted and responded to throughout the life cycle. Mannheim also noted that generations may be fighting different opponents — an observation that was confirmed in one study of age-group political attitudes, where it was reported that the majority of older persons were against giving atheists or Communists a public forum. These "enemies" for the older age group were not "opponents" for young and middle-age groups, the majority of whom supported civil liberties for such groups (Braungart & Braungart, 1982).

When political and social events are preceived and reacted to differently by the various contemporary cohorts, then generational conflict may arise. However, proponents of the cohort view contend that it is not the particular historical events, trends, and external–internal conflicts per se that are important, but, at a deeper level, the resulting patterns of thought and mentalities that take form within each cohort (Marias, 1970). Thus the entrance of young cohorts into society represents a genuine potential for social change, but, as Ryder (1965, p. 850) pointed out, "without specification of its content or direction." Much depends not only on the actual historical structure and conditions, but on how these are interpreted by the different age groups.

C. Life-Cycle Versus Cohort Explanations

Both the life-cycle and cohort models account for age-group disagreement over politics, but each model stresses different features. The life-cycle approach emphasizes growth, maturation, and change in political views as young people come into contact with politics and as they mature through the life cycle. The cohort explanation highlights the importance of historical circumstances as young people come of age and form their political views, which tend to be carried with them throughout their lives. Each model makes slightly different predictions about the political attitudes formed during youth: the life-cycle model predicts a change in political outlooks as individuals grow older and assume different responsibilities and roles; the cohort model indicates that the political attitudes and behavior formulated during the stage of youth are relatively enduring throughout life and provide a foundation for subsequent political interpretations.

Most of the empirical investigations comparing age differences in politics involve examinations of stability and change in liberalism–conservatism, political party identification, alienation, and voting behavior (M. Braungart, 1980; Hendricks & Hendricks, 1977; Hudson & Binstock, 1976). Numerous studies reported that young people were more likely to be politically liberal, while older people were more supportive of conservatism and Republican party identification (Lipset, 1981; Milbrath & Goel, 1977; Stacey, 1977). Crittenden (1962) interpreted these age differences in politics as indicating a systematic movement toward conservatism with advancing age. However, this view was not supported by others who favored a cohort interpretation, arguing that there is a tendency to retain those political orientations learned early in life (Abramson, 1975; Campbell, 1971; Foner, 1972; Glamser, 1974; Hudson & Binstock, 1976). According to the cohort explanation, at the time when many older people developed their political attitudes and opinions, they may have appeared relatively liberal in comparison with the older cohorts of their day, but because society changes, by contemporary standards, older people merely appear conservative relative to younger age groups (Campbell, 1971; Foner, 1972; Hudson & Binstock, 1976). Strong support for a cohort-historical interpretation was reported in a comparative election study, where the cohort that entered the political system in the Depression–New Deal years continued to have strong Democratic party identification throughout the life cycle (Campbell, Converse, Miller, & Stokes, 1960). Reanalysis and extension of the data base used by Crittenden did not confirm an increase in Republicanism with age. For example, Cutler (1969) reported a slight cohort effect, while Glenn and Hefner (1972) concluded that the cross-sectional data gathered at various times over the past 30 years — indicating a positive association between age and Republicanism — reflected generational or cohort differences rather than aging effect. A cohort effect on politics has also been identified for the declining relationship between social class and partisan choice during the years after World War II (Abramson, 1974).

One of the strongest proponents of the cohort-historical argument is Inglehart (1971, 1977, 1981). In a cross-national European survey, major differences in value orientation were evident for older versus younger cohorts. According to Inglehart, these differences appeared to be rooted in the historical condition of whether one came of age during times of economic depression in the 1930s or grew up under the relatively affluent post–World War II economy. Inglehart's central thesis is that the postwar affluence facilitated a shift from materialist (austerity and authoritarian) values to postmaterialist (hedonistic and liberation) values. His survey in the 1970s confirmed that older cohorts who experienced the economic depression of the 1930s had less favorable attitudes toward expressive values, such as free speech and life-style changes, when compared to younger cohorts socialized under a different set of historical circumstances where economic security was taken for granted. More recently, Inglehart (1981) argued that the pro- versus anti-nuclear power struggle in Europe is not a class struggle but a form of generational polarization based on materialist versus postmaterialist values.

Further support for a cohort interpretation can be found in studies of 1960s political activists. Despite a few activists who appeared to have changed their life-style and political orientation as they grew older, a comparison of follow-up surveys of former political activists and case studies of activist leaders revealed a lasting effect of having been politically active and radical in the 1960s. In general, left-wing activists and their leaders did not join the establishment and pursue careers in business, rather, they chose careers that were in keeping with their youthful social and political values, favoring jobs in education, social services, and government where they could at least implicitly work for their political goals. Second, only a minority of former activists abandoned politics, with most maintaining a high level of political commitment and interest throughout the 1970s. The follow-up surveys indicated that the great majority of former radicals remained liberal or far left in their political orientations; however, a number of case studies illustrated while their political goals changed little, their style of expression, strategies, and tactics selected to implement their goals mellowed considerably (Braungart & Braungart, 1980).

A cohort interpretation for political behavior is becoming increasingly popular. A recent analysis of European politics identified a new generation of activists who were born after World War II (Szabo, 1983a, 1983b). Labeled the "successor generation," they have no memory of the war and take affluence and political stability for granted. This new generation of Europeans is at odds with the "founder generation" (founders of the Atlantic Alliance), who grew up in pre–World War II Europe and remember a Europe divided by war, Stalinist Russia, Soviet threats to security, and view the United States as a "model of self-confident and dominant power whose values and social system contrasted favorably with those of Europe and the U.S.S.R." (Szabo, 1983a, p. 9). To the contrary, the successor generation views America as "excessively materialistic" and is deeply suspicious of American motives and power—"America does not connote to them the Marshall Plan and the Berlin Airlift, or even John Kennedy, but rather Vietnam and Watergate" (Szabo, 1983a, p. 9). University educated and eschewing traditional religion, the young European successor generation strongly supports left-wing politics, antinuclear peace movements and is disenchanted with both the United States and U.S.S.R. world superpowers. Opinion polls indicated that in the area of military defense, only 13% of university-trained Italians born after 1950 endorsed increased defense, as compared to 50% of university-educated Italians born prior to World War II. Generational divisions also were evident among the highly educated Western Europeans regarding their opinions about NATO, with the founder generation favoring NATO and the successor generation endorsing greater neutrality from NATO. Szabo (1983a, 1983b) argued that these findings may have important implications for Western foreign policy, especially as the members of the successor generation begin to assume more leadership and administrative positions in European governments.

The picture is not always clear, however, regarding life-cycle versus cohort effects on politics. Jennings and Niemi's (1981) panel study of adolescents and their parents—analyzed at both the aggregate and family levels—concluded in favor of mixed effects, finding both elements of stability (cohort effects) and change (life-cycle effects) in individual and group political views over time. They maintained that change in adult political outlooks, in particular, should be granted more significance than it has in the past. Jennings and Niemi (1981, p. 387) also took issue with the widespread notion that political attitudes tend to crystallize prior to late adolescence, contending that although young adults change their political views more frequently than older persons, and the likelihood of political change is less as one ages, the results of their panel study indicated that political views of older adults "are far from intractable."

The appropriateness of the life-cycle or cohort models in accounting for age differences in politics depends on a number of factors, including the particular political attitude or issue under study. As Abramson (1975) noted, the cohort explanation only holds for relatively stable attitudes; when attitudes are more malleable, change is likely to occur for all age groups. Samuels (1977) contended that the type of society also matters in interpreting age differences in politics. The life-cycle model may have greater applicability in slowly changing societies such as India, while the cohort explanation appears appropriate for rapidly changing societies – particularly those societies that have experienced nationalist struggles where the rise of new institutions and military units represents important benchmarks for political experiences and divides age groups into pre- and postnationalist generations.

D. Factors that Minimize Age-Group Differences in Politics

Both the life-cycle and cohort views predict that the young and old are likely to disagree politically, but the life-cycle model attributes the age differences to maturational changes over time, whereas the cohort model emphasizes the importance of historical experiences during the formative period. Other factors minimize age differences in politics. For example, pronounced age-group political disagreement may be more evident at certain times and places in history than others, and over some issue areas but not others. Despite the tendency to emphasize age-group differences in politics, generational politics also includes examinations of age-group similarities and agreement over politics. Of particular interest here are those factors that minimize, obscure, or override the effects of life cycle and cohort placement: period effects, intra-age variability, and lineage or political socialization effects.

1. Period Effects. The period effect occurs when current events and societal trends induce age groups to react to politics in a similar way. Dramatic events, such as a popular war, political scandal, or foreign threat (hostage crisis, terrorism, impending war), provide solidifying experiences which facilitate age-group agreement over politics (Rosow, 1978). Certain social and political trends too have an effect independent of age, where all age and cohort groups respond similarly. There are a number of ways period effects may influence politics, as some of the following examples illustrate.

Comparing life-cycle, cohort, and period effects has been a popular research design for investigations of alienation, conservatism, political party identification, and voting participation (Hudson & Binstock, 1976). The interpretation of findings is not always clear, but analysis and reanalysis of political data point to the growing importance of period effects in politics. As an illustration, the finding that young people are less likely to be Republican when compared to older persons has gone through several changes in interpretation. Initially, the positive association between advancing age and increased Republicanism was explained as a consequence of life-cycle changes; later, it was reinterpreted as a cohort effect, where those entering the electorate after 1928 were identified as less likely to be Republican. The question was then raised: why, given the failure of young people to become Republican, has the percentage of Republicans remained relatively constant (Abramson, 1983)? Closer examination of the data indicated that the largest increase in Democratic strength was for those who were in their twenties during the Great Depression, but by the 1950s the trend had run its course.

The cohorts that entered the electorate after the 1950s have been as Republican as the national electorate. Of interest here is the role that generational trends can play in political change (Bengtson & Cutler, 1976). In this case, a generational replacement trend appears to be occurring. That is, certain political events may affect the attitudes of new cohorts entering the electorate but not the attitudes of older cohorts. Cohorts entering the electorate since the 1950s had levels of Republican support similar to the national electorate, while the older cohorts that had strongly supported Republicanism had left the electorate by 1952; thus, the overall ratio of Republicans to Democrats remained relatively constant (Abramson, 1983).

Alienation is another factor that has been subject to period effects. Although it was hypothesized that high levels of alienation might be the result of life-cycle effects (young people and old people are not well integrated into modern societies and hence more alienated) or cohort effects (certain cohorts such as the "lost generation," the "beat generation," and the "1960s generation" have especially high levels of alienation), analyses of national opinion poll data clearly supported a period effect, with age groups and cohorts responding similarly to items designed to measure political alienation. More specifically, all age levels and cohorts evidenced a decrease in political alienation from 1952–1960, followed by an increase in alienation from 1960–1968 (Cutler & Bengtson, 1974). A correlational analysis of these data demonstrated that the changes in alienation could not be attributed to age, region, education, income, or gender (House & Mason, 1975). No doubt, the dramatic events and social trends of the 1960s — Vietnam war, assassinations, disenchantment with leadership, mass society — neutralized age and cohort differences (along with other demographic and social differences) to promote an increase in alienation expressed by all age groups.

A period effect also has been demonstrated for political efficacy, although, in this case, the results were somewhat mixed. Analysis of 12 SRC (Survey Research Center, University of Michigan) surveys from 1952–1980 confirmed a slight life-cycle effect in that older people were less politically efficacious, with a drop occurring around ages 60–70. However, despite the apparent life-cycle effect, period effects carried greater weight, with each cohort declining in feelings of political efficacy over time (Abramson, 1983; Searing, Wright, & Rabinowitz, 1976). Perhaps many of the same events and trends that promoted increased alienation among all age groups were associated with declines in feelings of political efficacy for each cohort.

Period effects may be evident when a generational trend occurs where one age group switches its support from one direction to another, while another age group shifts in the opposite direction, thus canceling out life-cycle or cohort differences. In a recent cohort study by Inglehart (1981), the youngest cohort declined in postmaterialist value orientation (a decrease in support for expressive values), while the older cohorts became less materialistic (increased support for expressive values) over the years. These investigations of period effects suggest that societal trends and events may play an important part in promoting shifts in political attitudes and behavior within all age groups and that an observed relationship between age and politics may change over time.

2. Intra-Age Variability. It has been argued that a wide diversity of political orientations and social backgrounds is represented within each age group. Consequently, the likelihood of an age group sharing similar political views is minimal. Mannheim (1952) clearly recognized that political differences within a generation may be as great or greater than those between generations. According to this line of thinking, although members of an age group are exposed to a common set of historical experiences at a similar stage in the life cycle, because they occupy diverse status positions and differ in other conditions of life, they interpret and react to the sociopolitical situation in a variety of ways. There is some support for this argument. During the politically volatile 1960s, a number of viewpoints and responses were identified within the ranks of the younger generation — left-wing activists (revolutionary, radical, reformist), hippies (communal, drug-oriented, "back-to-nature"), political moderates and conventionals (Democrats, Republicans, Independents), right-wing activists (conservative, reactionary, and violent), along with many apoliticals (Braungart, 1979; Yankelovich, 1972, 1974). These various political reactions, in turn, appeared to be partially the result of different family, class, and status backgrounds. For example, left-wing activist youth were more likely to come from affluent, minority ethnic and religious homes, while student members of right-wing organizations tended to be drawn from less affluent, majority ethnic and religious backgrounds (Braungart, 1979; Dunlap, 1970; Westby & Braungart, 1966).

Concern with the variation within age groups is related to two issues in generational politics: (a) whether the diversity of political opinion or attitudes within an age group is so wide that it overrides any possible inter-age group differences in politics; and (b) whether the political orientations and social status characteristics associated with these orientations are similar or different within the ranks of the young, middle-aged, and older adult groups. The argument concerning the first issue suggests that since social location factors — such as social class, ethnicity, education, and gender — differentiate the political views expressed within age groups, these social characteristics may cut across other age-group divisions to minimize the effects of age on politics (Bengtson, Kassachau, & Ragan, 1977; Fengler & Wood, 1972). The empirical question then becomes this: When age is considered relative to other social status factors, does it exert an independent effect on politics, when other social status dimensions are held constant?

This question was addressed in Inglehart's (1977) national European survey and in Braungart and Braungart's (1982) analysis of NORC (National Opinion Research Center, University of Chicago) data. Both studies employed path analysis and reported that age had a strong independent effect on political orientations and participation. Despite the wide range of political attitudes and social backgrounds within age groups, intra-age variability did not negate interage differences in politics—although this finding may vary, depending on the particular political variables under study.

It is important in the analysis of generational politics to consider not only political differences between age groups but also to make comparisons within age groups. Some of the intra-age examinations of politics have suggested important qualifications for the relationship between age and politics. First, there appears to be a greater likelihood of change over time and wider variation in the political attitudes and behavior of the young when compared to middle-aged and older age groups (Abramson, 1975, 1983; Braungart & Braungart, 1982; Jennings & Niemi, 1981). Second, the involvement and intensity of political views within each age group may vary, depending on the specific issue, wording and interpretation of questions, or time during which political research is conducted. In general, the more proximal the issue for the age group (health care represents a high priority issue for older persons but not for younger people), the greater the intensity of response (Douglass, Cleveland, & Maddox, 1974). And third, the effects of various social location factors on politics may be different for the young, middle age, and old. In one study, the social status dimensions that differentiated the politics of young adults were different from the social location factors that were associated with the politics of middle-aged and older adults (Braungart & Braungart, 1982). Furthermore, the social status and politics relationships may not be the same for subgroups of an age group—as in one study comparing the politics of college versus noncollege youth, or in another investigation contrasting the politics of the "young-old" with the "old-old" (Braungart, 1976; M. Braungart, 1980). These findings point to the importance of examining intra-age variability in generational politics, not only to determine whether the diversity in politics within age groups minimizes interage-group differences, but also to look for important political distinctions within young, middle-aged, and older age groups.

3. Political Socialization and Lineage Effects. Another factor that may temper age-group or generational differences in politics (minimizing life-cycle and cohort effects) involves the efforts of parents and adults to socialize the young into politics—what has been termed the lineage effect in generational analysis (Bengtson & Cutler, 1976). In most societies, parents and adults are responsible for teaching the younger members of society the values, norms, orientations, and proscriptions for everyday life. A sizable literature has accumulated in the area of political socialization, concerned with: (a) the extent of political similarities and differences between parents and offspring or adults and young people, and (b) the factors that influence the political socialization process (Dawson, Prewitt, & Dawson, 1977; Renshon, 1977).

As a point of clarification, in political socialization or lineage analysis, the concept of chronological age has less meaning than in cohort or life-cycle analysis. Lineage roles of parents or adults are not necessarily highly correlated with chronological age, since one person may become a parent at age 19, while others may not have their first child until their early 40s. It therefore becomes difficult to talk about the parent or adult "generation" in a life-cycle or cohort sense (Bengtson & Cutler, 1976). It is the social role of transmitting political values and behavior to the young that provides the significance of lineage or political socialization analysis.

The theoretical underpinnings of the socialization literature are drawn largely from the behaviorist, symbolic interactionist, and social-learning theories, which assume that children and adolescents learn their political orientations from "significant others" such as parents and authority figures. Adults tend to reward the attitudes and behavior of young people that correspond with their own, while they may attempt to extinguish (through nonreinforcement or punishment) political views that run contrary to the adult "definition of the situation." The political socialization efforts of parents and adults are not necessarily direct or intensive, but are nonetheless considered to have an impact on the politics of the young. In contrast, the psychodynamic theoretical position argues that because of the inherent generational animus between youngsters and parents or authority figures, young people develop their own unique, and perhaps rebellious, interpretations of society and politics. From this perspective, offspring and their parents are not likely to agree over politics.

The extent to which young people adhere to or break away from their parents' political beliefs has been a popular topic of research, with most investigations reporting that the correlation between parent–offspring politics is at best moderate (Cutler, 1977; Stacey, 1977). In one sense, the research indicates that the transmission of political orientations from parents to offspring facilitates stability in society, but on the other hand, it also implies that there is room for change in the politics of young people. Despite the modest correlation in family politics, some research has suggested that parents have a greater impact than peers in influencing adolescent political orientations (Jennings & Niemi, 1981; Tedin, 1974).

In the 1960s, the existence of a "generation gap" in politics was widely debated. From a psychodynamic perspective, it was argued that young people were disgusted with the older age group and were acting out a host of deep-seated emotional conflicts with their parents in the political arena. Other researchers maintained that activist youth were not rebelling against their parents per se but were merely carrying out the political orientations and values learned in the home. Much of the research conducted on student activists during the 1960s confirmed the socialization explanation for political behavior, or what Keniston (1968) termed the "red diaper" hypothesis (Braungart, 1971, 1979, 1980; Flacks, 1967).

The socialization or transmission of political orientations from parent to offspring, or from adults to youngsters, does not occur in a vacuum and is itself determined by a number of factors, such as the rate of social change, the complexity of the social structure, the degree of cultural integration and lag, social mobility, and the nature of the socialization relationship. The political socialization process is also influenced by affective and cognitive factors, including emotional ties and attachment bonds, gender and ethnic identity, and sibling placement (Bengtson & Black, 1973; Davies, 1977). Consequently, the extent of parent–offspring or adult–youth agreement over politics may fluctuate, depending on any number of factors.

The relationship between family or lineage socialization and politics changes over time. According to one panel study, the modest correlation in parent–youth political agreement when offspring were in high school declined following high school (Jennings & Niemi, 1981). No doubt, after offspring graduate from high school and leave home, other political socialization forces come into play that may weaken family political agreement. Newcomb's (1943) classic Bennington study indicated that the college experience may be one such important force, since the freshmen from Republican homes often changed their political views in keeping with the liberal orientation of Bennington College. Follow-up studies of Bennington graduates reported that many former students still adhered to the liberal politics of their college days — although the political orientations of spouses and friends in later adulthood had considerable bearing on whether Bennington graduates eventually changed their political views back in the conservative direction (Newcomb, Koenig, Flacks, & Warwick, 1967).

The formation of political attitudes and behavior on the basis of age-group membership takes place under different circumstances. On the one hand, the potentially divisive life-cycle and cohort-historical conditions can promote age-group differences and political change, while on the other hand, period effects, intra-age variability, and lineage political socialization may enhance age-group agreement and political stability. During so-called routine historical periods, youth cohorts come and go, incorporated into adult society without major political incident. These are the cumulative periods in world time, represented by recurring biological rhythms of birth, aging, and death. During routine or cumulative periods, adult society dominates the general direction of political development and change, the socialization process of the younger age groups, and the type of politics prevailing at the time.

However, when younger age groups experience the same historical location as they come of age and perceive inconsistencies in the adult world, they may mobilize to challenge adult hegemony in the form of intergenerational and intragenerational conflict. When age groups are both influenced by national and international forces through their collective exposure to historically conditioned structures, processes, and events, and they organize and exert their collective will on existing institutional forms to bring about radical political change, they become full-fledged political generations that represent eliminating periods in world time. During eliminating periods, political generations, often in the form of youth movements, dominate or significantly influence the structure and direction of social and political change, the socialization process, and the style of politics expressed at that time (Braungart, 1982a). The purpose of the following discussion is to outline why and how political generations take form.

IV. POLITICAL GENERATIONS

A political generation comes into existence when an age group rejects the existing order, joins together, and attempts to redirect the course of politics as its "generational mission." An important corollary question is why do political generations arise during certain periods in history but not others? Why were young people politically quiescent in the 1950s and 1970s in the United States but active during the 1930s and 1960s? Explanations for the formation of political generations have stemmed from two major sources: (a) those focusing on the importance of historical circumstances and social–structural conditions; and (b) those emphasizing the dynamics of mobilization into movements for political change. Thus far, many of the political–generational movements have been initiated by young people — based partially on their placement or stage in the life cycle which makes them receptive to the idea of change and engaging in "action." The focus of the discussion of political generations is on the young and the various youth movements that have erupted over the past 170 years. The question why political generations arise is addressed by outlining the historical circumstances that promote their development; the issue of how political generations take form is offered by drawing from the mobilization literature and discussions of intergenerational and intragenerational conflict. Included here are brief descriptions of some of the major political generations and generation units that have formed over the past 170 years. Finally, the factors associated with the decline of political–generational activity are mentioned, along with an assessment of whether political generations make any real difference in politics or history.

A. Historical Circumstances

A crucial force in the development of political generations are the historical circumstances in which young people find themselves as they are coming of age and about to enter into adult society. Generally speaking, the stage appears to be set for the formation of a political generation when young people come up against a disappointing set of conditions created by their elders. Social inconsistencies, societal breakdowns, and marked discontinuities influence the cognitive awareness of young people who are receptive to new possibilities and opportunities in a stagnating or contradictory society. Societal discontinuities in conjunction with surges in the youth population and increased higher education have been associated with the rise of youth movement activity (Greer, 1979; Gurr, 1970; Gusfield, 1979; Hamilton & Wright, 1975; Kornhauser, 1959; Meyer & Rubinson, 1972; Moller, 1972; Smelser, 1963, 1968; Weinberg & Walker, 1969). While space does not permit a full discussion of the historical circumstances related to political–generational activity, some of the more important social, political, economic, technological, and cultural conditions associated with youthful political activity briefly are outlined (Braungart, 1980, 1982a).

Social trends credited with providing the seedbed for youth unrest are modernization, nationalism, industrialization, urbanization, secularization, and bureaucratization. These are the forces which have both ignited young people's aspirations, yet segregated them from society. In general, modernization carries with it a number of problems — rural emigration, urban poverty, and discontent — making it difficult for political systems and elites to juggle limited resources with rising demands, especially those by idealistic youth (Gurr, 1970). Disenchanted with the performance of elites, young people have reacted by organizing antibureaucratic, antiregime, and university reform movements.

A major political factor in the lives of young people has been the drive for nationalism, which spearheaded the first youth movements in the nineteenth century known as the Young Europe movement. This generational movement later became the impetus for the anticolonial and nationalist struggles around the turn of the twentieth century in Asia, Latin America, and more recently in Africa and the Middle East (Lipset & Altbach, 1969; Snyder, 1982). Beginning with the American and French Revolutions, a consistent political force has been the quest for citizenship, suffrage, and egalitarianism, which provided the issues and tactics for student activism throughout the world.

War has been an important factor linked to youthful political generations in several ways. Wartime defeat results in political and social reorganization, as well as loss of national honor. The defeat of Napoleon at Waterloo and the desire for national unity spurred Young Italy and Young Germany in the 1800s. The disappointment of defeat in Germany after World War I was seen by Loewenberg (1974) and Hamilton and Wright (1975) as drawing young people toward right-wing fascism with its paramilitary appeals and simplistic violent solutions. War has provided an impetus for youthful political mobilization in another way: when young people decided that they did not want to fight and die — a triggering issue for massive antiwar protests in the United States in the 1930s and again in the 1960s (Draper, 1967; Starr, 1974).

Debilitating economic conditions, particularly depressions and unemployment, stimulated youth unrest in the 1930s in the United States and Europe. When economic times were hard (sinking GNP, lower production and consumption rates), young people became the most vulnerable to unemployment, particularly unskilled and college-educated youth. Draper (1967, p. 156) referred to young Americans of the 1930s as the Locked-Out Generation: "A whole section of the American middle class was being declassed; and the student movement was in part a result of this declassment." Young Europeans were having similar experiences, and Simon (1967) observed that during these troubled economic times people seemed to be looking for charismatic leaders who could turn their despair into hope.

Technological changes, too, have provided both a direct and indirect impetus for youthful political generations. Technology was a direct issue in the 1960s, 1970s, and 1980s ecology movements, ban-the-bomb, and antinuclear power rallies in the United States, Western Europe, and Japan. The upsurges in protest in the early 1980s were staffed not only by multitudes of young people but many former student radicals from the 1960s (Braungart & Braungart, 1980). Youth have reacted against technology by creating countercultural movements, such as the *Wandervögel* movement in Germany around the turn of the twentieth century, which urged young people to abandon the materialistic values and life-styles of their parents and return to a more simple, natural life. This same theme appeared again in the American 1950s Beat Generation and 1960s hippie movements. Rapid communications and transportation were other forces behind the youth movements, which spread quickly to every continent in the 1960s. It was this new technology that linked together enclaves of youth around the world and offered a vehicle for youth consciousness and mobilization. Capturing media attention became an important part of the youthful activists' political game (Gitlin, 1980).

There is a close tie between the cultural context and political generations. The marginality and isolation of youth, as an age-status group adrift and alienated in modern society, coupled with surges in the youth population have tended to produce a youth culture, where age peers rather than adults exerted the major socializing influence. Young people have reacted against adult values and norms by creating their own culture in opposition to conventional society. For example, the political conservatism and outmoded beliefs of the overly formalized nineteenth century, in conjunction with rising expectations among youth, resulted in the romantic notion of "student freedom fighters"—individualistic and antiestablishment—who would readily scale the barricades for "liberty, freedom, and equality." The youth culture of the 1960s (its music, dress, argot, drugs, and personal style) infused the political anti-war movement and created a combustible mixture of culture and politics (Altbach, 1967; Keniston, 1968).

Despite the numerous social, economic, and political reasons given for youth mobilization, both Mentré and Ortega contended it is intellectual thought and cultural forces that captivate young people's imaginations and play an overriding role in heightening their consciousness and potential for mobilization. During major turning points in history, there were identifiable influences from intellectual and creative works that inspired the hearts and minds of the young. Youth activity in the nineteenth century gained inspiration from the *Sturm und Drang* movement, Enlightenment philosophers, positivism, and utopian socialism. Turn-of-the-century youth movements were politicized by the works of Marx, the Russian novelists, the Progressives, and revolutions in art and music. Young people in the 1930s drew from the social criticism of H.L. Mencken, Sinclair Lewis, Dos Passos, Wolfe, Hemingway, Farrell, Dreiser, as well as the political "isms" of communism and socialism. In the 1960s, many activists had read and been influenced by Kerouac, Camus, Salinger, Marcuse, Che Guevara, Fanon, and Mao.

B. Dynamics of Mobilization

A political movement is not merely the passive response of a group of people to a disappointing set of historical circumstances. Political movements have to be deliberately initiated and directed; discontent must be focused and channeled through group consciousness and the belief that something can be done. A strong argument has been made that it is less social and historical disorganization and hardship that account for collective political action than solidarity and articulated interests (Etzioni, 1968; Nettl, 1967; Oberschall, 1973; Tilly, 1975; Tilly, Tilly, & Tilly, 1975).

One of the foremost proponents of the mobilization explanation of political movements has been Tilly (1975). According to Tilly, a group can be said to be mobilizing when it increases its collective control over: normative resources (commitments to ideals, groups, and other people); coercive resources (means of punishing and limiting alternatives); and utilitarian resources (all the rest, especially those things that are considered rewarding to acquire). The types of collective action that may be undertaken include competitive action (between rivals or enemies), reaction (claim is laid to a resource under the control of another group and that group resists or reacts), and proaction (a group claims a resource it was not previously accorded). The proactive behavior of one group often leads to reactive behavior by another group, with conflict and violence growing out of the interaction of organized groups. It is Tilly's view that government plays an important role in such interactions, since the withdrawal of commitment by moderate or weak governments opens the way for conflict, as both the left and right mobilize in response to the regime's insufficient ability to maintain legitimacy and effectiveness.

Very much a dynamic political process, generations have challenged and made historical differences by discrediting governments, toppling regimes, and bringing new coalitions to power. As Oberschall (1973) illustrated, the Nazi success in the 1930s was not only due to the structural conditions of a lost war, humiliation, and unemployment, but to the politicization and mobilized violence, as socialist workers and communists resisted the Nazi strong-arm tactics. Year after year of unending conflict, skirmishes, and street battles made the middle class increasingly receptive to the promises by the Nazi's to restore law and order.

Over the last two centuries, numerous historical changes, such as rapid population growth, expanding higher education, rising expectations, nationalism, depressions, and wars, produced periods of social and revolutionary change that were characterized by self-conscious and mobilized age cohorts. The historical dialectic between successive cohort flows and the existing social order tells us much about the socialization, opportunities, and political actions of young people in concrete situations. The political mobilization of youth during periods of rapid change may stem from three sources: (a) the exposure or experience of historical events, (b) the conscious interpretations of these events, and (c) the subsequent modes of responses to these events (Braungart, 1982a). Times of heightened political activity by young people represent a synthesis of historical, generational, and psychological forces that combine to produce a political generation having its own particular character and form. Once a political generation begins to materialize, its momentum is determined by political disagreement and conflict, not only between generations (intergenerational) but within generations (intragenerational) as well.

1. Intergenerational Conflict: Deauthorization and Authorization. When young people reject and/or extend significantly beyond the values, norms, and practices of their elders, a break in cohort succession results, such that adult values and norms cannot be easily transmitted to, or assimilated by, the young. The adult generation is deauthorized by the younger generation, who openly rejects and attacks tradition. The means employed to achieve deauthorization may be symbolic (verbal, written, defamation, nonviolent actions) and/or violent (destruction of property, assassination, terrorism). Intergenerational conflict involves also — and perhaps more important to the formation of a political generation — the dynamics of authorization, as the younger generation attempts to seize control and redirect the course of politics. During this process, vigorous attempts are made to create and validate the younger generation's own "indigenous" values and norms, which are perceived as transcending, superceding, and replacing those of the older generation. Authorization too may be achieved by symbolic and/or violent means.

Examples of political generations can be found in the formation of youth movements that began a little over 170 years ago in Europe. Although there were cultural and social components within each of these periods of heightened generational conflict in history, the overt thrust of much of the youthful activity was political. In surveying the various political youth movements during this time, a close relationship appears between historical change, generational mobilization, and youth movements. Historically, political generations have not represented random political behavior but have clustered around four periods in world time: the Young Europe Generation, Post-Victorian Generation, Great Depression, and 1960s Generation (Braungart, 1982a). Moreover, the structural features that produced the Young Europe Generation in 1815–1848 recurred as youth movements spread rapidly to other parts of the world — first to Latin America and Asia, then to the United States, and more recently to Africa and the Middle East. Four generational movements took form in Europe in the 1800s, and by the 1960s, at least 50 nations reported youth movement activity. The generic conditions that gave rise to the political activity of the nineteenth century European youth were conducive to similar kinds of political activity throughout the rest of the world at later periods in time. In each case, historical changes and discontinuities in society interacted with generational forces in the form of deauthorization and authorization to produce political generations. Briefly, these four periods of political–generational activity can be described as follows (for a more detailed description, see Braungart, 1982a, 1982b).

The Young Europe Generation included Young Germany, Young Italy, Young France, and Young Russia and represented a turning point in modern world time. The Young Europe movement initially involved a rejection of absolutism in favor of the modern nation-state. Inspired by the German student unions and led by Mazzini and later by Garibaldi's Red Shirts, European youth deauthorized the parent generation over their humiliating defeat at the hands of Napoleon. German and Italian youth reacted vigorously against any possibility of the return or restoration of Europe to the *ancien régime*. The young republicans and Saint Simonian socialists of France fought for greater liberty, freedom, and participated in the Revolutions of 1848. Inspired by French successes, bomb-throwing Russian students and nihilists led one of the most significant student movements recorded in world history. All across Europe, young people felt a new age was about to begin. The authorization of the younger generation was provided by university-based youth and intellectual circles, who comprised the network and nucleus for mobilizing the political rebellion that was about to become unleashed on the world. The youth revolution had begun and provided the blueprint for others to follow.

The insurrectionary patterns laid down in the mid-nineteenth century were repeated during *fin-de-siècle* Europe by the Post-Victorian Generation. Once again, youth were up in arms, deauthorizing the "backward world" of their parents and looking forward to a new modern future. *Wandervögel* youth reacted against the rigid formalism of Wilhelmine Germany and took to hiking through the romantic countryside. In other parts of the world, young revolutionary leaders like Mahatma Gandhi, Kemal Ataturk, and Mao Tse-tung were preparing to lead their countries and youthful supporters away from colonialism and despotism toward nationalism, modernization, and democracy. Young people are often at the forefront of movements for political change, and it was a young Bosnian youth who shot the heir to the Austrian throne in 1914 that triggered the onset of World War I. A third of the way around the world, young Latin American students were challenging a university system with a tradition that dated back to the Middle Ages. Paradoxically, as European colonialism was at its peak, the "serene confidence" of the Victorian colonial age was about to be challenged by mass democracy, nationalism, and socialism. Youthful intellectuals, such as the Bloomsbury circle, the revolutionary generation of Lenin, the Fabian socialists, and bohemians in the Paris of Toulouse-Lautrec opposed the stilted, conservatism of European society. Caught up in the political ferment from 1890–1918, youthful political generations, such as Young Wales, Young Ireland, youthful Czechs and Poles, and the Spanish Generation of '98, authorized themselves in the name of nationalism.

Another turning point in world time occurred during the 1930s, led in part by the Great Depression Generations. Unhappy with the Versailles Treaty, the faltering global economy, rising unemployment, the Bolshevik revolution, and unstable political systems, young people in a number of areas of the world once again mobilized for change. Youthful rejection of established authority in Europe, the United States, and Asia was widespread and intense. In order to redirect these rebellious tendencies, adult-sponsored youth groups like the *Hitler Jugend,* and Mussolini's Sons of the Wolf were created. These organizations were successful in directing the rebellious utopianism of youth into totalitarian and political service. Fascist-controlled youth groups quickly spread from the core fascist countries of Germany, Italy, and Spain throughout all of noncommunist Europe. During the same time, the United States experienced its first national student movement and one of its largest to date. American youth reacted against the depression, fascism in Europe, the threat of another impending world war, and fought for university reform. In Asia, Indian youth in unprecedented numbers participated in the national independence movement and were the most radical force in Indian political life during the 1930s. Chinese youth, who were angry over the Japanese invasion of Manchuria and Shanghai and the divided national leadership, began to look to communism for solutions to their problems.

The post-World War II years witnessed an unprecedented growth and spread of youth movements throughout Europe, Latin America, the United States, Asia, Africa, and the Middle East. Everywhere the signs and symbols of a new global malaise were the same. Youth mobilized over issues ranging from university reform and local problems to national and international issues. Young people were particularly concerned with three major issues: (a) the destruction and reform of the existing regime, (b) unity with workers and the poor, and (c) forming an international student movement. The primary means youth employed to achieve their goals were demonstrations, riots, strikes, and occupations. The consistency or similarity in both the goals and means of youth movements throughout the world indicated that the world had now become highly politicized, with an international political culture. These global themes were reinforced by the rapid rise of nationalism and the new political culture made possible by modern technology and communications systems. The 1960s represented a watershed in youth movement activity that occurred on every continent around the world. The 1960s Generation created a precedent for high levels of political activity among youth that did not completely dissipate in the decades that followed.

An examination of each of the four periods of heightened youthful political activity suggests that while there were a number of similarities and some differences in the patterns of historical factors related to youth movements, generational conflict was a common feature of all four periods. In each case, the younger generation deauthorized the older generation over such issues as defeat in war, colonialism, and lack of economic and political opportunities. At the same time, and perhaps more important, they authorized their own youthful generation to fight for nationalism, increased citizenship, university reform, and political ideology. The issues over which deauthorization and authorization emerged varied, but the generational conflict between the young and their elders appears to be a constant factor associated with the rise and fall of political generations.

2. Intragenerational Conflict: Political Generation Units. Not all members of a political generation share in the dominant generational mentality. Although exposed to the same set of historical experiences, members of a generation may react to the political situation in numerous ways, forming, as Mannheim (1952) said, competing generation units. Traditionally, generation units have often divided along both sides of the political spectrum, with some units representing utopian and extremist goals (radical left- and right-wing groups), while others are more ideological and moderate (liberal and conservative groups). The generation units that arise within any political generation may be youth-initiated, or sponsored directly or indirectly by adult organizations. Any number of spontaneous and sponsored generation units can emerge during a political generation on the political left and right (Braungart, 1982b). Spontaneous generation units usually erupt on the political left (Narodniks, Cordoba Movement, nationalist movements, the New Left), while sponsored generation units typically represent elitist, fascist, and religious organizations (pro-Royalist youth, *Hitler Jugend,* Islamic, Hindu, and Buddhist youth groups).

The divergent and often opposing generation units within a political generation do not negate the existence of a political generation, for beneath the generational diversity lies a generational unity (Esler, 1982). Each unit, in its own way, deauthorizes some aspect of society and politics. In the United States during the 1960s, left-wing youth groups reacted against the Vietnam war, U.S. imperialism, and the excesses of capitalism; right-wing youth deauthorized the New Deal liberalism, "creeping communism or socialism," and the loss of individualism. Young black activists rebelled against racism, blocked opportunities, and the oppression of minorities and the poor. While these generation units rejected the adult generation for different and sometimes similar reasons, their major point of departure was the way in which they authorized the members of their own generation unit to change the course of politics.

The dynamic pattern of intragenerational conflict generally begins with the emergence of generation units that favor radical or revolutionary change from the political left; these are insurgent left-wing or proactive generation units. Proactive or change-oriented generation units reject the ideological (liberal) status quo and embrace more radical or utopian alternatives. They usually precede and may stimulate the emergence of right-wing generation units that are against change and represent reactive or reactionary generation units. Like their left-wing counterpart, these right-wing reactive groups reject the ideological (conservative) status quo in favor of radical utopian solutions to their problems and perhaps the atavistic return to an earlier time in history. The specific historical changes and problems play a major role in determining the political direction and thrust of intragenerational conflict. Generational units can also emerge that actively represent the status quo or moderate ideological (center) positions in society, which are called active generation units. Active generation units are comprised of practical (moderate liberals, conservatives) groups that are either sponsored or in some way influenced by adult groups in society. Both proactive and reactive generation units reject the adult generation in favor of some idealized, utopian alternative, whereas active generation units accept the parent generation and are willing to compromise over principles in moderate fashion.

A survey of the literature on youth movements over the last 170 years resulted in the identification of more than 40 separate generational movements, with separate generation units (over 80 identified thus far) emerging within each political generation struggling to dominate their respective generation movements (Braungart, 1982b). For example, the Young Europe Generation began with the *Burschenschaften* ("Student Union"), which emerged and spread throughout Germany between 1815–1848. The *Burschenschaften* movement consisted of the liberal, progressive *Germania Burschenschaften* wing of the movement, which was countered by the *Arminia Burschenschaften* that preferred conservative, traditional values and politics. Both these generation units competed openly for the control of the larger movement.

During turn-of-the-century Germany, the *Blau Weiss Wandervögel* and *Alt Wandervögel* generation units squared off against each other over the growing issues of anti-Semitism, despite the fact that both groups remained loyal to the same objectives of the larger *Wandervögel* movement (Braungart, 1982b). During the Post-Victorian era in the Soviet Union, the Komsomol or Young Communist League, formed in 1918, sent "shock brigades" of youth throughout the countryside singing and preaching the virtues of communism. Unimpressed with Bolshevism, rural Soviet youth battled the Komsomol forces against collectivization of their farms.

At the time of the Great Depression Generation of the 1930s, intra-generational political conflict became particularly violent and bloody. Throughout Germany, Italy, and Spain, fierce street battles erupted between fascist generation units on the radical right versus young communist and socialist generation units on the left. Elsewhere around the world, revolutionary young communists in China confronted Kuomintang nationalists and Chiang Kai-shek's youthful supporters. The pro-Gandhian nationalist youth generation of India favored independence from England and was opposed by religious youth groups not concerned with Indian independence but with autonomous Muslim rights. In the United States, groups of young socialists and communists were countered by generation units on the right, such as the Paul Reveres and American Liberty League.

By the 1960s, intragenerational conflict spread to every region of the world. In Latin America, Cuba furnished the model for the decades of intragenerational conflict to follow. Socioeconomic problems such as poverty and university reform provided the issues over which youthful left- and right-wing generation units opposed each other. Despite the considerable media coverage and publicity given to left-wing youth groups in the United States and Europe (particularly in France, Germany, and Italy) in the 1960s, an equal number of right-wing youthful generation units existed in these countries as well. The intragenerational movements in Asia concerned themselves with national liberation (East Pakistan and South Vietnam), a political coup d'état (Indonesia), insurrection (Sri Lanka), and university and political reform (India and Japan). In each of these Far Eastern or Asian countries, generational units confronted each other in battle over numerous bitterly contested issues. More recently, intragenerational movements spread throughout Africa in the struggle against colonialism and aparthied and for independence, while in the Middle East, Marxist youth confronted fundamentalist Islamic student organizations for political control in Turkey and Iran. (For an expanded discussion of the generation units within each political generation, see Braungart, 1982b.)

3. The End of a Political Generation. Political generations decline when the historical and mobilizing forces that produced intergenerational and intragenerational conflict lose their potency. Intergenerational conflict comes to an end when: (a) the historical problems that precipitated the conflict lose their saliency and new issues emerge (new wars, postrevolutionary periods, inflation, prosperity); (b) the historical problems are corrected or ameliorated through institutional reforms; (c) generational movements lose their leadership, mobilization, solidarity; (d) adults and youth cooperate and compromise their differences, adults coopt the youth movement, and/or adults crush the youth movement (police or military force); and (e) political–generational movements succeed in their efforts to overthrow the opposition (topple regimes, win and are granted their demands, produce necessary changes), and/or split up, with some factions dissolving while other splinter groups go underground (guerrilla, terrorism, violence).

The conflict between generation units (intragenerational conflict) subsides when: (a) the historical or ideological issues are resolved or are replaced by new issues or objectives; (b) the competing generational units are unable to sustain momentum (loss of leadership, organization, resources, mobilization, solidarity), so the units tire and give up their cause; (c) competition between generational units continues until one unit emerges victorious (with or without adult support); and (d) a compromise is worked out between the competing units such that they are willing to coexist in a peaceful fashion. Once the historical, generational, and political forces decouple, the political–generational dynamic loses its momentum, and generational conflict declines (Braungart, 1982a).

With the periodic rise and fall of generational fervor, a nagging issue remains whether political generations have any significant influence or impact on society and politics? This is a difficult question to address, and the answer partially depends upon whether the impact of the political generation is assessed as direct or indirect, the change is viewed as short-term or long-term, and the lag in time considered between the actual movement and the appearance of change. In general, the extent of change brought about by political–generational movements can be determined by examining the scope and degree of change, along with the longevity of generational conflict. The scope of change includes the breadth or range of the generational conflict throughout society, and the levels (local, national, international) of society or regions that are affected by generational movements. The actual amount or degree of change involves the depth of institutional penetration and adjustment (the degree to which institutions, values, and norms were modified) brought about by generational movements. And finally, the duration of the political generation affects the ability of social institutions to withstand or resist generational conflict.

Actual attempts to evaluate the impact of political generations are few, although Esler (1982, pp. 122–126) contended that the likelihood of a successful outcome is greater for artistic, scientific, and intellectual generations than for political generations, which "seem to follow a rather more crooked road to victory—when they win at all." There does appear to be a consensus that despite youthful political intensity and goals, collective behavior on the part of young people is more likely to bring about change in culture rather than in politics, although in some circumstances the two are linked (Abrams, 1970; Yankelovich, 1974). When participating in larger social and historical change—separatist, national liberation or revolutionary movements—political generations are quickly absorbed into, or curtailed by, the new regime. Most students of political sociology would concur, however, that many of the effects of a political generation are realized long after the movement itself has subsided.

V.   CONCEPTUAL AND METHODOLOGICAL ISSUES IN GENERATIONAL POLITICS

A number of conceptual and methodological issues are involved in research on generational politics. One major conceptual problem is defining a generation and determining its boundaries. Another issue concerns the existence of generations as a genuine force for social and political change. The methodological difficulties in research on generational politics include the different levels of comparison suggested by generational theory, the problem of time as a dimension in research designs, and the logistical and ethical difficulties of studying a political generation.

A.   Conceptual Issues

The difficulty defining a generation is partially a semantic one, since the term generation has several meanings. There are at least four theoretical and empirical approaches to the study of generational politics, each with its own literature. Generation as a stage of life-cycle development represents one use of the concept, where the emphasis is on the maturation of the individual, the inherent "generational" conflict, and the different developmental tasks and roles that result in changes in political outlooks over the life span (Bettelheim, 1963; Erikson, 1968; Feuer, 1969). A second use of generation is as a cohort focusing on the "generational" experiences of being born during a certain period in history which plays a major part in structuring the individual's political orientations during youth and acts as a lens through which subsequent political events are perceived and interpreted throughout the life span (Mannheim, 1952; Rintala, 1979; Ryder, 1965). The third meaning comes out of the genealogical–ancestral approach, which defines generations as parents versus offspring or adults versus young people and focuses on the extent of political agreement between lineage groups, along with the ways political values, attitudes, and behavior are transmitted from one "generation" to the next (Dawson, Prewitt, & Dawson, 1977; Jennings & Niemi, 1981; Renshon, 1977). A fourth definition views a generation as a decisive age group (the interaction of life cycle and cohort forces) that mobilizes to bring about social, political, cultural, scientific, or intellectual change (Braungart, 1982a, 1982b; Esler, 1974, 1982; Heberle, 1951). Each of these approaches emphasizes a particular aspect of the relationship between generations and politics—from biopsychological (life cycle), historical (cohort), kinship (lineage), to sociopolitical (political generations).

Another difficulty in defining a generation involves determining its boundaries. Ortega, Mannheim, and Marias spent considerable effort quibbling over whether a generation is 5, 15, or 30 years in length—although more recently, it has been argued that since the pace of social change has accelerated, the time between generations is lessening (Berger, 1960; Cutler, 1977). Whether dealing with demographic cohorts or with dynamic political generations, in the succession of daily births, separating one group from another is no simple task (Cutler, 1977; Marias, 1970; Spitzer, 1973). Part of the problem is deciding what criteria to use in making age or generational divisions. Although quantitative criteria are often employed—such as traditional groupings by decade, election years, or a fixed interval of time—it has been suggested that generations be divided along qualitative lines such as distinct historical events or experiences (Rintala, 1979; Rosow, 1978). Whatever approach one prefers, the difficulty of delimiting age groups or generations remains a continual problem in generational analysis (e.g., what are the exact years that mark the beginning and end of the 1960s Generation?). Moreover, when qualitative criteria are used to identify a generation, the data may no longer meet the assumptions (equal intervals) necessary to perform certain mathematical operations. The problem of determining an age group or a generation's boundaries is not unlike making decisions about cutoff points for other kinds of social categories such as social classes, ethnic groups, or income levels. Careful and imaginative attempts at defining age groups and generations may well enhance our understanding of the dynamic relationship between generations and politics.

The problem of identifying the existence of a political generation partially concerns the difference between age group and generation — a distinction that has not always been made clear in the literature. In other words, at what point does an age group become a political generation? It is a generally accepted view that an age group is transformed into a generation when its members are aware of their uniqueness, solidarity, and join together to become an active force for social and political change. Part of the difficulty in political–generational analysis is recognizing — much less measuring — the phenomenon of "generational awareness" or "generational consciousness." The problem is not an insurmountable one, however, and by carefully considering historical factors, it is possible to differentiate and clearly document the rise and fall of political generations.

Assessing the existence of a political generation also entails knowledge of the dynamics of its formation and momentum — a process that is not well understood at this time. Arguments presented thus far suggest that certain historical circumstances, in conjunction with intergenerational (the politics of one age group must be resisted by another) and intragenerational (the competing units within a generation) conflict stimulate the formation of a political generation. Although the process of deauthorization and authorization is an important part of political generations, these are areas that have not been well researched. We know little about the development of shared collective mentalities and how these become activated into a genuine force for political change, nor do we understand fully the interplay between competing political generation units, the maintenance of a political generation's active thrust, and the actual changes that come about through protracted generational efforts.

While it has been demonstrated that political generations periodically have taken form to change the course of human history, to date their origin, mobilization, and impact remain unpredictable. Empirical examinations of political generations have been post hoc, and it is not yet possible to determine when and where a political generation will emerge. There exists throughout the world today a disappointing set of circumstances for many young people — high unemployment, blocked and constricted opportunities, low integration into political systems, political elites who are distant and isolated, environmental deterioration and destruction with a prognosis for worse to come, and the all-too-clear acceleration toward a possible nuclear holocaust. Life-cycle theorists indicate that young people are innately ripe for "action," with a natural propensity to deauthorize the older generation. The historical circumstances appear highly conducive to the formation of decisive political generations. What so far has been lacking is the authorization by youth, or any other age group, to seize the moment and take the political initiative — although there has been increasing political activity by young people throughout Europe (see Mushaben, 1983). Until the dynamic processes of intergenerational deauthorization and intragenerational authorization empirically are better understood, political–generational analysis will remain at best an incomplete theoretical exercise.

B. Methodological Issues

The methodological problems involved in research on generational politics are similar to other kinds of social science research, although perhaps more challenging. Many of the difficulties revolve around two assumptions inherent in generational political analysis: (a) the different levels of comparison (intergenerational, intragenerational, lineage, and intraindividual) suggested by generational theory, and (b) the dimension of time. In order to more completely understand generational politics, comparisons need to be made not only between age groups and political generations but within each group as well. Much of the research conducted thus far has examined either the extent of age or generational differences in politics, or the political orientations of a specific age group such as young people or older adults. Few studies have undertaken political comparisons both between *and* within age groups or generations in a single research design. Those research investigations that have done so have been able to identify some important distinctions within each age group that would have gone unrecognized had further breakdown of the age–politics relationship not been made.

The time dimension complicates research on generational politics in various ways, including such problems as changes in the meaning or interpretation of attitudinal and behavioral responses over time, sample mortality, or other aspects of external and internal reliability. The time dimension also presents statistical problems such as contamination, confounding, and identification (Baltes, Reese, & Nesselroade, 1977; Cutler, 1977; Harris, 1967).

There are a number of methodological techniques for handling time in research designs or generational politics: (a) longitudinal designs, which involve repeated measures on the same individual over time; (b) cross-sectional designs, which test or measure individuals of different age levels and draw a new sample for each time of measurement; and (c) time-lag analysis, such as comparing different cohorts at different points in time (comparing age groups or generations in the 1980s with those from the 1960s and 1970s). Each of these research designs, however, faces the problem of confounding, or not being able to disentangle the effects of life-cycle, cohort, or period effects. For example, in the cross-sectional design, life-cycle and cohort factors are intertwined — as a result, it cannot be determined how much variation is due to life-cycle factors or cohort effects; in the longitudinal design, life-cycle changes are confounded with period changes; and in time-lag analysis, cohort and period effects are entangled. Moreover, there may be contradictions in findings when trying to compare longitudinal with cross-sectional outcomes (Baltes, 1968; Baltes, Reese, & Nesselroade, 1977; Huyck & Hoyer, 1982).

One of the most popular research designs in investigations of the relationship between age groups and politics has been the combined life-cycle, cohort, and period (also referred to as age, generational, and time of measurement) design, the use of which has generated considerable debate in the methodological literature. One of the contested issues concerns the assumption of additivity, with some arguing that life-cycle, cohort, and period effects are quite likely to be interactive rather than additive (Foner, 1972; Riley, 1973). Even if the assumption of additivity appears justified, small amounts of measurement error or errors in specifying constraints for either life-cycle, cohort, or period effects result in highly inaccurate estimates (Rodgers, 1982). The statistical problem of identification (given the values of two of the parameters, the third value is determined automatically) is an important issue for this type of research design. A few suggested solutions to the dilemmas of the life-cycle, cohort, and period design have been offered (Rodgers, 1982; Schaie, 1965; Smith, Mason, & Fienberg, 1982). Some researchers have employed time-series analysis and borrowed econometric techniques such as curve fitting with ordinary least squares or maximum likelihood estimates, but the problems of handling the time dimension in research designs for generational politics have yet to be resolved satisfactorily (Knoke, 1982, 1984).

Another methodological consideration is the need to include important additional variables in the analysis to either uncover a spurious relationship between age group and politics or to qualify an apparent existing association (Allerbeck, 1977; Braungart & Braungart, 1982). Identifying those social and psychological characteristics that interact with or confound the age and politics relationship can enhance greatly the understanding of generational politics.

Undertaking the study of political generations presents its own methodological problems, especially if the research entails direct contact (participant or nonparticipant observations, interviews, surveys) with members of a political generation or generation unit. Gaining access or permission from these political groups can be a major obstacle, and there are important ethical considerations. Whenever one conducts research on political groups, there is always the possibility that findings and interpretation of data may be colored by researcher bias and deception of participants. Foremost among the ethical problems in political sociological research is the use that can be made of the empirical results—the possibility that the findings might be turned into a weapon for political repression or coercion.

VI. CONCLUSION

Generational politics is a rapidly growing area of inquiry in the social sciences. While concern with age and politics can be traced to antiquity, theoretical speculation over the social origins of generations and their impact developed in the late nineteenth and early twentieth centuries. More recently, the concept of social generations has been extended to include political generations. The contemporary literature on generational politics consists of two major areas of interest: the influence of age on political attitudes and behavior, and the formation of political generations.

In identifying the relationship between age and politics, political attitudes and behavior are seen as resulting from the maturational changes that occur with age, along with the particular demographic–historical circumstances experienced as a function of time of birth. The different concerns, roles, and tasks in life-cycle development lay the foundation for misunderstandings and conflict between the young, middle age, and old — which are exacerbated in modern and modernizing societies where the various age cohorts have grown up under dissimilar historical conditions. The impetus for political change has come from the young who, with their high levels of energy, new awareness of politics, and limited historical memory, have confronted and challenged the traditions of middle-aged and older members of society.

Generational conflict over politics has been more evident at certain times in history than others. Political disagreement between age groups is minimized when events and trends promote similar responses among age groups; the variation in politics within age groups is wide, with other social factors cutting across age-group lines as a basis for political divisiveness; and the political socialization efforts of parents and adults are successful. Periodically, historical circumstances interact with life-cycle and cohort effects to produce a heightened generational awareness among members of an age group. A political generation may mobilize as a "generation for itself," actively working for change when its members become discontented with the past, the performance of other age groups, and the thrust or drift of politics. While political generations exhibit intergenerational conflict, they also disagree with each other over concrete goals or objectives, forming intragenerational units that compete for political ascendency.

Historical patterns and changes provide the stage and scenery for age-based political activity, while political generations and generation units represent the actors who write the script and play out the parts. Through a process of social and political mitosis, generational consciousness takes form, and ideological–utopian generation units polarize on the political left and right to challenge other age groups and one another for political control. This dynamic pattern of political–generational activity dates back over 170 years and has been accelerating steadily on a worldwide scale. The cycles of intergenerational and intragenerational conflict represent barometers of social and political change, often bound up with local, national and global struggles. Increasing evidence suggests that political generations will become a more significant force in the future; therefore, the challenge to modern political societies is not to inhibit or destroy this age-old creative impulse for human revitalization and change, but to move it from a potentially violent arena to a more peaceful and rational political forum.

REFERENCES

Abrams, P. (1970). Rites de passage: The conflict of generations in industrial society. *The Journal of Contemporary History, 5,* 175–190.

Abramson, P.R. (1974). Generational change in American electoral behavior. *American Political Science Review, 68,* 93–105.

Abramson, P.R. (1975). *Generational change in American politics.* Lexington, MA: Lexington Books.

Abramson, P.R. (1983). *Political attitudes in America: Formation and change.* San Francisco: W.H. Freeman.

Adelson, J. (1975). The development of ideology in adolescence. In S.E. Dragastin & G.H. Elder, Jr. (Eds.), *Adolescence in the life cycle.* New York: John Wiley.

Allerbeck, K. (1977). Political generations: Some reflections on the concept and its application to the German case. *European Journal of Political Research, 5,* 119–134.

Altbach, P.G. (1967). Students and politics. In S.M. Lipset (Ed.), *Student politics.* New York: Basic Books.

Baltes, P.B. (1968). Longitudinal and cross-sectional sequences in the study of age and generation effects. *Human Development, 11,* 145–171.

Baltes, P.B., Reese, H.W., & Nesselroade, J.R. (1977). *Life-span developmental psychology: An introduction to research methods.* Monterey, CA: Brooks/Cole.

Baltes, P.B., & Schaie, K.W. (Eds.). (1973). *Life-span developmental psychology: Personality and socialization.* New York: Academic Press.

Bengtson, V.L., & Black, K.D. (1973). Intergenerational relations and continuities in socialization. In P.B. Baltes & K.W. Schaie (Eds.), *Life-span developmental psychology: Personality and socialization.* New York: Academic Press.

Bengtson, V.L., & Cutler, N.E. (1976). Generations and intergenerational relations: Perspectives on age groups and social change. In R.H. Binstock & E. Shanas (Eds.), *Handbook of aging and the social sciences.* New York: Van Nostrand Reinhold.

Bengtson, V.L., Kassachau, P.L., & Ragan, P.K. (1977). The impact of social structure on aging individuals. In J.E. Birren & K.W. Schaie (Eds.), *Handbook of the psychology of aging.* New York: Van Nostrand Reinhold.

Berger, B.M. (1960). How long is a generation? *British Journal of Sociology, 2,* 10–23.

Bettelheim, B. (1963). The problem of generations. In E.H. Erikson (Ed.), *Youth: change and challenge.* New York: Basic Books.

Borland, D.C. (1978). Research in middle age: An assessment. *Gerontologist, 18,* 379–386.

Botwinick, J. (1978). *Aging and behavior.* New York: Springer.

Braungart, M. (1980). *Generational alienation and politics: A social psychological model.* Unpublished doctoral dissertation, Syracuse University.

Braungart, M.M., & Braungart, R.G. (1982). The alienation and politics of older, middle-aged, and young adults: An inter- and intra-age group analysis. *Micropolitics, 2,* 219–255.

Braungart, R.G. (1971). Family status, socialization, and student politics: A multivariate analysis. *American Journal of Sociology, 77,* 108–130.

Braungart, R.G. (1974). The sociology of generations and student politics: A comparison of the functionalist and generational unit models. *Journal of Social Issues, 30,* 31–54.

Braungart, R.G. (1976). College and noncollege youth politics in 1972: An application of Mannheim's generation unit model. *Journal of Youth and Adolescence, 5,* 325–347.

Braungart, R.G. (1979). *Family status, socialization and student politics.* Ann Arbor, MI: University Microfilms International.

Braungart, R.G. (1980). Youth movements. In J. Adelson (Ed.), *Handbook of adolescent psychology.* New York: John Wiley.

Braungart, R.G. (1982a). Historical generations and youth movements: A theoretical perspective. Paper presented at the meetings of the World Congress of Sociology, Mexico City.

Braungart, R.G. (1982b). Historical generations and generation units: A global pattern of youth movements. Paper presented at the annual meetings of the Social Science History Association, Bloomington, IN.

Braungart, R.G., & Braungart, M.M. (1980). Political career patterns of radical activists in the 1960s and 1970s: Some historical comparisons. *Sociological Focus, 13,* 237–254.

Campbell, A. (1971). Politics through the life cycle. *Gerontologist, 11,* 112–117.

Campbell, A., Converse, P., Miller, W., & Stokes, D. (1960). *The American voter.* New York: John Wiley.

Conger, J.J. (1971). A world they never knew: The family and social change. *Daedalus, 100,* 1105–1138.

Crittenden, J.A. (1962). Aging and party affiliation. *Public Opinion Quarterly, 26,* 648–657.

Cutler, N.E. (1969). Generation, maturation, and party affiliation: A cohort analysis. *Public Opinion Quarterly, 33,* 583–588.

Cutler, N.E. (1974). Aging and generations in politics: The conflict of explanations and inference. In A.R. Wilcox (Ed.), *Public opinion and political attitudes: A reader.* New York: John Wiley.

Cutler, N.E. (1977). Political socialization research as generational analysis: The cohort approach versus lineage approach. In S.A. Renshon (Ed.), *Handbook of political socialization: Theory and research.* New York: Free Press.

Cutler, N.E., & Bengtson, V.L. (1974). Age and political alienation: Maturation, generation, and period effects. *Annals of the American Academy of Political and Social Science, 415,* 160–175.

Davies, J.C. (1977). Political socialization: From womb to childhood. In S.A. Renshon (Ed.), *Handbook of political socialization: Theory and research.* New York: Free Press.

Dawson, R.E., Prewitt, K., & Dawson, K. (1977). *Political socialization.* Boston: Little, Brown.

Douglass, E.B., Cleveland, W.P., & Maddox, G.L. (1974). Political attitudes, age, and aging: A cohort analysis of archival data. *Journal of Gerontology, 29,* 666–675.

Draper, H. (1967). The student movement of the thirties: A political history. In R.J. Simon (Ed.), *As we saw the thirties.* Urbana: University of Illinois Press.

Duncan, M. (1980). Radical activism and the defense against despair. *Sociological Focus, 13,* 255–263.

Dunlap, R. (1970). Radical and conservative student activists: A comparison of family backgrounds. *Pacific Sociological Review, 13,* 171–181.

Eisenstadt, S.N. (1956). *From generation to generation: Age groups and social structure.* London: Free Press of Glencoe.

Eisenstadt, S.N. (1963). Archetypal patterns of youth. In E.H. Erikson (Ed.), *Youth: change and challenge.* New York: Basic Books.

Elder, G.H., Jr. (1974). *Children of the Great Depression.* Chicago: University of Chicago Press.

Elder, G.H., Jr. (1980). Adolescence in historical perspective. In J. Adelson (Ed.), *Handbook of adolescent psychology.* New York: John Wiley.

Erikson, E.H. (1968). *Identity: Youth and crisis.* New York: Norton.

Esler, A. (Ed.). (1974). *The youth revolution.* Lexington, MA: D.C. Heath.

Esler, A. (1982). *Generations in history: An introduction to the concept.* Williamsburg, VA: William and Mary College.

Etzioni, A. (1968). *The active society.* New York: Free Press.

Fengler, A.P., & Wood, V. (1972). The generation gap: An analysis on contemporary issues. *Gerontologist, 12,* 124–128.

Feuer, L.S. (1969). *The conflict of generations.* New York: Basic Books.

Feuer, L.S. (1974). *Einstein and the generations of science.* New York: Basic Books.

Flacks, R. (1967). The liberated generation: An exploration of the roots of student protest. *Journal of Social Issues, 23,* 52–75.

Foner, A. (1972). The polity. In M.W. Riley & A. Foner (Eds.), *Aging and society.* New York: Russell Sage.

Gallatin, J. (1980). Political thinking in adolescence. In J. Adelson (Ed.), *Handbook of adolescent psychology.* New York: John Wiley.

Gitlin, T. (1980). *The whole world is watching.* Berkeley: University of California Press.

Glamser, G. (1974). The importance of age to conservative opinions. *Journal of Gerontology, 29,* 549–554.

Glenn, N.D., & Hefner, T. (1972). Further evidence on aging and party identification. *Public Opinion Quarterly, 36,* 31–47.

Goldman, P., & Lubenow, G. (5 September 1977). Where the flowers have gone. *Newsweek,* pp. 24–30.

Goulet, L.R., & Baltes, P.B. (Eds.). (1970). *Life-span developmental psychology: Research and theory.* New York: Academic Press.

Greer, S. (1979). Discontinuities and fragmentation in societal growth. In A. H. Hawley (Ed.), *Societal growth.* New York: Free Press.

Gurr, T.R. (1970). *Why men rebel.* Princeton, NJ: Princeton University Press.

Gusfield, J. (1979). The modernity of social movements: Public roles and private parts. In A.H. Hawley (Ed.), *Societal growth.* New York: Free Press.

Hamilton, R.F., & Wright, J. (1975). *New directions in political sociology.* Indianapolis: Bobbs-Merrill.

Harris, C.W. (Ed.). (1967). *Problems in measuring change.* Madison, WI: University of Wisconsin Press.

Heberle, R. (1951). *Social movements.* New York: Appleton-Century-Crofts.

Hendin, H. (1975). *The age of sensation.* New York: W.W. Norton.

Hendricks, J., & Hendricks, C.D. (1977). *Aging in mass society.* Cambridge, MA: Winthrop.

House, J.S., & Mason, W.M. (1975). Political alienation in America, 1952–1968. *American Sociological Review, 40,* 123–147.

Hudson, R.B., & Binstock, R.H. (1976). Political systems and aging. In R.H. Binstock & E. Shanas (Eds.), *Handbook of aging and the social sciences.* New York: Van Nostrand Reinhold.

Huyck, M.H., & Hoyer, W.J. (1982). *Adult development and aging.* Belmont, CA: Wadsworth.

Inglehart, R. (1971). The silent revolution in Europe: Intergenerational change in post-industrial societies. *American Political Science Review, 65,* 991–1017.

Inglehart, R. (1977). *The silent revolution: Changing values and political styles among Western publics.* Princeton, NJ: Princeton University Press.

Inglehart, R. (1981). Post-materialism in an environment of insecurity. *American Political Science Review, 75,* 880–900.

Jansen, N. (1975). *Generation theory.* Johannesburg: McGraw-Hill.

Jennings, M.K., & Niemi, R.G. (1981). *Generations and politics: A panel study of young adults and their parents.* Princeton, NJ: Princeton University Press.

Keniston, K. (1968). *Young radicals.* New York: Harcourt Brace and World.

Keniston, K. (1977). An American Ishmael. In L.R. Allman & D.T. Jaffe (Eds.), *Readings in adult psychology.* New York: Harper and Row.

Knoke, D. (1982). Methods for the quantitative analysis of historical change. Paper presented at the annual meetings of the Social Science History Association, Bloomington, IN.

Knoke, D. (1984). Conceptual and measurement aspects of the study of political generations. *Journal of Political and Military Sociology, 12,* 191–201.

Kornhauser, W. (1959). *The politics of mass society.* Glencoe, IL: Free Press.

Lauer, R.H. (1977). *Perspectives on social change.* Boston: Allyn and Bacon.

Lipset, S.M. (1981). *Political man: The social bases of politics.* Baltimore: Johns Hopkins University Press.

Lipset, S.M., & Altbach, P.G. (Eds.). (1969). *Students in revolt.* Boston: Houghton, Mifflin.

Loewenberg, P. (1974). A psychohistorical approach: The Nazi generation. In A. Esler (Ed.), *The conflict of generations in modern history.* Lexington, MA: D.C. Heath.

Lowenthal, M.F., & Chiriboga, D. (1977). Transition to the empty nest. In L.R. Allman & D.T. Jaffe (Eds.), *Readings in adult psychology.* New York: Harper and Row.

Mannheim, K. (1952). *Essays on the sociology of knowledge.* London: Routledge and Kegan Paul.

Marias, J. (1968). Generations: The concept. In D. Sills (Ed.), *Encyclopedia of the social sciences.* New York: Macmillan.

Marias, J. (1970). *Generations: A historical method.* University, AL: The University of Alabama Press.

Martin, W.C., Bengtson, V.L., & Acock, A.C. (1974). Alienation and age: A context-specific approach. *Social Forces, 53,* 266–282.

Mentré, F. (1920). *Les Générations sociales.* Doctoral dissertation, University of Paris (Sorbonne).

Meyer, J.M., & Rubinson, R. (1972). Structural determinants of student political activity: A comparative interpretation. *Sociology of Education, 45,* 23–46.

Milbrath, L.W., & Goel, M.L. (1977). *Political participation.* Chicago: Rand McNally.

Moller, H. (1972). Youth as a force in the modern world. In P.K. Manning & M. Truzzi (Eds.), *Youth and sociology.* Englewood Cliffs, NJ: Prentice-Hall.

Murphy, H.B.M. (1974). Mass youth protest movements in Asia and the West: Their common characteristics and psychiatric significance. In W. Lebra (Ed.), *Youth socialization and mental health.* Honolulu: University Press of Hawaii.

Mushaben, J.M. (1983). The forum: New dimensions of youth protest in Western Europe. *Journal of Political and Military Sociology, 11,* 123–143.

Muuss, R.E. (1968). *Theories of adolescence.* New York: Random House.

Nash, L.L. (1978). Concepts of existence: Greek origins of generational thought. *Daedalus, 107,* 1–21.

Nesselroade, J.R. (1977). Issues in studying developmental change in adults from a multivariate perspective. In J.E. Birren & K. W. Schaie (Eds.), *Handbook of the psychology of aging.* New York: Van Nostrand Reinhold.

Nettl, J.P. (1967). *Political mobilization.* New York: Basic Books.

Newcomb, T.M. (1943). *Personality and social change.* New York: Dryden.

Newcomb, T.M., Koenig, K.E., Flacks, R., & Warwick, D.P. (1967). *Persistence and change: Bennington College and its students after 25 years.* New York: John Wiley.

Oberschall, A. (1973). *Social conflict and social movements.* Englewood Cliffs, NJ: Prentice-Hall.

Ortega y Gasset, J. (1961). *The modern theme.* New York: Harper and Row.

Ortega y Gasset, J. (1962). *Man and crisis.* New York: W.W. Norton.

Ortega y Gasset, J. (1974). The importance of generationhood. In A. Esler (Ed.), *The youth revolution.* Lexington, MA: D.C. Heath.

Piaget, J. (1967). *Six psychological studies.* New York: Random House.

Piaget, J., & Inhelder, B. (1969). *The psychology of the child.* New York: Basic Books.

Pratt, H.J. (1976). *The gray lobby.* Chicago: University of Chicago Press.

Renshon, S.A. (Ed.). (1977). *Handbook of political socialization: Theory and research.* New York: Free Press.

Riley, M.W. (1973). Aging and cohort succession: Interpretations and misinterpretations. *Public Opinion Quarterly, 37,* 35–49.

Riley, M.W., & Foner, A. (1968). *Aging and society.* New York: Russell Sage.

Rintala, M. (1968). Generations in politics. In D. Sills (Ed.), *Encyclopedia of the social sciences.* New York: Macmillan.

Rintala, M. (1979). *The constitution of silence: Essays on generational themes.* Westport, CT: Greenwood Press.

Rodgers, W.L. (1982). Estimable functions of age, period, and cohort effects. *American Sociological Review, 47,* 774–787.

Rose, A.M. (1965). The subculture of the aged: A framework in social gerontology. In A.M. Rose & W. Peterson (Eds.), *Older people and their social world.* Philadelphia: F.A. Davis.

Rosow, I. (1978). What is a cohort and why? *Human Development, 21,* 65–75.

Ryder, N.B. (1965). The cohort as a concept in the study of social change. *American Sociological Review, 30,* 843–861.

Samuels, R.J. (Ed.). (1977). *Political generations and political development.* Lexington, MA: D.C. Heath.

Schaie, K.W. (1965) A general model for the study of developmental problems. *Psychological Bulletin, 64,* 92–107.

Schorske, C.E. (1978). Generational tension and cultural change: Reflections on the case of Vienna. *Daedalus, 107,* 111–122.

Searing, D.D., Wright, G., & Rabinowitz, G. (1976). The primacy principle: Attitude change and political socialization. *British Journal of Political Science, 6,* 83–113.

Simon, R.J. (Ed.). (1967). *As we saw the thirties.* Urbana, IL: University of Illinois Press.

Smelser, N.J. (1963). *Theory of collective behavior.* New York: Free Press.

Smelser, N.J. (1968). *Essays in sociological explanation.* Englewood Cliffs, NJ: Prentice-Hall.

Smith, H.L., Mason, W.M., & Fienberg, S.E. (1982). More chimeras of the age-period-cohort accounting framework: Comment on Rodgers. *American Sociological Review, 47,* 787–793.

Snyder, L.L. (1982). *Global mini-nationalisms.* Westport, CT: Greenwood Press.

Spiegel, L.A. (1951). A review of contributions to a psychoanalytic theory of adolescence: Individual aspects. In R.S. Eissler, et al. (Eds.), *The psychoanalytic study of the child* (Vol. 6). New York: International Universities Press.

Spitzer, A.B. (1973). The historical problem of generations. *American Historical Review, 78,* 1353–1385.

Stacey, B. (1977). *Political socialization in Western society: An analysis form a life-span perspective.* New York: St. Martin's Press.

Starr, J.M. (1974). The peace and love generation. *Journal of Social Issues, 30,* 73–106.

Szabo, S.F. (1983a). The successor generation in Europe. *Public Opinion, 6,* 9–11.

Szabo, S.F. (1983b). *The successor generation: International perspectives of postwar Europeans.* Woburn, MA: Butterworths.

Tedin, K.L. (1974). The influence of parents on the political attitudes of adolescents. *American Political Science Review, 68,* 1579–1592.

Tilly, C. (1975). Revolution and collective violence. In F.I. Greenstein & N.W. Polsby (Eds.), *Handbook of political science.* Reading, MA: Addison-Wesley.

Tilly, C., Tilly, L., & Tilly, R. (1975). *The rebellious century, 1830–1930.* Cambridge, MA: Harvard University Press.

Vaillant, G.E. (1977). The climb to maturity: How the best and the brightest came of age. *Psychology Today, 11,* 107–110.

Weinberg, I., & Walker, N. (1969). Student politics and political systems: Toward a typology. *American Journal of Sociology, 75,* 77–96.

Westby, D.L., & Braungart, R.G. (1966). Class and politics in the family backgrounds of student political activists. *American Sociological Review, 31,* 690–692.

Wohl, R. (1979). *The generation of 1914.* Cambridge: Cambridge University Press.

Yankelovich, D. (1972). *The changing values on campus.* New York: Washington Square Press.

Yankelovich, D. (1974). *The new morality: A profile of American youth in the 70s.* New York: McGraw-Hill.

3

Public Opinion

Stanley Feldman
Department of Political Science
University of Kentucky

I.   INTRODUCTION

The study of mass belief systems and public opinion has generated a vast amount of research over the past 10 to 15 years. As noted by Bennett (1977), however, the accumulation of new research only seems to introduce new uncertainty in our knowledge of this subject. Concepts and methods that were once taken for granted are now questioned, and once sacred conclusions about the nature of public opinion are more frequently challenged. In a recent review of the subject, Kinder (1983) has even suggested that researchers may be asking the wrong questions. In part, such confusion may be attributed to the difficult nature of the enterprise. Public opinion is not an easy phenomenon to come to grips with and the underlying concepts of political attitudes, beliefs, and values can be measured only indirectly by instruments that often seem to obscure as much as they illuminate. In fact, many of the problems in the study of mass belief systems may be traced directly to issues of conceptualization and measurement, issues that are typically not directly addressed in much of the empirical research that has been done in recent years.

   In this chapter I will review the major lines of research in the study of mass belief systems and public opinion over the past ten years. In undertaking this task, it was necessary to be somewhat selective. Therefore, the focus of this chapter will be the question of how public opinion develops and is structured. This attention to belief system structure means that a large body of research on the specific content of public opinion will not be dealt with here. Instead, broader questions of the underlying basis of public opinion, trends in opinion over time, and basic issues of the study of public opinion will be considered. In the final section of the chapter, I will review recent attempts to suggest new directions for the study of belief systems and public opinion.

II. BACK TO THE ROOTS: CONVERSE AND MASS BELIEF SYSTEMS

It is difficult to begin a paper on the subject of mass belief systems without acknowledging the contribution of Phillip Converse. Building on research first presented in *The American Voter* (Campbell, Converse, Miller, & Stokes, 1960), Converse's (1964) major paper on the topic continues to set the agenda for much of the research still done 20 years later. Perhaps as much as anything else, that paper demonstrated to many that mass belief systems are amenable to rigorous empirical study. Beyond this, many of the empirical techniques currently used by researchers were introduced by Converse. For this reason, it is important to briefly go back over this paper one more time in order to adequately set the stage for a review of the more recent literature.

Converse's expressed goal in the paper was to explore differences in the belief systems of members of the general public on the one hand, and elites on the other. Converse's theoretical analysis of belief systems led him to expect that mass and elite belief systems would not closely resemble each other. Preferring to deal with belief system constraint rather than the "muddied" term ideology, Converse initially discussed three sources of constraint: logical, psychological, and social. Although acknowledging that belief systems may be organized at least in part by logical and psychological mechanisms of constraint, Converse immediately focused his attention on social mechanisms of constraint, in particular, the diffusion of information through society. Social mechanisms of constraint originate from the actions and statements of political elites, who "package" political beliefs and preferences into coherent structures, which are then presented to the public for general consumption. If belief systems are constrained socially, then two major consequences should follow: to the extent that people's belief systems show evidence of constraint, the pattern should be that of the dominant pattern of political beliefs in society (liberalism–conservatism); and the extent of constraint should rapidly decline as we move away from the most politically informed segments of society. Two important points should be noted here. First, the conclusion that constraint is largely social in nature is not only an important theoretical assumption but has a powerful impact on the way in which belief systems are empirically studied. Second, Converse was not concerned with empirically examining the relative prevalence of logical, psychological, and social sources of belief system constraint. Sociological constraint was accepted as a working hypothesis to guide the empirical analysis.

Converse's empirical analysis proceeded in a series of steps each designed to counter possible objections to preceeding methodological procedures. Several of these empirical strategies have defined major lines of research on belief systems. The paper begins by presenting data for the levels of conceptualization measure first developed in *The American Voter*. Relying on a complete reading of open-ended responses to likes and dislikes questions about the two major parties and the presidential candidates (asked of a national sample in 1956, 1958, and 1960), individuals were placed into one of four major categories based on the criteria underlying their evaluations: ideologues, group benefits, nature of the times, and no issue content. The major conclusion of this analysis was that even with a generous reading, only 12% of the population in 1956 responded to the candidates and parties in ideological terms. Converse went on to show that when asked directly about the term "liberal" and "conservative," a large percentage of the population either had little or no understanding of the terms or conceived of them in a very narrow manner (i.e., spend–save). Moreover, there was a substantial correlation between the levels of conceptualization measure and the degree of understanding of the ideological symbols.

Since one criticism of measures like these is that they are biased toward finding ideological responses among the more articulate members of the public, Converse needed a measure of constraint among belief elements that did not require respondents to verbalize their conceptions of ideology. The approach he employed was to examine the matrix of intercorrelations among issue positions in the sample. Converse reasoned that if the belief systems of members of the public were in fact organized along liberal–conservative lines, this should be observable through the degree of coherence among their positions on major policy issues. The items used dealt with both domestic and foreign policy issues and the magnitude of the correlations was found to be generally low. Moreover, Converse compared the correlations from the mass sample with comparable issue items drawn from an elite sample (candidates for the House of Representatives in 1958). The comparison showed uniformly higher correlations in the elite sample compared to the mass sample. From this, Converse concluded that the absence of ideological responses from most members of the public was more than just a problem of a lack of articulation. The absence of strong correlations among the issue items indicated a more general lack of constraint in mass belief systems. The lack of correlation among issue positions found by Converse soon proved to hold in other national setting as was demonstrated in a similar analysis by Butler and Stokes (1969) in Britain.

Before concluding that the evidence strongly supported his conclusion, Converse examined one last possibility. Perhaps the lack of correlation among the issue items was not a result of a lack of constraint in mass belief systems but was rather a result of the aggregation of numerous or even idiosyncratic belief systems. In this scenario, belief systems may in fact be highly constrained, but in a way that would be obscured when aggregated across the public. If this is so, argued Converse, we should at least find that the individual elements of mass belief systems should be stable over time. However, examining over time correlations of issues positions in the 1956–1960 panel study, Converse found remarkably low stability coefficients for virtually all of the issues examined. This conclusion was reinforced in a later paper (Converse, 1970), in which Converse argued that the pattern of correlations fit a model in which some small portion of the public possessed perfectly stable issue positions, while the majority of people responded randomly over time — revealing "non-attitudes." This was interpreted as strong evidence against the possible existence of idiosyncratic belief systems. How could constraint exist among belief elements that exhibited little or no stability over time?

In one published paper, Converse thus effectively set the agenda for research on mass belief systems for at least two decades. His research was significant for two different reasons. First, the major conclusion — that the vast majority of people in this country do not think about politics in anything remotely resembling an ideological manner — became widely accepted as the appropriate description of the character of public opinion. Research has been set against this conclusion ever since. Second, most of the research on belief systems since the Converse paper has been based on some variant of one of the three methodological strategies employed there: the levels of conceptualization, intercorrelations among issue positions, and attitude stability.

A. An Alternative Perspective on Political Ideology

It should be noted, however, that even as Converse was writing there were alternative perspectives on belief systems and public opinion. The most clearly articulated and significant of these perspectives was advanced by Robert Lane (1962) in *Political Ideology*. Converse and Lane differed on many fundamental issues. The most obvious of those differences was in their ways of studying belief systems. For Lane, attitudes, beliefs, or opinions could not be studied apart from the larger cognitive system they are imbeded in. As opposed to Converse, Lane was less interested in demonstrating the existence of (or lack of) liberal–conservative constraint than in uncovering the ways in which ordinary people reasoned about political affairs. Based on this, Lane's approach was in depth interviews with a relatively few people (15 working-class men).

Although Lane's analysis is usually seen as a direct challenge to Converse, in many respects the two were looking at two very different sets of questions. While Converse was generally searching for some overall (ideological) coherence to public opinion and mass belief systems, Lane was most concerned with the way people understand various aspects of politics and the social world. In particular, Lane devoted a great deal of attention to how basic values such as freedom and equality are reflected in people's attitudes toward politics and social change. In fact, one of Lane's overall conclusions paralleled Converse's findings: most people seem to view the political world from relatively narrow perspectives rather than employing some overarching perspective.

Seen in this way, Lane is not in direct conflict with Converse, but picks up where Converse leaves off. If people do not evaluate politics from a general ideological perspective how do they make sense of the political world? Lane's analysis suggests that people do make sense of politics and that they make use of identification beliefs, values, and strategies to do so. Although much of the empirical literature has largely ignored Lane's work (in part because of the subjective nature of his methods), we will see in the last section of this chapter that recent research is returning to many of the questions that Lane was concerned about 20 years ago.

III. A GROWTH IN IDEOLOGY?

Although research on mass belief systems continued in the 1960s, the volume of literature increased markedly beginning in the mid-1970s. The theme of much of this research was that the level of ideological thinking among the American public became more pronounced in the 1960s and early 1970s compared to the relatively nonideological 1950s that Converse examined. The view that ideology was on the rise coincided with other observed trends in American political behavior that included increasing perceptions of differences between the two parties (Pomper, 1972), an increase in issue voting (Nie, Verba, & Petrocik, 1976), and declines in party identification (Hill & Luttbeg, 1980). Clearly, the most significant research on this point was Nie with Anderson (1974) and Nie, Verba, and Petrocik (1976).

Nie and his colleagues replicated Converse's analysis of the correlations among issue positions in a mass sample using National Election Study data from 1956 to 1972. In 1956 and 1960, their results were the same as Converse: there seemed to be little evidence that people organized their issue positions in a manner indicative of liberal–conservative constraint. The picture appeared to be very different in 1964, 1968, and 1972. The correlation matrices for those years showed consistently stronger relationships among the issue positions. With the single exception of the size of government issue in 1972, correlations among the issues were uniformly higher in the years after 1964 than were observed before. Converse's conclusion that belief systems in the mass public showed little or no evidence of ideological organization seemed to be quickly done in by the new evidence.

Nie et al. did not, however, argue that Converse had been wrong after all. In fact, in one major respect this new evidence was seen to be consistent with Converse: ideological constraint *was* lacking in the 1950s. The explanation advanced for the increase in ideological constraint involved changes in the political environment. That environment in the 1950s, according to Nie, was decidedly nonideological (see also Pomper, 1972). This was reflected at one level by the moderate presidency of Eisenhower, and at another level by scholarly accounts of the "end of ideology." The result was that the public developed a relatively nonideological perspective on politics. The dozen years after Kennedy's election changed all of this. The civil rights movement and later the women's rights movement, the Vietnam war, violence in the cities, and assassinations of political figures all increased the level of conflict in politics and society and made ideological differences more apparent to more people (see Miller & Levitin, 1976). The elections of 1964 and 1972 pitted candidates with ideological differences more pronounced than any for 20 years before. The result of all of this, according to Nie, was a substantial increase in the public's ability to organize the political world along ideological lines. Converse was not wrong; his conclusions were just time bound.

The acceptance of Nie's interpretation of these findings was helped along by other trends that seemed to similarly reflect the heating up of the political environment. Several of these were previously mentioned — increases in issue voting, declines in party identification, and increased perceptions of party differences. A particularly important finding reported by Nie et al. (1976) was that a second measure of ideological content in belief systems used by Converse, the levels of conceptualization, also increased dramatically over this same period. Using a somewhat different measure than the one initially developed in *The American Voter,* Nie et al. argued that not only were the issue positions of the public more consistent along liberal–conservative lines, but in addition, evaluations of the parties and presidential candidates were decidedly more ideological.

Led by the research of Nie and his associates, analysts soon came to conclude that the level of ideological thought in the public was determined to a great degree by the ideological quality of the political environment. Belief system constraint, ideological evaluations of candidates and parties, and even the amount of issue voting could all be quite pronounced if political elites would only argue about issues in a more pronounced ideological manner. Although these conclusions were decidedly more optimistic about the quality of political thought in the mass public than were the earlier judgments reached by Converse, the basic continuity of the research had been maintained (see Converse, 1975). The worst that could be said was that Converse had overgeneralized from a limited slice of observation. In fact, the thesis of increasing ideological sophistication was entirely consistent with the social constraint argument. As political debate and discussion of issues became more packaged in ideological terms, constraint was able to penetrate deeper into the mass public. The process remained the same, openly the parameters changed slightly.

Into this happy state of affairs fell a bomb. It just so happened that in 1964 and again in 1968 the issue questions on the CPS-SRC National Election Studies that researchers used to measure belief system constraint were altered. What had been five-point, Likert-type items were changed into forced alternative formats and then into the now familiar seven-point scales. Although these changes seemed minor at the time, analysis has shown that impact on the observed intercorrelations among the issue items was far from trivial (Bishop, Oldendick, & Tuchfarber, 1978a, 1978b). Most devastating to the increasing constraint argument was evidence from split half-surveys using both the old and new question formats presented simultaneously to different samples of respondents (Sullivan, Marcus, & Piereson, 1978; Brunk, 1978).

The Sullivan, Marcus, and Piereson study was based on two random samples of people in the Minneapolis-St. Paul area. One of these samples received issue items in the form used prior to 1964 (Likert format). The other sample received the post-1968 form of the issue questions (seven-point scales with labeled alternatives). The results strongly suggest that the observed increases in issue constraint from 1960 to 1964 were not due to changes in the political environment, but rather to changes in the survey instrument. The intercorrelations among the issue items for those who received the pre-1964 format mirrored closely those reported by Converse and Nie for 1956 and 1960 — even though the data were collected in 1976. The sample receiving the newer version of the issue questions generated substantially higher intercorrelations — in this case very similar to those obtained from 1964 on. Clearly the differences in these two sets of correlations could not be explained by any differences in the political environment. The more plausible conclusion is that the change in the issue questions was responsible for much or all of the reported increase in issue consistency.

The weight of the evidence now seems to run counter to the conclusions that Nie and his associates reached (for rejoinders to this date see Nie & Rabjohn, 1979; Petrocik, 1980). Although other aspects of mass political behavior may have been affected by the political environment of the 1960s and early 1970s (such as issue voting and party identification), it appears that actual levels of such constraint (as measured by correlations among issue positions) did not increase substantially. Converse's initial conclusions seem to hold up well after all.

But maybe not. If the new and old versions of the issue questions produce substantially different results when administered to equivalent samples in the 1970s, would they have produced equally different results if both sets were used in the 1950s? In the absence of any reason to believe otherwise, we must answer that question in the affirmative. This puts us in the uncomfortable position of having two sets of estimates of the degree of constraint in mass belief systems. The items that Converse relied on seem to show that constraint is quite low, while the new issue items produce somewhat more optimistic estimates of constraint. Which do we believe?

There are reasons for believing that the newer question formats were in fact the better ones. Sullivan, Marcus, and Piereson (1978) have shown that the older Likert format items seem to contaminated by agreement response set (see also Jackson, 1979a). Moreover, such a response set is the only plausible explanation for an otherwise strange result. Comparisons of the distribution of responses to similar issue questions from 1960 to 1964 seems to show that the public grew significantly more *conservative* over this time period. Given other indicators of changes in the climate of public opinion over this period, such a result seems odd at best. The anomoly disappears by noting that the effect of agreement response set on the earlier questions would have substantially increased the proportion of "liberal" responses. If the newer questions were not so bothered by response set, the result of the change in question wording would make it look like the public had grown more conservative. This evidence of agreement response set thus casts some doubt on the earlier questions.

In addition, it is important to consider the more general question of why different items relating to the same issues should produce different levels of correlation. Perhaps the most reasonable response would be that one form of the questions produced more *reliable* indicators of issue positions. Assuming no change in the true correlation among the constructs (and this is a very reasonable assumption since we have estimates using both sets of questions at the same point in time), more reliable indicators will produce higher estimates of the correlation. We can therefore conclude that the newer seven-point measures are more reliable indicators of the public's positions on issues that are the Likert format items.

This line of reasoning leads to the conclusion that the estimates of issue constraint derived from the newer questions are in fact "better" estimates than those originally obtained from the pre-1964 formats. Furthermore, there is every reason to believe that had Converse employed the seven-point versions instead of the Likert format items he would have found higher levels of constraint in 1950s (a classic case of Monday morning quarterbacking).

After all of this methodological bickering it would thus seem that levels of issue constraint in the mass public are not nearly as puny as was originally indicated.

IV. STUDYING MASS BELIEF SYSTEMS: THE MEASUREMENT PROBLEM

A. The Measurement of Issue Positions

Although the previous discussion suggests that issue constraint in the American public of the 1950s was probably higher than Converse's initial estimates, it is still not clear what the "true" degree of issue constraint is. If we completely reverse Nie and Anderson's arguments and conclude that there has been *no* increase in issue constraint from the 1950s to 1970s, it is possible to use the interitem correlations from the more recent election studies as "better" (more reliable) estimates of issue constraint. These correlations are certainly higher than the earlier estimates, but do they justify a conclusion that there is a great deal of issue constraint in the American public? Although it is tempting to use these larger correlations to say that issue constraint is high, that conclusion may not be warranted on the basis of these correlations. The mean gamma correlation between issue positions in the 1964 election study is 0.41 compared to 0.13 for 1960 (Nie et al., 1976). This seems like a very large increase but two things must be kept in mind. First, even an average intercorrelation of 0.41 is far from a demonstration that issue positions are tightly interconnected. At this level, issue positions are still to a considerable degree independent of each other. Second, the interpretation of the magnitude of these relationships must be tempered by the strong tendency of the gamma coefficient to produce (substantially) larger estimates of relationships than other such measures of association (see Bruner, 1976). Thus, even if we accept the post-1960 estimates of the interitem correlations, it still appears as if issue constraint is at best modest.

It is possible, however, that the more recent estimates are still problematic. The trouble with accepting the correlations at face value is directly related to dispute over observed changes in the correlations over time. The methodological explanation offered for the increase in interitem correlations is that the new issue items may be "better" measures of political belief. By better we mean less prone to measurement error. All else being equal, as the amount of random measurement error in a pair of indicators goes up, the correlation between the two will go down. But if the new (post-1964) measures of issue positions are more reliable than the old measures it is likely that the new measures are still contaminated by measurement error. If so, it is possible that a correction for measurement error would yield substantially higher estimates of the correlations among the issue positions.

This logic has been pursued by several researchers (Achen, 1975; Erikson,

1978, 1979; Jackson, 1983). The results of these attempts to estimate the random error components of the issue questions have been quite startling. Rather than the low or even moderate estimates of issue constraint produced by uncorrected correlations among the various forms of the issue questions, the corrected estimates are very large. By these estimates, the degree of liberal–conservative constraint in the American public is very high — and was very high in the 1950s. According to these analyses, the reason that Converse and others found low levels of issue constraint is that the items used to measure constraint were highly unreliable. Estimates of the reliability of some of the pre-1964 items hover around 0.5. Reliabilities of this magnitude indicate that half of the variance in the issue items is simply random noise.

In addition to challenging previous estimates of interitem correlations, corrections based on reliability assessments also produce drastically different conclusions about the stability of issue positions over time. Recall that one of the most far reaching of Converse's findings was that the issue items exhibit very low levels of temporal stability. If issue positions are not even stable over time it is hard to imagine that any form of belief system constraint is possible. After taking into account measurement error, the stability coefficients go from quite low to very high. Corrected estimates of the two- and four-year correlations show many of them approaching one. By these calculations, issue positions may be almost perfectly stable over time for those people expressing an opinion.

These attempts to estimate the reliability of the issue questions have not gone unchallenged. Although virtually all researchers acknowledge that there is a substantial random component to the issue items the critical question is the identification of the source of the random variation. Those who use various psychometric techniques to assess the reliability of the questions are assuming that the source of the error is inherent in the questions. Consistent with classical measurement theory (Nunnally, 1967), responses to an indicator are seen to be a function of trues scores on the underlying construct and a random error component. The reliability of the indicator is the ratio of the true score variance to the total variance of the indicator. By these assumptions, better measurement will lead to a relative decrease in the error component and thus to a more reliable measure. A direct consequence of a large error component is the attentuation of correlation coefficients.

An alternative perspective is that the source of the random error is not the questions themselves but the public. This is Converse's original interpretation as formalized in his black and white model (Converse, 1970). According to this model, the public can be divided into those people who have perfectly stable issue positions and those who respond in an essentially random manner. This second group of people, according to Converse, really have no attitudes on the issue being assessed but choose a position on an issue scale when asked to do so. This choice is basically random and accounts for all or most of the random component in the issue items. If this interpretation is accepted it means that attempts to estimate and correct for unreliability in the issue items are misguided. The model underlying these analyses would be wrong and errors that are inherent in people would be attributed instead to the questions.

Although it would at first glance seem like a relatively simple matter to choose between these two sets of assumptions, in practice it has proven to be very difficult. A direct test of the alternative hypotheses has yet to be done, and the data on hand seems to be roughly compatible with both interpretations. There are reasonable arguments on both sides, although little direct evidence exists. Achen (1975), for example, regressed the error component for each issue position on several independent variables to determine if the size of the random component was larger for the less educated and less politically interested. He found no strong relationships. On the other hand, this analysis has been criticized because the dependent variable — the random error component — is itself unreliable (Hunter & Coggin, 1976). Moreover, it may not be general political interest or education that determines the probability of responding randomly, but actual political involvement or the salience of the specific issue to the respondent (see Converse, 1975; Kinder, 1983).

Another line of argument tries to deal with this problem by comparing the issue questions with other measures of political attitudes. Although acknowledging that some of the random error in the issue items is due to measurement error, Kinder (1983) wonders why the reliability of measures of issue positions for the mass public should be so much lower than comparable measures for elites or measures of other political attitudes for the public. For example, measures of party identification have been shown to be very reliable in comparison to the issue questions. And substantially higher estimates of the reliability of issue questions used in elite samples have been found (Putnam, Leonardi, & Nanetti, 1979). If other attitudes can be measured reliably and issues can be measured reliably for elites, then perhaps the problem is with nonattitudes rather than measurement error. There are several problems with this argument, however. First, it may not be appropriate to compare the reliability of measures of partisanship with measures of issue positions. Compared to the complexity of most issues, party identification involves a simple choice. In addition, party identification is a symbolic attitude and measures of partisanship need only to gauge people's reactions to the symbols of the Democratic and Republican Parties. In fact, it has been shown that the high reliability of measures of partisanship is due to the simple choice of party support; the reliability of the strength component of partisanship is in fact no higher than the reliability of the issue items (Feldman & Zuckerman, 1982; Marcus, 1983).

Comparisons of issue questions used in mass and elite samples is also somewhat problematic. Such comparisons never involve identically worded questions. This raises the possibility that differences in the wording of the questions may be responsible for some of the differences in the wording of the questions may be responsible for some of the difference in reliability estimates. The 1960 to 1964 changes in the issue items on the National Election Studies shows clearly how much impact question wording and form may have on responses. Moreover, there may very well be an interaction effect between level of political expertise and issue complexity. Elites probably understand issues in more complex terms and likely in somewhat different ways than the public. Issue questions written for elites (or for the public by elites) may be quite reliable for elite samples yet miss the mark for mass samples, not because the public does not have true attitudes toward that issue, but because the issue is understood in different terms. A question that may be valid and reliable for those with political expertise may be inappropriate for the public more generally.

A possible example of this is the question that has been used for a number of years in National Election Studies to measure attitudes toward social welfare policy. The question asks people whether they think the government should see to it that everyone has a job and a good standard of living or whether people should get ahead on their own. For elites, this may be a perfectly adequate item to tap fundamental attitudes toward government involvement in social welfare. On the other hand, people who look at the question more narrowly may find three distinct positions to react to. First there is the question of the government providing jobs for people who need them. Beyond that is the issue of the government seeing to it that everyone has a good standard of living. And the single alternative that the question provides is that people should get ahead on their own. This alternative position is in fact a basic cultural value (and therefore a position that is symbolically loaded) and ignores other possible alternatives to federal government action (state and local governments, private organizations). Although there is no empirical evidence that people interpret the question in this way (just as there is no evidence that people interpret it as researchers would often like to believe), one may be reasonably skeptical that instability in responses to this question is simply due to nonattitudes.

Two other analyses show how difficult it is (and will be) to determine whether the random component in the issue items is due to nonattitudes or poor questions. First, Jackson (1979b) has shown that it is possible to obtain a perfect fit for Converse's black and white model with data from a sample of people with perfectly stable attitudes. Jackson shows that responses representing an underlying continuous dimension that are projected, along with some measurement error, on to an ordinal scale, will produce a group of people who appear to be perfectly stable in their attitudes and another who appear to vary randomly. Since these data fit Converse's model perfectly, there seems to be no simple way of determining whether the underlying problem is nonattitudes or measurement error. In a second analysis, Achen (1983) has shown that estimates of the reliability and stability of the issue items derived from simple measurement models are very sensitive to alternative model specification. One approach, which assumes a simple first-order autoregressive model for the observed variable, yields estimates that show that the issue items have low reliability and that the true (unobserved) variables are very stable. A second model adds the assumption that the error terms for the observed variables are themselves autocorrelated. Estimates from this model show the issue items to be much more reliable than previous estimates and, more significantly, the responses to be even more unstable over time than Converse originally found. Moreover, with just three waves of data both of these models fit perfectly, and there is no way to choose one set of estimates over the other.

It is clear that the solution to this problem is not going to be simple. The answer, however, is critical for our understanding of public opinion. As Converse noted 20 years ago, it is difficult to imagine any pattern of belief system organization characterizing a set of attitudes that very randomly over time. As several researchers have shown, estimates of liberal–conservative constraint among issues positions depends directly on estimates of the reliability of the measures used. We know for certain that the most popular measures of issue positions contain a sizeable random component. Is this due to poor questions or to attempts to measure nonattitudes? Without being able to provide a simple answer to this question, it is interesting to note that political scientists have consistently gone about measuring issue positions through the use of single questions. Psychometricians, on the other hand, argue that attitudes in general require a large number of items combined into a scale to insure reliable measurement. From this perspective, any single item is going to be in part a reflection of the underlying attitude as well as some idiosyncratic or random component. Is there any reason to believe that the measurement of, for example, cynicism requires a multi-item scale, while attitudes toward issues can be successfully measured by single questions?

B. The Levels of Conceptualization

When Nie et al. sought to show that ideological thinking in the American public increased from the mid-1960s to the early 1970s, they looked not only at changes in inter-item correlations among issue positions but at changes in levels of conceptualization as well. Again using Converse's analysis as a point of departure, Nie and his associates argued that the number of people who evaluated the parties and presidential candidates in ideological terms increased substantially during the 1960s from the low levels reported by Converse in the 1950s. It is important to note that in demonstrating this, Nie et al. did not use the same coding procedures used by Converse. In the original analysis, the full verbatim responses given by the respondents were examined in order to determine which level he/she would be placed in. In constructing their measure, Nie et al. used the content coding of the responses in the election study data sets. Thus their measure reflected more the content of the responses than the ideological structure of the comments. Compared to the original coding, the content coding produces significantly higher estimates of the proportion of the public at the ideological level. Since the Nie et al. analysis, the original coding of the levels of conceptualization has been replicated by Pierce and Hagner (Pierce & Hagner, 1982; Hagner & Pierce, 1982) for the years since 1960. Their analysis also shows increases in the use of ideological evaluation but the increases are not nearly as striking as those produced by the Nie et al. content coding.

Nie et al. interpret the increases in ideological conceptualization as support for the thesis that the American public became more ideologically sophisticated in the 1960s and consistent with their findings of increases in issue constraint. A comparison of their surrogate measure of the levels of conceptualization with the original measure shows that ideological thinking in the public may have increased, but not nearly at the rate advertised by Nie et al. In fact, the increases in the original levels measure seems to be remarkably small given the presumably more ideological environment of the 1960s and 1970s.

Although the levels of conceptualization measure has been relied upon heavily as an indicator of the extent of ideological thinking in the American public, it has recently become the focus of a debate over its usefulness as an indicator of enduring cognitive processes. Taking aim at the surrogate levels of conceptualization measure, Smith (1980) argues that it is an unreliable measure, with a great deal of individual level movement across the categories over a four-year period from 1972 to 1976. In accounting for this instability in placing people on the measure, as well as the overall increase in the ideological categories from 1950s, Smith goes on to argue that the levels of conceptualization measure is not only unreliable but invalid. Rather than tapping a stable property of political sophistication, the measure is actually indicating the public's tendency to mimic contemporary political rhetoric. With little ideological debate in the 1950s the public evaluated the candidates and parties in nonideological terms. As debate heated up in the mid-60s, the language of the political elites was reflected in the public's comments on politics. The public had not become more ideologically sophisticated, although the political environment was producing more ideological cues for people.

Smith's criticism of the levels of conceptualization was directed at the content-coded version used by Nie et al. rather than the original coding direct from the interview protocols used by Converse. It is still possible that the original measure, relying as it did on an actual reading of the respondents' comments, may be a more reliable and valid measure of ideological sophistication. However, in a second paper, Smith (1983) examines the original coding of the levels of conceptualization and argues that it is plagued by the same problems as the surrogate measure. In particular, Smith finds that the original measure appears to be no more reliable than the surrogate measure. Turning to the question of the validity of the measures, Smith suggests that the levels of conceptualization is not measuring the ideological content of people's evaluations of politics at all. Rather, all that is being measured is the number of responses people give to the open-ended questions about the candidates and parties. According to his logic, there is a certain probability that any comment a person gives concerning politics will have some ideological content. Thus the more comments a person makes the more likely he/she will be classified as an ideologue. Smith concludes that the levels of conceptualization is not tapping qualitatively different aspects of political cognition but instead a "continuous function of knowledge, range of opinions, and talkativeness" (Smith, 1983, p. 19).

Smith's analysis seems to show that the levels of conceptualization measures are to an annoying degree unreliable. There is far too much individual level flux in the measures to sustain our confidence that they are really tapping stable individual differences in understandings of politics. Moreover, there is evidence consistent with Smith's claim that the measures are overly sensitive to changes in the political environment. Recall that the content coding used by Nie et al. produced both larger proportions of ideologues in general and more substantial changes in the proportion of ideologues over time than the verbatim coding developed by Converse and replicated by Pierce and Hagner. This suggests that the language that people can use to evaluate politics can be greatly affected by the political rhetoric of the time. Although the original coding of the levels of conceptualization seems somewhat less subject to transient influence from the political environment, there is no reason to believe that it is immune. If one believes that issue constraint has not increased substantially in the past 20 years, it appears more likely that the observed changes in conceptualization are *not* indicative of fundamental changes in the structure of mass political thought. (Although some change may be expected as a consequence of increases in educational levels.)

It is somewhat less clear how to deal with Smith's more sweeping conclusion that the underlying logic of the levels of conceptualization is faulty. In the 1983 paper, Smith goes as far as to say that virtually all measures based on the content of open-ended questions will be invalid. Clearly, the levels of conceptualization is correlated with the number of responses a person gives to the eight like–dislike questions. But is this because, as Smith argues, the levels of conceptualization reflect nothing more than the number of responses made, or because people with higher levels of conceptualization have more to say about politics? The answer may lie somewhere between these two positions. In a recent paper, Knight (1983) demonstrates that several measures of ideological sophistication show pronounced differences between the ideological level of conceptualization and the other three levels. Differences in ideological sophistication between the other three levels are nowhere near as large. And Lau (1984), using a very different content coding of the open-ended responses, shows that the ways in which people evaluate politics (their political schemas) influence the ways in which they process and organize political information.

In evaluating these various findings, it is important to remember what the critical question is. The most significant claim made by the proponents of the levels of conceptualization is that they directly tap the underlying structures of political evaluation: the persisting bases and logic people use to perceive and evaluate politics. Research based on the various codings of the levels of conceptualization will be far less significant if the measure is rather a indicator of short-term variations in the acquisition and processing of political information or the willingness of respondents to chat with the interviewer.

V. THE SUBSTANCE OF POLITICAL THINKING

The previous discussion may lead the reader to think that the study of mass belief systems and public opinion is concerned only with the methodological problems of our measurement instruments and not with the substantive properties of public opinion. Attempts to draw conclusions about the structure of political thinking seem to be quickly followed by a spate of methodological criticisms. A consideration of why this is so leads to the important conclusions. First, these methodological debates, far from being trivial, demonstrate the difficulties researchers face in the measurement of political cognition (Bennett, 1977). Far too often it is assumed that one or two simple questions will reliably and validly tap a political opinion, attitude, or belief. The results are often superfically comforting: ask respondents a question and they will usually give you an answer. In far too many cases, however, it is simply assumed that those questions are measuring the construct of interest and demonstrations of reliability and validity are rare. As the examples just discussed clearly show, these measurement problems are likely to be difficult ones. Moreover, the quality of the empirical research done on the subject of public opinion will depend directly on the ability of investigators to adequately measure the phenomenon. This is especially true when researchers attempt to devise measures that directly tap the utilization of ideological modes of thought.

Second, a major reason why these methodological debates have been so prominant is a preoccupation with a single question: does the American public think ideologically? Along with Kinder (1983), I think the accumulated research answers this question well. If by ideological we mean political evaluation supported by a breadth of information and reasoned from an abstract and well integrated set of principles, then the vast majority of people cannot be considered ideological. This conclusion seems to hold irrespective of the time period considered. In fact, by almost any reasonable standard of ideology it would be quite extraordinary to find that politics is important and understandable to enough people to generate widespread ideological reasoning. But it is one thing to say that people do not evaluate politics ideologically and another to say that they are unable to understand politics or to form political opinions. People clearly do attend to politics and arrive at political judgments. Researchers need to stop finding that such political cognition is nonideological and begin to investigate its origins.

A. The Meaning of Ideological Self-Identification

Given what has just been said, it would seem odd to begin a discussion of the origins of public opinion by considering the meaning of ideological concepts. In fact, for a period of time after Converse's demonstration that many people did not have sophisticated understandings of the meaning of liberalism and conservatism, national surveys did not even ask respondents whether they consider themselves liberals or conservatives. Researchers simply assumed that ideological self-identification can be of little political significance for people who do not understand the meaning of the liberal–conservative continuum. Research has recently shown that this assumption is wrong; ideological self-identification can have a pronounced impact on political evaluation in the absence of a full-blown ideology (Levitin & Miller, 1979; Holm & Robinson, 1978).

The clearest demonstration of the impact of liberal–conservative self-identification comes from Levitin and Miller (1979). They constructed a summary measure of ideological identification based on self-placement and attitudes toward liberals and conservatives. This summary measure is shown to be substantially more stable than individual issue positions and almost as stable as party identification. Although ideological identification is clearly correlated with party identification, Levitin and Miller show that ideology has an impact on vote choice that is independent of party. Yet the effect of ideological identification on political evaluation is not a result of a connection between ideology and issue positions. Levitin and Miller show clearly that liberal–conservative self-identification is not strongly anchored in a knowledge of the linkage between issues and ideological labels (see also Hamill and Lodge, 1984). Another intriguing observation is that, on average, the public saw more of a difference in 1976 between Ford and Carter in their general ideological position than on any specific issue (Page, 1978); this in an election that has been described as nonideological. And Feldman and Conover (1983) have found that placements of candidates on the liberal–conservative continuum are used by voters to infer where the candidates stand on specific issues, but perceived issue stands of the candidates seem to have little impact on those ideological judgments.

This research shows that people's identification of themselves as liberal or conservative is an important element in the evaluation of politics and political candidates but, in the absence of a strong connection with issues, the meaning and origins of self-identifications remain a puzzle. In an attempt to resolve these consistent findings on the impact of ideological identification with the accumulated evidence that most people are not ideologically sophisticated, Conover and Feldman (1981) argue that for most people liberal–conservative self-identification is symbolic in nature. People's positions on the liberal-conservative continuum are most immediately a function of their evaluations of the symbols "liberal" and "conservative." Moreover, these ideological symbols are, for the most people, only barely seen as opposites; elites may perceive an ideological continuum defined by the poles of liberal and conservative, but most people tend to see no such continuum, making rather distinct evaluations of the two ideological symbols.

What do people mean when they talk about liberals and conservatives? Liberalism is associated with change; evaluations of liberals are strongly related to evaluations of reformist and radical leftist groups in society. On the other hand, conservatism reflects attitudes toward the status quo and traditional values: capitalism, social control, and small government. The symbols of liberal and conservative thus represent, in simplified terms, the major lines of political conflict in society.

Since most people are not ideologues, that is, only one of the two symbols is salient for them, it should be the case that liberals and conservatives will define ideological labels in different ways. In fact, they do. Liberals are more likely than conservatives to think of ideological labels in terms of change, equality, and recent social issues. Conservatives in turn base their evaluations on fiscal concerns, the size of government, and economic issues. For most people then, liberalism–conservatism is not a bipolar continuum, but distinct evaluations of political symbols. And liberals and conservative interpret ideological debate from very different perspectives rather than from opposite sides of the same world view.

B. Symbolism and Explanations of Politics

Besides clarifying the meaning of ideological labels in the mass public, this analysis has some major implications for the study of public opinion and political evaluation more generally. First the basis of much of public opinion can be traced to symbolic evaluations of politics. Symbols are objects or words that possess meaning that goes beyond the immediate definition of the object. In many cases symbols also generate strong affective and emotional reactions (see Elder & Cobb, 1983). For example, the American flag is in one sense nothing more than a multicolored piece of cloth with 50 stars and 13 stripes. For most people, however, the flag reflects a sense of patriotism and nationalism and triggers a powerful positive reaction. Many of the major conflicts of politics have been described as strongly symbolic in nature (Edelman, 1964; Elder & Cobb, 1983). Looking at the symbolic side of politics helps to explain why people often react so strongly to certain political issues in the absence of a well-informed view of politics. Some of the most significant conflicts of recent years, for example race and busing (Kinder & Sears, 1981; Gatlin, Giles, & Cataldo, 1978; Sears, Hensler, & Speer, 1979) and the women's equality movement and conservative reaction (Conover & Gray, 1983), have been profitably explored from a symbolic perspective. Attempts to find clear evidence of a self-interest basis for public opinion often find personal concerns dwarfed by symbolic evaluations (Sears, Hensler, & Speer, 1979; Sears, Lau, Tyler, & Allen, 1980). The widespread hostility to busing among whites cannot be easily explained on the basis of personal impact of busing on parents of school-aged children (Gatlin, Giles, & Cataldo, 1978; Sears, Hensler, & Speer, 1979).

The recent research on ideology also demonstrates that it can be dangerous to assume that all people see the political world in the same terms (for a similar demonstration with party labels see Weisberg, 1980). There are a number of ways of organizing political information and there is no strong evidence that these come in directly opposing pairs (Conover and Feldman, 1984a). The view of politics as the clash of opposing political philosophies is more an elite perspective than an accurate description of the public. One example of the absence of an overarching ideological mode of organization is found in studies of issue constraint that isolate not one but several dimensions along which the public clusters political issues (Axelrod, 1967; Knoke, 1979). Social issues, racial issues, and economic issues tend to go together with much less evidence of strong interrelationships across domains (Knoke, 1979; Kritzer, 1978). Even in elite samples, issue positions tend to cluster together along relatively narrow substantive lines rather than exhibiting simple liberal-conservative constraint (Herzon, 1980). It is only one step beyond this to suggest that the salience of these dimensions varies across people, with important consequences for the ways in which people organize and process political information (Marcus, Tabb, & Sullivan, 1974; Feldman & Conover, 1984).

A consideration of individual differences in the organization and salience of political concerns leads us further from an ideological perspective of public opinion. People can make sense of politics in a number of different ways that do not require a high degree of political sophistication. But if people do not possess broad ideological conceptions of politics, how do they come to understand the political world? Some research has begun to suggest that we begin to look at people's *explanations* of politics and political problems. The most immediate need for people is to make some sense of the world around them. Social psychologists have shown that, to a great extent, people rely on simple causal explanations to provide that understanding (Jones & Davis, 1965; Kelley, 1971). For some people these explanations may be part of a coherent world view that justifies the label ideology. For most people, though, explanations may be more or less isolated, used only for some issues and not others.

Although systematic research yet needs to be done on the explanations that people rely on to make sense of the political world, some intriguing evidence is beginning to accumulate. For example, people use a variety of explanations to explain inequality in society. There are a number of different ways that people apparently go about understanding racial inequality (Apostle et al., 1983; Kinder & Sears, 1981) and poverty in general (Feldman, 1983): the poor (blacks) don't work hard enough, they have some character defects, or they have been discriminated against by society, among others. Explanations of inequality seem to have a great deal of texture to them, with people employing different explanations for political or economic inequality (Hochschild, 1981), and often varying in their account of gender and racial inequality (Sears, Huddy, & Schaffer, 1984). People also account for changes in the economy in a number of different ways, employing explanations of unemployment, inflation (Kinder & Mebane, 1983), and even causal understandings of changes in their own economic well-being (Kinder & Mebane, 1983; Feldman, 1982). In each of these cases, it has been shown that the different explanations held for a specific problem have a significant effect on the way that problem is perceived, who is held accountable, and what, if anything, should be done.

C. Values and Group Identification

Explanations provide a relatively simple way of dealing with the complexity of politics and societal problems. Where do these explanations come from? Although virtually no research has attempted to deal directly with this question some bits of evidence are available. As just discussed, explanations may be heavily based on symbolism. Simple causal accounts built around a few salient symbols may be a popular way of dealing with political information (Elder & Cobb, 1983). Evidence for two other sources of political beliefs is slowly accumulating: group identification and values.

In the early days of the behavioral study of public opinion and political behavior, group identification was an important explanatory concept (Lazarsfeld, Berelson, and Gaudet, 1948; Berelson, Lazarsfeld, & McPhee, 1954). After years of benign neglect, group identification is making a comeback as a key element in the study of public opinion and political mobilization (Conover & Feldman, 1983; Miller, Gurin, & Gurin, 1978). In some cases, group identification is seen as simply attitudes toward salient groups in society (Kinder, 1983). Defined more consistently with recent treatments in the political science and social psychology literature (Miller et al., 1978), group identification has two major components: (a) a self-awareness of one's membership in a group; and (b) a feeling of psychological closeness to the group (Conover & Feldman, 1984b). Group identification is therefore not equivalent to group membership, nor does it necessarily imply a sense of group consciousness.

Group identification helps to shape political opinions by making the group identified with part of people's self-concept. As a result, the group's perspective becomes personally salient. Political attitudes therefore become declarations of social identity; stands on public policies reflect evaluations of how those policies affect the group's interest (Kinder, 1983). Evidence suggests that group identification has long been an important source of political evaluation and public opinion. Group-oriented comments have constituted a major response category in open-ended evaluations of presidential candidates and political parties (Kagay & Calderia, 1975) and a large proportion of people fall into the group benefits category of the levels of conceptualization measure (Hagner & Pierce, 1982). More specifically, racial identities appear to be a major source of attitudes on issues involving the interests of different racial groups (Carmines & Stimson, 1982).

Values are another potentially important source of public opinion that has been until recently largely ignored in the empirical literature, although other, more descriptive accounts of American public opinion and political behavior have consistently used basic values and beliefs as central explanatory concepts (see for example, Lipset, 1963). Like group identification, values make up an important component of people's self-concept. Compared to opinions, attitudes, and beliefs, values should be more central components of belief systems and more stable over time (Rokeach, 1973). Values function as standards that guide behavior and thinking. Thus the development of political beliefs and attitudes should be consistent with people's basic values. Recent empirical research suggests that values may in fact be a basis of public opinion and policy preferences.

One value that has occupied center stage in some accounts of American public opinion is individualism: an umbrella concept for commitments to liberty, opportunity, freedom of expression, and upward mobility (see Lipset, 1963; Kinder, 1983). Somewhat more narrowly defined, economic individualism—a commitment to the hard work and self-advancement—has been strongly linked with attitudes toward social welfare policy and support for racial integration (Feldman, 1983; Kinder & Sears, 1981). The companion value to individualism, equality, may also be a key to understanding fluctuations of support for social welfare and antipoverty measures in this country. Over 20 years ago, Lane (1962) demonstrated how people's "fear of equality" limited their support for redistributive policy. More recent research has supported the relationship between equalitarianism and support for policies to improve the condition of the poor, women, and blacks (Hochschild, 1981; Sears et al., 1984). Rokeach (1973) has shown that the relative priority assigned to equality is strongly related to support for the civil rights movement and desegregation efforts more generally. Moreover, ideological differences and candidate support was more related to equality than to any other value that Rokeach investigated.

The recent study of economic and social change has brought to light another value domain that appears to have significance for the study of public opinion: materialism–postmaterialism (Inglehart, 1977). Materialist values include physical sustenance and safety while postmaterialist values emphasize belonging, self-expression, and the quality of life. Inglehart's studies indicate that postmaterialists differ significantly from materialists in their political attitudes and behaviors, particularly with respect to support for environmental and antinuclear policies, and other recent social issues (Inglehart, 1977).

D.   Schemas and Political Understanding

One of the most serious defficiencies of research on mass belief systems and public opinion has been the absence of a general theoretical framework for understanding how people organize their political beliefs and process political information. Recent advances in cognitive social psychology may provide such a theoretical framework. The mainstream of social psychology has moved away from cognitive consistency theories and their assumption that people seek cognitive consistency and hence are "rationalizing, motivating, face-saving, and justifying" (Taylor, 1981, p. 192). From this heavily motivational view of people, a different perspective has gradually evolved: that of people as "cognitive misers" who have a limited capacity for dealing with information, and who therefore must use cues and previously stored knowledge to reach judgments and decisions as accurately and efficiently as possible. This shift in perspective has led psychologists to focus more on how knowledge is stored and how such information subsequently influences the perceptual processes. To accomplish this, the concept of a "schema" has come to the forefront (Taylor & Crocker, 1977).

A schema may be defined as a cognitive structure of "organized prior knowledge, abstracted from experience with specific instances" that guides the processing of new information and the retrieval of stored information (Fiske & Linville, 1980, p. 543). Schemas perform a variety of functions. First, they lend organization to an individual's experience in the sense that people order the elements of their environment to reflect the structure of relevant schemas. Second, schemas influence "what information will be encoded or retrieved from memory" (Taylor & Crocker, 1981, p. 98). Third, the structure of a schema constitutes a basis for "filling in" missing information and thus going beyond the information given. Fourth, schemas provide a means for problem solving by supplying short cuts or heuristics that simplify the problem solving process. Finally, by generating expectations against which reality is compared, schemas provide a basis for evaluating one's experience (Taylor & Crocker, 1981).

Schema theory can be useful for the study of mass belief systems and public opinion in several ways. First, schema theory provides a basis for describing the organization of political knowledge that does not require the assumption that people are ideologues. For many people, beliefs about politics are organized in relatively small "chunks" (for example, schemas about racial inequality, economics, foreign affairs). For some people these individual schemas may be organized in ways that approach an ideological structure, while for others the schemas may be relatively independent (Conover & Feldman, 1984a). Second, schema theory offers a way of understanding the development of political belief systems. A schema develops as a consequence of interaction with the environment, and subsequently as an existing internal structure it influences the way new information is organized, thus shaping its own further development (Neisser, 1976). Finally, schema theory provides an important link between the structure of political belief systems and the processing of political information. This necessary link between structure and content has been neglected by those who study political belief systems, despite the fact that Converse (1964) cast his seminal work in dynamic terms. Most research has viewed belief systems as static structures. Schema theory, however, directs our attention to the ways people deal with new information. Simply put, schemas provide a way of understanding new situations or events by supplying a context or explanation for the event. Schemas provide people with implicit theories for understanding the political world. Thus the political schemas that people possess should help to determine what stimuli they attend to, how information will be processed, and how judgments and evaluations will be reached.

Research on mass belief systems and political evaluation is beginning to take advantage of schema theory. Significant differences have been shown in how political "experts" and "novices" process political information (Fiske, Kinder, & Larter, 1983). Political belief systems have been described in schematic terms (Conover & Feldman, 1984a). And the ways in which people organize political knowledge, process political stimuli, and perceive political candidates has been related to the political schemas they hold (Lau, 1984; Hamill & Lodge, 1984; Feldman & Conover, 1983).

VI. CONCLUSION

In a chapter of this length it is not possible to summarize all of the research on public opinion and mass belief systems that has been done over the last ten years. I have not tried to do so. Much research on the substance of public opinion on specific issues has not been dealt with at all here. Rather, the discussion has attempted to highlight the major directions and controversies in the study of the structure and dynamics of mass belief systems. It is in this body of research that the slow but steady movement toward a general understanding of public opinion has been made.

A great deal of the discussion in this chapter has dealt with methodological issues, specifically the problem of measurement. In part, this emphasis is simply a reflection of the published work in this area. However, it is important to recognize that attention to measurement issues is not an idle diversion from more significant and substantive issues. Perhaps more than in other areas of political science, the validity of empirical research on mass belief systems and public opinion hinges on the reliability and validity of the measures used. As this research demonstrates, substantively important conclusions about the structure of public opinion have often been overturned by closer attention to measurement. Further progress in this area will come in part from advances in the measurement of political cognitions. As history demonstrates, however, this is likely to be a difficult enterprise.

Theoretically, researchers must begin to look beyond the field's preoccupation with the question of ideology. The continuing search for evidence of ideological thinking in the mass public only detracts from the really important questions: How do people organize political information and understand the political world? An abundance of evidence suggests that, although few people think about politics ideologically, most people do make sense of the political world in some way. Some interesting attempts to probe the sources of political understanding were discussed in the last section of this chapter: symbolism, explanations of politics, values, and group identification. Each of these lines of research leads us further away from the ideology question and closer to an understanding of public opinion. In order to tie together these diverse factors underlying public opinion, researchers will need to think more seriously about a general theoretical approach to the study of political cognition. Schema theory may provide that approach. In its ability to link the structure of cognitions with the processing of political information, schema theory may lead to a better understanding of the origins and dynamics of public opinion.

REFERENCES

Achen, C.H. (1975). Mass political attitudes and the survey response. *American Political Science Review, 69,* 1218–1231.

Achen, C.H. (1983). Toward theories of data: The state of political methodology. In A.W. Finifter (Ed.), *Political science: the state of the discipline.* Washington, D.C.: The American Political Science Association.

Apostle, R.A., Glock, C.Y., Piazza, T., & Suelzle, M. (1983). *The anatomy of racial attitudes.* Berkeley: University of California Press.

Axelrod, R. (1967). The structure of public opinion on policy questions. *Public Opinion Quarterly, 31,* 51–60.

Bennett, W.L. (1977). The growth of knowledge in mass belief systems: An epistemological critique. American Journal of Political Science, 21, 465–500.

Berelson, B.R., Lazarsfeld, P.F., & McPhee, W.V. (1954). *Voting.* Chicago: University of Chicago Press.

Bishop, G.F., Oldendick, R.W., & Tuchfarber, A.J. (1978a). Effects of question wording and format on political attitude consistency. *Public Opinion Quarterly, 42,* 81–92.

Bishop, G.F., Oldendick, R.W., & Tuchfarber, A.J. (1978b). Change in the structure of American political attitudes: The nagging question of question wording. *American Journal of Political Science, 22,* 250–269.

Bruner, J. (1976). What's the question to that answer: Measures and marginals in crosstabulation. *American Journal of Political Science, 20,* 781–804.

Brunk, G.G. (1978). The 1964 attitude consistency leap reconsidered. *Political Methodology, 5,* 347–360.

Butler, D., & Stokes, D. (1969). *Political change in Britain.* New York: St. Martin's Press.

Campbell, A., Converse, P.E., Miller, W.E., & Stokes, D.E. (1960). *The American voter.* New York: John Wiley.

Carmines, E.G., & Stimson, J.A. (1982). Racial issues and the structure of mass belief systems. *Journal of Politics, 44,* 2–28.

Conover, P.J., & Feldman, S. (1981). The origins and meaning of liberal-conservative self-identifications. *American Journal of Political Science, 25,* 617–645.

Conover, P.J., & Feldman, S. (1984a). How people organize the political world: A schematic model. *American Journal of Political Science, 28,* 95–126.

Conover, P.J., & Feldman, S. (1984b). Group identification, values, and the nature of political beliefs. *American Political Quarterly, 12,* 151–175.

Conover, P.J., & Gray, V. (1983). *Feminism and the New Right.* New York: Praeger.

Converse, P.E. (1964). The nature of belief systems in mass publics. In D.E. Apter (Ed.), *Ideology and discontent.* New York: Free Press.

Converse, P.E. (1970). Attitudes and non-attitudes: Continuation of a dialogue. In R.R. Tufte (Ed.), *The Quantitative Analysis of Social Problems.* Reading, MA: Addison-Wesley.

Converse, P.E. (1975). Public opinion and voting behavior. In F. Greenstein & N. Polsby (Eds.), *Handbook of Political Science* (Vol. 4), Reading, MA: Addison-Wesley.

Edelman, M. (1964). *The symbolic uses of politics.* Urbana: University of Illinois Press.

Elder, C.D., & Cobb, R.W. (1983). *The political uses of symbolism. New York: Longman.*

Erikson, R.S. (1978). Analyzing one variable-three wave panel data: A comparison of two methods. Political Methodology, 5, 151–166.

Erikson, R.S. (1979). The SRC panel data and mass political attitudes. *British Journal of Political Science, 9,* 89–114.

Feldman, S. (1983). Economic individualism and American public opinion. *American Politics Quarterly, 11,* 3–30.

Feldman, S., & Conover, P.J. (1983). Candidates, Issues and Voters: The role of inference in political perception. *Journal of Politics, 45,* 810–839.

Feldman, S, & Conover, P.J. (1984). The structure of issue positions: Beyond liberal-conservative constraint. *Micropolitics, 3,* 281–308.

Feldman, S., & Zuckerman, A.S. (1982). Partisan attitudes and the vote. *Comparative Political Studies, 15,* 197–222.

Fiske, S.T., Kinder, D.R., & Larter, W.M. (1983). The novice and the expert: Knowledge-based strategies in political cognition. *Journal of Experimental Social Psychology, 19,* 381–400.

Fiske, S.T., & Linville, P.T. (1980). What does the schema concept buy us? *Personality and Social Psychology Bulletin, 6,* 543–557.

Gatlin, D.S., Giles, M.W., & Cataldo, E.F. (1978). Policy support within a target group: The case of school desegregation. *American Political Science Review, 72,* 985–995.

Hagner, P.R., & Pierce, J.C. (1982). Correlative characteristics of the levels of conceptualization in the American public: 1956–1976. *Journal of Politics, 44,* 779–809.

Hamill, R., & Lodge, M. (1984). Cognitive consequences of political sophistication. Paper presented at the 19th Annual Carnegie Symposium on Cognition, Carnegie-Mellon University.

Herzon, F.D. (1980). Ideology, constraint, and public opinion: The case of lawyers. *American Journal of Political Science, 24,* 233–258.

Hill, D.B., & Luttbeg, N.R. (1980). *Trends in American voting behavior.* Itasca, IL: F.E. Peacock.

Hochschild, J.L. (1981). *Whats fair? American beliefs about distributive justice.* Cambridge: Harvard University Press.

Holm, J.D., & Robinson, J.P. (1978). Ideological identification and the American voter. *Public Opinion Quarterly, 42,* 235–246.

Hunter, J.E., & Coggin, T.D. (1976). A reanalysis of Achen's critique of the Converse model of mass political belief. *American Political Science Review, 70,* 1226–1229.

Inglehart, R. (1977). *The silent revolution.* Princeton, NJ: Princeton University Press.

Jackson, J.E. (1979a). Statistical estimation of possible response bias in close-ended issue questions. *Political Methodology, 6,* 393–423.

Jackson, J.E. (1979b). Issues and answers: Estimating individuals' preferences with survey data. Paper presented at the 1979 meeting of the American Political Science Association.

Jackson, J.E. (1983). The systematic beliefs of the mass public: Estimating policy preferences with survey data. *Journal of Politics, 45,* 840–865.

Jones, E.E., & Davis, K.E. (1965). From acts to dispositions: The attribution process in person perception. In L. Berkowitz (Ed.), *Advances in experimental social psychology* (Vol. 2). New York: Academic Press.

Kagay, M.R., & Calderia, G.A. (1975). I like the looks of his face: Elements of electoral choice, 1952–1972. Paper presented at the annual meeting of the American Political Science Association.

Kelley, H.H. (1971). *Attribution in social interaction.* Morristown, NJ: General Learning Press.

Kinder, D.R. (1983). Diversity and complexity in American public opinion. In A.W. Finifter (Ed.), *Political science: The state of the discipline.* Washington, D.C.: The American Political Science Association.

Kinder, D.R., & Mebane, W.R. (1983). Politics and economics in everyday life. In K. Monroe (Ed.), *The political process and economic change.* New York: Agathon.

Kinder, D.R., & Sears, D.D. (1981). Prejudice and politics: Symbolic racism versus racial threats to the good life. *Journal of Personality and Social Psychology, 40,* 414–431.

Knight, K. (1983). Ideology in the 1980 election: Sophistication does matter. Paper presented at the annual meeting of the American Political Science Association.

Knoke, D. (1979). Stratification and the dimensions of American political orientations. *American Journal of Political Science, 23,* 772–791.

Kritzer, H.M. (1978). Ideology and American political elites. *Public Opinion Quarterly, 42,* 484–502.

Lane, R.E. (1962). *Political ideology.* New York: The Free Press.

Lau, R.R. (1984). Political schemas, candidate evaluations, and voting behavior. Paper presented at the 19th annual Carnegie Symposium on Cognition, Carnegie-Mellon University.

Lazarsfeld, P.B., Berelson, B., & Gaudet, H. (1948). *The people's choice.* New York: Columbia University Press.

Levitin, T.E., & Miller, W.E. (1979). Ideological interpretations of presidential elections. *American Political Science Review, 73,* 751–771.

Lipset, S.M. (1963). *The first new nation.* New York: Basic Books.

Marcus, G.E., Tabb, D., & Sullivan, J.L. (1974). The application of individual differences scaling to the measurement of political ideologies. *American Journal of Political Science, 18,* 405–420.

Marcus, G.E. (1983). Dynamic modeling of cohort change: The case of political partisanship. *American Journal of Political Science, 27,* 717–740.

Miller, A.H., Gurin, P., & Gurin, G. (1978). Electoral implications of group identification and consciousness: The reintroduction of a concept. Paper presented at the annual meeting of the American Political Science Association.

Miller, W.E., & Levitin, T.E. (1976). *Leadership and change.* Cambridge, MA: Winthrop.

Neisser, U. (1976). *Cognition and reality.* San Francisco: Freeman.

Nie, N.H., & Anderson, K. (1974). Mass belief systems revisited: Political change and attitude structure. *Journal of Politics, 36,* 540–591.

Nie, N.H., & Rabjohn, J.N. (1979). Revisiting mass belief systems revisited. *American Journal of Political Science, 23,* 139–175.

Nie, N.H., Verba, S., & Petrocik, J.R. (1976). *The changing American voter.* Cambridge: Harvard University Press.

Nunnally, J.C. (1967). *Psychometric theory.* New York: McGraw-Hill.

Page, B.I. (1978). *Choices and echoes in presidential elections.* Chicago: University of Chicago Press.

Petrocik, J.R. (1980). Contextual sources of voting behavior: The changeable American voter. In J.C. Pierce & J.L. Sullivan (Eds.), *The Electorate Reconsidered.* Beverley Hills, CA: Sage.

Pierce, J.C., & Hagner, P.R. (1982). Research update: Conceptualization and party identification, 1956–1968. *American Journal of Political Science, 26,* 377–387.

Pomper, G.M. (1972). From confusion to clarity: Issues and American voters, 1956–1968. *American Political Science Review, 62,* 415–428.

Putnam, R.D., Leonardi, R., & Nanetti, R.Y. (1979). Attitude stability among Italian elites. *American Journal of Political Science, 23,* 463–494.

Rokeach, M. (1973). *The nature of human values.* New York: Free Press.

Sears, D.O., Hensler, C.P., & Speer, L.K. (1979). Whites' opposition to "busing": Self-interest or symbolic racism?. *American Political Science Review, 73,* 369–384.

Sears, D.O., Huddy, L., & Schaffer, L.G. (1984). Schemas and symbolic politics: The cases of racial and gender equality. Paper presented at the 19th Annual Carnegie Symposium on Cognition, Carnegie-Mellon University.

Sears, D.O., Lau, R.R., Tyler, T., & Allen, A.M. (1980). Self-interest versus symbolic politics in policy attitudes and presidential voting. *American Political Science Review, 74,* 670–684.

Smith, E.R.A.N. (1980). The levels of conceptualization: False measures of ideological conceptualization. *American Political Science Review, 74,* 686–696.

Smith, E.R.A.N. (1983). The measurement characteristics of the levels of conceptualization and what they can tell us about ideological thinking (not much). Paper presented at the annual meeting of the American Political Science Association.

Sullivan, J.L., Piereson, J.E., & Marcus, G.E. (1978). Ideological constraint in the mass public: A methodological critique and some new findings. *American Journal of Political Science, 22,* 233–249.

Taylor, S.E. (1981). The interface of cognitive and social psychology. In J.H. Harvey (Ed.), *Cognition, social behavior, and the environment.* Hillsdale, NJ: Erlbaum.

Taylor, S.E., & Crocker, J. (1981). Schematic bases of social information processing. In E.T. Higgins, C.P. Herman, & M.P. Zanna (Eds.), *Social cognition: The Ontario symposium* (Vol. 1). Hillsdale, NJ: Erlbaum.

Weisberg, H.A. (1980). A multidimensional conceptualization of party identification. *Political Behavior, 2,* 33–60.

4

Electoral Behavior

Charles L. Prysby

Department of Political Science
University of North Carolina
at Greensboro

I. INTRODUCTION

The research literature on electoral behavior is prodigious. Even specific subtopics in this area have enormous bibliographies. Hence it is impossible in this brief essay to summarize everything that has been done, and we shall concentrate instead on a selective review. First, our focus shall be on very recent scholarly research, on the grounds that older studies have had sufficient opportunity to be disseminated, although reference to some research milestones will be necessary. Second, our concern will be with the behavior of voters; candidates, parties, and other actors in the electoral process are equally important, but they deserve a separate essay. Third, we shall concentrate on summarizing major findings and concerns of the research dealing with American electoral behavior, emphasizing topics that have received recent attention. Our description of the current state of the field is organized around three major areas: turnout, the social-psychology of the vote, and electoral dynamics.

II. TURNOUT

Participation in elections has been a subject of considerable academic research. The scholarly fascination with American turnout patterns is due in large part to the relatively low rates of voting in this country. The question of who votes, and for what reasons, increases in importance as turnout decreases. Questions of representation and influence that would be of little significance if turnout were high become extremely relevant when turnout is low. Scholarly interest and concern with electoral participation also has been stimulated by the decline in American turnout patterns over the past twenty years. Not only are our rates of voting low, relative to other democracies, they also seem to be moving in the wrong direction, all of which makes turnout a fascinating and relevant topic for electoral research.

A. Basic Aspects of Turnout

Before analyzing who votes and why, some basic descriptive information on turnout needs to be summarized. Perhaps the most basic question is what we mean by turnout—i.e., how is it defined and measured. It also will be useful to quickly sketch out the historical patterns and recent trends in turnout and to compare American turnout rates with those in other democracies.

1. **Measurement of Turnout.** American turnout rates normally are calculated by taking the vote total as a percentage of the voting-age population. These estimates of the turnout rate are subject to error, as the census figures for the voting age population may be inaccurate and the official vote tallies may ignore disqualified or write-in ballots. Indeed, one usually can find several "official" estimates of the turnout rate for a given election, all slightly different. Perhaps more importantly, the voting-age population includes groups who are legally ineligible to vote in most states (e.g., aliens, convicted felons, institutionalized individuals), so our usual estimate of turnout understates the proportion of eligible members of the electorate who actually voted (Crotty, 1977). It obviously is possible to adjust the voting-age

population for the presence of ineligible individuals, thus allowing for a more meaningful calculation of voters as a proportion of eligible adults, but this is almost never done.

Whatever the deficiencies of measuring turnout as a proportion of the voting-age population, it is superior to some common alternative definitions. Calculating turnout as a proportion of registered voters, the common method in many other countries, is generally inappropriate in the American context, given the large numbers of people who are eligible to register but fail to do so. In fact, the available research indicates that most nonvoters are not registered and that registering these nonvoters would result in most of them going to the polls (Erikson, 1981). But there are situations where focusing on the percentage of registered individuals who actually vote is theoretically and methodologically appropriate. One investigation of the impact of early media projections of the presidential contest on turnout in western states where the polls have not closed (DuBois, 1983) correctly points out that earlier research on this topic employed the traditional measure of turnout, when in fact the focus should be on the percentage of registered individuals who go to the polls on election day, as media projections are only capable of affecting this, not registration or absentee voting.

Estimating turnout from responses to postelection surveys results in substantial exaggeration of the true turnout rate, in large part because of overreporting by respondents. In some years the SRC/CPS American National Election Studies have validated the respondent's report of voting by checking the official records, and the findings have shown misreporting of both registration and voting to be over ten percentage points (Katosh & Traugott, 1981). Even the validated turnout rate among survey respondents is higher than the estimate derived from vote totals and census figures, however. This probable occurs because sample surveys inevitably exclude some chronic nonvoting groups, such as transients, institutionalized individuals, and those who travel considerably (the census presumably is less likely to miss such individuals) and also because any preelection interview (used in the SRC/CPS surveys) stimulates some election interest in the respondent and increases the likelihood of his or her voting.

Although the turnout rate found in a survey will not be a good estimate of the true population figure, this inflation of electoral participation appears to be an across-the-board phenomenon. The correlates of reported voting and actual voting are remarkably similar, as examinations of the data from SRC/CPS validated surveys have shown (Katosh & Traugott, 1981; Sigelman, 1982). We thus can confidently examine the sources and causes of voting and nonvoting by working with reported voting, making the research task easier.

2. **Turnout Patterns and Trends.** Measuring turnout as a proportion of the voting-age population makes sense when most adults have

the right to vote. This has not always been so. Blacks, women, and the propertyless all have been prohibited from voting in the past. But since the enactment of the Nineteenth Amendment in 1920 virtually all adults over 21 have had the legal right to vote. However, while universal adult suffrage has constitutionally existed throughout most of the twentieth century, it has been compromised by the electoral laws and practices within the states, especially the deliberate exclusion of blacks (and to some extent poor whites) in the South through such legal subterfuges as the poll tax and literacy test. Less pernicious but still significant were other impediments, such as lengthy residency requirements, which were employed throughout the country. Congressional actions (especially the Voting Rights Act) and court decisions during the 1960s and 1970s reformed registration procedures by wiping out these undesirable practices (Crotty, 1977), and the contemporary situation is one of minimal legal restrictions on the right to vote (see Crotty, 1977, for existing exclusions).

Despite the election reforms of the 1960s and 1970s, turnout (measured as a percentage of the voting-age population) dropped during these decades. Figure 1 charts the turnout in presidential and off-year congressional elections over this time period, and the consistent downward trend is evident. A slight upturn in 1982 may suggest that the decline has bottomed out, but even if it has, it is at a relatively low level. When one considers that in 1960 a sizable number of people of voting age were effectively excluded by the aforementioned practices, the decrease in turnout becomes more significant. Had the reforms not been enacted, turnout surely would have declined even more. The one reform that did serve to lower turnout was the 1971 enactment of the Twenty-Sixth Amendment, which extended the suffrage to the 18- to 21-year-old group, an action that probably produced a three percentage point decline in the turnout rate (Shaffer, 1981), but the effect of the other reforms more than compensated for this action.

Current turnout rates are low when compared to those of the recent past. They also may be low when compared to late nineteenth century rates. Burnham (1982) argues that participation flourished in the highly partisan atmosphere that existed before the turn of the century, and fearful elites successfully worked to discourage such mass involvement. Others see the high turnout rates of this earlier era as the result of substantial electoral fraud, which was eliminated by the Progressive reforms. Unfortunately, the data available to us are inadequate to definitively determine which of these explanations is more accurate, but the debate suggests the significance that can be attached to changes in turnout.

3. **Turnout in Comparative Perspective.** The turnout rates displayed in Figure 1 compare poorly to those of other democracies. One study of turnout in recent national elections found the United States to rank 23rd

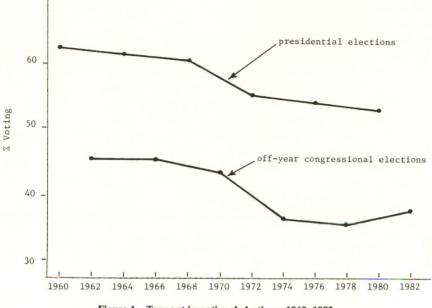

Figure 1   Turnout in national elections, 1960–1982.

of 24 western democracies (Glass, Squire, and Wolfinger, 1984). Turnout rates frequently exceed 80% in other democracies, and while it is true that elsewhere the rate is calculated as a percentage of registered voters rather than of the voting age population, correcting for this still leaves most countries with substantially greater turnout rates (Glass et al., 1984). This disparity between American and European turnout rates tells us very little about differences between citizens but a great deal about differences between political systems, especially the registration systems. People in other democracies vote more not because their attitudes are closer to that of the model democratic citizen, but because they live in a different legal and political context, a topic that we shall pursue in more depth later in this essay.

B.   Voters and Nonvoters

Turnout can be approached in two ways. Most research has focused on the individual characteristics that are related to voting, examining both attitudinal and socio-demographic correlates of turnout. Another approach, which has received more attention recently, is to explain turnout in terms of contextual characteristics, broadly defined. This approach emphasizes the impact of the legal, political, and social context on individual behavior. We shall look first at the individual or microlevel relationships, then consider the systemic or contextual effects.

1. Political Orientations and Voting. Widespread agreement exists on the political attitudes that lead to voting. Early research (Campbell, Converse, Miller, and Stokes, 1960) identified interest in the campaign, concern over the outcome, political efficacy, and sense of civic duty as the major motives propelling voters to the polls, and more recent research has confirmed and refined these earlier findings. While these orientations are interrelated, they each have a separate and independent impact on turnout. Interest and concern clearly are relevant variables, and they explain why those with strong partisan attachments are more likely to vote (Campbell et al., 1960). Political efficacy, especially a feeling that one's vote really counts, also has a significant impact. Finally, even the uninterested and unconcerned may vote if they feel it is their civic duty to do so. Not only do these variables explain voting quite well, similar variables are useful in explaining other forms of political participation, adding to our theoretical understanding (Verba & Nie, 1972).

These variables are extremely useful for distinguishing voters from nonvoters in any given election. They also are useful for explaining the decline in turnout during the 1960s and 1970s. A declining sense of political efficacy probably accounts for much of this drop (Cassel & Hill, 1981; Shaffer, 1981; Abramson & Aldrich, 1982). Weaker party attachments also have played a role by reducing levels of concern over the election outcome (Cassel & Hill, 1981; Abramson & Aldrich, 1982). In fact, most of the decline in turnout can be attributed simply to changes in political efficacy and partisan attachments (Abramson & Aldrich, 1982). But while these attitudinal variables are useful for explaining individual-level differences and changes over the past two decades, they are not very helpful in explaining cross-sectional geographical differences in turnout. The sizable differences in turnout among the states, or between the United States and other countries, generally are not accounted for simply by population attitudinal differences.

2. Social Factors and Voting Turnout has long been linked to several social and demographic characteristics. These characteristics also can be linked to the attitudinal variables discussed above, yielding a model in which social factors affect attitudes, which in turn affect electoral participation (Verba & Nie, 1972). This model works fairly well, but some residual influences of social factors on voting appears to exist even after attitudinal factors are taken into account (Verba & Nie, 1972; Cassel & Hill, 1981).

Socioeconomic status is the social factor most often cited as a determinant of electoral participation. While there is an enormous body of empirical research supporting this relationship, most of the studies have not carefully unravelled the components of socioeconomic status to determine exactly how and why SES is related to voting. Fortunately, a recent study (Wolfinger &

Rosenstone, 1980) has addressed these concerns. Working with data from the Current Population Surveys conducted by the Census Bureau, which provides a very large number of respondents, Wolfinger and Rosenstone were able to examine the independent impact of education, income, and occupation. They found education to be the most important SES component affecting turnout. Income has only a slight impact, once education and occupation are controlled for, and this impact is limited to the low end of the income spectrum. Occupation has a clear effect, but more in terms of specific aspects of occupations than in terms of overall job status.

It appears that the effect of SES on turnout is not due to any overall notion of status. Rather, it represents the impact of specific experiences or attributes on an individual's political sophistication and understanding. The fact that education is the component of socioeconomic status that has the greatest effect on turnout reflects the effect that education has on an individual's ability to comprehend abstract ideas and complex information. Many occupations develop the same skills in individuals, and it is this that causes an independent effect of occupation, apart from the effects of education and income, which are strongly related to occupation.

Besides SES, age is the other important social characteristic affecting the likelihood of voting. Almost all studies have emphasized the familiar curvilinear relationship in which turnout is lowest among the very young, rises and peaks among the middle-age groups, then declines among the old. Perhaps the best examination of this relationship is a cohort analysis by Hout and Knoke (1975) that attempts to separate aging, generational, and period effects and finds that aging itself is related in a curvilinear fashion to turnout. A few studies (Wolfinger & Rosenstone, 1980; Verba & Nie, 1972) have examined the relationship between age and voting after controlling for education and other relevant demographic characteristics that are correlated with age, and they have found that the decline in turnout among the elderly is much less than what one observes from the simple bivariate relationship. On the other hand, the lower turnout rates among the young are not explained away by controls for education or other demographic characteristics; in fact, the relationship is strengthened. But the more interesting finding is that the most highly educated young people vote at relatively high rates and do not show much increase as they become older, whereas poorly educated young people vote at very low rates and display substantial increases in turnout as they reach middleage (Wolfinger & Rosenstone, 1980, p. 59). Age apparently substitutes for formal education as a source of political awareness and understanding.

The relationship between age and turnout helps to explain the decline in electoral participation that has occurred over the past two decades. Not only were the 18- to 20-year-olds brought into the eligible electorate by the Twenty-Sixth Amendment, but the age structure of the population changed in the direction of a younger adult population. Boyd (1981) estimates that one-fourth of the decline in participation in presidential elections that occurred in the 1960s and 1970s can be accounted for by changes in the age structure for the electorate.

C. Contextual Influences on Turnout

While most existing research on electoral participation has focused on the influence of individual social and attitudinal characteristics, increasing emphasis recently has been placed on analyzing contextual effects. Contextual effects refer to influences on an individual's behavior that are attributed to characteristics of the geographical context in which the individual resides. The state normally is the geographical unit of greatest interest when it comes to turnout, but county or community level effects also have been examined. Two general sets of characteristics have attracted the attention of researchers: (a) legal arrangements, especially registration procedures, and (b) political factors, especially those relating to competition (Kim, Petrocik, and Enockson, 1975).

1. The Legal Context. Registration procedures are cited as the single most important contextual or institutional factor affecting turnout. Kelley, Ayres, and Bowen (1967) argued that turnout differences among communities largely represented differences in registration levels, which in turn were affected by registration procedures. Erikson (1981) claims that registration is the key to voting and that even individuals who have the social characteristics of nonvoters are likely to vote once they are registered. As evidence of this, he cites the fact that the usual correlates of turnout (education, etc.) predict registration quite well but are poor predictors of turnout among the registered. Erikson's point is important, because it implies that registering low SES groups will boost their turnout, not just add nonvoters to the registration rolls.

A thorough and systematic examination of the impact of the registration procedures in the 50 states (Wolfinger & Rosenstone, 1980) concluded that turnout in the 1972 presidential election could have been almost ten percentage points greater if every state had registration procedures as lenient as the least restrictive state. Especially important aspects of registration laws were: (a) how close to election day one could register and (b) whether one could register during evenings or weekends. On the whole, the easier it is to register, the greater the turnout. The same arguments can be extended to cover the legal arrangements on voting day, as Conway (1981) found that longer poll hours increased turnout. Of course, such arguments have been at the heart of criticisms of American legal arrangements, as compared to European laws. The substantially higher turnout rates in most European democracies can be attributed to extremely high registration rates, which result from the fact that the election officials actively attempt to register all eligible citizens.

Other legal arrangements concerning elections may affect turnout. Boyd (1981) argues that declining turnout in the U.S. is partially attributable to the disaggregation of the election calendar. While there is no doubt that many states have attempted to separate or insulate elections for state office from presidential elections (and even from all national elections for a few states), and while there are some cross-sectional data that support Boyd's conclusion, a more careful quasi-experimental analysis by Cohen (1982) finds little evidence to justify such a conclusion. Even if the timing of elections does not explain the decline in turnout that has occurred, it still seems justified to conclude that when an election is held has an impact on the turnout. Kenney (1983), for example, finds that gubernatorial primaries held in conjunction with presidential primaries elicit higher turnout, other variables being controlled for.

2. The Political Context. Characteristics of the political context also influence turnout. Competition is widely cited as an important factor, on the assumption that voters are less interested in voting in lopsided elections. Most research has been focused at the state level, examining the connection between the level of partisan competition and turnout in state-wide elections. For example, Patterson and Caldeira (1983) find that turnout in gubernatorial elections is related to the level of partisan competition, even when other factors are controlled for. While state-wide partisan elections have received the most attention, the arguments appear to apply more broadly. Caldeira and Patterson (1982) examined state legislative races in California and Iowa and found some evidence that the competitiveness of the legislative district was related to turnout, which they unfortunately had to measure as a percentage of registered voters. Kenney's (1983) analysis of gubernatorial primaries from 1968 to 1980 finds that intraparty competition is one of the best predictors of turnout, indicating that it is competition in general, not just partisan competition, that exerts an influence on turnout.

The other important characteristic of the political context involves the mobilization of voters by campaign activities. Turnout may be increased by direct efforts of campaign organizations to register potential supporters and bring them out on election day. Apart from such direct efforts, turnout may be affected by the general level of campaign activity, which may serve to heighten voter awareness and interest. Lack of appropriate data prevents a thorough and systematic analysis of these activities, but some recent research is suggestive. Focusing on campaign spending as a measure of activity and effort, two studies conclude that higher spending leads to higher turnout: Patterson and Caldeira (1983) find this to be the case for gubernatorial elections, and Caldeira and Patterson (1982) find that in state legislative elections spending has an effect, at least up to a threshold figure.

D. Conclusions

Turnout most commonly has been explained in terms of individual-level social and attitudinal characteristics. The effects of these individual-level factors appear to be well-understood, and they are useful not only in explaining who votes and who does not, but also for explaining recent changes in turnout. More recently, increasing attention has been paid to contextual-level influences, especially from legal, institutional, and political factors. These appear quite useful for explaining variations in turnout among the states (or other geographical units) and for explaining why turnout is lower in the U.S. than in other Western democracies. These institutional and legal factors do not explain recent changes in turnout, however, except for the rise in southern turnout rates. The overall decline in turnout over the past twenty years has taken place despite legal and institutional changes that should have increased overall turnout.

Attempts to explain turnout inevitably lead to one basic question: What significance should be attached to the turnout rate? Some analysts claim that it makes little difference what the turnout level is, citing as support for their position the fact that most survey analyses have found little difference in the political orientations of voters and nonvoters (Abramson, Aldrich, and Rohde, 1982, p. 89; Wolfinger & Rosenstone, 1980, p. 109). Others argue that higher turnout would benefit the Democrats, as nonvoters are disproportionately located among lower SES groups, but two recent analysis show that this view, while commonly expressed, is questionable. Drawing on the distinction between core and peripheral voters, DeNardo (1980) argues that increased turnout may actually benefit the Republicans. Petrocik (1981) concludes that, rather than systematically benefiting the Democrats, higher turnout simply would add to the short-run oscillation and volatility of the vote.

Regardless of the partisan implications of a higher turnout rate, analysts are agreed on one point: lower SES groups are underrepresented among voters, and the extent of this underrepresentation has increased with the decline in turnout over the past two decades (Cassel & Hill, 1981; Conway, 1981; Reiter, 1979). Moreover, this differential representation along class lines is not characteristic of other Western democracies, where social differences in turnout are fairly minimal in most cases (Burnham, 1982, p. 183). This leads some to suggest that there is at least a long-run, if not a short-run, significance to the turnout rate, and comparisons of the views of voters and nonvoters in a particular year fail to reveal the full implications of higher turnout. It is this point, however, that is most in need of further research.

III. SOCIAL PSYCHOLOGY OF THE VOTE

Explanations of individual voting behavior have been greatly influenced by a single pioneering study, *The American Voter* (Campbell et al., 1960). Most scholarly research in this area during the 1960s adopted the ideas and approach of this work, and while later research often was critical of many of the conclusions drawn by *The American Voter,* its heavy influence was still evident in the concepts and framework that were the subject of debate. Because of the impact of this study on subsequent research, our discussion of the social psychology of the vote is best organized by first considering the basic ideas of this work, and then examining the revisions and findings of recent research.

The American Voter explained individual voting decisions in terms of three basic influences: party identification, candidate characteristics, and issues. Party identification assumed the central role in this model, influencing all other perceptions and attitudes. Issues were seen as relatively uninfluential. Voters cast ballots in line with their partisan dispositions, and when they did not, it was more likely to be a result of their evaluation of candidate characteristics than a result of positions on specific issues. In fact, most voters were incapable of casting a ballot according to issue orientations because they lacked the information that would be necessary to behave in that fashion (Campbell et al., 1960, p. 183).

An enormous amount of research has followed the paths blazed by *The American Voter,* and much of it has supported, reinforced, and elaborated the ideas of this work. But criticisms have emerged. Some appear to have been motivated by a normative reaction against what seemed to be a very unflattering picture of the average voter as an individual motivated largely by habitual partisan dispositions and superficial views of candidate characteristics. Other criticisms and revisions have a more scholarly base. Some have focused largely on the fact that the *The American Voter* was based on the analysis of survey data from the 1952 and 1956 presidential elections, and consideration of data from different years, or from nonpresidential elections, might yield different results. Other criticisms have focused directly on the concepts and framework employed by Campbell and his colleagues, arguing that fundamental revisions are required. The two areas that have received the greatest attention in the recent literature are: (a) the concept of party identification and (b) the extent and nature of issue voting. These are related topics, and both are important for our understanding of decision-making processes among voters.

A.   Party Identification
Party identification normally is measured by: (a) asking respondents whether they consider themselves to be a Democrat, Republican, or inde-

pendent; (b) asking a follow-up question for those calling themselves Democrats or Republicans that categorizes these respondents as strong or weak partisans; and (c) asking a follow-up question for those calling themselves independents that determines whether these respondents can be classified as leaning toward one of the two parties. The result of all this questioning is that respondents can be classified on the familiar seven-point scale (strong Democrat, weak Democrat, independent Democrat, pure independent, independent Republican, weak Republican, strong Republican). However, many researchers choose not to employ the full seven-point scale, working instead with a more condensed version, such as a three-point scale (Democrat, independent, Republican), a practice that can lead to many problems as we shall see later.

The view of Campbell and his colleagues was that party identification was a stable and basic orientation toward the political world that not only affected the individual's vote, but also influenced his attitudes and perceptions. Thus party identification played an important role in opinion formation, and it therefore was necessary to consider party identification in any attempt to explain orientations or reactions to political issues, events, or personalities. Party identification also was seen as extremely stable. Individuals acquired it early, with family influence being quite substantial, and changed it infrequently (if at all), with the likelihood of change diminishing with age.

The usefulness of this concept was twofold. First, party identification was an essential variable for microlevel explanations of individual voting behavior. Second, it was useful at the macro-level for the study of electoral dynamics. Since partisan loyalties were stable attachments, outcomes for a particular election that deviated from what would be expected, given the distribution of party identification (i.e., what can be termed the "normal vote"), necessarily represented the influence of short-term forces. This partitioning of influences into short-term and long-term was essential to the understanding of electoral dynamics.

Recent research has suggested many modifications of earlier ideas concerning party identification. Some studies have focused on the influence of party identification on attitudes or behavior, while others have more carefully analyzed the concept itself.

1. **Decline of Partisanship**   Beginning in the 1960s, partisan loyalties began to weaken in intensity, with fewer people calling themselves strong partisans and more identifying as independents. This trend, summarized in Figure 2, can be seen as part of a more general weakening of the American political party system, a development widely commented on in the mass media. The change is real and significant, but it has been exaggerated, especially by reports in the popular media suggesting that independents now outnumber Democrats or Republicans. This is true only if one counts all

independents; in fact, most independents feel themselves to be closer to one of the two parties, and pure independents (i.e., those not closer to either party) have never constituted more than 15% of the electorate. When one realizes that the independent learners are very similar to the weak partisans (as we shall see later), the decline in partisan loyalties may seem somewhat less dramatic than has been suggested by some reports (LeBlanc & Merrin, 1979). It also appears that there has been a slight strengthening of partisan loyalties in the past few years. Still, the number of strong partisans has declined substantially, and there are twice as many pure independents now as in the early 1950s.

The weakening of partisan loyalties is significant because it implies that party identification will have less influence on voting behavior, and therefore the short-term forces of issues and candidates will be more important. Numerous studies have noted this, and the analysis by Nie, Verba, and Petrocik (1976) nicely summarizes the various dimensions of this phenomenon: increased ticket-splitting, increased defections in both presidential and congression voting, and increased associations between issue orientations and voting behavior — in general, a more volatile electorate easily affected by short-term forces. Of course, this revision of Campbell et al. (1960) is not a fundamental rejection of their findings, merely an indication that the behavior of voters in the 1950s should not be generalized too quickly to other time periods.

2. Stability of Partisanship. Declining partisanship also stimulated consideration of the stability of party identification. Of course, changes in the overall level of party identification can occur even if party identification is perfectly stable at the individual level, and it is clear that much of the decline in partisanship has resulted from generational replacement (Nie et al., 1976). However, a careful analysis of this phenomenon reveals that period effects produced a weakening of loyalties among older voters as well (Norpoth & Rusk, 1982). The impact of the 1960s and 1970s on individual partisan loyalties suggests that party identification is something more than a stable habit; it is responsive to political events and forces.

Numerous studies have suggested that earlier research too often assumed an incorrect causal order between party identification and other political attitudes. Rather than stemming from an individual's party identification, various political orientations can form the basis for the individual's party identification. Cassel's (1982) analysis of party identification from 1956 to 1980 finds that when demographic and social characteristics are controlled for, policy attitudes predict party identification quite well; but demographic and social characteristics are not good predictors of party identification once policy attitudes are controlled for. Howell's (1981) analysis of the 1972–1974 American National Election Study panel data concludes that changes in

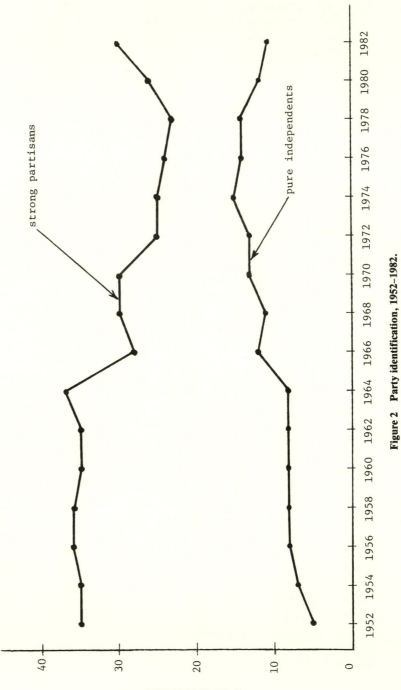

Figure 2 Party identification, 1952–1982.

124

party identification are caused, or at least preceded by, changes in voting. Fiorina (1982, p. 89) sees party identification as a "running tally of retrospective evaluations," especially those evaluations concerning the handling of domestic and foreign matters at the national level.

Recent research has painted a new picture of party identification, but we should recognize the limits of these revisions. First, while party identification may be less stable than had been assumed, it still is a fairly stable orientation; the difference we are referring to is between very stable and moderately stable. Second, although party identification can be influenced by the performance of office holders and the responses of individual candidates to specific issues, it also is true that party identification affects perceptions and attitudes. This reciprocal causation is troublesome for researchers, but it undoutbedly is more reflective of reality. Third, even though party identification plays a less central role in the determination of the individual's vote, it nevertheless is one of the important influences, and cannot be ignored.

3. Concept Reformation While the criticisms just discussed accept the basic notion of party identification, questioning only its stability or its relationship to attitudes or behavior, others have argued that the concept itself is fatally flawed. The crux of most of these criticisms is that the seven-point scale is not a unidimensional ordinal scale. Many researchers have noted that the independent leaners do not differ very much from the weak partisans (of the same partisan direction) in their voting behavior, and in other attitudes and behavior the similarities between weak partisans and partisan leaners are readily evident (Abramson et al., 1982, pp. 167–183; LeBlanc & Merrin, 1979; Valentine & VanWingen, 1980). The greatest conceptual problems seem to involve the independents, who cannot be simply labeled as less partisan than some of the partisans.

There are a number of reasons for these conceptual inadequacies. Miller and Wattenberg (1983) emphasize the fact that the independent category includes two types of respondents: those who call themselves independents in response to the opening question used to measure party identification ("Do you think of yourself as. . .") and those who indicate no preference. More fundamentally, Weisberg (1980) argues that the concept of party identification is a multidimensional concept. At the very least, there are two dimensions: a Democratic/Republican dimension and an independent/not-independent dimension. This appears to be the position favored by Valentine and VanWingen (1980). An alternative is to view party identification as involving three dimensions: attitude toward Democrats, attitude toward Republicans, and attitude toward independents (Weisberg, 1980). Once the multidimensional nature of party identification is recognized, most of the anomalies are readily explained. For example, the tendency for independent Democrats to be as Democratic in their voting as weak Democrats is understandable once we realize that the independent Democrats are not less positive in their orientation toward Democrats, just more positive in their orientation toward independents.

Recognizing the inadequacies of the traditional party identification scale is easier than determining a superior alternative. Attempts to refine the concept of party identification by making it multidimensional also make it more complex, thereby limiting its utility. Efforts to construct alternative measures of partisanship that would be unidimensional have not progressed very far. Weisberg (1983) formulates a measure of party support, using different questions, that yields a five-point scale of party support (which can be extended to a ten-point scale by adding a positive/negative reaction toward independents). However, while his new scale better predicts some things, the old scale is a superior predictor of other things. Furthermore, the new scale results in about one-third of the respondents being classified as not closer to either party, which seems to be a disadvantage when compared with the traditional scale.

Actually, the traditional measure of party identification is quite suitable, provided that: (a) all seven categories are used and (b) we recognize the similarity between the weak partisans and the independent leaners. Unfortunately, this often is not done. Substantial scholarly research exists in which party identification is trichotomized into Democrats, Republicans, and independents, with the last category including the independent learners. Despite the popularity of this approach, it is indefensible. It both arbitrary divides weak partisans from the neighboring independent leaners, when in fact these two groups are much more similar to each other than any other combination of groups, and it combines together independent Democrats, independent Republicans, and pure independents — three quite dissimilar groups. If it is necessary to trichotomize party identification, it would be far preferable to include the independent leaners with the strong and weak partisans of the same direction, and leave only the pure independents as the middle category. All of this follows logically from the findings of recent research, and given the attention that has been paid to inadequacies in the traditional handling of party identification, it is surprising to see these implications ignored by other researchers.

B. Issue Voting

No topic in the study of voting behavior has generated more controversy than the question of issue voting. In part this is due to normative associations with the phenomenon: it is "good" or "desirable" for voters to cast their ballots on the basis of issue positions; it is "bad" or "undesirable" or at least "unfortunate" when voters decide whom to vote for without reference to political issues. Even the scholarly literature is not immune from such judgments — for example, Key's (1966) well-known study of issues and voting claims that "voters are not fools." Scholarly controversy also arises from the variety of approaches and methods used to measure or determine the extent of issue voting, the result being that scholars analyzing the same data set often arrive at different conclusions.

The conclusion of *The American Voter* was that issue voting was quite limited. Most voters lacked the information necessary to cast a ballot on the basis of issues, as many of those who had an opinion on what the government should do on a particular matter did not know either what the government actually was doing or what differences existed between the parties or candidates on the issue. Moreover, voters seemed more inclined to evaluate the candidates in terms of general personal characteristics or partisan loyalties. Additionally, the analysis by Campbell et al. (1960) emphasized the extremely nonideological nature of the electorate. Voters displayed low levels of attitude constraint, even when it came to domestic issues, indicating that there was no ideological structure to their ideas. They also were remarkably unsophisticated in their evaluations of the parties and candidates, with only a small minority employing abstract concepts, such as references to liberalism or conservatism. It appeared that voters viewed the political world in terms of simple concepts of self-interest and isolated and unstructured values. But, just as with the traditional view of party identification, scholarly research in the 1970s increasingly began to challenge and modify the conclusions of *The American Voter*.

1. The Rise of Issue Voting.   An enormous amount of literature has been devoted to the topic of issue voting. The basic theme of most of the recent literature is that issue voting has increased substantially from the levels found in the 1950s by Campbell et al. (1960). Probably the best-known study is Pomper's (1972) article, which argues that there was a significant change in American electoral behavior in the 1960s. Beginning in 1964, voters began to see clearer differences between the parties and to align their partisan choices with their issue orientations. Similar conclusions are put forth by Nie et al. (1976), which is the most comprehensive analysis of issue voting. These and other studies did not argue that the findings of *The American Voter* were wrong; rather, they claimed that the situation changed from the 1950s.

Not all scholars agreed with these conclusions. Some argued that changes in the extent of issue voting were being exaggerated, usually because of inadequate or biased methodology. For example, Margolis (1977) criticized Pomper's (1972) study on such grounds. But many different studies, employing different methods and approaches, have concluded that issue voting is more pervasive than traditionally has been assumed, and the evidence appears compelling. This increase in issue voting also appears to be a relatively permanent shift, as substantial levels of issue voting have persisted in presidential elections, including the 1980 contest (Abramson et al., 1982).

The rise in issue voting naturally has led to investigations of the source of this change. Most have emphasized the nature of the choices offered to the voter (Pomper, 1972; Nie et al., 1976). Thus the rise of issue voting is not primarily a result of changes in the electorate (although some of the rise can be attributed to increases in education); it is a result of changes in the political context. The low level of issue voting observed by Campbell et al. (1960) reflects the fact that the 1956 presidential election was relatively issueless. By contrast, the 1964 presidential contest offered a clear choice to the voters. Thus, if more voters satisfy the conditions for issue voting, it is because the candidate choices and party differences are sharper. Carmines and Gopoian (1981), on the other hand, suggest that issue voting results less from the character of the campaign and more from partisan coalitions that form out of differences in the policies pursued and the general performance of officeholders, a view that is similar to the retrospective voting theories we shall consider shortly.

Now that it seems clear that issues play a substantial role in the vote decision, research attention has focused on refining and elaborating our understanding of this process. Some research has been concerned with more thoroughly understanding the conditions necessary for issue voting (Meier & Cambell, 1979). Other research has considered different types of issues and the implications for issue voting (Carmines & Gopoian, 1981). And a considerable amount of research has simply looked at the role of issues in nonpresidential elections, a worthwhile avenue for exploration, given the heavy concentration on presidential elections among studies of this area. Gopoian (1982), for example, analyzed data from exit polls conducted during the 1980 presidential primaries and found very modest relationships between ideological orientation and candidate choice, especially among Democratic voters. Also some analyses of congressional elections suggest that voters often are influenced less by issues and more by perceptions of general candidate characteristics (Hinckley, 1980; Jacobson, 1983). Thus there is general agreement that the extent of issue voting will vary, both over time and across different races, and the task for future research is to explain more fully when and why issue voting will be higher or lower.

2. **Ideological Thinking.** Related to increases in issue voting are increases in the ideological nature of the electorate. Changes in the ideological nature of the electorate imply two things. First, there is greater attitude constraint, so that orientations on issues are more closely tied together along liberal–conservative lines. Many studies have noted this increase, with the most thorough description and analysis presented by Nie et

al. (1976). This rise in attitude constraint or consistency is related to the increases in issue voting. Substantial attitude constraint permits voting along liberal–conservative lines, while little or no attitude constraint hampers issue voting, because many voters will have difficulty in finding candidates who match their pattern of issue orientations (Nie et al., 1976).

Increases in the ideological nature of the electorate also involve greater sophistication in evaluations of candidates and parties, and recent research has found that voters now are more likely to employ abstract terms and ideological concepts (loosely defined) in their evaluations (Nie et al., 1976). Other studies reinforce the view that voters are more ideological than previous work had assumed. Levitin and Miller (1979) argue that even when voters have an incomplete understanding of what liberal and conservative mean, they still may find meaning in these terms and employ them in their evaluations. Sears, Lau, Tyler, and Allen (1980) find that views on most issues reflect general ideological values and are fairly unrelated to individual self-interest. While the mass public certainly is not ideological in the fullest sense of that term, these findings underscore the fact that many members of the electorate are comfortable with abstract and complex ideas, and it is surely incorrect to claim that most voters evaluate the political world solely in terms of simple ideas of self-interest or unrelated and disorganized value systems.

In sum, recent research finds a new American voter. Levels of ideological thinking are higher, both in terms of attitude consistency and in terms of the use of ideological concepts in reasoning. More voters possess the information necessary for issue voting, and more actually cast their ballot on this basis. Again, it is important not to exaggerate the situation. Some of the change may be an artifact of the data or methods employed, and the methodological arguments in this area are fierce. But the overall weight of evidence suggests that real change has taken place, and such findings have stimulated increased research in this area.

3. Retrospective Voting. Theories of retrospective voting provide the most promising and fruitful development in the study of issues and voting. Actually, retrospective voting theories deal with more than issue voting; they really attempt to synthesize or integrate issues, candidates, and parties into explanations of voting behavior. The central idea of retrospective voting is that voters react to what they have observed; for presidential elections, this means that evaluations of the performance of the incumbent administration are crucial.

Key's (1966) analysis of "switchers" and "standpatters" in presidential elections was the stimulus for more recent and more sophisticated treatments, such as Fiorina (1982). Proponents of retrospective voting theories point out that this view demands less of the voter, and therefore seems more realistic. Rather than having to judge the relative merits of the campaign promises of competing candidates, voters have only to assess the performance of officeholders. Others, such as Page (1978), argue that candidates often stress such orientations in their campaigns (with incumbents defending their performance and challengers attacking it) and that candidates often are deliberately ambiguous about where they stand on particular issues. Such campaign behavior encourages retrospective voting and discourages prospective voting.

Theories of retrospective voting have been most thoroughly employed to explain the role of economic issues in national elections, so we shall concentrate on this body of research. Until the 1970s, very little research was done on the impact of economic conditions on voting, but Kramer's (1971) article stimulated a flood of research on this topic, with Kiewiet's (1983) study providing the best single summary, synthesis, and elaboration of the research findings.

Two basic types of studies are found. One type, represented by such studies as Kramer (1971) or Tufte (1978), relies on aggregate time-series data and attempts to relate fluctuations in election outcomes to fluctuations in economic conditions. The findings of these studies generally are extremely positive. Both Kramer (1971) and Tufte (1978) find that changes in real per capita income are significantly related to changes in the distribution of the vote, and Kramer claims that one-half of the variance in congressional voting can be attributed to this variable.

A second type of study examines the impact of economic conditions on voting through the cross-sectional analysis of survey data (e.g., Klorman, 1978; Kinder, 1981). These studies generally have found that the relationship between the individual's personal financial situation and his vote is a much more modest one, raising the question of whether researchers have made unwarranted inferences from aggregate-level analyses. While the data show that perceptions of government economic performance, especially in terms of who would better manage the economy, play a strong role in voting, the effect of individual economic situations on these perceptions often is weak.

Several reasons can be suggested for this discrepency between the survey and aggregate findings. One possibility is that voters are "sociotropic," reacting not to their own individual financial situation, but to their perception of the economic situation of the society (Kinder, 1981). Another likelihood is that many individuals simply do not feel their own situation is a result of government policy, either because they have an individualistic economic ideology (Feldman, 1982), or because in fact their situation is the result of purely personal factors (Kramer, 1983). Jacobson (1983) suggests that the effects of economic conditions on congressional elections may operate largely in an indirect manner, through effects on the quality of candidates and the extent of their resources, rather than through direct effects on the voters. All of these suggestions have some validity. It also is important to realize that the discrepency between the survey and aggregate findings can be explained, at least partially, in methodological terms. The strength of individual-level cross-sectional relationships will not normally equal the strength of aggregate-level longitudinal relationships, even if both sets of relationships are accurate representations of the underlying dynamics. Thus closer inspection of the various studies indicates more agreement among the findings than has been suggested, and the most recent research seems to have successfully synthesized the two sets of findings (Kiewiet, 1983; Kramer, 1983).

Recent research also has gone beyond the simple question of whether fluctuations in economic conditions affect national election outcomes. Theoretical refinements have included making distinctions between different elections, different types of candidates, and different economic issues. Kiewiet (1983, p. 126) finds the impact of economic conditions to be greater for presidential elections than congressional elections, and Kuklinski and West (1983) find that among congressional elections, Senate elections are more affected than House elections. Hibbing and Alford (1981) argue that the blame or credit for economic conditions that voters attach to the incumbent party should not equally affect all congressional candidates from that party, and a consideration of the difference between incumbent and nonincumbent candidates resolves some of the anomalies observed in earlier analyses.

Perhaps the most interesting analyses have been attempts to synthesize the retrospective and policy voting approaches (Kiewiet, 1983; Weatherford, 1983). For example, while voters are likely to blame the party in power for poor economic performance, there also is a perception that the Democrats are more likely to do something about unemployment and the Republicans are better able to handle inflation, and these considerations influence voter reactions. Thus voters react somewhat differently to high levels of unemployment or high levels of inflation, depending on whether a Democrat or Republican administration is involved.

C. Conclusion

Impressive strides in understanding the social psychology of the vote have been made over the past 10–15 years. Especially significant is the work done on issue voting and retrospective voting. Perhaps the area that now needs the most research involves the effects of campaigns on individual voting. We understand the orientations and evaluations that determine the vote, but we are less clear about how those psychological factors are shaped or influenced by the behavior of the candidates and the events of the campaign. In large part, this involves understanding the effects of the mass media, as that is the primary source of information for national elections. Unfortunately, much of the research in this area has not been very successful in identifying and explaining media influences (Wagner, 1983). Much of the problem may lie in the difficulties of assessing influence through secondary analyses of cross-sectional surveys. Significantly, one of the best investigations of media effects during a presidential campaign (Patterson, 1980) relied on a specially-designed panel survey in two communities. It appears that more research designs of this type will have to be employed if we are to really understand the dynamics of opinion formation during the campaign.

IV. ELECTORAL DYNAMICS

The study of electoral dynamics traditionally has been concerned with examining the impact of long-term and short-term forces. Long-term change in partisan attachments is seen as occurring primarily through realigning elections. Short-term fluctuations are seen as the result of forces unique to the particular elections. Normal vote analysis can be used to distinguish between these two types of change. Deviations from the election outcome that is predicted on the basis of the normal vote represent the effect of short-term forces, whereas changes in the normal vote parameters represent long-term change. However, the usefulness of a normal vote analysis seems more dubious, given the previously discussed agreement that party identification is less stable than had been thought and actually is affected by short-term forces.

During the 1960s and 1970s, considerable scholarly attention was focused on the possibilities of partisan realignment. Precipitated in large part by the nature of the presidential elections and the political events from 1964 through 1972, analysts began to more fully explore the nature of realignment, and major theoretical contributions were made by Burnham (1970) and Sundquist (1973). But the absence of substantial realignment during this period, despite what some observers felt were propitious conditions, diminished concern with critical realignments and focused research attention on less dramatic electoral change.

A. Explaining Electoral Dynamics

Fundamental and lasting change in electoral behavior does not have to occur through a critical realignment. The slow accumulation of more modest changes over a period of time can achieve the same result. The possibilities for such secular realignment are widely recognized, and Carmines and Stimson (1981) attempt to construct a theoretical model for such a process. Other studies have empirically examined actual shifts among various population subgroups, such as the thorough description and analysis of changes in the party coalitions by Petrocik (1981). Most such analyses conclude that while substantial changes have occurred for some groups, such as white southerners, the likelihood of a fundamental realignment occurring through the cumulative effect of such change is slim. Critical realignment seems even less likely, so the prospect is for continuation of a dealigned electorate that is buffeted by short-term forces. Given this view, it is not surprising that recent attention has been on the effects of short-term forces.

Substantial research has been done on the dynamic relationship between election outcomes and economic conditions. We have already discussed these studies, but it is worthwhile here to underscore the fact that both aggregate time-series data and cross-sectional survey data have been used in this area of research, and the synthesizing of both methods of analysis represents a successful integration of micropolitical behavior with macropolitical dynamics.

While there has been enormous concern with issue voting, most of the work has focused on the ability to explain individual voting, not election outcomes. There is a difference. An issue may be extremely important in affecting the votes of many voters, but it may be relatively unimportant in affecting the election outcome. If, for example, one-half of the voters felt one way on the issue and the other one-half felt the other way, and both groups were equally influenced by the issue, the net impact would be zero. Relatively little work has been done on this aspect of issues and elections, but there are some notable exceptions. Kelley (1983) uses four concepts to help identify the role that an issue plays in affecting the election outcome: salience (how many voters use the issue to evaluate the candidates); bias (how much the evaluations favor one candidate over the other); pull (a combination of bias and salience); and marginal impact (the effect that the issue has on the election outcome). These appear to be relevant considerations, and future research along these lines should be quite fruitful.

B. Forecasting Elections

One of the most interesting trends in recent electoral research is the construction of models that can be used to predict election outcomes. Such models have been used to successfully predict the outcome of midterm congressional elections (Tufte, 1978). Also, Rosenstone (1983) has recently put forth a model for the forecasting of presidential elections. Although the work in this area is very limited, it is an encouraging development. Attempts to forecast election outcomes are useful and worthwhile because they force us to construct models to explain elections, not just individual voting behavior. Future research in this area, especially if it builds on the substantial knowledge we have about the social psychology of the vote, should fill a large lacuna in the research literature.

REFERENCES

Abramson, P.R., & Aldrich, J.H. (1982). The decline of electoral participation in America. *American Political Science Review, 76,* 502–521.

Abramson, P.R., Aldrich, J.H., & Rohde, D. (1982). *Change and continuity in the 1980 elections.* Washington: Congressional Quarterly Press.

Boyd, R.W. (1981). Decline of U.S. voter turnout: Structural explanations. *American Politics Quarterly, 9,* 133–160.

Burnham, W.D. (1970). *Critical elections and the mainsprings of American politics.* New York: Norton.

Burnham, W.D. (1982). *The current crisis in American politics.* New York: Oxford University Press.

Caldeira, G.A., & Patterson, S.C. (1982) Contextual influences on participation in U.S. state legislative elections. *Legislative Studies Quarterly, 7,* 359–382.

Campbell, A., Converse, P., Miller, W., & Stokes, D. (1960). *The American voter.* New York: John Wiley.

Carmines, E.G., & Gopoian, J.D. (1981). Issue coalitions, issueless campaigns: The paradox of rationality in American presidential elections. *Journal of Politics, 43,* 1170–1191.

Carmines, E.G., & Stimson, J.A. (1980). The two faces of issue voting. *American Political Science Review, 74,* 78–91.

Carmines, E.G., & Stimson, J.A. (1981). Issue evolution, population replacement, and normal partisan change. *American Political Science Review, 75,* 107–118.

Cassel, C.A. (1982). Predicting party identification, 1956–1980: Who are the Republicans and who are the Democrats? *Political Behavior, 4,* 265–282.

Cassel, C.A., & Hill, D.B. (1981). Explanations of turnout decline: A multivariate test. *American Politics Quarterly, 9,* 180–195.

Cohen, J.E. (1982). Change in election calendars: A test of Boyd's hypotheses. *American Politics Quarterly, 10,* 246–254.

Conway, M.M. (1981). Political participation in midterm congressional elections. *American Politics Quarterly, 9,* 221–244.

Crotty, W.J. (1977). *Political reform and the American experiment.* New York: Crowell.

DeNardo, J. (1980). Turnout and the vote: The joke's on the Democrats. *American Political Science Review, 74,* 406–420.

Dubois, P.L. (1983). Election night projections and voter turnout in the west. *American Politics Quarterly, 11,* 349–364.

Erikson, R.S. (1981). Why do people vote? Because they are registered. *American Politics Quarterly, 9,* 259–276.

Feldman, S. (1982). Economic self-interest and political behavior. *American Journal of Political Science, 26,* 446–466.

Fiorina, M.P. (1982). *Retrospective voting in American national elections.* New Haven: Yale University Press.

Glass, D., Squire, P., & Wolfinger, R. (1984). Voter turnout: An international comparison. *Public Opinion, 6,* 49–57.

Gopoian, J.D. (1982). Issue preferences and candidate choice in presidential primaries. *American Journal of Political Science, 26,* 523–546.

Hibbing, J.R., & Alford, J.R. (1981). The electoral impact of economic conditions: Who is held responsible? *American Journal of Political Science, 25,* 423–439.

Hinckley, B. (1980). The American voter in congressional elections. *American Political Science Review, 74,* 641–650.

Hout, M., & Knoke, D. (1975). Change in voting turnout, 1952–1972. *Public Opinion Quarterly, 39,* 52–62.

Howell, S.E. (1981). Short term forces and changing partisanship. *Political Behavior, 3,* 163–180.

Jacobson, G.C. (1983). *The politics of congressional elections.* Boston: Little, Brown.

Katosh, J.P., & Traugott, M.W. (1981). The consequences of validated and self-reported voting measures. *Public Opinion Quarterly, 45,* 519–595.

Kelley, S. (1983). *Interpreting elections.* Princeton: Princeton University Press.

Kelley, S., Ayres, R., & Bowen, W. (1967). Registration and voting: Putting first things first. *American Political Science Review, 61,* 359–379.

Kenney, P.J. (1983). Explaining turnout in gubernatorial primaries. *American Politics Quarterly, 11,* 315–326.

Key, V.O., Jr. (1966). *The responsible electorate.* Cambridge: Harvard University Press.

Kieweit, D.R. (1983). *Macroeconomics and micropolitics.* Chicago: University of Chicago Press.

Kim, J.O., Petrocik, J., & Enockson, S. (1975). Voter turnout in the American states: Systemic and individual components. *American Political Science Review, 64,* 107–131.

Kinder, D.R. (1981). Presidents, prosperity, and public opinion. *Public Opinion quarterly, 45,* 1–21.

Klorman, R. (1978). Trend in personal finances and the vote. *Public Opinion Quarterly, 42,* 31–48.

Kramer, G.H. (1971). Short-term fluctuations in U.S. voting behavior, 1896–1964. *American Political Science Review, 65,* 131–143.

Kramer, G.H. (1983). The ecological fallacy revisted: Aggregate versus individual-level findings on economics and elections and sociotropic voting. *American Political Science Review, 77,* 92–111.

Kuklinski, J.H., & West, D.M. (1981). Economic expectations and voting behavior in United States House and Senate elections. *American Political Science Review, 75,* 436–447.

LeBlanc, H.L., & Merrin, M.B. (1979). Independents, issue partisanship, and the decline of party. *American Politics Quarterly, 7,* 240–256.

Levitin, T.E., & Miller, W.E. (1979). Ideological interpretations of presidential elections. *American Political Science Review, 73,* 751–771.

Margolis, M. (1977). From confusion to confusion: Issues and the American voter (1956–1972). *American Political Science Review, 71,* 31–43.

Meier, K.J., & Campbell, J.E. (1979). Issue voting: An examination of individual necessary and jointly sufficient conditions. *American Politics Quarterly, 7,* 21–50.

Miller, A.H., & Wattenberg, M.P. (1983). Measuring party identification: Independent or no partisan preference? *American Journal of Political Science, 27,* 106–121.

Nie, N.H., Verba, S., & Petrocik, J. (1976). *The changing American voter.* Cambridge: Harvard University Press.

Norpoth, H., & Rusk, J. (1982). Partisan dealignment in the American electorate: Itemizing the deductions since 1964. *American Political Science Review, 76,* 522–537.

Page, B.I. (1978). *Choices and echoes in presidential elections.* Chicago: University of Chicago Press.

Patterson, S.C., & Caldeira, G.A. (1983). Getting out the vote: Participation in gubernatorial elections. *American Political Science Review, 77,* 675–689.

Patterson, T.E. (1980). *The mass media election.* New York: Praeger.

Petrocik, J.R. (1981). *Party coalitions.* Chicago: University of Chicago Press.

Pomper, G.M. (1972). From confusion to clarity: Issues and American voters, 1956–1968. *American Political Science Review, 66,* 415–428.

Reiter, H.L. (1979). Why is turnout down? *Public Opinion Quarterly, 43,* 279–311.

Rosenstone, S.J. (1983). *Forecasting presidential elections,* New Haven: Yale University Press.

Sears, D.O., Lau, R., Tyler, T., & Allen, H. (1980). Self-interest vs. symbolic politics in policy attitudes and presidential voting. *American Political Science Review, 74,* 670–684.

Shaffer, S.D. (1981). A multivariate explanation of decreasing turnout in presidential elections. *American Journal of Political Science, 25,* 68–95.

Sigelman, L. (1982). The nonvoting voter in voting research. *American Journal of Political Science, 26,* 47–56.

Sundquist, J.L. (1973). *Dynamics of the party system.* Washington: The Brookings Institution.

Tufte, E.R. (1978). *Political control of the economy*. Princeton: Princeton University Press.

Valentine, D.C., & VanWingen, J.R. (1980). Partisanship, independence, and the partisan identification question. *American Politics Quarterly, 8,* 165–186.

Verba, S., & Nie, N.H. (1972). *Participation in America: political democracy and social equality*. New York: Harper & Row.

Wagner, J. (1983). Media do make a difference: The differential impact of mass media in the 1976 presidential race. *American Journal of Political Science, 27,* 407–430.

Weatherford, M.S. (1983). Economic voting and the "symbolic politics" argument: A reinterpretation and a synthesis. *American Political Science Review, 77,* 158–174.

Weisberg, H. (1980). Multidimensional conceptualization of party identification. *Political Behavior, 2,* 33.

Weisberg, H. (1983). A new scale of partisanship. *Political Behavior, 5,* 363–376.

Wolfinger, R.E., & Rosenstone, S.J. (1980). *Who votes?* New Haven: Yale University Press.

Chapter 5

Theory and Research in Social Movements: A Critical Review*

Aldon Morris

Department of Sociology
University of Michigan

Cedric Herring

Department of Sociology
Texas A&M University

I. INTRODUCTION

There has been an explosion of theoretical and empirical writings on social movements and collective action within the last decade. These writings have triggered debates, a new school of thought, defenses of old schools of thought and theoretical advances. Moreover, important research on social movements is being conducted in various disciplines including sociology, political science, history, economics and communications. For example, The Central States Speech Journal (1980) recently devoted an entire volume to social movement articles. Studies of movements and protest transcend national boundaries as epitomized by the Conflict Research Group of the European Consortium for Political Research. This group (Webb et al., 1983) is developing New European perspectives based on a six-nation study of 180 protest groups over a 20-year period (1960–1980) using a resource mobilization perspective. The field of social movements is thriving and contributions are being made from diverse camps.

The purpose of this chapter is three fold: to review and evaluate theory and research on social movements; to establish whether a theoretical shift has occurred and if so how; and to identify several key unresolved theoretical problems and suggest promising lines research should take to solve some of them. To accomplish these three purposes the chapter will be divided into three parts. First, we will critically discuss the main theoretical formulations within the field and evaluate them in terms of empirical evidence. In the second part we will raise the issue as to whether there has been a theoretical shift within the study of movements. We will then present evidence that a shift has indeed occurred and attempt to distill those factors responsible for the shift. Finally, in the last part of the chapter we will briefly identify some of the major unresolved issues in the field and point to the kind of research that we believe will lead to their resolution.

The availability of excellent review articles is one indication that a field is undergoing a renaissance. Review articles on movements from the perspectives of collective behavior (Marx & Wood, 1975; Turner, 1981; McPhail & Wohlstein, 1983; Zurcher & Snow, 1981) deprivation approaches (Gurr, 1980), and resource mobilization (Oberschall, 1978; Jenkins, 1983) have appeared recently. Our discussion is based on these and other published works and ten interviews with major formulators of collective behavior theory (Ralph Turner, Lewis Killian, Neil Smelser, and Kurt and Gladys Lang) and resource mobilization theory (Charles Tilly, William Gamson, Anthony Oberschall, Mayer Zald, and John McCarthy). It is important to point out at this juncture that the chapter will concentrate on the sociological literature concerning social movements. However, we will pay attention to those economic, political, psychological, philosophical, and historical writings that sociologists self-consciously take into account in their analyses.

The taped interviews for this chapter lasted approximately an hour and fifteen minutes each.* They addressed important issues, including the theorists backgrounds, their participation in movements, the social and intellectual factors that shaped their theoretical approaches, whether they believe a theoretical shift has occurred, and what they consider to be the outstanding unresolved theoretical problems. We will draw on these interviews throughout, and they will provide core data for our discussion of a theoretical shift. Before proceeding we need to address an important question — what is a social movement?

II. Conception of Social Movements

No definition of social movement enjoys a scholarly consensus and there probably will never be such a definition because definitions inevitably reflect the theoretical assumptions of the theorists. There are a number of competing frameworks in the field and each conceptualize movements differently. Even scholars within the same "school" define movements differently depending on their particular theoretical formulation. Rather than attempting the difficult task of defining movements we will examine various conceptions of social movements advanced by the major schools and distinguish between conceptions within schools when they differ fundamentally. Thus, we will explore conceptions of social movements embedded in marxian, weberian, collective behavior, mass society, relative deprivation, and resource mobilization approaches. Much of the discussion in this chapter is relevant to the study of revolutions. Indeed scholars often analyze revolution as a particular kind of social movement or as one possible outcome of political movements. Nevertheless, because revolutions are complex and have been studied in their own right we refer the interested reader to Brinton (1938), Moore (1966), Gurr (1970), Paige (1975), Tilly (1978), Skocpol (1979) and Goldstone (1982). Additionally, this chapter restricts its focus to political movements rather than the wide variety of social movements often discussed in the literature.

A. Marx's View of Social Movements

Marx was primarily interested in the causes and dynamics of revolutionary movements aimed at dismantling the capitalist system. He argued that movements grow out of basic social and economic relations which establish the bases of power in a society. Thus, he focused attention on how capitalism

*We are indebted to William Gamson, Lewis Killian, Kurt and Gladys Lang, John McCarthy, Anthony Oberschall, Neil Smelser, Charles Tilly, and Ralph Turner for graciously allowing us to interview them. We also express gratitude to our many friends and colleagues who provided us with critical feedback. Finally we thank Mary Hartness, Janet Somers and Sheila Wilder for typing the manuscript.

generates the necessary conditions for a revolutionary reconstruction of capitalist societies.

Marx viewed revolutionary movements as both normal and inevitable under capitalism because capitalism generates endemic structural contradictions. The main contradiction that inevitably leads to efforts geared toward structural change is the existence of two classes with mutually exclusive interests. Marx argued that as they were faced with falling rates of profit, the capitalists — "owners of the means of social production and employers of wage labour" (Marx & Engels, 1968, p. 35) — would attempt to maintain their profits by increasing their rate of exploitation of workers because higher rates of exploitation mean higher rates of profit for them. Hence, it is in the interests of capitalists to exploit workers as much as possible; it is in the interests of workers to resist as much exploitation as possible. These diametrically opposed interests produce inherent class antagonisms which culminate in a revolutionary conflict between workers and capitalists.

Workers — the revolutionary class — would engage in several stages of intendedly rational activity to resist further efforts of exploitation. Those stages coincide with progressions in working class consciousness, as the working class advances from being merely a class-in-itself to acting as a class-for-itself: Initially workers who constitute only an incoherent, uninformed mass experience self-estrangement and powerlessness. They engage in such misdirected strategies as attacking their machinery and setting factories on fire. However, as they begin to put their struggles in political-economic contexts, they form trade unions against the bourgeoisie through which they demand higher wages, better working conditions, and other limited objectives while engaging in sporadic rioting and localized violence. Next, workers create national and international networks which link them across localities and enable local struggles to take on national and international significance. In the next stage, workers recognize their true class interests and organize themselves into a class for itself. At this time, legislatures begin recognizing the interest of workers, and internal differences among the bourgeoisie intensify. In the next stage, enlightened segments of the bourgeoisie join the ranks of the proletariat. And finally, the proletariat engages in successful revolution against the bourgeoisie, gain control over the means of production, does away with the basis of class antagonism — private ownership of the means of production — and class conflict dissipates.

Marx's theory calls attention to a number of factors often overlooked by alternative theories of social movements. For example, Marx linked inequality and other properties of the society to the rise of revolutionary movements. He pointed out the centrality of interests, especially class interests. Thus, he made the case that participation in movements is intendly rational, purposive activity. Nevertheless, he did not deny that consciousness, especially class consciousness plays a central role in movement activities. Marx also emphasized the necessity of internal organization and networks. And finally, by showing how movements are products of the societies in which they arise, Marx, showed that revolutionary movements are not abnormal occurrences unconnected to the larger society. Because of its focus on class, however, Marx's analysis may have limited explanatory power for social movements where other factors play prominent roles.

B. Weber's View

Weber's (1947, 1968) treatment of charismatic authority provides an overview of his conception of charismatic movements. He conceptualized the charismatic movement as a social change force. He argued that "within the sphere of its claims, charismatic authority repudiates the past and is in this sense a specifically revolutionary force" (1947, p. 362). Furthermore, "in a revolutionary and sovereign manner, charismatic domination transforms all values and breaks all traditional and rational norms . . ." (1968, p. 1115). For Weber, the struggle for power and change are the main objectives of charismatic movements.

Charismatic movements originate in social systems that are undergoing great stress and are unable to meet the needs of a significant number of people (Weber, 1968, p. 1121). Charismatic leaders are paramount because their extraordinary personal qualities lead people in stressful situations to treat them as if they possess superhuman powers. The charismatic leader attracts followers because they identify with his divine mission and believe that its realization translates into their own well being. Thus, the leader's personal magnetism and world view serve as the recruiting forces that pull people into the charismatic community where they establish an emotional and communalistic form of existence.

For Weber charismatic movements are nonroutine forms of collective action that emerge outside of preexisting social organizations, norms, and bureaucracies. Such movements are inherently unstable because the pure charismatic element provides them with resources and solidarity only during their early stages. Hence, Weber advanced a life cycle scheme in which he argued that if charismatic movements are to endure, they must routinize their activities because of the economic, administrative, and leadership succession problems they inevitably face. When routinization occurs, the charismatic movement establishes a sound organizational base and become integrated into the society.

Weber's analysis calls attention to (a) charismatic leadership, (b) belief systems, (c) social systems undergoing stress, (d) routinization of charismatic authority, and (e) the revolutionary nature of charismatic movements.

C.   Collective Behavior View

Collective behavior theorists view social movements as noninstitutionalized social change efforts (Jenkins 1983, p. 529). Thus, Blumer (1951, p. 199) defined "social movements as collective enterprises to establish a new order of life "and maintained that in the beginning," a social movement is amorphous, poorly organized and without form." Lang and Lang (1961, p. 490) defined the social movement as "a large-scale, widespread, and continuing, elementary action in pursuit of an objective that affects and shapes the social order in some fundamental aspect." Finally, Turner and Killian (1972, p. 246) define a social movement as:

> Collectivity acting with some continuity to promote or resist a change in the society or group of which it is a part. As a collectivity a movement is a group with indefinite and shifting membership and with leadership whose position is determined more by the informal response of the members than by formal procedures for legitimizing authority.

The "social movement" is the unit of analysis in these definitions. Turner (1981, p. 3) wrote "the primary focus of interests for students of collective behavior is the social movement as a sociological phenomenon and as a form of collective behavior." Therefore, the movement in collective behavior approaches is conceptualized as a phenomenon sui generis with its own properties, processes, and internal logic.

In short, collective behaviorists view social movements as non-routine forms of collective action geared toward social change. They cannot be explained by prior social organization, norms, and culture because movements are emergent forms that acquire organization during their life cycles. Once such forms become institutionalized they cease to be objects of inquiry as social movements. The tasks, then, are to identify the origins of movements; investigate how they give rise to change; analyze the fluid processes, dynamics, life cycles of movements; and group movements into comprehensive classificatory schemes.

D. Mass Society View

Mass society theorists view social movements as phenomena which occur when previously unorganized individuals band together to change some part of their social millieu (e.g., Kornhauser, 1959; Arendt, 1951; Lipset, 1963; Hoffer, 1951; Cantril, 1941; King, 1956). Mass society definitions of movements are not vastly different from those of collective behaviorists. For example, King (1956, p. 27) defines a social movement as "a group venture extending beyond a local community or a single event and involving a systematic effort to inaugurate changes in thought, behavior, and social relationships," and Toch (1965, p. 5) defines a social movement as "an effort by a large number of people to solve collectively a problem they feel they have in common."

Mass society theorists usually emphasize the characteristics of "mass societies" which make movements possible: cultural confusion, social heterogeniety, weak cultural integration mechanisms, and a lack of attachments to secondary group structures. Thus, they are less likely than collective behaviorists to examine movements directly. Instead, they analyze the properties of societies, specify the "personality traits" and psychological states which those societies produce, and explain how these factors generate movements. Their conception of social movements calls attention to the interface between social structure and personality.

E. Relative Deprivation View

Unlike collective behaviorists and mass society theorists, relative deprivation proponents generally have not focused attention on social movements, per se. Rather, they study episodes of political violence and revolution; thus their interest are more limited than collective behaviorists and mass society theorists.

Gurr (1970, pp. 3–4), a leading proponent of relative deprivation, states that his research is concerned with political violence – "all collective attacks within a political community against the political regime, its actors . . . or its policies." He further elaborates on the forms of political violence with which he is concerned:

Turmoil: Relatively spontaneous, unorganized political violence with substantial popular participation, including violent political strikes, riots, political clashes, and localized rebellions.

Conspiracy: Highly organized political violence with limited participation, including organized political assassinations, small-scale terrorism, small-scale guerrilla wars, coups d'etat, and mutinies.

Internal war: Highly organized political violence with widespread popular participation, designed to overthrow the regime or dissolve the state and accompanied by extensive violence, including large-scale terrorism and guerrilla wars, civil wars, and revolutions. (p. 11)

Thus, most behaviors discussed in the relative deprivation literature qualify as "social movement" activity as defined by other approaches and will be included in this review. Moreover, theorists using variants of the relative deprivation framework have also analyzed social movements (e.g., Lipset and Raab, 1978 and Pettigrew, 1964). However, because relative deprivation perspectives focus on the genesis of political violence instead of social movements, per se, there are two points to keep in mind: relative deprivationists examine the *genesis* of political violence but do not focus on the *dynamics* of such violence; and they focus on political *violence,* while not analyzing other forms of political protest.

F. Resource Mobilization View

Resource mobilization approaches have produced conceptions different from those reviewed above, and substantially different conceptions of movements exist within the school. To capture the external and internal differences we will examine the approaches of McCarthy–Zald and Tilly.

McCarthy and Zald have formulated an organizational-entrepreneural model of social movements. In their view (1977, p. 1217–1218), "a social movement is a set of opinions and beliefs in a population which represents preferences for changing some elements of the social structure and/or reward distribution of a society." This definition excludes both organizational factors and the struggle for power. Indeed, the definition implies that latent movements are forever present in societies because no society lacks individuals who possess preferences for change. In McCarthy and Zald's logic social movements are nothing more than preference structures directed toward social change (1977, p. 1218).

For McCarthy–Zald, the social movement can serve as one unit of analysis because analysts may investigate "who holds the beliefs" and/or "how intensely are they held?" But different units of analyses are needed to explain open conflict, mobilization, or outcomes of collective action. To understand those issues the unit of analysis shifts to movement organizations, industries, sectors, and entrepreneurs. Later it will be clear that McCarthy–Zald utilize these additional units of analysis when they investigate the dynamics between these various groups and preference structures for changes. Their definition of movements, however, differs sharply from previous ones by explicitly excluding actual conflict, mobilization, and social change activities.

Charles Tilly (1973) advances a "political process" view of movements arguing that collective action derives from a population's central political processes. Tilly (1979, p. 12) defines a social movement as:

> A sustained series of interactions between national powerholders and persons successfully claiming to speak on behalf of a constituency lacking formal representation, in the course of which those persons make publicly — visible demands for changes in the distribution or exercise of power, and back those demands with public demonstrations of support.

For Tilly the focus is sustained interactions rather than the "social movement" as a phenomenon sui generis. Tilly (1978, p. 49) breaks from previous definitions by refusing to treat the social movement as the unit of analysis; instead, he argues that a movement is not a group that emerges and transforms over time.

Tilly roots the concept of "social movement" in historical time and space. The social movement is argued to be a nineteenth-century creation generated by the nationalization of politics and the rise of special purpose associations. During that century political parties, unions, and other associations became the chief vehicles through which groups struggled for power and institutionalized their interests. Still large groups remained disenfranchised without their interests routinely satisfied through elections and labor–management negotiations. Tilly argues that these people constitute social movements and like their institutionalized counterparts, they struggle for national power through special purpose associations. What distinguishes social movements from their institutionalized counterparts is their political situation which causes them to rely heavily on a repertoire of disorderly tactics such as strikes, demonstrations, violence, and protest meetings to accomplish political ends.

Nevertheless, social movements and formal political parties are mirror images because both are political actors pursuing power. In short, both set of actors are propelled by the same political process wherein the social movement is a party with broad aspirations and a unifying belief system and the political party is a tamed, nationalized social movement (Tilly 1979, p. 11).

Tilly paints two views of a movement: that of national power structures and that of movement participants. Social movements from the "perspective of national power structures . . . are coherent phenomena; they exist so long as they offer a challenge to dominant interests and beliefs." But "seen from the bottom up, . . . [social movements] . . . are usually much more fragmented and heterogeneous: shifting factions, temporary alliances, diverse interests, a continuous flux of members and hangers on" (Tilly 1979, p. 19). The task of the analyst, therefore, has three prongs: (a) investigate the response of power holders to social movements, especially their ability to protect their interests through repression, forming coalitions, bargaining, and cooptation; (b) investigate the dynamics through which movement actors advance their interests by creating the illusion of unity, mobilizing large numbers of supporters, and making strategic choices; and (c) combine these two perspectives into a dynamic analysis of collective action. The next section focuses on the conceptual framework in which these conceptions are embedded.

III. CLASSICAL MODELS: COLLECTIVE BEHAVIOR, DEPRIVATION, AND MASS SOCIETY

Classical models differ in their approaches to social movements. Our strategy is to explore the common premises underlying classical models while highlighting their important differences. In our view, classical models explain the origins, development, and outcomes of social movements by focusing attention on (a) structural breakdown that leads to noninstitutionalized social change efforts, (b) psychological states of movements participants, and (c) the role shared beliefs play in guiding movements.

Classical theorists occasionally refer to the role that prior social organization and strategic choices play in movements. However these are not central variables and do not constitute the central message of the classical approach. Following Patinkin (1983, p. 314) the central message of a theory can be identified because it is announced early in the work (and frequently in its title) and by repetition, either verbatim or modified in accordance with the circumstances (1983, p. 14). Our discussions of classical models are concerned with their central messages regarding origin, development, and outcome of movements.

A. Chicago School of Collective Behavior

The "irrationalist" school of crowd psychologists (e.g., Le Bon, 1960; McDougall, 1908; Ross, 1916; and Freud, 1955) which was dominant between the 1890s and the 1920s, tended to view movements as irrational and guided by group minds. The Chicago School of collective behavior which borrowed from and went beyond the "irrationalist" school, displaced crowd psychology as the dominant approach to social movements during the 1920s. Among the numerous proponents of collective behavior are Park and Burgess (1921), Blumer (1951), Turner and Killian (1957, 1972), and Lang and Lang (1961). The collective behavior approach is social psychological in orientation and rooted in symbolic interaction theory (Turner 1981, p. 6). Thus, social structures have no existence independent of subjective meanings actors attach to them. Symbolic interactionists focus on the processes by which actors continuously construct meanings through social interactions, and thereby provide the basis for human action. They argue that human behavior cannot be understood with grand theories and positivist methodologies (Coser 1977, p. 575). Rather, it is to be grasped through careful description and synthesis of concepts which capture the "crucial processes by which actors endow the forces acting upon them as well as their own behavior with meaning" (Ritzer 1983, p. 301).

For Chicago theorists, social order is tenuous, always evolving, and changing. Nevertheless, they argue that everyday conventional behavior is guided by prior social organization and culture, while collective behavior is not. Collective behavior analyses began with the assumption that societies consist of two coherent realms — institutionalized behavior and collective behavior. Building on Park and Burgess, Blumer provided the guiding conception of collective behavior: It "is not based on the adherence to common understandings or rules" (1951, p. 171), rather, it is behavior "formed or forged to meet undefined or unstructured situations" (1957, p. 130). The central message of the Chicago School is that "collective behavior occurs when the established organization ceases to afford direction and supply channels for action" (Turner & Killian, 1972, p. 30). Therefore, collective behavior arises under some form of structural or cultural breakdown — dramatic event, migration, natural disaster, urbanization, rapid social change, etc. — that leads to noninstitutionalized efforts aimed at reconstituting ruptured social struc- tures or shared meaning system. This distinction between institutionalized and collective behavior leads Chicago theorists to argue for a special sociol- ogy with its own theoretical principles to explain collective behavior.

Social movements are one form of collective behavior. Other forms in- clude panics, mobs, riots, fads, sects, cults, religious revivals, and revolu- tions. For collective behaviorists, an inner logic permeates these forms and binds them into a coherent family. The logic consists of unstructured situa- tions in which social organization and meaning systems no longer provide a basis for social action.

Chicago theorists focus on how people in collective behavior situations act collectively in the absence of guiding cultural definitions and social organiza- tion. They investigate the cognitive and social psychological processes by which actors formulate a new basis for action when confronting unstructured situations. Thus, collective behaviorists:

> have tended to work from the inside out; that is, looking at people and working from there. (Turner, 1983).

Killian (1983) captured the puzzle collective behavior is thought to give rise to:

> The situation becomes unstructured. The people don't have their usual sources of information, and then they know something is wrong, but they don't have any clear guidelines as to what. They have to start reconstructing a picture of re- ality to enable them to act.

The emergence and development of a movement is, therefore, contingent on actors formulating a shared understanding which makes collective action possible. Chicago theorists (Park & Burgess, 1921; Blumer, 1951; Lang & Lang, 1961) have argued that crude, nonrational, psychological communica- tion processes form the new basis for collective action. Drawing from crowd psychologists (e.g., Le Bon, 1960; Tarde, 1903; Sighele, 1898), they posited that contagion, circular reaction, imitation, suggestibility, and convergence constitute the mechanisms through which actors reconstitute ruptured com- munication systems and social structures. Under such influences actors are often portrayed as releasing frustrations, insecurities, alienation and inner tensions. In a characteristic statement, Blumer (1951, p. 171) wrote:

> Externally, the activity is likely to be erratic, lacking in consistency, and rather similar to a sort of indefinite prowling; internally, it is likely to take the form of disordered imagination and disturbed feelings. In its most acute form it is char- acteristic of neurotic behavior.

In this view movements, especially in their early stages, are characterized by spontaneity, emotionality, and nonrational behavior.

Turner and Killian (1972) rejected the veiw that collective behavior is irrational and emotional. Following Park and Burgess and Blumer, Turner and Killian attempted to account for the new definition enabling people to act collectively when the structure or communication system break. However, they differed from Park and Burgess and Blumer by arguing that collective behavior is guided by a property of social structure — an emergent norm. Such a norm provides "a common understanding as to what sort of behavior is expected in the situation," and it can explain why people with a great variety of motives come to act collectively (Turner & Killian 1972, p. 22). Accepting the view that collective behavior occurs in unstructured situations, they argue that "since the norm is to some degree specific to the situation, differing in degree or in kind from the norms governing noncrowd situations, it is an emergent norm" (p. 22). The new, revised, or reapplied norm that guides social movements creates a sense of injustice and provides a "vital sense that some established practice or mode of thought is wrong and ought to be replaced" (Turner & Killian 1972, p. 259).

The emergent norm approach suggests that movements are not fundamentally different from organized behavior. Nevertheless, Turner and Killian do not explicitly link movements with prior social organizations and ongoing power struggles. Thus, Killian (1964, p. 427) wrote that the study of social movements "is not the study of stable groups of established institutions, but of groups and institutions in the process of becoming." Moreover, the emergent norm approach accepts the idea that crude communication processes are central to movements because the norm develop through a process of rumor which "is the characteristic mode of communication in collective behavior" (Turner & Killian, 1972, p. 32).

Chicago theorists argue that organization and tactics are important in the growth and spread of movements. However, these factors are not central because in terms of emphasis and treatment they take a back seat to spontaneity, construction of meaning frames, and social psychological processes. Thus, Lang and Lang (1961, p. 497) argue that movements are largely spontaneous and characterized by contagion, but coordinated by core groups. The organized core group crystalizes the vague unrest of the movement, but even here the role of the core group in movements is never planned (1961, p. 495). The assumption of an uneasy fit between movements and organization is so entrenched in classical approaches that Heberle (1951, p. 8), who pays considerable attention to organizational factors, concludes that "movements as such are not organized groups." He distinguishes movements from political parties by arguing that the latter is formally organized (1951, p. 19). For Blumer, social movements do not come into existence with structure and organization already established; instead, he argues, organization and culture develop in the course of the movement's career. This formulation ties organization to a movement's development but rules organization out as a causal factor in the genesis of movements.

The emergent norm approach does not come to grips with the role of organization in movements. Turner and Killian maintain "movements are in a state of flux, their character changing from day to day . . ." (1972, p. 252). The emergent norm itself . . . matures and crystallizes with the development of the movement. Turner and Killian argue (1972, p. 247) that effective organization is crucial in sustaining movements, but they provide no explanatory framework to assess and analyze organizational factors. In short collective behavior theory is geared to the central message that movements break from preexisting organization and that movement organizations are always in a state of emerging and becoming. Hence, this perspective "is decreasingly applicable to movements as they become formalized and institutionalized" (Turner, 1981, p. 8). Additionally, collective behavior theory provides little insight into the causal connections between movement emergence and prior social organization.

Collective behaviorists have not provided theoretically specific statements of movement outcomes. Pointing to this gap, Marx and Wood (1975, p. 403) concluded ". . . most statements about the consequences of social movements are primarily descriptive or taxonomic." The view that movements progress through stages is the most widely used descriptive account collective behaviorists have produced to assess outcomes. This natural history approach (Dawson & Gettys, 1929; and Hopper, 1950) maintains that successful movements pass sequentially through the preliminary stage of social unrest to the popular stage, formal organization stage, and finally, the institutional stage. Summarizing this strategy, Turner and Killian (1972, p. 254) wrote it "permits us to discover the additional conditions that have to be present if a movement is to proceed from any given stage to the next." Thus, it can provide explanations "for movements that make impressive beginnings and then fail and for movements that have weak beginnings and suddenly burst into rapid development" (1972, p. 254). However, as Turner and Killian note, the natural history approach has serious limitations because the variety of social movements do not lend themselves to typical sequences and it is difficult to predict when movements may move backward, foreward, or skip stages.

The influence of symbolic interaction leads collective behaviorists to stress the fluidity and changing character of movements. According to Turner (1981, p. 5) "collective behaviorists see goals arising, evolving, and constantly changing through the interplay of collective definition among movement adherents and public opinion." Thus, ". . . the complex and volatile nature of movements make assessments of success and failure difficult, and collective behaviorists often find it more meaningful to develop theory concerning process than concerning movement success" (1981, p. 5). But symbolic interaction imagery can be misleading because movements often pursue stable goals as did the civil rights movement which did not swerve from desegregating public facilities and enfranchising Southern Blacks. Nor did the antiwar movement swerve from its goal of ending the Viet Nam war. However, as symbolic interaction stresses, some goals, priorities, and tactics often shift and change during movements. This too was clearly the case in the civil rights and antiwar movements. Therefore, a fruitful theory of movement outcomes must account for the structural and social psychological conditions under which movements fail or succeed to accomplish stable goals and the conditions under which goals become unstable, or change entirely.

Thus, the collective behavior perspective has directed attention from assessing movement outcomes because it often view movements and activists as creative victims of fluidity and evolving realities rather than as controllers of those processes. Tilly (1983) had this in mind when he concluded:

> The idea that people are making some kind of a tactical choice itself, even if that is an implicit choice, is a liberation . . . There has been a lot of complaint in the literature recently about the weakness of our statements about outcomes. Why didn't we make that complaint for fifty years before? It is because we had a framework that didn't require it. In fact, even blocked us from thinking of these events as having outcomes . . .

B.   Smesler's Structural Approach to Collective Behavior

Neil Smelser's *Theory of Collective Behavior* (1962) was a landmark in the field. Yet, Chicago theorists (e.g., Killian, Turner, Lang, and Lang) argue that Smelser's work does not reflect the collective behavior tradition. Turner (1983) stated:

> That view [Smelser's] is not from the collective behavior viewpoint . . . they [critics] accepted that [Smelser's work] as the definition of what the collective behavior tradition is and I would suggest that they look back at the real collective behavior tradition.

Smelser broke from the Chicago School in two ways. First, his aim was to analyze collective behavior with a distinctively sociological approach (1962, p. IX), and he explicitly rejected the claim that collective behavior and conventional behavior constitute seperate coherent realms of reality. He argued it is "possible to use the same theoretical framework to analyze both conventional and collective behavior" (1962, p. 23). Second, Smelser's theoretical framework and style differed from the Chicago approach. Smelser utilized grand theory to arrive at a theoretical synthesis of collective behavior by explaining these phenomena with Parsonian structural/functionalism. He was interested in identifying the specific structural conditions that make it possible to predict and explain the occurrence of specific forms of collective behavior.

The Chicago School maintains that such a goal cannot be accomplished. Killian (1983) stated:

> I think its dangerous . . . to develop grand theory . . . Some people think you
> should not do it prematurely. I think that anytime in sociology it is premature.

At bottom, these different theoretical outlooks stem from the debate between Chicago symbolic interactionists and structural functionalists during
the 1950s. The latter viewed society as a functionally integrated system rest-
ing on a value consensus. In contrast, the Chicago School:

> followed . . . Robert Park's view of society as . . . a loose system of accomo-
> dation not a functionally integrated system . . . [For] Park, . . . conflict and
> competition [are] the fundamental processes. (Turner, 1983)

In short Smelser rejected the idea that collective behavior has unique characteristics that must be explained by a special branch of sociology, and he
adopted a structural functionalist approach to collective behavior.

For Smelser collective behavior can be explained and predicted with his six
variables value-added model. This model maintains that the interaction of
structural conduciveness, strains, generalized beliefs, precipitating factors,
mobilization, and social control produces collective behavior episodes.

In Smelser's treatment only conduciveness, strain, and social control were
explicitly structural (Smelser, 1983). Conduciveness refers to the extent that
structural characteristics permit or encourage collective behavior. Social
control refers to how authorities encourage, prevent, interrupt, deflect, or inhibit collective behavior. The "strain" variable is most prominent because it
links Smelser's analysis to Parson's structural/functionalist framework.
Smelser (1962, p. 47) defines strain "as an impairment of the relations among
and the consequently inadequate functioning of the components of social action. Those four components of social action are: values, norms, mobilization into organized roles, and situational facilities (1962, pp. 24–34). Thus
Smelser focuses on "structural strain" rather than individual strain. Hence,
there is "value strain," "normative strain," "mobilization strain," and "facilities strain." In Parson's terms, such strain occurs when the components of an
integrated social system become malintegrated. In Smelserian terms, this is
the strain that "must be present if an episode of collective behavior is to occur" (1962, p. 48).

Mobilization for Smelser is the process by which participants are mobilized for action. Similar to Chicago theorists, Smelser argued that movements proceed through stages and that preexisting or newly created organizations facilitate the growth and spread of movements after they emerge.
Smelser distinguished between the mobilizing role of preexisting and newly
created organizations (1962, p. 276), but his central message was that strain
and generalized beliefs were the driving forces of movements. Organizations
and leaders facilitated the process after being drawn in. In his words:

I felt that the mobilization dimension in my own book was rather undeveloped. It was kind of acknowledged to be an important variable but it was not developed.

Smelser's social control variable focused almost exclusively on how authorities block or prevent collective behavior. His basic message was that if authorities vacillate, appear weak, or refuse to use necessary force, they facilitate the growth and spread of movements (1962, pp. 73, 261–266). After serving as chief negotiator for Berkeley's administration during the Free Speech movement, Smelser realized the limitation of stressing only repressive and permissive dimensions of social control agents.

What I came to define as much more important was the negotiation between the authorities and movement leaders . . . If I were to rewrite that section on social control, I would make it more of a two way business. (Smelser, 1983)

Smelser's approach shares basic premises and intellectual roots with the Chicago School. The first link between the two is a common definition of collective behavior. Following Blumer, Smelser writes, "collective behavior...is not institutionalized behavior. According to the degree to which it becomes institutionalized, it loses its distinctive character. It is behavior "formed or forged to meet undefined or unstructured situations" (1962, pp. 8–9). Smelser argues that conventional and collective behavior can be explained with a common theory, but follows the Chicago School by viewing movements as noninstitutionalized behavior geared toward repairing a ruptured social structure.

The second link between the two approaches is the common argument that collective behavior forms—panics, fashion cycles, revivals, riots, movements and revolutions—constitute coherent phenomena explainable with a single theory. Like the Chicago School, Smelser fails to confront the idea of whether the differences between the various forms of collective behavior are so great as to warrant different theoretical explanations. That is, can the same theoretical formulation be used to explain both revolutions and the hula hoop phenomenon?

The third crucial link between Smelser and Chicago theorists is the view that a special cognitive definition provides the basis for collective action in unstructured situations. Thus, Smelser (1968, p. 8) defined collective behavior as "mobilization on the basis of a belief which redefines social action." A central role is attributed to the "generalized belief" because "collective behavior is *guided* by various kinds of beliefs.." These beliefs are the basis for uninstitutionalized mobilization as well as the criterion by which collective behavior forms can be distinguished. The generalized belief serves the same function as Blumer's "circular reaction," Lang and Lang's "collective redefinition" and Turner and Killian's "emergent norm": It provides the shared definition that enables people to act collectively in the task of re-constituting some aspect of the social order.

However, generalized beliefs differ from collective behavior accounts stressing rationality, especially Turner's emergent norm approach. For Smelser (1962, p. 72), generalized "beliefs differ . . . from those which guide other types of behavior. They involve a belief in the existence of extraordi-nary forces . . . which are at work in the universe . . . The beliefs on which collective behavior is based . . . are thus akin to magical beliefs." Moreover, "adherents to such movements exaggerate reality because their action is based on beliefs which are both generalized and short-circuited" (1962, p. 72). This stress on non-rational beliefs had led some Chicago theorists to reject Smelser's formulation because it brings Le Bon and related accounts of irrationality back to center stage. Moreover, it does matter whether rational-ity or irrationality is stressed. For example, Tilly (1983) distinguished Turner and Killian's approach from Smelser's:

> You don't really have the Smelserian cycle of irrational response to strain. What you have is people who are creatively trying to reconstruct reality . . . It has people trying to recognize reality so that it makes sense and constitute a basis for action.

Similarly, in Park's (1928) view structural breakdown may free individuals by enabling them to become emancipated, enlightened and cosmopolitan. Yet, Smelser's stress on nonrational processes is not incongruent with most ac-counts of the Chicago School. In his words:

> I suppose . . . I did not deny that process like suggestions, . . . milling, and con-tagion took place.

Rather, Smelser's objective was to:

> improve our theory about understanding these processes by seeing when and under what [structural] conditions they take place.

Smelser's central message that collective behavior is non-institutionalized, guided by and mobilized on the basis of beliefs and produced by strain and breakdowns also links him with the Chicago School. This message restricted his structural analysis and prevented him from moving the field into main-stream sociology. Yet, the thrust of criticisms leveled at Smelser's formula-tion did not stress structural features. Why then did Smelser's approach re-ceive disproportionate attention and foreshadow theoretical breakthroughs?

Our interview data revealed possible answers. Ralph Turner (1983) ad-vanced an "intellectual snobbery" explanation. He argued that critics:

> are snobs when they look toward Harvard on the East Coast, [and that] may ac-count for the fact that they then accepted that [Smelser's] as the definition of what collective behavior is and what the collective behavior tradition is.

Tilly's (1983) reflections suggest Smelser's style of theorizing may account for the attention:

> In a way the other collective behavior people got a bum rap from Smelser. Because Smelser did a far more elegant job of synthesizing the literature than any of them had ever done. Even though his basis for synthesis was one that they would reject. [Smelser gave] dignity to what had previously seem to be a marginal phenomenon.

Finally, Gamson (1983) concluded that the attention Smelser received is linked to the academic reward system:

> What is going on is that Smelser is getting this focus of attention because he's a student of Parsons . . . one confronts [structural/functionalism] because of its influence and centrality. There are more points for overthrowing Smelser than for Lang and Lang.

Whatever the reasons for the one-sided attention, it directs the focus from versions of collective behavior theory that may contain useful ideas about social movements.

Smelser's analysis foreshadowed breakthroughs because it included mobilization and social control as central variables and argued against the need for a special field to study collective behavior. Two resource mobilization scholars — Oberschall and Gamson — were critical of the thrust of Smelser's analysis but concluded that its structural aspects were steps in the right direction. According to Obershall (1983):

> Smelser said some rather interesting things about social control, mobilization, structural conduciveness. Certain pages there about social control, mobilization, and structural conduciveness are useful.

Gamson (1983) maintained:

> I thought Smelser's theory of collective behavior was really a big step forward and I still think that way. It had a couple of features that were different from the traditional collective behavior approach . . . It tried to integrate it [collective behavior] into a more general theory [and] it didn't have so sharp a separation [between] normal institutionalized behavior . . . and "crazy" behavior . . . It began to suggest . . . an interaction [between] social control strategies of authorities and the outcomes of collective behavior.

Later we will examine resource mobilization analyses and their focus on structural variables. Presently we will address mass society and deprivation theories of movements.

C.   Mass Society and Relative Deprivation Approaches

The mass society perspective, another variant of the classical model, shares some similarity with collective behavior approaches and draws from similar intellectual roots (e.g., Le Bon, 1960; Tarde, 1903; Sighele, 1899; and Durkheim, 1933). More recent proponents include Hopper (1950), Hoffer (1951), Kornhauser (1959), Lipset (1963), King (1956), and Arendt (1951).

Mass society theorists (e.g., Kornhauser, 1959) argue that "mass societies" are characterized by detachment and isolation. In contrast to pluralist and well-integrated societies, mass societies lack strong networks of secondary groups which cross check their members and lead them to be selective in their political participation. Mass societies have few structures which facilitate attachments between elites and masses that usually serve to moderate demands made on elites. These societies have relatively few secondary groups which socialize citizens to accept their lot and compromise rather than raise challenges. Moreover, such societies have a shortage of intermediate groups to penalize individuals for engaging in illegitimate means to attain their (often fanatical) goals. Finally, because the levels of group memberships are so low, high levels of alienation and anxiety are pervasive, and the detached members of these societies are inclined toward extremist activities.

Proponents argue that, given these characteristics, contemporary mass societies cannot effectively prevent people from participating in mass movements during periods of rapid change. Thus, religious groups, political parties, community organizations, trade unions, and voluntary associations, which ordinarily restrain antisocial behaviors, breakdown and become ineffective. Primary group attachments become increasingly weaker, and atomization of the individual occurs. It is the inability of mass societies to integrate and restrain people during periods of rapid change, then, that is the underlying source of mass social movements and other non-routine collective action.

Hence, movements grow and spread because numerous individuals become detached and susceptible to proselytization and suggestibility (e.g., Hoffer, 1951). Mass society theorists usually view movement participants as fanatical, irrational, malintegrated, alienated, and even psychopathological. Thus, participants are interchangeable from movement to movement; i.e., they are discussed as "rebels without a cause" who are as likely to participate in radical movements as reactionary ones (e.g., Hoffer, 1951; Hopper, 1950). Again, movements proliferate when societal institutions are unable to serve their integrative functions in light of rapidly changing conditions: The more anomic the conditions, the more likely movements of all types will flourish.

Organizations, in this view, play a conservative role because they are integrating mechanisms which hinder rather than promote movements. As movements evolve, successful ones eventually *become* organizations. However, organization is not a prior nor concommitant facilitative condition in the development of movements. In general, mass society theorists ignore movement dynamics, and like collective behaviorists, they have relied on life cycle and natural history explanations to account for movement processes and outcomes.

A final variant of the classical model is the relative deprivation perspective which can be traced to such theorists as Mosca (1939), Pareto (1935), and Durkheim (1933). Recent proponents include Gurr (1968; 1970; 1973), Runciman (1966), Huntington (1968), Davies (1962), Pettigrew (1964), and Crosby (1976). This approach focuses on the relationship between social conditions, perceptions of those conditions, and behaviors resulting from those perceptions. In most versions (e.g., Gurr, 1970; Davies, 1971; and Lipset and Rabb, 1978; and Crosby 1976), proponents offer frustration-anger-aggression explanations. They argue that when people perceive great discrepancies between the power and privileges they possess and the amount they *ought* to possess, they become frustrated, angered, and subsequently participate in movements and protest to offset feelings of deprivation.

Relative deprivation theorists differ over the sources of felt deprivation and over the forms of deprivation (e.g., progressive/J-curve, aspirational/v-curve, status, decremental, and egotistical) that are important in predicting protest. Nevertheless, they agree that changes in felt deprivation result from rapid social changes which cause incongruencies between what people expect and what the society delivers. Rapid changes which generate relative deprivation include socioeconomic changes (e.g., depressions or economic booms [e.g., Olson, 1963]), industrialization (e.g., Feierabend et al., 1969), urbanization (e.g., Hibbs, 1973), political modernization (e.g., Huntington, 1968), and increased exposure to mass media and education (e.g., Parvin, 1973).

Therefore, it is important to examine unusually rapid and dramatic changes because they lead to: (a) changes in expectations; (b) frustrations about discrepancies between expectations and outcomes; (c) political anger resulting from frustrations; and (d) politicized anger which finds expression through participation in movements and protest. In short, periods of rapid change followed by changes in expectations give rise to social movements.

Relative deprivation theories do not claim that participants differ from nonparticipants (i.e., participants are not alienated rebels without a cause); rather, participants find themselves in different circumstances which cause them to act differently. Nevertheless, relative deprivation shares with mass society theories the claim that movement and protest activity: (a) are a result of the structural strain of rapid changes in societies, (b) are preceded by changes in the psychological state of those who participate, (c) are guided by emotional rather than meaningful tactical considerations, (d) are relatively rare and short-lived, (e) are abnormal because they are not structurally defined by the normal operation of institutions, and (f) is inherently different from institutional activity.

Because these theorists focus on macro changes and subsequent psychological changes in individuals, they have paid little attention to the "nuts and bolts" of social movements. They have not explained how participants coalesce, nor how activities spread between locales. Rather, collective action is treated as the result of aggregates of individuals who engage in similar forms of protest at the same time. Moreover, because episodes of collective action are treated as independent, unrelated events, they are not related to each other or to larger social movements. Finally, like other classical models, this perspective has not illuminated movement outcomes.

Relative deprivation approaches have been criticized methodologically and substantively. One problem stems from using aggregate indicators to make inferences about psychological states of participants. Second, no direct evidence has been produced on the actual feelings of participants prior to protest participation (see for example, Orum, 1978; Oberschall, 1978a, b; Tilly, 1978; and Marx & Wood, 1975). Furthermore, critics have questioned how analysts know a priori what determines which comparison groups or equity norms a person will select in deciding whether he is relatively deprived. Third, because these approaches explain the genesis of movements on the basis of individual deprivation, they have not elaborated the process by which the relatively deprived come to act collectively. Finally, critics point to occasions in which rapid changes occur, but no protest emerges, or when protest occurs in the absence of rapid change. Thus, critical problems remain for relative deprivation theories of social movements and political protest. We turn now to resource mobilization formulations which challenge the classical approach.

IV. RESOURCE MOBILIZATION MODELS: RATIONAL ACTION, ORGANIZATIONAL-ENTREPRENEURIAL AND POLITICAL PROCESS

The recently formulated resource mobilization approach has become central in the analysis of social movements and collective action. It has produced models that challenge the classical approach. As with classical approaches these models differ in emphases and explanations. Yet, they share the following central message: There is no fundamental difference between movement behavior and institutionalized behavior; movement participants and their actions are rational; social movements pursue interests; movement mobilization occurs through an infrastructure or power base; outcomes of collective action are central, and they are products of strategic choices made by participants; either support or repression by elite groups can affect the outcomes of movements.

Components of the central message are by no means shared equally by all resource mobilization models. By treating the models separately we will examine how each explains the origins, development, and outcomes of movements.

A.   Rational Action Approach

In marked contrast to the view that movement and protest activities are motivated by irrational impulses, the rational approach argues that movement participation is guided by utilitarian cost–benefit calculations. This approach is akin to formulations by Mill (1950) and other utilitarians (e.g., Smith, 1910; Bentham, 1789) which explain collective action in strictly self-interested, individualistic terms. Such analyses are ultimately reducible to choice which *individuals* make while pursuing some goal which they share with others. Thus, in its "pure" form, the rational action approach explains movements and collective action as consequences of rational choices made by individuals in pursuit of goals which could not be achieved as efficiently through other means.

Rational action proponents differ in the degree to which they relax the claim that utilitarian logic explains protest and movement activity. Some give prominence to utilitarian logic in their models and argue that self-interests are sufficient for explaining virtually all aspects of collective action (e.g., Granovetter, 1978; Olson, 1965). For others the assumption that movement participants are rational is just one part of a more general approach which gives far more weight to group, organizational, strategic, and political considerations (e.g., McCarthy & Zald, 1977; Tilly, 1978; Gamson, 1975; Oberschall, 1973). Nevertheless, there is agreement "that the lower the risks and the higher the rewards for an individual and members of a group or social stratum, i.e., the lower [the] risk/reward ratio, the more likely are they to become participants in a social movement of opposition, of protest, or of rebellion" (Oberschall, 1973, p. 162).

Rational actionists reject the idea that movements result from system breakdowns, relative deprivation, irrational motivations, and rises in the levels of grievances. Instead, movements occur because individuals and groups resort to participation in movement activity to realize their interests. The McCarthy–Zald (1973, p. 1215) version argues that, given enough power and resources, "grievances and discontent may be defined, created, and manipulated by issue entrepreneurs and organizations" which reinforce major interest cleavages in the society. In other words, social movement activity can be (and on occasion is) manufactured and generated by those with vested interests in the occurrence of such activity.

Similarly, rational action proponents argue that participation in social movement and protest activity is based on a cost–benefit calculus: A person will participate when the perceived benefits of doing so exceed the perceived costs. Granovetter (1978, p. 1422), posits a "threshold model" of collective action in which he defines one's threshold as "the proportion of the group [one] would have to see join [in a collective action] before he would do so." For Granovetter, a person will participate in collective behavior only when a sufficient number of others participates such that the risks of participation become reduced to the point where net benefits exceed net costs. He argues that because each individual is activated into collective action only when his particular threshold is exceeded, the key to understanding the spread of collective action is the *frequency distribution* of thresholds, not the average preference for collective action. Thus, collective action occurs when thresholds are distributed in a manner such that "contagion" can occur. When lower level thresholds are absent from a distribution, higher level thresholds will not be triggered: thus the spread of collective action becomes impossible.

Granovetter's formulation has several limitations. His approach explicitly assumes that collective action participants are "rational actors with *complete* information" (1978, p. 1433, emphasis added) who *always* act to maximize their utility. An obvious shortcoming of such assumptions is that they draw attention from behaviors which do not fit economic, means–ends or risk–reward schemes in which individuals are all-knowing. Another deficiency is the omission of an explanation of how and why actors come to be in the same location at the same time. Furthermore, it claims that "all crowds are simple random samples from the population at risk" (1978, p. 1431) and thus, it erroneously assumes that crowds that are socially and demographically different will, nevertheless, have similar (normally distributed) threshold distributions. A related problem is the model's lack of method for determining individual's thresholds a priori, and thus, after-the-fact thresholds can be invoked to explain collective participation. Finally, no explanation of why collective action ceases once everyone's threshold has been activated is provided.

In contrast to Granovetter's arguments concerning mobilizing participants for collective action when the number of participants is too small, Olson (1965) points to the difficulties involved once the pool of potential participants is sufficiently large and the goal at hand is not a tangible product which can be divided up only among those who participate. Olson argues that it is not rational for a person to contribute to or participate in collective action when (a) the contribution of no one person will make a significant difference to the group or any of its members, and (b) all members will receive the same collective goods regardless of their level of participation; therefore, *only* the provision of "selective incentives" — distinct, divisible benefits (or costs) — will provide a solution to their "free-rider" problem. Thus, given Granovetter's and Olson's claims, it becomes difficult for people to participate in movements without receiving selective incentives. In the early stages, not enough people have become involved to make participation cost-effective for an individual; similarly, when the number of people who could make contributions is so great that an additional participant would not make a noticeable difference, participation is not cost-effective, especially for an individual who will receive access to collective goods any way.

Nevertheless, participation in the absence of selective incentives does occur (Marwell and Ames, 1979), and social movements do grow and spread. Rational actionists who relax the assumption that strict, individual self-interest and utilitarianism are of paramount importance explain collective action by arguing that "collective interests" exist which have varying degrees of conflict with individual interests (Tilly, 1978), by pointing to "collective incentives" (Jenkins, 1982), and by calling attention to "bloc recruitment" of preexisting solidary groups (Oberschall, 1973). Rational action theorists who do not relax the assumption of strict individual interest (e.g., Granovetter, 1978; Olson, 1965) are silent on the issues of increases in participation without increases in rewards to risk ratios.

Rational action theorists who discuss outcomes of social movements and collective action have done so with (at least) three slightly different emphases: McCarthy and Zald (1977) focus on movement organizations' choices of support bases as being critical to understanding their successes and failures. For them, the selection of a support base is a strategic task which has implications for the amount of resources which can be aggregated, the ranking of priorities and goals, the range of tactics which can be used, and the relation of the movement to authorities and other parties. All of these factors, in turn, affect the success of social movement organizations in realizing their preferences. In a similar vein, Tilly (1978) focuses of groups' repertories of contention" as one key in explaining outcomes of collective action. He argues that "actors approach defined objectives with strategy and tactics . . ." but action and outcome "cannot be explained by looking at the challenging groups alone . . . they result from the interplay of interests, organization, and mobilization, on the one side, and on repression/facilitation, power, and opportunity/threat, on the other" (p. 138). Given these factors, participants decide which action will be least costly but effective in the accomplishment of objectives. To the extent that these actors are correct, collective action episodes have higher probabilities of success. Finally, Oberschall (1978) maintains that those involved in confrontations have three options which affect their outcomes: (a) They can submit to their adversaries and abandon their cause, (b) they can make a conciliatory move, or (c) they can make a coercive move. He posits that at each point in the confrontation, those involved will choose the alternative which maximizes their expected benefits. Thus, outcomes, too, are determined by cost–benefit analyses.

In sum, rational action approaches explicitly reject the notion that movement activities are motivated by irrational impulses. Instead, they argue that a movement's genesis, participants, dynamics, and outcomes can all be understood by examining the rational choices of individuals in pursuit of goals. In their pure form, however, they are virtually incapable of explaining occurrences which are not consistent with the notion of individual self-interests. Hence, those who use rational action formulations have had to look to other factors to accommodate such occurrences.

B. Organizational-Entrepreneurial Approach

McCarthy–Zald's organizational-entrepreneurial model has become one central focus within the resource mobilization approach. This model has received attention because it seeks to explain modern American movements. Indeed, the model argues that these movements are best conceptualized as professional movements relying on the affluent middle class for funds, entrepreneurial leadership, and professional movement organizations. Moreover, this model has stimulated research by including political scientists (Walker, 1983) interested in the rise and fall of interest groups and comparative analysts (e.g., Tarrow, n.d.) interested in movements across western societies.

McCarthy–Zald's model can be traced to three intellectual antecedents: organizational sociology, political science interest group theory, and micro economics. McCarthy and Zald's heavy stress on formal movement organizations derive from classical organizational studies including Weber (1947), Michels (1962), Selznick (1960), and Zald–Ash (1966).

McCarthy–Zald easily transfer insights from organizational studies to formal movement organizations because such analyses take formal organizations as the unit of analysis. The model also draws heavily on Salisbury's (1969, p. 12) exchange theory of interest groups by adopting its claim that "the entrepreneur in any organizational situation is the initiater of the enterprise." Finally, from economics McCarthy–Zald accept Olson's (1965) "free rider" dilemma as a major underlying problem that analysts of collective action must solve (McCarthy & Zald, 1977, p. 1216).

A main thrust of the model is to solve the "free rider" problem by utilizing organizational and economic concepts. For Olson the only way to entice rational individuals to engage in collective action is by providing each with selective incentives. In McCarthy–Zald view (1977, p. 1226) this solution hardly works for movements because such groups with serious objective deprivations and preexisting preferences for change, tend to be very limited in their control of discretionary resources which are crucial to collective action.

Nevertheless, such groups are confronted with the problems of aggregating resources for collective purposes and building at least minimal forms of organizations. Hence, social movements groups must solve this mobilization problem in spite of being unable to provide their members with selective incentives. McCarthy and Zald's arguments suggest that this problem is not serious because modern movements depend on affluent individuals and organizations from outside the oppressed groups.

By defining movements simply as preference structures for change, McCarthy–Zald focus specifically on the outside organizations and individuals which, in their view, make mobilization possible. Key actors in the organizational-entrepreneurial model are social movements (SMs), social movement industries (SMIs), social movement sector (SMS) mass adherents, conscience constituents, professional cadre, workers, and transistory teams.

SMOs, SMIs, and SMS are the social structures through which preferences for change (SMs) can be mobilized and activated. The social movement sector "consists of all SMIs in a society no matter to which SM they are attached (McCarthy & Zald, 1977, p. 1220). The level of resources within the SMS determines the emergence and viability of SMIs and SMOs. The SMS must compete with other sectors and industries but is at a distinct disadvantage because it is a low-priority competitor which flourishes only after the satiation of other wants occur. The SMS is supported by discretionary resources which includes money and time that can easily be reallocated to social movements. It is affluent middle class individuals who have discretionary resources that are donated to the SMS. These resources determine the likelihood that new SMIs and SMOs will develop and be able to compete. Thus societal wealth and donations by affluent individuals determine the capacity of the SMS.

The Social Movement industry consists of all SMOs organizations that have as their goal the attainment of the broadest preferences of a social movement (McCarthy & Zald, 1977, p. 1219). A social movement is usually represented by a number of SMOs belonging to the same industry, but such industries are not necessarily dependent on any particular movement because firms within industries may produce products that can be used across industries. Nonetheless SMIs which are dependent on the SMS provide crucial resources that support the efforts of a social movement. "A social movement organization (SMO) is a complex, or formal organization which identifies its goals with the preferences of a social movement or a countermovement and attempts to implement those goals" (1977, p. 1218). However, in order to accomplish goals SMOs must possess resources. Herein lies the problem because SMOs represents groups with few discretionary resources needed to keep the organizations in business, and members of such groups are not likely to participate in collective action on their behalf because of the "free rider" dilemma.

In McCarthy and Zald's view many modern American movements have solved this problem. They argue (1973, p. 18) that, in contrast to major classical social movements of the past which depended on its membership for money, manpower, and leadership, "modern movements can increasingly find these resources outside of self-interested memberships concerned with personally held grievances." That is, these resources can be drawn from outside elites because it is they "who control larger resource pools" (McCarthy & Zald, 1977, p. 1221). Therefore modern movements are led by professional movement organizations such that "it is increasingly possible that their financial support is totally separate from their presumed beneficiaries" (McCarthy & Zald, 1973, p. 18). In short, SMOs, SMIs, and the SMS are the structural configurations that give rise to and provide money and manpower for modern movements.

Modern social movements, like classical ones, involve mass constituents, adherents, bystander publics, and opponents. Yet these groups cannot generate and sustain movements because of their limited resources. In the organizational-entrepreneurial model conscience constituents provide the money and resources that generate and sustain movements. "Conscience constituents are direct supporters of the SMO who do not stand to benefit directly from its success in goal accomplishment" (1977, p. 1222). Such individuals have discretionary wealth which can be "made available to causes beyond the direct self-interest of the contributor." These individuals donate money to movements because they get satisfaction by sympathizing with the goals of the underdog. By attributing a central financial role to conscience constituents Zald–McCarthy solve one aspect of Olson's free rider problem. Indeed, Olson (1965, pp. 159-160) argues that "the theory is not at all sufficient where philanthropic lobbies, that is, lobbies that voice concern about some group other than the group that supports the lobby, or religious lobbies are concerned." Thus philanthropic groups avoid the free rider problem because their rewards are derived from the heart rather than on the basis of rational individual interests. For McCarthy–Zald it is these philanthropic conscience constituents that support the efforts of professional movement organizations.

In the model, professional movement organizations are the vehicles of modern movements. These organizations direct resource appeals primarily toward conscience adherents and tend to utilize few constituents for organizational labor (McCarthy & Zald, 1977, p. 1223). Other key characteristics of the professional movement organization include (a) a small professional entrepreneur cadre who provide leadership and accomplish tasks through small transitory teams; (b) a very small or nonexistent membership base; (c) outside money and resources from elite groups (e.g., foundations, churches, and the government) that largely support the organization and its staff; and (d) professional entrepreneurs who define, create, and manipulate the grievances associated with oppressed groups (1973, p. 20).

Social movement entrepreneurs loom large because they represent the movement's cause (at time create it) and form the organization that pursues the cause (1977, p. 1226). Given that the leadership and small transitory teams are hypothesized to perform the work of modern movements, McCarthy–Zald have solved another aspect of the free rider problem on two fronts. First, movement entrepreneurs receive selective incentives because the available discretionary funds from the affluent provide them with the resources to pursue professional movement careers. If the entrepreneur is unsuccessful in linking to or creating grievances among the oppressed, s/he may switch to another SMI where the grass is greener. Oberschall (1973, p.

159) has developed a similar view of movement leadership in his argument that leaders are to be understood in terms of the "individual incentives, gains, risks, and opportunities for advancement that participation in a social movement represents for them. Social movement leaders are political entrepreneurs just as politicians are." Second, movement workers comprise small voluntary, transitory teams which perform the bulk of the movement's tasks. They receive selective incentives because small face-to-face groups receive solidary incentives-selective benefits of a nonmaterial sort (McCarthy & Zald, 1977, p. 1227). In the McCarthy–Zald model, modern movements, then, have solved the free-rider problem pertaining to movement financial support, leadership, and workers.

The central message of this model is that the growth and spread of modern movements is a function of societal wealth available to SMOs, SMIs, and SMS. Moreover, the efficiency and achievements of such movements depend on the efforts of small professional movement organizations guided by entrepreneurs rather than the intensity of grievances held by the oppressed group. Indeed, the model argues that "in accounting for a movement's successes and failures there is an explicit recognition of the crucial importance of involvement on the part of individuals and organizations from outside the collectivity which a social movement represents" (McCarthy & Zald, 1977, p. 1216). Joining McCarthy and Zald in this important claim are Oberschall (1973), Jenkins and Perrow (1977), and Lipsky (1968). All of these theorists are contributors to the resource mobilization approach. A similar claim was advanced earlier by Lenin (1975) who argued that workers will not spontaneously develop a revolutionary consciousness and mobilize for more than limited economic goals without the leadership provided by intellectuals in a disciplined vanguard organization with a clear vision and analysis to lead them. For McCarthy–Zald, the conditions of modern society are such that the fates of oppressed groups hinge on the activity of outside groups.

This provocative model raises a number of issues. First, should groups that McCarthy–Zald discuss — AFL-CIO lobbyists, National Union for Social Justice, and National Council for Senior Citizens — be conceptualized as movement organizations or interest groups? It is well known that many problems social movements groups face — mass mobilization and solidarity, loyalty, intense grievances, repressive authorities, etc. — often differ from those faced by interest groups so that an important distinction needs to be made between the two. Oberschall (1983) pointed to this problem:

> Zald comes at this study from organization theories. A lot of things that he describes are actually interest groups, and they are really what he calls professional social movements . . . He always tends to emphasize the social movement organization rather than the whole movement.

Second, the model directs attention from mass-based movements that may be "quietly emerging" on the modern scene. Such conceptual neglect in the 1950s allowed the mass movements of the 1960s to catch social scientists by surprise. Third, is the McCarthy–Zald view that poor oppressed groups are always without the resources needed to conduct collective action an accurate portrayal? This view according to Perrow (1983) and Zald (1983) is relevant to resource-starved, impoverished, groups, rather than stable working class communities. This may be the case but presently this view has not established "how poor is poor?", and the analytical grounds on which such potentially valuable distinctions can be determined. This is important because even poor groups have established organizations, institutions, leaders, networks and skills. A key question is what are the conditions and minimum resource level that lead such groups to mobilize and pursue their collective interests? A theory that does not take these factors into account can fall victim to what Morris (1984) calls the outside bias. Nevertheless, McCarthy and Zald have directed attention to the unique forms that some modern movements may take.

C. Political Process

Major formulations of the political process model include Charles Tilly (1979), William Gamson (1975; Gamson, Fireman, & Rytina, 1982) and Anthony Oberschall (1973). These theorists are uncomfortable with the term "resource mobilization" because it fails to capture crucial aspects of their approaches (interviews, 1983). Thus Tilly (1983) stated:

> . . . It [resource mobilization] brings together the idea that manipulators are somehow central to all kinds of social movements, which I think is in fact a variable . . . Second, it identifies the amassing or spending of resources as the absolutely central phenomenon, and to that extent, distracts attention away from power struggles and from group organization . . . The term itself . . . just makes me worry that one of the least structural feature of this line of thought should be the thing that is singled out.

For Gamson, Oberschall, and Tilly the study of movements is the study of the political process and the collective action it generates.

Political process theorists do not view the social movement as the unit of analysis. In Tilly's view,

> the different forms of collective action are part of the regular processes of struggle. The coherent phenomenon is a process that has an orderly side and a disorderly side. The central process is a process of sets of people acting together on their interest, and that is what we ought to be theorizing about.

The dependent variable for political process theorists is collective action. Oberschall (1983) maintained:

> I feel that by emphasizing terms like resource mobilization or social movements, you tend to cut yourself off from the larger theory . . . I feel very strongly that what the real dependent variable should be is collective action . . .

> Collective actions are generated by interest groups. Some are by just routine politics, some are by social movements, others are by just crowds. So there is a theoretical core around the dependent variable, and it is not the term social movement or mobilization; its collective action.

Focusing on continuous political struggles, these theorists reject collective behaviorist's claim that social movement analyses require unique concepts and theories. According to Gamson (1983):

> . . . you don't have to have some fundamentally different set of processes to explain it . . . Resource mobilization tries to apply or to incorporate into a single theory both conventional political behavior and unconventional political behavior.

In contrast to collective behaviorists, political process theorists focus on political movements rather than cults, religious revivals, and the like. In Gamson's view, the model focuses on movements engaged in political conflict and:

> its useful . . . to treat it as a conflict between insurgents and authorities. That's . . . the core of the dynamics.

Tilly argues that fads, changes in style, panics, etc., are a different set of phenomena than wars, revolutions, and political movements. Tilly breaks from collective behavior and objects to their bases of synthesis

> because they are putting into the same box, things . . . [which] are not in the same family.

As to the advantages of studies focusing on political movements Tilly maintains that

> the next ones that come out are much less likely to be Seventh-Day-Adventists, or people who believe that we are at the crack of doom . . . There will be less kookie stuff and more interest in explaining what Common Cause is doing or where the anti-abortion forces are coming from.

Having identified the central dynamics we can now explore how political process theorists analyze the key dependent variable — collective action.

Why do groups engaged in collective action typically subscribed to social movement tactics such as demonstrations, boycotts, strikes, violence, riots, and sit-ins? Political process theorists argue that it is the political situation of movement group that give rise to "unruly" tactics and strategies. In the "polity model" (Tilly, 1978; Gamson, 1975), it is argued that challengers — movement groups — are excluded from the polity which means they lack routine, low cost access to resources controlled by the government. Thus, the interests of challenging groups cannot be realized through "legitimate" means because governments respond to the interests of polity members only. Collective action, and its accompanying tactics, are the vehicles of groups who rationally pursue group interests. It is the struggle for power between polity members and challenges that give rise to collective action.

Focusing on the excluded interests of movement groups, this model investigates the social structures and processes enabling challengers to pursue power through collective action. The first requirement is that challenging groups have internal organization. Organization is the extent of common identity and unifying structure among members of the challenging group (Tilly, 1978, p. 54). The relevant internal organization consists of various forms including established institutions, professional and informal networks, and formal movement organizations (Morris, 1981). Some formulations imply that a centralized bureaucratic organization is the hallmark of a movement. But this need not be the case because the theory has greater power when "the type of organization that works best is treated as an empirical issue . . . It is more infra-structure than a particular form of organization that is emphasized in resource mobilization theory—particularly structures of solidarity and communication" (Gamson & Schmeidler, 1984). Contrary to the claims of classical approaches, many of these forms exist prior to the movement and play a distinct role in generating large volumes of collective action. Organization is important because, through it, movements groups are able to collectively plan and strategize, hold meetings, organize and coordinate demonstrations, raise money, and facilitate the mobilization process. In this approach, organization is crucial to both the emergence and success of movements.

Though potential movement groups usually possess organizational structures and resources, they must be mobilized if challengers are to contend for power. Mobilization refers to the process by which challenging groups gain collective control over resources that make collective action possible (Tilly, 1978, p. 84). For example, in the Baton Rouge bus boycott of 1953 the cars of private citizens had to be collectively mobilized into an alternative transportation system; money from the pockets of black church members and from other black organizations had to be raised on a consistent and rapid basis to finance the entire struggle; and, black leaders including ministers and other organizational actors had to coalesce and provide the boycott with collective leadership (Morris, 1984). These internal resources were brought under the collective control of the newly created umbrella movement organization — United Defense League — that constituted the backbone of this effective boycott which was central to the rise of the civil movement. Thus, "mobilization is a process of increasing the readiness to act collectively by building the loyalty of a constituency to an organization or to a group of leaders" (Gamson, 1975, p. 15).

The political process model analyzes the link between the mobilization process of movement groups and their preexisting structures and resources. Unlike classical models which often portray new movement groups as having the awesome tasks of creating new symbolic systems and constructing new organizations, political process theorists argue that the task is usually much easier because these groups already have many of these resources. "Thus the conflict group escapes, to some extent, from the great cost of starting at zero mobilization" (Tilly, 1978, p. 81). Preexisting organization rather than its breakdown, facilitates mobilization. The model predicts that individuals who are well integrated into preexisting community structures constitute the bulk of the early participants of collective action (Oberschall, 1973). When preexisting social organization and the mobilization process are cojoined they generate collective action.

Under ideal circumstances it is an increase in the organizational and resource capacity of a subordinate group coupled with mobilization that give rise to movements. However, resource mobilization theorists have not formulated precise theoretical statements of movement causation. This has led Smelser to argue:

> they don't talk much about what starts them, they talk about it once they have gotten started.

Similarly, Gamson concluded:

> Resource mobilization is really not much concerned with why people engage in collection action. It tends to take the "why" for granted and doesn't treat it as problematic. Resource mobilization doesn't really offer a separate theory of that. It basically assumes that there are injustices or some condition that people are concerned about and the issue is "how". What's the process by which they try to get what they want. In that sense, it doesn't confront [the causal] issue directly.

Nevertheless, in the political process approach organizational capacity and mobilization are preconditions that must be present if sustained collective action is to occur.

Circumstances, are usually not ideal for collective action by movement groups. The extent of repression by social control agents and the power position of challenging groups play an important role in determining whether movements materialize (Tilly, 1978, p. 100). High levels of repression and low power can force challengers to withdraw from power struggles because they raise the cost of mobilization and collective action. In Tilly's view, repressive action aimed at demobilizing the challenging group is an effective strategy against collective action:

> . . . Raising the costs of mobilization is a more reliable repressive strategy than raising the costs of collective action alone. The antimobilization strategy neutralizes the actor as well as the action, and makes it less likely that the actor will be able to act rapidly when the government suddenly becomes vulnerable, a new coalition partner arises, or something else quickly shifts the probable costs and benefits of collective action. (Tilly 1978, pp. 100–101).

Demobilization may occur when authorities disrupt the challenger's organization and communication system and freeze crucial resources that make a challenge possible.

Therefore, interest, organization, mobilization, and the opportunity to act are major variables in the analysis of collective action. Moreover, the model attributes an active role to participants and leaders, for their strategic choices will affect the growth and spread of collective action. In Gamson and Schmeidler's view "collective action is a craft; there are skills and routines for carrying it out" (1984). Thus Gamson is concerned with conditions enabling challenging groups to pursue successful rebellious careers (Gamson, 1982). Similarly Tilly (1983) maintains that:

> we are much more serious now about discovering the point at which people turn to forms of action that authorities or even most other people disapprove of.

Hence, the model focuses on the varied strategic choices that confront movement participants and the likelihood of their success.

Movement participants are confronted with organizational choices. They must decide whether to adopt formal or informal, centralized or decentralized forms of organization, and they must deal with internal factionalism. Collective actors must make tactical choices including decisions about whether to adopt "mild unruly" tactics such as boycotts and strikes or whether mass demonstrations and violence would be more instrumental in reaching goals. The careful and explicit study of violence reflects the willingness of political process theorists to analyze and empirically investigate the instrumental role that disruptive tactics play in collective action. With respect to violence, Tilly (1978, p. 183) argues that "out of the entire stream of collective action, only a small part produces violence" and when violence occurs, it usually grows out of strategic interactions among groups rather than heightened emotions. Thus, violence is normal and usually results from prior nonviolent confrontations. Confronting the issue head-on, Gamson (1975, p. 81) concluded that "violence should be viewed as an instrumental act, aimed at furthering the purposes of the group that uses it when they have some reason to think it will help their cause." Thus, Gamson (1975) presents evidence which suggests that groups who use violence and other unruly tactics are more likely to succeed.

In addition to organizational and tactical choices, movement groups must decide whether to pursue limited or radical goals or some combination. This choice will affect the degree to which authorities employ extensive repression against the group. Finally, participants make decisions as to whether they will rely on money and resources from outside or within. In Oberschall's version, subordinate populations are often portrayed as resource-deficient groups who must depend on outside resources if their efforts are to be successful. Gamson's (1975, p. 63, 66) systematic test of this proposition reveals that outside resources minimize the free-rider problem but that such groups "are only very slightly more successful than the others." Moreover, when the size of the movement group increases and when it overcomes the free-rider problem, "the help of rich or powerful sponsors is largely irrelevant in determining outcome." More studies documenting the relative advantages and disadvantages of outside resources are sorely needed.

In short, the central message of the political process model is that political movements emerge within the organizational and resource base of subordinate groups pursuing group interests and that mobilization of resources make collective action possible. Furthermore, the growth, vitality, and success of movements are associated with strategic choices made by movement participants and leaders. Likewise, repression by authorities and unfavorable political realities increase the chances that challengers will be forced to demobilize and withdraw from collective action.

The question can be raised as to whether the resource mobilization framework with its emphasis on organization, strategic choice, coalition-building, rationality and solidary groups is applicable to radical right movements. It is comforting for some to view these movements as the work of fanatics and the atomized. Yet resource mobilization theorists contend that radical right movements do not differ in essentials (although the goals may differ) from other movements and can be explained within the resource mobilization framework. Tilly, echoing other resource mobilization theorists interviewed argued that they have been reluctant to extend the same kind of analysis to the right for political rather than analytical reasons. Tilly stated:

> They [resource mobilization theorists] may even have stayed away from it [right wing movements] precisely because they were worried about glorifying most of the things they were unsympathetic to . . . but I certainly don't think it is true that somehow this [resource mobilization] is a line of thought that only applies to left wing movements.

Moreover, resource mobilization theorists (e.g., Liebman & Wirthnow, 1983) have begun to analyze right wing movements thereby demonstrating clearly the utility of resource mobilization concepts for such movements.

Resource mobilization models in general and the political process approach in particular are attractive because they address what McCarthy calls the "nuts and bolts of movements" by examining realities and choices that actually confront movement participants. However, the political process model needs a theoretical account that specifies the variable conditions which give rise to heavy volumes of collective action within given periods. Moreover, the preexisting organizations and resources of challengers do not always give rise to collective action. The political process model needs explicit statements about the links between mobilization and prior organization. Here the role of ideology may be significant in providing the bridge that links the two (Smelser, 1983). Then too, great movements often give rise to charismatic leaders such as Martin Luther King, Mao Tse-Tung, Cesar Chavez, Gandhi, and Hitler. The political process model needs either to investigate the role that charisma plays in the mobilization and success of movements or to demonstrate its irrelevancy. We will return to these issues at the end of the chapter. Presently the task is to assess the empirical support for both classical and resource mobilization approaches.

V. EVIDENCE: CLASSICAL AND RESOURCE MOBILIZATION MODELS

With respect to recent empirical findings and theoretical formulations, a number of issues remain unresolved. This lack of resolution is attributable to a combination of epistemological and methodological disputes over what constitutes evidence and disagreements about which factors are central to understanding social movements. For example, proponents of the classical approach have produced studies supporting their claims (e.g., Gurr & Duvall, 1973); however, they have not escaped methodological and substantive criticisms by other scholars operating within the classical framework and by those raising fundamental challenges to the basic premises of the approach. Similarly, resource mobilization theorists have marshalled substantial evidence in support of their various perspectives but have come under attack for neglecting aspects of movements which others claim are central. Hence, a number of disagreements exist among proponents of the competing theoretical formulations. The areas of controversy include theories of social movement causation, distinctions between conventional and collective behavior and between social movement and interest groups, explanations of movement dynamcis, formulations concerning the role of organization, characterizations of movement participants, and specifications of the determinants of movement activities and outcomes. The evidence relevant to these debates is discussed below.

A. Emergence of Movements

There is little empirical support for the claim that movements emerge from conditions of structural breakdown and social or psychological strain accompanying rapid change and catastrophe. Contrary to the classical approach, Bwy (1968) reports a negative relationship between the rate of economic growth and political violence and protest in Latin American countries. Tilly (1969) found no support for the claim that rapid urbanization, per se, leads to political violence. Flanigan and Fogelman (1970) report a negative relationship between the rate of economic development and the occurrence of political violence. And finally, Zimmerman (1980) concludes that the sources of change covered (including economic growth, economic decline, urbanization, and modernization) proved to be unreliable predictors of political protest. Thus, the rapid change–breakdown–protest nexus proposed by virtually all classical theories is weak in explanatory power and lacks empirical verification.

Research on the genesis of social movements has not fundamentally undermined resource mobilization explanations of when protest actions will occur; however, not much in the way of supporting evidence has been produced either. For example, McCarthy and Zald's (1973) argument that discontent can be created and manipulated by social movement entrepreneurs has not been established. McCarthy and Zald have modified their claim that grievances are basically irrelevant in generating social movements to a modest claim that grievances are "sometimes a secondary component in the generation of social movements" (McCarthy & Zald, 1977, p. 1215). No study, however, has directly addressed the issue of whether discontent and grievances can be manufactured by movement entrepreneurs. Other resource mobilization theories which argue that grievances are virtually always present in certain populations (and thus are not a very powerful variable) argue that movements will occur when there is an opportunity to act. This position is both circular and untestable to the extent that, by definition, movement activity occurs when (and *only* when) there is an opportunity to act. In order for this formulation to become more theoretically fruitful, it must specify more concretely *when* and *why* opportunities to act occur, and to what degree actors create their own opportunities to act. Similarly, Granovetter's thesis is so difficult to operationalize that there has been no rigorous test of his threshold model. In short, the resource mobilization approach has shown that classical formulations regarding the emergence of movements and protest are lacking; however, they have failed to substantiate their alternative explanations and to specify the combination of variables that give rise to movements.

B. Distinctions between Conventional, Collective, and Interest Group Behavior

Traditional distinctions between "conventional" and "collective" behavior have been effectively challenged. There is little support for the claim that major discontinuities exist between the two. Major formulators of classical (especially collective behavior) approaches (e.g., Turner & Killian, 1957, 1972; Smelser, 1962) have maintained that one can understand a great deal about movements by employing the same theoretical models used to analyze conventional behavior. Hence, Weller and Quarantelli (1973) argue against viewing collective behavior as the flip side of conventional behavior and offer a framework stressing continuities between the two. Moreover, Marx and Wood (1975, p. 365) argue that the tendency to show the continuities between conventional behavior and noninstitutionalized behavior has accelerated to a point where important aspects of collective and conventional behavior can be conceptualized within a common framework.

Distinctions have become so blurred and undefined, in fact, that some resource mobilization scholars are vulnerable to the charge that they study political parties, interest groups, and formal organizations rather than social movements. Such controversies cannot be resolved until a consensus definition of "social movement" is established, and movement scholars agree on what it is that they study. As pointed out earlier, no such definition now exists nor probably ever will.

C. Nature of Participants

Evidence concerning movement participants is both substantial and contrary to those approaches which posit that participants are detached or isolated, malintegrated and psychopathological, suffering from psychological strain or frustration, and less than rational vis-a-vis nonparticipants. Numerous studies show that individuals who first participate in social movements and protest are well-integrated into collectivities (e.g., Morris, 1981; Flacks, 1967; Paige, 1971; Freeman, 1973; Fogelson & Hill, 1968). Several studies have refuted the notion that movement participants are psychopathological and malintegrated (e.g., Keniston, 1968; Flacks, 1967; Kerpelman, 1972; Abramowitz, 1973). No direct evidence has been presented which demonstrates that participants suffer from strain or frustration, and Orum (1972) found no relationship between feelings of deprivation and participation in his study of the black student movement. And finally, no evidence demonstrates that movement participants are any less rational than nonparticipants. In short, most claims about movement participants that theorists within the classical approach have presented have not been supported empirically.

Nevertheless, debates about the nature of movement participants continue. One debate has resolved around the "suprarational" participant advanced by some rational action theorists. Hence, the question has been "when will people participate in collective action?" Extreme rational action views posit that individuals will participate in/contribute to collection action *only* when it is cost-effective for them individually; others claim that loyalty and solidarity factors override the utilitarian logic. Experimental evidence supports the latter view; evidence from an actual movement, however, suggests that a large majority of aggrieved individuals did indeed choose to "free ride" on the efforts of a few activists (Walsh & Warland, 1983). A second area of controversy involves the contention by the organizational-entrepreneurial perspective that movements among underdog groups do not rely on indigenous leadership, mass participation, and resources from grass root sources. Bailis (1974) and Jenkins and Perrow (1977) have provided support for their claims; however, Morris (1981, 1984) and McAdam (1982) have presented evidence to the contrary. Clearly though, this controversy is concerned with the sources of resources (leadership skills, manpower, funding, etc.) rather than their centrality to movements.

D.   Dynamics, Growth, and Spread of Movement Activity

Explaining the dynamics of social movements and protest activity has been one of resource mobilization's strong points. Meanwhile, classical approaches that rely on "natural history" and "life cycle" formulations to explain movement dynamics have been found to have limited explanatory power, as numerous studies have demonstrated that movements spread and are mobilized through friendship, familial, and organizational networks which precede movement activities (e.g., Freeman, 1973; Morris, 1981; Gamson, 1975; McCarthy & Zald, 1973). In explaining the process by which movement activity spreads from one location or occurrence to another, the arguments offered by classical theorists — contagion (Lang & Lang, 1961), imitation (Tarde, 1903), suggestion (Le Bon, 1960), circular reaction (Blumer, 1951), and emergent norms (Turner, 1964) — have been challenged by collective behaviorists (McPhail, 1973; McPhail & Wohlstein, 1983) and theorists employing a resource mobilization perspective (Freeman, 1973; Morris, 1981; Molotch, 1979). Numerous studies have documented the centrality of leadership, skills, "know-how," and strategizing and planning. All of these factors are consistent with resource mobilization explanations of movement dynamics. The resource mobilization approach, then, in contrast to the classical approach has made significant, empirically verifiable contributions to understanding the dynamics of social movements.

E.   Role of Organization

Generally, the notion that organization is an after-the-fact outcome of prior movement stages has not been supported, and the available evidence clearly suggests that organization facilitates rather than hinders the efforts of social movements. Numerous studies have pointed to preexisting organizations as crucial in mobilizing participants for protest activities (e.g., Morris, 1981; Gamson, 1980; Freeman, 1973; Gerlach & Hine, 1970; Aveni, 1978). For the most part, debates about organization have changed from *whether* organization to *what kind* of organization. The emerging concensus suggests a conditional relationship; that is, it depends on the goals pursued, the strategies employed, the nature of membership, the tactics that social control agents employ, and other factors. In short, findings on the role of organization in movements are counter to what classical approaches predict; therefore, future debates about the role of organization will center around issues well within the domain of the resource mobilization perspective.

F. Determinants of Movement Outcomes

Research on movement outcomes has shown that the life cycle approach is at best incomplete. In fact, there is now general agreement that organization, resources, strategic choices, and political context affect movement outcomes; however, there has been little empirical research to confirm or refute most formulations. Notable exceptions include Gamson (1975), Snyder and Kelly (1976), Isaac and Kelly (1981), and Gamson et al. (1982). Gamson (1975) for example, found that several factors are associated with movement success – the attainment of tangible goal-related benefits and formal acceptance by movement antagonists: reliance on bureaucratic organization, use of selective incentives, pursuit of narrowly defined goals, and use of "unruly" tactics. However, Goldstone (1980) challenged these findings by arguing that Gamson's analysis involved simple (bivariate) relationships, and that by controlling for the political context and the nature of goals, these relationships disappear. Also, Piven and Cloward (1977) argue directly counter to Gamson by claiming that poor people's movements realize gains from mass defiance, not organization. Moreover, organizations in the Piven–Cloward view are antithetical to gains for the poor because they de-radicalize movement demands, channel mass insurgency, and thereby limit the gains of movement. Their argument that mass insurgency itself produces gains has received empirical support (e.g., Isaac & Kelley, 1981); however, contrary to their thesis, organization facilitated the gains of the Civil Rights movement (Morris, 1981; 1984; McAdam, 1982) and the worker's movement (Gamson & Schmeidler, 1984).

Other factors also influence movement outcomes. Gamson et al. (1982) provided experimental evidence showing that available leadership skills, know-how, and other resources have positive effects on mobilization of collective action and thus on outcomes. Others (e.g., Marx, 1974; Oberschall, 1978b; Tilly, 1978) have argued that the nature of repression/facilitation by authorities affect outcomes. And a number of tactics and strategies have proven to promote successful outcomes. In sum, it is clear that organization, resources, strategies, and the nature of repression/facilitation affect movement outcomes depending on the nature of goals pursued. What is not clear, however, is *how* these factors affect outcomes and what their relative importance is in determining outcomes.

G. Assessments

Collective Behavior. In light of the empirical findings where do collective behavior explanations of social movement stand? In general, they lack support for many of their fundamental arguments including the notion that structural breakdowns and subsequent strains give rise to movements. Fewer collective behaviorists now argue that there are inherent, clear-cut distinctions between collective behavior and conventional behavior. The life cycle and natural history formulations have been found lacking in explanatory power. And some collective behaviorists concede that their formulations underestimated the positive, facilitative role that preexisting organization plays in the genesis of movements. In short, while there is not sufficient reason to reject collective behavior explanations of social movements, there is definite need for major reformulation of this basic approach. Indeed promising reformulations are underway (see McPhail, 1973; Snow, Zurcher, & Peters, 1981; Pinard, 1983).

Mass Society. The mass society approach has, for the most part, been disconfirmed by scholars because of the overwhelming negative evidence against its basic tenents. Its claim that movement participants are psychopathological, irrational, malintegrated, etc. has been shown false and research repeatedly shows that the argument that organizations impede social movements is untenable. Mass society formulations also share some of the same limitations as the collective behavior approach: lack of support for the notion that breakdown leads to movements; lack of evidence for the claim of discontinuities between conventional and non-institutional behavior; and problems with using the life cycle approach to account for movement dynamics and outcomes. Clearly, the evidence does not support the central claims of mass society approaches.

Relative Deprivation. Though relative deprivation fares better than the mass society approach, it too needs convincing evidence for many of its fundamental premises. For example, research using individual level data (as an accurate test of the theory requires) has demonstrated that relative deprivation, is neither a necessary nor sufficient precondition for the genesis of movements and protest. Moreover, the approach is ineffective in explaining how group behaviors result from psychological and individual tendencies; in other words, relative deprivation theorists have not sufficiently accounted for movement dynamics nor group activities within movements. In terms of organizations and the determination of movement outcomes relative deprivation theorists have offered little meaningful theory, and thus, their analyses are also lacking in this regard. Unlike other classical models (especially mass society theories), however, this approach does not necessarily preclude the role of organization or tactics, nor does it require life cycle explanations to account for movement dynamics or outcomes. Nevertheless, because of theoretical gaps and contradictory empirical findings, the relative deprivation approach, like the other classical theories, is in need of major reformulation and correction.

Rational Action. The rational action perspective lacks hard evidence for many of its central claims. For example, there has been no rigorous test of (and thus no support for) Granovetter's threshold explanation of the origins of collective action and participation. Nor has there been a test of the

McCarthy–Zald claim that grievances can be manufactured by movement entrepreneurs, nor the general claim that participation is a function of strict, cost–benefit calculations. Marwell and Ames (1979) provided experimental evidence which contradicted Olson's claim that selective incentives are necessary to overcome the "free-rider" problem, and thus challenged his portrayal of collective action participants. However, Walsh and Warland (1983), focusing on the community mobilization following the Three Mile Island Accident, report that only 12 percent of the population at risk contributed time or money to efforts to close the plant. There are no data to support the "suprarational" model of participants posited by extreme versions of this perspective. However, findings about other aspects of movements — distinctions between social movements and other phenomena, dynamics of movement activity, the role of organization, and the determinants of movement outcomes — are not incompatible with rational action formulations, but neither are they central to many of these formulations (especially Granovetter's and Olson's). In short, there is a lack of evidence concerning rational action formulations about the emergence of movements, disconfirming evidence about the nature of participants, and compatible evidence about other aspects of social movements.

Organizational-Enterpreneurial. Research investigating the central formulations of the organizational entrepreneurial perspective has produced mixed results. For example, research has shown both support for and evidence against the McCarthy-Zald contention that movements among underdog groups no longer rely on indigenous participation and support. Other unresolved issues which directly involve organizational-entrepreneurial perspectives include controversies over the nature of participants (e.g., suprarational vs. intendedly rational, indigenous vs. "conscience constituents," and self-interested vs. group interested), and the type of organization which facilitates movement success (centralized bureaucracy vs. loosely structured, informal networks vs. no organization). There is also continued debate over how movements are mobilized (through bloc recruitment vs. through selective incentives vs. through solidarity and/or loyalty to causes). Most of these debates are occurring within the resource mobilization framework, and thus will not undermine the resource mobilization approach.

Political Process. Research on social movements has provided support for the political process perspective; nevertheless, there have been critics. Critics have raised questions about the model's tendency to focus on organization, resources, and strategies to the neglect of grievances and deprivations (Gurr & Duvall, 1973; Zimmerman, 1980; Pinard, 1983; Walsh & Warland, 1983) and the occurrence of crises (Goldstone, 1980). Citing evidence from a number of empirical studies (e.g., Legget, 1964; Pinard & Hamilton, 1977; Isaac, Mutran, & Stryker, 1980), Pinard (1983) claims that political process proponents have prematurely dismissed the effects of socioeconomic deprivations on movement participation and support for collective action. He argues that because political process theorists concluded that deprivations do not give rise to movements, they wrongly rejected the argument that the relatively deprived are more likely to support and participate in non-routine collective action. Pinard's criticism of this perspective's tendency to blur distinctions between "emergence" issues and "participation/support" issues is valid. However, the characterizations of movement participants offered by political process theorists are, for the most part, consistent with the existing evidence.

As pointed out earlier, Goldstone's (1980) claim that organizational and strategic matters are insignificant in determining outcomes does question the fundamental premises of the political process perspective. Gamson (1980), however, has questioned the validity of Goldstone's findings on the grounds that they are based on faulty definitions, operationalizations, and codings of key concepts. Thus, Gamson's (1975) analysis of organization, strategies, and resources is still a major statement providing empirical support for key arguments of the political process model. In the next section, we raise the question of whether there has been a shift in the theoretical orientation of social scientists who study movements. We present evidence which bears on this issue, and we point out those factors which may account for our findings.

VI.   Has a Theoretical Shift Occurred?

This section attempts to determine whether a theoretical shift in how social scientists theorize about social movements and non-routine collective action has occurred. More specifically, it investigates whether the resource mobilization perspective has become dominant in the study of social movements and collective action. In doing so, it compares how frequently articles published in major social science journals since 1949 have employed the resource mobilization approach versus the classical model's and others over the last four decades.

A.   Method

The first task is to determine whether most movement analyses have shifted from the classical approach to the resource mobilization approach when explaining the causes, dynamics, and outcomes of social movements and other non-routine collective action within the period. To address this issue, articles concerning social movements and related phenomena in the 1949–1983 volumes of the *American Sociological Review,* the *American Journal of Sociology,* the *American Political Science Review,* and *Social Forces* were reviewed and categorized according to the theoretical approaches they used. Though our method has the limitation of excluding other important measures of change in theoretical emphasis such as additional journals, dissertations, books, social movement course syllabi, and other media outside of the major social science journals, we, nevertheless, believe that our indicator is a reliable one because journal publications reflect the work of many of those who actively contribute to the literature on movements. As will be seen shortly, our limited data strongly suggest that there has been an increase in the proportion of the literature that employs the resource mobilization perspective. We believe that a more comprehensive methodological strategy would provide even more evidence consistent with this conclusion.

To classify journal articles, ideal types for the classical approach and the resource mobilization approach were constructed. Table 1 summarizes these ideal types by illustrating how "pure type" articles would address questions about the properties of social movements and non-routine collective action. Using these ideal types as the standards, articles were classified as "classical approach" if the majority of their explanations were consistent with classical responses, "resource mobilization" if they were predominantly consistent with resource mobilization explanations, and "other" if a majority of their explanations were consistent with neither the classical nor the resource mobilization approach.

Articles included in the analysis are those which discuss aspects of the following subject matter: social movements, strikes, riots, revolutions, crowds, rebellions, protests, political violence, civil conflict, and various forms of demonstration (e.g., sit-ins, marches, boycotts). The greatest difficulty involved deciding which activities traditionally studied by collective behaviorists (e.g., panics, fads, crazes, revolutions, riots, religious cults) to include. Such activities were included only when the case was made that they share with social movements similar causes, dynamics, and consequences. This decision is arbitrary; however, results are biased toward finding that the resource mobilization approach has gained dominance *only* if there has been an increase in the proportion of studies which investigate such "collective behavior" from a non-resource mobilization perspective. There is little reason to believe this is the case (see, for example, Weller & Quarantelli, 1973; Marx & Wood, 1975).

B.   Results

Table 2 presents the percentage distribution of social movement and non-routine collective action articles appearing in major social science journals by theoretical approach and period of publication. This table shows that in recent years, there has been a major increase in the percentage of journal articles using the resource mobilization approach, and a parallel decrease in the percentage of articles which have employed the classical approach. By the 1970's, over half of the social movement and collective action articles in the major journals (56%) used the resource mobilization approach. In the 1980s, more than 2 out of 3 of these articles (71%) used the resource mobilization approach. This is in sharp contrast to the 1950s when over 80% of these arti-

Table 1 Summary of How the Various Approaches Would Respond to Questions About the Properties of Social Movements

| | Responses of Approaches | | |
Question	Chicago School-Collective Behavior	Structural/Collective Behavior	Mass Society
1. Are movements discussed as infrequent, unusual phenomena?	1. Yes	1. Yes	1. Yes
2. What are the causes of movements?	2. Crisis situations which require collective redefinitions of reality	2. Structural breakdowns	2. Rapid changes which lead to cultural lag, stress, and alienation
3. Is movement behavior more similar to or different from "conventional" behavior?	3. Very different, as it is guided by cognitive definitions that emerge in unusual situations.	3. Very different, as it is guided by a belief in extraordinary forces.	3. Very different, as it is irrational, spontaneous, emotional, or psychopathological
4. What is the nature of participants?	4. They lack the guidance that cultural definitions usually provide	4. They exaggerate reality. Their action is based on generalized, short-circuited beliefs	4. Fanatical, psychopathological, irrational, and alienated
5. Why do people participate?	5. To reconstitute a new social order	5. In response to the psychological strains of structural breakdowns	5. Because they are malintegrated, irrational, and fanatical
6. How is it that movements grow and spread?	6. Emergent norms. *OR* contagion, circular reaction, and diffusion	6. Mobilization on the basis of generalized beliefs	6. Proselytization and suggestibility
7. What role does organization play in social movement?	7. Successful movements *become* organizations, but are not central in the initial stages	7. Organizations are not initiators of movement, but facilitate their growth and developments	7. Hinder the development of movements
8. Is there attention to strategies and resources?	8. Limited attention	8. Limited attention	8. No
9. What accounts for the outcomes of movement activities?	9. Unpredictable occurrences, and the "natural history" of movements	9. The response of authorities	9. "Natural history" of movements

		Responses of Approaches		
Relative Deprivation	**Rational Action**	**Organizational/ Entrepreneurial**	**Political Process**
1. Yes	1. No	1. No	1. No
2. Changes which bring about feelings of deprivation of injustice	2. Pursuit of individual self-interests which cannot be attained as efficiently through other means	2. Rises in discretionary resources and the availability of movement entrepreneurs	2. Unequal distribution of power & resources leading to the pursuit of interests unattainable through "legitimate" means
3. Not necessarily different, but it is guided by emotional rather than rational considerations.	3. Very similar, as both are guided by rational pursuit of benefit maximization.	3. Very similar as both are guided by institutional and organizational factors	3. Similar, but involves the "disorderly" side of the political process
4. Frustrated by sense of injustice	4. Rational, self-interested individuals	4. Rational, well-integrated members of organizations	4. Well-integrated members of organizations and solidarity groups who are intendedly rational & (sometimes) ideologically committed
5. To relieve their individual frustrations	5. To realize individual interests	5. To realize individual or group interests	5. To realize group interests
6. No specifications of these dynamics	6. By making it rational to participate	6. Through the accumulation and expenditure of resources	6. Through mobilization of members of challenging groups & the strategic use of resources & tactics
7. Organization is not a central variable	7. Organization is not a central variable	7. It exists prior to and during movement activities. It is central to realization of movement gains	7. It exists prior to and during movement activities. It is central to realization of movement gains
8. No	8. Limited attention	8. Yes, attention to these is central in terms of hypotheses and propositions	8. Yes, attention to these is central in terms of hypotheses and propositions
9. No specifications of outcomes	9. Ability to persuade actors to participate in or contribute to collective action	9. Nature of goals, organizations, and strategies	9. Nature of goals, organizations, strategies, repression, power, and opportunities to act

Table 2   Social Movement and Collective Action Articles Appearing In Major Social Science
           Journals by Theoretical Approach, 1949-1983[a]

| Years | Theoretical Approach Used | | | |
	Classical Theory	Resource Mobilization	Other	Total
1949–1959	83%	6%	11%	100%
	(15)	(1)	(2)	(18)
1960–1969	79%	17%	4%	100%
	(41)	(9)	(2)	(52)
1970–1979	38%	56%	6%	100%
	(24)	(28)	(2)	(54)
1980–1983	21%	71%	8%	100%
	(5)	(17)	(2)	(24)
Total	57%	37%	6%	100%
	(85)	(55)	(8)	(148)
$\chi^2 = 36.24$	$df = 6$	$p < .001$		

[a]Major journals include the *American Sociological Review*, the *American Journal of Sociology*, *Social Forces*, and the *American Political Science Review*.

cles used some variant of the classical approach, and fewer than 6 out of 100 used the resource mobilization approach. A chi-square statistic of 36.24 with 6 degrees of freedom suggests that these differences are statistically significant at $p < .001$. The remainder of this section will discuss the major social and intellectual factors which facilitated this theoretical shift in particular, and the optimal conditions for theoretical innovations in general.

C. Social Factors

The 1960s movements were critical in the shift from classical models to the resource mobilization approach. The civil rights movement, student movement, and women's movement rocked America with such force that they attracted the attention of movement scholars. Moreover, these movements had major campus components which enabled scholars to become sympathizer/ participants and attain a close-up view of movements not possible through secondary sources.

Movement participation led future resource mobilization proponents to sharpen their criticisms of existing theories and to accentuate their specific limitations. For example, Oberschall maintained that his participation resulted in a better understanding of movements and:

> even when I read other people's descriptions of them, I understood a lot better what they were describing and in fact not describing.

Referring to prior theories and his participation, McCarthy stated:

> they weren't wrong so much as they didn't resonate. I read extensively and I didn't know more about what I had taken part in than I knew before my reading.

The view that participation allowed one to observe movement phenomena usually ignored by prior theories was a common theme of the interviews.

Second, participation by collective behaviorists and resource mobilization theorists generated greater appreciation for the complexity of movements. Participation alerted scholars to the significant ideological, tactical, and goal divisions within movements and the necessity of coalition building. Thus Tilly relates that:

> one thing that I learned was how phony most notions of a unified movement are.

He continued:

> this notion that you begin with a unified population and then some people mobilize that population on behalf of a set of beliefs they already have and that this group is a social movement . . . I became skeptical about that way of portraying the whole thing.

Tilly's participation in part, led him to a line of reasoning that says:

> look for organizing groups, look for recruiters, look for the making of coalitions, look for people deciding that the enemy of my enemy is my friend.

It is these kinds of dynamics that occupy a central place in resource mobilization theory and direct participation was crucial in revealing their significance.

Third, participation and sympathy with the 1960s movements led resource mobilization theorists to reject ideological biases often inherent in classical models. Gamson explained:

> when you are participating, you inevitably look at it from the standpoint of participants in social movements.

Additionally,

> collective behavior theories engage in a slightly insulting or put down quality by denigrating the motives of the participants.

They emphasized

> psychological motives rather than the collective goals of the movement. The natural tendency is to look around for some theoretical explanation that really reflects the experiences that one is having, addresses the problems that ones experiencing as a participant.

Again, this theme was prevalent among most resource mobilization theorists interviewed, and reflects, in part, their inclination to analyze movement goals, organization, and outcomes.

This discussion suggests that the movements of the 1960s were crucial to the theoretical shift. Gamson summed it up:

> If there hadn't been a civil rights movement there might not have been an anti-war movement, if there hadn't been these movements there might not have been an environmental movement. Without these movements there wouldn't have been people coming into the field who were receptive to a new orientation.

D.   Intellectual Factors

The 1960s movements highlighted the limitations of previous theories but subsequent intellectual activity pushed the field in new directions. Specifically, intellectual criticism and the incorporation of ideas from other fields were important in the formulation of resource mobilization theory.

Intellectual criticism of dominant orientations is crucial to breakthroughs. In the 1950s and 1960s structural functionalism and related frameworks were attacked by conflict theorists (Mill, 1956; Coser, 1956; Dahrendorf, 1959; Pilisuk & Hayden, 1965) who argued that conflict and change were endemic to societies rather than abnormal or marginal. Future proponents of resource mobilization absorbed and contributed to the conflict literature. However, that literature, as Tilly argued:

> so clearly took on the lineaments of the theories they were criticizing...It is useful polemically but what is the alternative structure that they give you that can then organize reality?

Conflict theory provided the critical mood conducive to formulating an alternative perspective.

Our data strongly suggest that alternative theories emerge slowly from a series of polemical statements and internal criticisms. In terms of resource mobilization theory, Tilly's experience was fairly typical:

> What I was trying to do is play this negative game of showing that the standard notions about marginalization, mass society, and so forth were wrong . . . for a long time I found myself getting somewhere, but not very far, mainly by attacking existing ideas.

The period of negative statements and groping is only the first step toward providing an alternative theory. Tilly recalled:

> I am saying, look I can't settle for that. Other people are saying, alright put up or shut up. What is your alternative? But I am saying to myself the same thing.

Thus, the stage is set for further theorizing. Tilly continued:

> In that process of struggle with my own schemes I started trying to map out the organization and the basis of collective action for the groups that I was looking at.

These data suggest that theoretical breakthroughs result not from inspirational flashes but a long process of internal criticisms and reworking of ideas.

The interview data revealed that the major formulators of resource mobilization borrowed and incorporated ideas from disciplines other than sociology. Even within sociology ideas were often borrowed from outside the social movement area, especially from organizational sociology. Similarily, ideas from anthropologists and historians of revolutions (e.g., Rude, 1964; Hobsbawn, 1959; Soboul, 1958; Wolf, 1966) were crucial in the formulation of resource mobilization. According to Oberschall:

> what greatly helped intellectually was that very prominent historians like George Rude and a whole bunch of historians were rewriting history of popular uprising in Britain and France and Western Europe. It wasn't just something happening in sociology intellectually. It was being sustained at the edges of sociology.

We have already seen how public choice theories (e.g. Olson, 1965) in economics and entrepreneurial theories in political science (e.g. Salisbury, 1969) played a central role in the development of resource mobilization.

In short, related or parallel ideas developed in other disciplines facilitate the formulation of an alternative perspective within a given field. As McCarthy put it:

> you are in an intellectual environment and you are picking what you can find and trying to stir it together.

Thus, both external and internal criticisms coupled with the borrowing of ideas from other disciplines were the intellectual soil from which resource mobilization emerged.

E. Institutional Factors

An alternative set of ideas do not take root in a field simply because of intellectual merit. This seems especially true in the social sciences where there are no "real answers" to problems as there are in mathematics and physical sciences [Hagstrom: 1965 and Weingart: 1974]. Thus, institutional factors including the prestige and resources of universities, informal networks of scholars, and the academic reward system are particular central to theoretical shifts in the social sciences.

Students of the sociology of science (e.g., Merton 1973; and Hagstrom 1965) have demonstrated that academic prestige is important to theoretical shifts. Thus, innovative scholars are in a good position to trigger a theoretical shift if they hold appointments in prestigious universities. Tilly (1983) maintained that:

> there is a tremendous advantage of being at the big, rich, prestigious university.

He explained:

> I spent my first six years at the University of Delaware, wishing I were somewhere else and having no opportunity to go anywhere else. I felt acutely what it was like to think that you have pretty good ideas and get no recognition for it. Moving to Princeton and then to Harvard as I did, gave me a sounding board that I didn't have before that time. It was astounding how much difference that made in contacts.

Other resource mobilization theorists (e.g., Gamson and Oberschall) also concluded that a prestige effect is usually central to theoretical shifts.

Second, prestigious universities provide well prepared students and faculty who facilitate theoretical shifts (Griffith and Mullins: 1972). Oberschall explained that

> you get students who understand you and can work for you and you don't have to explain everything to them. And you get support from faculty who recognize what you are doing.

Gamson maintained that at a university like Michigan you

> can attract good students who will start writing and citing that work. Tilly is on something like 48 dissertations. These are people who start writing books and become visible using the new orientation.

Finally, Tilly underscored the centrality of faculty at prestigious universities:

> You tend to be surrounded by people who know how to work the system. That is how they got there. They are often willing to tell you how to work the system.

Informal networks within a scholarly community facilitate theoretical shifts (Griffith and Mullins: 1972). The majority of the original formulators of resource mobilization were only vaguely aware of each others work before the orientation took root. Oberschall stated:

> it wasn't people getting together in a smoke-filled room and saying this is the party line and we are going to push it. We got to know each other really afterwards, and we discovered that we had some common interest and views.

Tilly pointed out how informal contacts solidified the new orientation:

> these people have means of making contact with each other. They send each other papers, they introduce each other, they form conferences and so forth. These are network building events that establish the credibility of a person for the next round of contacts.

Finally, the academic reward system facilitate theoretical shifts especially among scholars who are dissatisfied with the dominant orientation. Tilly explained that academicians:

> are very sensitive to a demonstration of originality. All it takes is a relatively small number of people getting recognized as a tour de force for having done something original and coherent, bright and so forth, for other people to say, gee I want to be in on that one too.

In a similar vein, Mullins and Griffith (1972, p. 961) argued that, "In addition to sounding a battle cry, a theoretical break provides personal motivation for fellow scientists." Gamson also pointed out that scholars who adopt the new orientation get socially rewarded because they get things published using it and so forth. In Smelser's (1983) view the academic reward system generates theoretical shifts in a cyclical fashion across generations:

> The generation effect is not 20 years but of 5 to 10 years or variable. People have to make their own way in the world. They can't simply say that this is the given and received view of things. The new orientation has to be different. It has to provide some alternative and there has to be some rejection of what went before.

Thus a bandwagon effect whereby additional scholars join the original formulators and publish works that give the new orientation visibility is necessary for theoretical shifts to occur.

Drawing from the above discussion and from our interview data, we conclude: the rise of a school of thought occurs when scholars, usually working independently, formulate a set of coherent premises capable of generating a theoretical shift, and when scholars other than the original formulators label the original group as a distinct school and act accordingly by producing research that either supports or undermines the new orientation. In general, the optimal conditions for a theoretical shift include (a) a social environment that provides a natural laboratory in which to observe theoretically problematic phenomena, (b) a field that is viewed as obviously deficient theoretically by some critical and creative scholars who are aware of fruitful ideas in other fields and who occupy appointments in leading academic institutions, and (c) the availability of ambitious scholars capable of triggering a bandwagon effect because of the compelling logic of a new orientation that clearly breaks from previous formulations.

F.   Resource Mobilization: Fad or Substance?

Is resource mobilization a new theory of social movements that will endure over time? Or, is it an intellectual fad masquerading under new labels? These are especially important questions because as Hagstrom (1965, p. 181) has pointed out the social sciences often lack rigorous theories and acceptable criteria for determining the relative importance of problems. Moreover, he argued that this situation allows more play to fashion because scientists must rely more on the direct social validation of their own judgment. Collective behaviorists who we interviewed (e.g., Turner, Killian, Lang, and Smelser) maintained that resource mobilization is not a theory but a re-emphasis because it fails to incorporate ideology, the social construction of reality, deprivation and grievances and causal factors all of which they believe important in explaining movements. Resource mobilization proponents concede that their approach is not a comprehensive theory but argued that it has provided verifiable theories concerning mobilization, nature of movement participants, social organization, and outcomes. Tilly agreed with this position but came down on the side of collective behaviorists by arguing that resource mobilization at this stage is not a theory. He (1983) stated:

> What we have right now is some interesting concepts, some pretty good ways of matching observations with those concepts, some apprehensions about how the processes involved work, and an empirical program of a kind. That's not bad, a lot of enterprises in social sciences operate for awhile on nothing much more than that.

Turner, Killian, and K. Lang maintain that much of the resource mobilization work is faddish behavior because it simply relables old ideas and concepts. This charge was directed toward those engaged in what we earlier called the bandwagon effect rather than the original formulators. Again resource mobilization proponents argue that some faddish behavior is involved and reflected through labels. McCarthy stated:

> part of why Zald and I get so much play is that we have generated a number of terms. Scholars find those useful, so we get cited, importantly, because we invented and coined some phrases.

However, Gamson's (1983) response captured the overall reaction of resource mobilization proponents:

> I'm admitting that there is a degree of faddishness in it, but I think that what happens with renaming is that it really puts it into a different overall organizing framework and gives it a different meaning. It's more than relabeling in the sense that its a rethinking and a reconceptualization of some phenomena that they [collective behaviorists] have been concerned with.

Moreover, as Turner noted, theoretical shifts in general generate some faddish behavior. Indeed, faddishness facilitates theoretical shifts and provides them with visibility that assist in attracting scholars who make important substantive contributions.

Given that resource mobilization has generated some theoretical breakthroughs as well as faddish behavior, will it endure? Tilly addressed the issue: "If we want to keep this game together, we need two things desperately. We need some unifying theory, and we need some empirical demonstration. A school of thought that has neither isn't going to last very long. It is going to be a fad, a temporary coalition." Similarily Zald remarked, "I wouldn't make a lot of large claims for what the long term payoffs are. At this point, I think it's a little early to say that we are not just a fad and fashion." Zald concluded that the staying power of resource mobilization hinges on whether it is able to provide scholars with useful tools for their research on specific issues. Another possibility, of course, is that some variants of resource mobilization theory may endure while others prove to be not very useful. From this vantage point it is too early to make predictions regarding such outcome. We shall let history be the judge.

Our empirical analysis demonstrated that there are a vast number of scholars contributing to the resource mobilization literature. This theoretical shift, whether permanent or short-lived, has changed the field of social movements by theoretically illuminating factors (e.g., tactics and strategies, organization, rationality, mobilization, outcomes, etc.) undeveloped in classical approaches. Indeed, new perspectives on social movements will have to take these important contributions of resource mobilization into account if they are to be comprehensive and deal with the realities of real social movements.

G.   Theoretical Problems and Conclusions

The field of social movements is divided between two theoretical streams. There is the classical approach which stresses social psychological variables including ideology, deprivation, strain, and social construction of reality, as well as structural breakdown. On the other side is resource mobilization with its stress on structural variables including social organization, interest, resources, group conflict, mobilization, and tactics and strategies along with rational, utilitarian logic. All of the theorists we interviewed on both sides of this theoretical divide maintain that both social psychological and structural variables are crucial to understanding social movements although they differ over how they should be combined into a comprehensive theory. The issue is whether it is possible to erase this bipolarity and combine the two approaches.

Our interview data reveal that the majority of the major formulations of collective behavior and resource mobilization theory will not work toward such a synthesis. Turner (1983), who believes such a synthesis is possible, made the case for collective behavior:

> I think we are going to move toward a better theory which takes a balanced account. But to me collective behavior is the comprehensive term. Resource mobilization is a statement that narrows the field. It has to do with a part of it. But there is a stream to integrate it [resource mobilizaton] in. That stream [collective behavior] can't simply be wiped out and discarded.

Tilly (1983), making the case for resource mobilization, rejected Turner's basis for synthesis:

> First of all we don't want to. I mean as a matter of scientific strategy we don't want to integrate everything else into collective behavior theory because by and large, it rests on a premise that we ought to reject. That is the premise of a break in social structure and a reconstitution. I think it is one of the most misleading notions that sociologists have propounded, and I think that is the 19th century heritage right there.

Gamson (1983) supported Tilly's view. He contended:

> I don't see how a theory is very comprehensive if it doesn't tell you anything about the organization and strategy of movement organizations; how they go about doing it, what strategies are successful or not successful. Collective behavior has a selective focus. I favor integrating collective behavior into resource mobilization to make it a comprehensive theory rather than the other way around. I think resource mobilization has the potential for being a comprehensive theory. Maybe it would have a different name.

Thus, from this standpoint it seems that the most to hope for is that this theoretical clash will generate additional insight from which a comprehensive theory can be formulated in the future.

However, several theorists we interviewed (Oberschall, Turner, McCarthy and Smelser) stressed the view that there is continuity between the various theoretical traditions discussed in this chapter. Smelser captured this view when he stated,

> It is in the nature of the case that different people use these several approaches to address qualitatively different kinds of problems, and for that reason the approaches are to be regarded in part as complementary or alternative rather than opposed to one another.

It is also possible that in the future some theorists will attempt the difficult task of synthesizing the various perspectives and unit of analyses in quest of a balanced and comprehensive view of movements. In any case there are some unresolved questions that future research must address. The remaining discussion is geared toward identifying some of those issues.

All the theorists we interviewed emphasized the crucial need for a theory that explains the role of ideology in movements. Turner concluded that we need to know:

> how certain world views become credible and vital at some times but not others.

Similarily Tilly concluded,

> a shared conception of what the world is about and of where a conflict group fits into the world underlies the whole process of collective action.

To explain the role of ideology there are several directions research should take. First the connection between ideology and prior social organization needs to be explicated. Thus Smelser argued that movement groups are often situated in prior organizations but they are not necessarily organized in the name of a social movement. He explained that:

> you don't get mobilized just because you are in an organization. You get mobilized because your organization gets talked into believing that your organizational goals are important from the standpoint of the movement.

Hence:

> the link is between the particular social movement and the preexisting organization. My belief is that is an ideological link.

Preexisting social organization among oppressed groups often contain dormant ideologies that can be activated to support social protest. Morris (1984) found that mobilization in the civil rights movement was often accomplished by ministers who activated the dormant revolutionary aspects of black religion already institutionalized within the black church. Blacks were pulled into the movement through the refocusing of the cultural content of the Bible, songs, prayers, and sermons in such a way that they facilitated the mobilization of protest. Moreover, changing attitudes by refocusing the cultural content of institutions is much more effective than changing the attitudes of separate individuals, because this procedure enables organizers to reach large numbers of people simultaneously. Thus research on institutional ideologies may shed light on what Turner refers to as the relationship between objective circumstances and the definition of the situation on which people actually act.

Second, Tilly maintains that an understanding of ideology and movements may be accomplished by investigating the process of struggle. That is:

> a significant part of the definition and redefinition comes out of the process of struggle itself.

Thus:

> ideology is not something that people acquire individually and somehow bring to a struggle.

If the struggle itself redefines the identities of the parties:

> it means that the history of a struggle or series of struggles will contain at least proximate answers to the questions of where world views come from.

Tilly's view implies that to understand how the ideologies of "black power" and "black is beautiful" emerged during the mid 1960s one would investigate prior confrontations between blacks, southern white power structures, and the national government. Prior struggles might have revealed to blacks that the ideology of "black and white together" yielded few substantive gains and that an independent black power base could be more effective. By the same logic many whites recognized the implications of "black power" and thus generated the ideology of "white back lash." Therefore, examining the process of ongoing struggles may shed light on the link between ideology and movements.

Resource mobilization arguments pertaining to mobilization are often limited by a utilitarian bias. This can be overcome in part by returning to the central role that charisma often play in movements so well understood by Weber. However, Weber failed to link charisma with prior social organizations and the mobilization of resources because his theory stressed an antithetical relationship between charisma and preexisting organization. To the contrary, Morris (1984) found that in the civil rights movement charisma and organization were cojoined from the very beginning and were mutually reinforcing. Moreover, he found that the movement did not create charismatic leaders out of a vacuum, charisma as a social form already existed in the black church long before the movement. The movement provided a large stage for the further development of preexisting charismatic relationships which enabled charisma to become an additional powerful force in the mobilization process. Further research is needed on the link between charisma and the development of social movements.

The field of social movements needs a theory of what Tilly calls salient interests. By this he means an explanation of the potential advantages and disadvantages within a population that become repeatedly important to collective action. This sphere of theorizing is especially suitable to Marxian analyses because they have illuminated the role of class interest in revolutionary movements (see Paige, 1975). However, Marxists have failed to provide potent theoretical analysis of the movements of the 1960s. We need a clearer understanding of the array of interests that fueled those movements as well as a general theory of salient interests.

Finally, as McCarthy–Zald pointed out, there is a need for a theory of the variable relationships between social movements and state structures. For example, do some state structures contain characteristics that are more likely to generate movements and revolutions? (see Skocpol, 1979). A related question is whether a national state should be conceptualized as a monolithic entity or whether local contradictions within a state structure generate movement activity? (See James, 1981.) This is ripe territory for both marxian and weberian schools of the state.

These are some of the important theoretical issues confronting movement scholars. Since the field has become so vibrant we may not have to wait long for answers.

REFERENCES

Abramowitz, S.I. (1973). The comparative competence-adjustment of student left social-political activists. *Journal of Personality, 41,* 244–260.

Arendt, Hannah (1951). *Totalitarianism.* New York: Harcourt, Brace and World.

Aveni, Adrian F. (1978). Organizational linkages and resource mobilization. *Sociological quarterly 19,* 185–202.

Bailis, Leonard (1974). *Bread or Justice.* Lexington, MA: Heath.

Bentham, Jeremy (1830). *Principles of Legislation.* New York: Boston, Wells and Lilly.

Blumer, Herbert (1951). Collective behavior. In Alfred McClug Lee (Ed.), *New Outline of the Principles of Sociology.* New York: Barnes and Noble.

Blumer, Herbert (1957). Collective behavior. In J.B. Gittler (Ed.), *Review of Sociology: Analysis of a Decade.* New York: Wiley.

Brinton, Crane (1938). *Anatomy of Revolution.* New York: Vintage.

Bwy, Douglas (1968). Dimensions of political conflict in latin america. *American Behavioral Scientist 11,* 39–50.

Cantril, Hadley (1941). *The Psychology of Social Movements.* New York: Wiley.

The Central States Speech Journal. (1980, Winter). Volume 31, No. 4.

Coser, Lewis (1956). *The Functions of Social Conflict.* New York: Free Press.

Coser, Lewis (1977). *Masters of Sociological Thought,* 2nd ed. New York: Harcourt Brace Jovanovich.

Crosby, Faye (1976). A mode of egotistical relative deprivation. *Psychological Review 83,* 85–113.

Dahrendorf, Ralf (1959). *Class and Class Conflict in Industrial Society.* Stanford, CA: Stanford University Press.

Davies, James C. (1962). Toward a theory of revolution. *American Sociological Review 27,* 5–19.

Davies, James C. (1971). *When Men Revolt and Why.* New York: Free Press.

Dawson, C.A., & Gettys, William A. (1929). *An Introduction to Sociology.* New York: Ronald Press.

Durkheim, Emile (1933). *Division of Labor in Society.* New York: MacMillan.

Feierabend, Ivo K., Nesvold, Betty A., & Feierabend, Rosalind L. (1969). Social change and political violence: Cross-national patterns. In H.D. Graham & T.R. Gurr (Eds.), *Violence in America: Historical and Comparative Perspectives.* New York: Praeger.

Feuer, Lewis (1969). *The Conflict of Generations.* New York: Basic Books.

Flacks, Richard (1967). The liberated generation: An exploration of the roots of student protest. *Journal of Social Issues 23,* 52–75.

Flanigan, W.H., & Fogelman, E. (1970). Patterns of political violence in comparative historical perspective. *Comparative Politics 3,* 1–20.

Fogelson, Robert, & Hill, Robert(1968). Who riots? A study of participation in the 1967 riots. In *Supplemental Studies for the National Advisory Commission on Civil Disorders.* Washington,DC: U.S. Government Printing Office.

Freeman, Jo (1973). The origins of the women's liberation movement. *American Journal of Sociology 78,* 792–811.

Freud, Sigmund (1955). Psychology and the analysis of the ego. In J. Strackey (Ed.), *The Standard Edition of the Complete Psychological Works of Sigmund Freud.* London: Hogarth.

Gamson, William A. (1975). *Strategy of Social Protest.* Homewood, IL: Dorsey.

Gamson, William A. (1980). Understanding the careers of challenging groups. *American Journal of Sociology 85,* 1043–1060.

Gamson, William A. (1983, September) Interview.

Gamson, William, Fireman, Bruce, & Rytina, Steven (1982). *Encounters with Unjust Authority*. Homewood, IL: Dorsey.

Gamson, William & Schmeidler, Emilie (1984). Organizing the poor. *Theory and Society 13:* 567–585.

Gerlach, Luther P. & Hine, Virginia (1970). *People, Power, Change: Movements of Social Transformation*. Indianapolis: Bobbs-Merrill.

Goldstone, Jack (1980). The weakness of organization. *American Journal of Sociology 85,* 1017–1042.

Goldstone, Jack (1982) The comparatives and historical study of revolutions. *Annual Review of Sociology 8,* 187–207.

Granovetter, Mark (1978). Threshold models of collective behavior. *American Journal of Sociology 83,* 1420–1443.

Griffith, Bolver C., & Mullins, Nicholas C. (1972). Coherent social groups in scientific change. *Science 177,* 959–964.

Gurr, Ted (1968). A causal model of civil strife: A comparative analysis using new indices. *American Political Science Review 62,* 1104–1124.

Gurr, Ted (1970). Why Men Rebel. Princeton, New Jersey: Princeton University Press.

Gurr, Ted (1973). "The Revolution-social Change Nexus: Some Old Theories and New Hypotheses." Comparative Politics 5: 359–392.

Gurr, Ted (1980). *Handbook of Political Conflict*. New York: Free Press.

Gurr, Ted, & Duvall, Raymond (1973). Civil conflict in the 1960's: A reciprocal theoretical system with parameter estimates. *Comparative Political Studies 6,* 135–170.

Hagstrom, Warren O. (1965). *The Scientific Community*. New York: Basic Books.

Herberle, Rudolf (1951). *Social Movements: An Introduction to Political Sociology*. New York: Appleton-Century-Crofts.

Hibbs, Douglass (1973). *Mass Political Violence: A Cross-National Causal Analysis*. New York: Wiley.

Hobsbawn, E.J. (1959). *Primitive Rebels*. Manchester, England: Manchester University Press.

Hoffer, Eric (1951). *True Believer*. New York: American Library.

Hopper, Rex (1950). The revolutionary process: A frame of reference for the study of revolutionary social movements. *Social Forces 28,* 270–279.

Huntington, Samuel (1968). *Political Order in Changing Societies*. New Haven, CT: Yale University Press.

Isaac, Larry, & Kelly, William (1981). Racial insurgency, the state and welfare expansion. *American Journal of Sociology 86,* 1348–1386.

Isaac, Larry, Mutran, E., & Stryker, Sheldon (1980). Political protest orientations among black and white adults. *American Sociological Review 45,* 191–213.

James, David (1981). *The Transformation of Local State and Class Structures and Resistance to the Civil Rights Movement in the South*. Unpublished Doctoral Dissertation, Madison: University of Wisconsin.

Jenkins, J. Craig (1982). The transformation of a constituency into a movement. In Jo Freeman (Ed.), *Social Movements of the Sixties and Seventies*. New York: Longman.

Jenkins, J. Craig (1983). Resource mobilization theory and the study of social movements. *Annual Review of Sociology 9,* 527–553.

Jenkins, J. Craig, & Perrow, Charles (1977). Insurgency of the powerless: Farm worker movements, 1946–1972. *American Sociological Review 42,* 249–268.

Keniston, Kenneth (1968). *Young Radicals*. New York: Harcourt, Brace, and World.

Kerpelman, Larry C. (1972). *Activists and Nonactivists*. New York: Behavioral Publications.

Killian, Lewis (1964). Social Movements. In Robert Faris (Ed.), *Handbook of Modern Sociology*. Chicago: Rand McNally.

Killian, Lewis (1983, September). Interview.

King, C. Wendell (1956). *Social Movements in the United States*. New York: Random House.

Kornhauser, William (1959). *The Politics of Mass Society*. New York: Free Press.

Lang, Kurt, & Lang, Gladys (1961). *Collective Dynamics*. New York: Crowell.

Lang, Kurt, & Lang, Gladys. (1983, September.) Interview.

Le Bon, Gustave (1960). *The Crowd*. New York: Viking.

Legget, John C. (1964). Economic insecurity and working-class consciousness. *American Sociological Review 29,* 226-234.

Lenin, V.I. (1975). *What is to be Done?* Peking, China: Foreign Language Press.

Liebman, Robert C., & Wirthnow, Robert (1983). *New Christian Right: Mobilization and Legitimation*. New York: Aldine.

Lipset, Seymour Martin. (1963). *Political Man*. Garden City, Doubleday.

Lipset, Seymour Martin, & Raab, E. (1978). *Politics of Unreason: Right-wing Extremism in America 1970-1977*. Chicago: University of Chicago Press.

Lipsky, Michael (1968). Protest as a political resource. *American Political Science Review 62,* 1144-1158.

Marx, Gary (1974). Thoughts on a neglected category of social movement participant: The agent provocateur and the informant. *American Journal of Sociology 80,* 402-442.

Marx, Gary (1979). External efforts to damage or facilitate social movements: Some patterns, explanations, outcomes, and complications. In John D. McCarthy & Mayer Zald (Eds.), *Dynamics of Social Movements*. Cambridge, MA: Winthrop.

Marx, Gary, & Wood, James L. (1975). Strands of theory and research in collective behavior. *Annual Review of Sociology 1,* 363-428.

Marx, Karl, & Engels, Friedrich (1968). Manifesto of the Communist Party. *Selected Works 1,* 31-63.

Marwell, Gerald, & Ames, Ruth (1979). Experiments on the provision of public goods. *American Journal of Sociology 84,* 1335-1360.

McAdam, Doug (1982). *Political Process and the Development of Black Insurgency, 1930-1970*. Chicago: University of Chicago Press.

McCarthy, John (1983, September). Interview.

McCarthy, John D., & Zald, Mayer N. (1973). *The Trends of Social Movements in America: Professionalization and Resource Mobilization*. Morristown, NJ: General Learning Press.

McCarthy, John D., & Zald, Mayer N. (1977). Resource mobilization and social mvements: A partial theory. *American Journal of Sociology 82,* 1212-1241.

McDougall, W. (1908). *Introduction to Social Psychology*. London: Methuen.

McPhail, Clark (1973). The assembling process: A theoretical and empirical examination. *American Sociological Review 38,* 721-735.

McPhail, Clark, & Wohlstein, Ronald T. (1983). Individual and collective behaviors within gatherings, demonstratons and riots. *Annual Review of Sociology 9,* 579-600.

Merton, Robert K. (1973). *The Sociology of Science: Theoretical and Empirical Investigations*. Chicago: University of Chicago Press.

Michels, Robert (1962). *Political Parties*. New York: Free Press.

Mill, John Stuart (1950). *Utilitarianism, Liberty, and Repressive Government*. London: J.M. Dent.

Mills, C. Wright (1956). Power Elite. New York: Oxford University Press.

Molotch, Harvey (1979). Media and movements. In John D. McCarthy & Mayer Zald (Eds.), *The Dynamics of Social Movements*. Cambridge, MA: Winthrop.

Moore, Barrington, Jr. (1966). *Social Origins of Dictatorship and Democracy*. Boston: Beacon.

Morris, Aldon D. (1981). Black southern student sit-in movement: An analysis of internal organization. *American Sociological Review 46,* 755-767.

Morris, Aldon D. (1984). *Origins of the Civil Rights Movement: Black Communities Organizing for Change.* New York: Free Press.

Mosca, Gaetano (1939). *The Mind and Society.* Andrew Bongiorno (trans.). New York: Harcourt, Brace.

Oberschall, Anthony (1973). *Social Conflict and Social Movements.* Englewood Cliffs, NJ: Prentice-Hall.

Oberschall, Anthony (1978a). Theories of Social Conflict. *Annual Review of Sociology 4,* 291–315.

Oberschall, Anthony (1978b). The decline of the 1960s social movements. *Research in Social Movements, Conflict, and Change 1,* 257–289.

Oberschall, Anthony (1983, September). Interview.

Olson, Mancur (1963). Rapid growth as a destabilizing force. *Journal of Economic History 23,* 529–552.

Olson, Mancur (1965). *The Logic of Collective Action.* Cambridge, MA: Harvard University Press.

Orum, Anthony (1972). *Black Students in Protest.* Washington, DC: American Sociological Association.

Orum, Anthony (1978). *Introduction to Political Sociology: The Social Anatomy of the Body Politic.* Englewood Cliffs, NJ: Prentice-Hall.

Paige, Jeffery (1971). Political orientation and riot participation. *American Sociological Review 36,* 810–120.

Paige, Jeffery (1975). *Agrarian Revolution.* New York: Free Press.

Pareto, Wilfredo (1935). *The Mind and Society.* Andrew Bongiorno (trans.). New York: Harcourt, Brace.

Park, Robert (1928). Human migration and the marginal man. *American Journal of Sociology 33,* 881–893.

Park, Robert, & Burgess, Ernest. (1921). *Introduction to the Science of Sociology.* Chicago: University of Chicago Press.

Parvin, Michael (1973). Economic determinants of political unrest: An economic approach. *Journal of Conflict Resolution 17,* 271–296.

Patinkin, Don. (1983). Multiple discoveries and the central message. *American Journal of Sociology 89,* 306–323.

Perrow, Charles (1984, February). Letter to Aldon Morris.

Pettigrew, Thomas (1964). *A Profile of the Negro American.* Princeton, NJ: Van Nostrand.

Pilisuk, Marc, & Hayden, Thomas (1965). Is there a military industrial complex which prevents peace? *Journal of Social Issues 21,* 67–117.

Pinard, Maurice (1983). *From deprivation to mobilization. Parts 1 and 2.* Papers presented at the annual meetings of the American Sociological Association in Detroit, Michigan.

Pinard, Maurice, & Hamilton, Richard (1977). The independence issue and the polarization of the electorate. *Canadian Journal of Political Science 10,* 215–259.

Piven, Frances Fox, & Cloward, Richard (1977). *Poor People's Movement.* New York: Pantheon.

Ritzer, George (1983). *Sociological Theory.* New York: Knopf.

Ross, E.A. (1916). *Social Psychology.* New York: MacMillan.

Rude, George (1964). *The Crowd in History.* New York: Wiley.

Runciman, W.G. (1966). *Relative Deprivation and Social Justice,* Berkeley, CA: University of California Press.

Salisbury, Robert H. (1969). An exchange theory of interest groups. *Midwest Journal of Political Science 13,* 1–32.

Selznick, Philip (1960). *The Organizational Weapon.* Glencoe, IL: Free Press.

Sighele, Scipio (1898). *Psychologie des sectes.* Paris: M. Giard et Cie.

Skocpol, Theda (1979) *States and Social Revolution.* Cambridge, MA: Cambridge University Press.

Smelser, Neil (1962). *Theory of Collective Behavior.* New York: Free Press.

Smelser, Neil (1968). Social and psychological dimensions of collective behavior. In *Essays in Sociological Explanation.* Englewood Cliffs, NJ: Prentice-Hall.

Smelser, Neil (1983, September). Interview.

Smith, Adam (1910). *The Wealth of Nations.* London: Dent.

Snow, David, Zurcher, Louis, & Peters R. (1981). Victory celebrations as theatre: A dramaturgial approach to crowd behavior. *Symbolic Interaction 4,* 21–42.

Snyder, David, & Kelly, William R. (1976). Industrial violence in Italy, 1878–1903. *American Journal of Sociology 83,* 131–162.

Soboul, Albert (1956). The French rural community in the eighteenth and nineteenth centuries. *Past and Present 10,* 78–95.

Tarde, Gabriel (1903). *The Laws of Imitation.* E.C. Parsons (trans.). New York: Holt.

Tarrow, Sidney (n.d.). Struggling to Reform: Social movements and policy change during cycles of protest. *Western Societies Papers: Cornell Studies in International Affairs.*

Tilly, Charles (1973). Does modernization breed revolution? *Comparative Politics 5,* 425–447.

Tilly, Charles (1978). *From Mobilization to Revolution.* Reading, MA: Addison-Wesley.

Tilly, Charles (1979). Social movements and national politics. *CRSO Working Paper 197.* Ann Arbor, MI.

Tilly, Charles (1983, September). Interview.

Toch, Hans (1965). *The Psychology of Social Movements.* Indianapolis: Bobbs-Merrill.

Turner, Ralph (1964) Collective Behavior. In Robert E.L. Faris (Ed.), *Handbook of Modern Sociology.* Chicago: Rand McNally.

Turner, Ralph (1981). Collective behavior and resource mobilization as approaches to social movements: Issues and continuities. *Research in Social Movements, Conflict and Change 4,* 1–24.

Turner, Ralph (1983, September). Interviews.

Turner, Ralph, & Killian, Lewis (1972). *Collective Behavior,* 2nd ed (1s ed., 1957). Englewood Cliffs, NJ: Prentice-Hall.

Walker, Jack, L. (1983). Origins and maintenance of interest groups in America. *American Political Science Review 77,* 390–407.

Walsh, Edward J., & Warland, Ren H. (1983). Social movement involvement in the wake of a nuclear accident: Activists and free riders in the TMI area. *American Sociological Review 48,* 764–780.

Webb, Keith, Zimmerman, Ekkart, Marsh, Michael, Aish, Anne-Marie, Mironesco, Christina, Mitchell, Christopher, Morlino, Leonardo, & Walton, James (1983). Etiology and outcomes of protest: New European perspectives. *American Behavioral Scientists 26,* 311–331.

Weber, Max (1947). *Theory of Social and Economic Organizations.* Talcott Parsons (Ed.). New York: Free Press.

Weber, Max. (1968). *Economy and Society.* Guenther Roth & Claus Wittich (Eds.). New York: Bedminster Press.

Weingart, Peter (1974). On a sociological theory of scientific change. Richard Whitley (Ed.), *Social Processes of Scientific Development.* Boston: Routledge and Kegan Paul.

Weller, Jack, & Quarantelli, Ernest L. (1973). Neglected characteristics of collective behavior. *American Journal of Sociology 79,* 665–685.

Wolf, Eric (1966). *Peasants.* Englewood Cliffs, NJ: Prentice-Hall.

Zald, Mayer (1983, September). Interview.

Zald, Mayer (1984, February). Memo to Aldon Morris.

Zald, Mayer N., & Ash, Roberta (1966). Social movement organizatoins: Growth, decay, and change. *Social Forces 44,* 327–341.

Zimmerman, Ekkart (1980) Macro-comparative research on political protest. In T. Gurr (Ed.), *Handbook of Political Conflict.* New York: Free Press.

Zurcher, Louis, & Snow, David (1981). Collective behavior: Social movements. In Morris Rosenberg & Ralph Turner (Eds.), *Social Psychology: Sociological Perspectives.* New York: Basic Books.

Chapter 6

Politics and Communication

Robert G. Meadow

Annenberg School of Communications
University of Southern California

I. INTRODUCTION

In recent years, it has become fashionable among popular critics of the media, and even among political and other social scientists, to describe how television has eroded the electoral system. Electronic media, we are told, have been responsible for general trends, such as the decline of the party system (Polsby, 1980; Everson, 1982) or the rise of political inefficacy (Robinson, 1976), as well as for specific events, ranging from the electoral success of John Kennedy, following the televised debates, to the drop in public support for the Vietnam War, to the resignation of Richard Nixon during the Watergate hearings, to the election of "the great communicator", Ronald Reagan. Surely anything that can be responsible for these diverse activities must be an important determinant of political behavior (see Ranney, 1983).

Author after author has laid the transformation at the foot of new media. Rubin (1981) writes that media coverage of the primaries has contributed to changes in the structure of the political parties by rearranging the influence of the political elites. The impact of television has significantly changed the ability of the parties to manage conflict.

Barber (1978) writes of how media define and select "serious" presidential candidates. Tannenbaum and Kostrich (1983) write how election night broadcasts of returns effect turnout. And M. Robinson (1976) holds television responsible not only for the "video malaise" of the electorate, but for the simultaneous growth of social liberalism and political conservatism (Robinson, 1977). Perhaps Saldich (1979, p. ix) summarizes the complaints best, writing that "television has restructured the political process by weakening parties and conventions, personalizing power, [and] increasing campaign costs." Yet to limit the discussion of the relationship between politics and communication to the short-term effects of television on politics is to severely understate the depth of the connections between politics and communication.

The linkages of politics and communication are far more complex. Messages from the political environment enter into our private worlds every day. News broadcasts provide limited information on a portion of the events that have occurred. Campaign messages arrive in our mailboxes or, in the form of political commercials, interrupt our entertainment programs. Public service announcements urge us to prevent forest fires or conserve energy. These messages come from a variety of sources. Most frequently, perhaps, explicit political messages come to us in the form of news from the political world. But messages are also found in rituals and symbols as well. The police patrol car cruising the neighborhood may provide us with a message of the stability of the social order. A simple hand signal from a person wearing a badge and a uniform can stop a ten-ton truck. The pledge of allegience in school enables us to ritualistically reconfirm our commitment to the regime. Popular cultural forms such as television entertainment may offer us graphic portrayals of the horrors of nuclear war. Governments may require that we communicate with them in a language that may not be our native tongue. And governments may send a flurry of diplomatic messages back and forth while negotiating a peace settlement.

All of these activities and more are part of the relationship between politics and communication. The purpose of this chapter is to explore the relationship between politics and communication by taking a broader view of both politics and communication than has been taken by researchers focused narrowly on media effects during elections.

Regardless of what our definition of politics may be, politics and communication are intimately intertwined. If politics is about power, then those who wield power must convey this. If politics is about participation, then citizens must present their desires to leaders. If politics is about legitimacy, then symbols of this legitimacy must emerge. And if politics is about choice, then policy options must be made known. Each of these (and other) conceptualizations of politics has a communication linkage that goes beyond the simple concern of the effects of television during elections. A broader view of the reciprocal relations between politics and communication will emerge from this perspective.

This chapter will be divided into four sections. First, I shall work toward a definition of the relationship between politics and communication. The second and major portion of the chapter will review the origins and major approaches to the study of politics and communication. Third, I will identify the most common theories employed in the study of politics and communication. Finally, I will examine some of the trends in politics and communication research. Although much political communication research will be cited and referenced, this chapter is not intended to serve solely as a literature review of politics and communication research. Adequate summaries can be found elsewhere (Kraus & Davis, 1976; Nimmo, 1977, 1981; Sanders & Kaid, 1978; Larson & Weigele, 1979; Jackson-Beeck & Kraus, 1980; Mansfield & Weaver, 1981). And a *Handbook of Political Communication,* which contains essays and a number of literature reviews, has already been written (see Nimm Sanders, 1981).

II.   DEFINITION

Most researchers looking at the relationship between politics and communication have considered political behavior as the dependent variable, concerning themselves generally with, as Sanders and Kaid (1978) suggest, the "role of communication in the acquisition and distribution of power." Few have considered that communication may be the dependent variable in the relationship, but there is ample evidence to suggest that communication itself — be it the communication policy expressed by a regulatory body, or the recognition of a second language as an official language — may depend on the political environment. In this chapter, I choose to consider the relationship between politics and communication from both perspectives, recognizing that political processes, behaviors, and institutions have implications for patterns of communication, and that communication processes, behaviors, and institutions have important consequences for political systems and relations. Thus, for our purposes, politics and communication is concerned with communication activity, such as the exchange of messages or symbols that to a significant extent have been shaped by or have consequences for the functioning of political systems.

III.   THE ORIGINS OF POLITICS AND COMMUNICATION
STUDIES

In their overview of political communication research, Nimmo and Sanders identify seven key areas that have been the focus of inquiry in politics and communication. Historically, from Aristotle's time to the present, speech and rhetoric traditionally have been a part of politics and communication. The making of a political orator, the motives of speakers, and analysis of the styles of public discourse developed with an eye toward understanding persuasion of audiences have been at the center of this mode of inquiry. But speech and rhetorical analysis have been inaccessible to political scientists in part because analysis has been tied to the formal characteristics of speech and the uniqueness of rhetorical interpretations rather than to general laws of social behavior. Indeed, rhetorical analysis has come under considerable criticism from Trent (1975) and others who identified the theoretical and methodological problems of formal speech analysis.

A second type of inquiry has been propaganda analysis, and its linkage to public opinion (Smith, Lasswell, & Casey, 1946). Mass movements in Europe raised suspicions in democratic circles about the average citizen's ability to make wise political choices. The rise of dictatorships in Europe led observers such as Harold Lasswell (1927) to question how symbols emerged for easy manipulation by emerging leaders. Assumptions developed about the passivity of audiences, which enabled them to be manipulated. Walter Lippmann (1925) suggested that since mass media failed to deliver information to citizens, elites could conjure up "phantom publics" who they claimed to support their positions. The result was a manipulated mass public, with one-way communication between elites and nonelites.

As all these fears about the wisdom of the common person were growing, social psychological researchers (Hovland, Lumsdaine, & Sheffield, 1949; Hovland, Janis, & Kelley, 1953) were finding that there were identifiable communication variables which could enhance the potential to manipulate audiences. In large part, this concern for manipulation of audiences still characterizes much research into communication and politics.

Many of the earliest empirical communications studies used the political environment as the laboratory for testing communications effects. In particular, voting studies were used as typical information campaigns to determine short-range media effects. These studies asked the simple question that even today guides politics and communication research: Do campaign communications make a difference on voting choice?

A fifth area for political communication research cited by Nimmo and Sanders is the government–news media relationship. Questions about the role of the press and the nature of the relations between public officials and reporters still abound. Rarely a year goes by without a new account of the news gathering processes, or of the government–news media relations.

Sixth, Nimmo and Sanders refer to functional and systems analysis of political communication derived from the comparative politics analysis of the 1960s. Structures and functions of political communication across systems are compared in these studies by Fagen (1966), Almond (Almond & Verba, 1963; Almond & Powell, 1966), and others.

Finally, Nimmo and Sanders refer to developments in political communication derived from changes in technology. The arrival of new media are shown to play a role in transforming politics; new techniques of policial campaigning and new research methods to enhance our understanding of political communications are lumped together under the heading of technology.

The identification of these seven areas, though not without merit, fails to reflect the relative attention paid to each area. Moreover, these seven areas do not identify the variety of assumptions and theories that have been the basis of most research in politics and communication. And these seven areas do not exhaust the frameworks which have been used to explore the relationship of politics and communication.

To some extent, the Nimmo and Sanders outline understates the contribution of Harold Lasswell (1948), who, more than any other political scientist, set the tone for much of the modern politics and communication research. His basic question of "Who says what in which channel to whom and with what effect" neatly packaged the issues for researchers. Much of the existing research has already been categorized through slight refinements to the question. Indeed most previous reviews of the political communication literature (Nimmo, 1977; Sanders & Kaid, 1978; Mansfield & Weaver, 1981) have outlined the existing research through an updated version of the basic questions. These reviews have looked at the "who" question by considering "political communicators," whom they define as politicians, journalists and activists. The "what" question has been studied by looking at political messages, including the languages of politics, the symbols used, and the techniques used to transmit political messages. The "channel" question has led to research on both interpersonal and mass media, including studies that have looked at the relative effectiveness of electronic, print, or interpersonal sources of information for message transmission and reception. The "to whom" and "with what effect" questions have been combined to underlie audience research focused on the roots of varying responses to political stimuli.

In their review of the literature, Jackson-Beeck and Kraus (1980) show that an overwhelming plurality of political communication studies emphasize the effects questions. But despite decades of research there are still no definitive answers as to what constitutes media effects. Increasingly, studies find new intervening variables or contingent conditions to modify the question of effects. Yet basic processes to link theoretically communications and political behavior remain misunderstood. Even though hundreds of studies can be identified to fit under the Lasswellian questions, it is remarkable that the range of political activities in which the questions are put forth is so limited. Most studies seek to answer the Lasswellian questions during the course of election campaigns. The result has been less research and theoretical progress than we might have hoped.

For all practical purposes, political communication research has been the study of mass mediated messages about politics. Researchers developed strategies to look at the "effects" of political messages on a wide range of political variables from party identification to information about political candidates, to voting choice. For the first decade of this research (Klapper, 1960), the results were more or less the same: direct effects of exposure to campaign information were limited because voters would selectively expose themselves to information from candidates toward whom they were favorably disposed. Although other important concepts such as the two-step flow of opinion emerged from these early studies to spur communication research, the investigation of mass media effects during elections defined politics and communication research for over a decade.

That there has been less research and theoretical advancement than desired does not mean that research approaches have been altogether absent. In culling the literature elsewhere, (Meadow, 1980b) I have identified six different theoretical and research approaches to the study of politics and communication. But in reviewing the voluminous American literature for this chapter, it is clear that most researchers have chosen to pursue one of three basic perspectives on politics and communication. First and most common has been the event-based research, characterized by considerable empirical, but often atheoretical work. Second has been the symbolic–linguistic approach, more theoretical than event research, but less empirical. Third have been the organizational and institutional studies of the communication patterns and organization of the communications industries and government communication policies and institutions. In the next sections, these three research traditions are reviewed.

IV. EVENT-BASED RESEARCH IN POLITICS AND COMMUNICATION

Despite the claims of Nimmo and Sanders that there is a broader tradition of political communication research, findings in the early voting behavior literature (Lazarsfeld, Berelson, & Gaudet, 1948; Berelson, Lazarsfeld, & McPhee, 1954), gave the discipline an empirical, election-based focus before the development of underlying theory. Perhaps more than anything, the quest for data without well-grounded theory has characterized much of the research since that time.

The findings of this early "Columbia School" research were simple: voters make firm decisions early in campaigns, and mass media reinforce those decisions. Mass media were shown to have little influence on changing voter intentions; indeed when voters did change their minds, it was largely because of personal influence. Subsequent research by "Michigan School" researchers (Campbell, Gurin, & Miller, 1954; Campbell, Converse, Miller, & Stokes, 1960) implicitly supported these findings by failing to inquire extensively about media influences on campaigns until the Center for Political Studies decided to incorporate media questions on the national election studies 20 years later.

These findings of no or very limited effects were somewhat problematic for social science researchers (though not for journalists: Katz, 1978), because conventional wisdom had it that there must be more direct effects than reinforcement alone. Fortunately, data became available (Nie, Verba, & Petrocik, 1976; DeVries & Tarrance, 1972) that suggested there was no evidence that media had no direct effects. Instead, voters were more partisan and less concerned with issues in the 1940s and 1950s than in the 1960s and 1970s, and information from mass media played a more significant role with respect to issues than partisanship.

Since 1970, there have been hundred of studies on the general effects of mass media during election campaigns, each specifying a new set of conditions enhancing or limiting media effects. Suffice it to say that a deep understanding is limited because the effects of media during election campaigns vary tremendously, depending on prior information, motivation, interpersonal interaction, predispositions, socialization, partisanship, level of election, media use, race, sex, education, social status, and dozens of other variables. Many of the smaller additional studies are cited and reviewed by Kraus and Davis (1976) and O'Keefe and Atwood (1981); recent books by Graber (1980), and Patterson (1980) cover the topic as well.

Without doubt, these research efforts offer insights into political communication as long as the study of political communication is limited to the effects of mass communication on political behavior. Yet following several decades of exploration, as more and more studies have been completed, political communication researchers are increasingly confident of only one thing—their uncertainty about the effects on voting decisions of exposure to campaign information. Continuing additional research in this direction would certainly yield only marginal further insights about the conditions under which one type of information exposure effects political choice.

Most event studies focus on the relationship of election campaign news to voting choice. But the concern for the effects of campaign news on voters spurred a second tradition of research—investigations into campaign news itself. Although even the earliest studies incorporated content analyses (Lazarsfeld, Berelson, & Gaudet, 1948), and numerous research efforts looked at the relationship between election news coverage and editorial preference, (Klein & Maccoby, 1954; Stempel, 1961, 1965, 1969; Graber, 1971) later studies were either cross-media comparisons (Meadow, 1973) or based entirely on content-analytic research of television news. A somewhat acrimonious debate about the alleged anti-Republican bias in television news (in marked contrast to the pro-Republican biases found in the Columbia studies) begun during the Nixon administration led to a series of studies focused not on the effects of campaign news, but on the texture of the news itself (Efron, 1972; Frank, 1973; Hofstetter, 1976; Adams & Schreibman, 1978; Adams, 1983; Robinson & Sheehan, 1983). Some, though not all of these studies concluded that there were indeed biases in the news, but they were not partisan or political biases. Instead, in both print and electronic media, structural and institutional biases limited coverage to trivia and campaign hoopla, or in the case of Congress, incumbents (Clarke & Evans, 1983). Qualitative studies (Barber, 1978) described the crucial role of news organizations and journalists in identifying "front-running" and serious candidates. These studies offered us few insights into political behaviors, but they provided some basis for understanding what messages formed the political terrain on which voters traveled on their way to the polls.

Beyond the general media effects during campaigns, other specific campaign events have been considered in the quest for knowledge about the media's role in campaigns. Numerous studies have considered the effects of campaign debates (Ellsworth, 1965; Kraus, 1962, 1979; Bishop, Meadow, & Jackson-Beeck, 1978; Ranney, 1979; Ritter, 1981). But the evidence shows the effect of debates on voter choice is limited. Again the quest for contingent conditions characterizes most of the research. Perhaps most intriguing about all the studies (see the reviews by Katz & Feldman, 1962; Sears & Chaffee, 1979) is that there is increasing evidence that the direct effects on a voter of exposure to a debate is less important than the effects of interpretation of the debate event by news media commentators (Lang & Lang, 1978, Steeper, 1978, Graber, 1984).

Other campaign events which have been studied include exposure to televised paid political advertising. Once again, developing a list of contingent conditions seems to have been the fruit of this research. The credibility of the narrator (Anderoli & Worchel, 1978; Meyer & Donohue, 1973), the duration of the ad (O'Keefe & Sheinkopf 1974; Kaid & Sanders, 1978), the video techniques used (Meadow & Sigelman, 1982), viewer involvement (Rothschild, 1978; Hofstetter & Buss, 1980) or motivation (Garramone, 1983), among other variables, might have some bearing on the effectiveness of political advertising. Even then, the effects might vary from increased cognition (Patterson & McClure, 1976) about the issues to affective or behavioral effects. Reviewing all of the literature on political advertising conducted over two decades, Kaid (1981) could only come to six very weak conclusions: (a) political advertising contains issue information; (b) channel variables interact with source variables in that some sources are more effective on one medium than other; (c) advertising overcomes partisan selective exposure; (d) advertising is most effective when voter involvement is low; (e) advertising has important cognitive effects on candidates and issues; and (f) there are some influences on voting behavior.

Still other campaign events have been investigated, including the activities ranging from literature drops (Miller and Richey, 1980) to the effects of broadcasting on the west coast election returns from the east coast (Fuchs, 1965, 1966; Lang & Lang, 1968; Mendelsohn & Crespi, 1970; Wolfinger &

Linquitti, 1981; Epstein & Strom, 1981; Dubois, 1983; Tannenbaum & Kostrich, 1983). The mixed results suggest that the findings of these studies are inconclusive.

Not content with mixed findings about the effect of campaign events, researchers have also looked at the coverage or effects of other political events, ranging from general television coverage of Middle East diplomacy (Adams, 1981) to international affairs (Adams, 1982), televised Watergate hearings (Lang & Lang, 1983; McLeod, Brown, Becker, & Ziemke, 1977; Robinson, 1974), riots (Singer, 1970), energy crises (Dangerfield, McCartney, & Starcher, 1975), assassinations (Hofstetter, 1969; Mendelsohn, 1964), bombings (Lever, 1969), and press conferences (Paletz & Entman, 1981).

Reviewing all of this literature, it is safe to say that there are some observable political behaviors that appear to be, under specified conditions, correlated with media coverage of certain events. But no comprehensive theory has emerged to explain these correlations. Do voters or citizens respond to the media coverage of political phenomena, or are they responding to the phenomena themselves? Thus far, research projects, with few exceptions, have not been designed to answer this question. Research has been piecemeal, looking at an election here or there, or a specific communication event. There have been few studies that have much to say about enduring effects. There have been fewer studies that view communication as an interactive process. There has been little research that offers clues to the cumulative consequences of exposure to information from a variety of sources. And perhaps most problematic, for event-based research, there has been no theory to guide research. Other approaches to politics and communication have been more theory driven.

V. SYMBOLIC POLITICS, LANGUAGE, AND COMMUNICATION

A second major approach to politics and communication has been the symbolic approach. Politics, like communication, can be viewed largely as a symbolic interchange. The origins of leadership and the maintenance of unequal distributions of social rewards are exercised through the manipulation of symbols and the distribution of symbolic rewards. The processes through which these symbols are created and disseminated serve as the focus for this perspective on politics and communication. Unlike event-based research, the emphasis is less on individual political behavior, and more on systemic qualities.

Political reality has been described through symbolic politics. Elites (organized participants who perceive of political participation instrumentally) gain successful outcomes over the unorganized spectators for whom politics is largely expressive. The result is that tangible rewards go to elites, while symbolic rewards are offered to maintain mass quiescence. Symbolic political struggles may replace instrumental politics. Evidence on some social conflicts (Gusfield, 1963) has shown political movements often to be symbolic.

Symbols in the political processes have a lengthy history. Beginning from the psychoanalytic tradition, Lasswell (1935) demonstrated how symbols help to synthesize meanings for individuals, and help them to attribute meaning to social interaction. Simultaneously, they preserve social stability by communicating power and authority relations.

Modern students of political symbols have recognized the power of symbols and the mythology and rituals accompanying them. Most influential has been the work of Murray Edelman (1964, 1971, 1977). Edelman chooses to emphasize the linguistic aspects of political symbols, drawing a distinction between referential symbols (Sapir, 1934), which are shorthand signs to identify objects (e.g., a journalist referring to the White House as a way of invoking the president and his staff), and condensational symbols, which have more ambiguous and emotional meanings. The flag, for example, can act as a referential symbol, standing for a country. As a condensational symbol, it may represent patriotism, love of country, and similar values. Symbols serve several political functions, including enhancing the ease of comprehending politics. In the absence of symbols, politics may be seen as too complicated, too abstract, and too difficult an activity in which to engage.

Recently, other scholars such as Combs (1980) and Nimmo (Nimmo & Combs, 1980) have chosen to focus on the symbolic basis of political drama. Deriving some of their insights from Burke (1945, 1950), Duncan (1968), and European literary theorists, these researchers have taken a semiotic approach to analyzing political events.

Unlike other areas of politics and communication research, the study of political symbols has been more descriptive and explanatory than empirical. Only a few researchers have even attempted to empirically measure the growth and potency of symbols. Prothro and Grigg, (1960), for example, found that abstract symbols were central in holding together the social fabric. When abstract, symbolic principles were stripped of their abstractions and citizens were forced to confront their underlying meanings, social consensus appeared to break down. Other recent research by Elder and Cobb (1983) explores anew how symbols effect political outcomes.

Symbols, of course, are intertwined with language. Both are ultimately concerned with social control. Language is viewed as a vehicle through which access to political processes and institutions is limited. Politics, for some analysts, is largely a matter of words (Graber, 1976) or talk (Bell, 1975). Negotiations are held, speeches are made, debates take place, and bargains are struck. All political talk takes place through languages, which are media through which ideas are symbolically expressed.

Perhaps there is no better or more appropriate example of the relationship between language and politics than that offered by George Orwell. In *1984,*

Orwell describes "Newspeak" as a language molded to impose thoughts on speakers. To control language, Orwell argues, is to control thought. The abolition of certain terms such as freedom, liberty, and honesty presumably eliminates them as values, and raises the question of whether or not it is possible to recognize concepts if there is no term for them. Writing more in the tradition of political philosophy, Shapiro (1981) has suggested that language, in political discourse, does not simply enable us to understand or describe politics. In many ways, he argues, it constitutes politics.

Two distinct lines of research have characterized the study of language and politics. One has been the development and elaboration of control models. In this line of research, language is seen not only as capable of constraining thought, it can also limit political action. Politics is conducted in a unique language. Proponents of a language-based theory of social control such as Mueller (1975) argue that decision-makers in society carry out their activities with unique languages. A specialized vocabulary, both literally and figuratively, is required in the political arena, but certain groups (the linguistically deprived) who speak in what Bernstein (1962) calls restricted codes, do not have the required vocabulary to participate effectively in politics. These groups are politically inarticulate, unable to present their demands to government decision-makers. Groups most likely to be politically inarticulate are those already socially, educationally, economically, or otherwise deprived. Their limited vocabularies, needs for immediate gratification, insensitivity to generalization, and otherwise arrested communications effectively precludes dialogue with middle-class politicians or more educated citizens.

Elites who are outside of decision-making circles speak in elaborated codes, in essence speaking the same languages as decision-makers. Hence their demands are heard and understood by authorities. As a result, political relationships and systems are stabilized, with a bias toward maintenance of the status quo. Differential access to the political world follows from the enhanced communication of the elites, while political power is maintained by elites because no voices can be raised to press demands or challenge legitimacy. Occasionally, there are those who are politically bilingual, able to communicate with the politically inarticulate as well as the articulate. Yet it may be the case that those who are politically bilingual are more similar to the decision-making, middle-class articulates by virtue of their training and socialization. Moreover, the very act of translating demands of the inarticulate to the language of the articulate may impose a structure on those demands not desired by the inarticulate.

Occasionally, political inarticulates make demands known without acquiring traditional political language. Indeed, much nontraditional political participation (strikes, riots, and terrorist activities) provide new languages for political discourse, and offer the politically inarticulate modes of expression with which the traditionally articulate are uncomfortable. Yet according to Gitlin (1980), dominant elites seek to maintain ideological (and to a lesser extent, linguistic) hegemony not only by rejecting new modes of discourse by breaking up demonstrations with police force, but also by linguistically undermining the seriousness of attempts to create a new language of political discourse. In general, the costs of nontraditional participation are high because they are illegal and/or repressed. Ultimately, in the absence of revolutionary success, changes are negotiated, so the need for political articulateness still stands.

Edelman's (1964) work on the hortatory, administrative, bargaining, and legal language used in political discourse has attempted to demonstrate the relationships between language and social control. Later, his work drew a bridge between the creation of political symbols, and the creative use of political language (Edelman, 1977). Language use and metaphor have been shown to vary even within political regimes, depending on the political conditions at the time (Frank, 1972).

Although sociolinguists have often cited the relationship between language and social class and social control (Tonkin, 1979), few have written as clearly of the symbolic political hierarchies that emerge from language use as clearly as has Lakoff (1974). Her work on gender-based power relations suggests that men have dominated women because of language differences resulting from differential socialization. But political domination through language is not limited to the differences between men and women. Social hierarchies established through the use of colonial languages in independent nations have been drawn by political scientists such as Laitin (1977). Indeed, the linguistic perspective on politics and communication offers the opportunity to look at how politics effects communication policy.

Although not always conducted by political scientists, there have been numerous studies (Mackey, 1979) that have focused on the political aspects of language policy, particularly with respect to the creation of official languages and bilingual planning. Virtually all these studies (Lieberson, 1970; Savard, 1975; Weinstein, 1982) have concluded that familiarity with the dominant language has been the basis for all political and economic distinctions. Major linguistic conflicts in nations as diverse as India, Nigeria, Canada, Belgium and the Soviet Union, and other linguistic conflicts, such as over bilingual education in the United States, testify to the political significance attached to language use. Deutsch (1953) has argued that patterns of communication, and particularly language use, define political boundries. Excluding natural geographic borders, language continues to be the basis for most national political boundries.

Overall, there are a variety of linkages among symbols, language, and politics. To summarize, language is necessary to express symbolically political relationships such as power and authority for maintaining social control and stability. Through the development of specialized languages for political discourse, political outsiders may be denied access to politics. And perhaps most important are the symbolic aspects of language use, for language expresses status, values, and hierarchies that may be independent of message substance.

VI. ORGANIZATIONAL AND INSTITUTIONAL APPROACHES TO POLITICS AND COMMUNICATION

After event-based election studies, no research in politics and communication has been as popular as have organizational and institutional studies. This research has focused on the political and communication organizations and institutions that are responsible for production and transmission of messages, and the relationships among these organizations. The two most actively studied communicating institutions have been governments and news organizations.

Government communications have been looked at a number of ways. The organization of intragovernmental and intergovernmental patterns of information exchange has occupied some researchers, while others have focused on political concepts, and the role that communications plays in maintaining political relationships.

Many important political activities such as the expansion of, and eventual management of conflict have led to the creation of structures to enhance communication. Schattschneider's (1960) model of conflict expansion, and its later elaboration by Cobb and Elder (1983) implies that political organizations are built around their capability to mobilize through effective communications. Political development as well has depended on the creation of communications institutions as much as it has on economic development. Although the ideological underpinnings of early development work (see Lerner, 1959) have been questioned, there have been few arguments with the claim that there can be no political development independent of evolving communication infrastructures.

As Deutsch (1963) points out, one of the most important functions of government decision-makers is to manage information, and to survey the environment to preserve the system from internal and external threats. The control of information and communications is indeed the source of power in government organizations. Elsewhere, it has been argued (Stinchcombe, 1968; Meadow, 1980b) that political behavior may be defined by strategic location in the information environment to control the flow of messages. Even in primitive cultures (Wirsing, 1973), control over the flow of information has been argued to be more important than the quantity of information in establishing political leadership.

In the United States, Lyndon Johnson (1971) in his memoirs refers to his "vantage point", confirming Neusdadt's (1976) contention that the source of presidential power is the ability to persuade. Persuasion itself depends on the president's ability to get various bureaus and personnel to compete in reporting to him. Not only does the executive have access to information from various perspectives. His reputation as a perceptive leader is enhanced by enabling him to "anticipate" the needs and demands of subordinates, because these demands have already reached him from other sources. Presidents who administer differently may not have the same power. Rather and Gates (1974) report, for example, that subordinates in the Nixon administration were able to wield exceptional power because they severely restricted the flow of information to the Oval Office.

The centrality of information and its perceived importance in governmental organizations, especially for the executive branch, has been behind much of the controversy over privacy and secrecy. Much public discussion followed the long series of Watergate revelations (e.g., government break-ins to acquire information, phone taps of questionable legality for national security, and other illegal actions).

As with language policy, controversies over secrecy demonstrate the effect of politics on communication. Following the Watergate revelations, several works on executive privilege (Berger, 1974; Dorsen & Shattuck, 1974) discussed the relationship of governance to privileged communication. Other researchers (Dorsen & Gillers, 1974) have addressed the implications of the openness of government communications in terms of open meetings, access to records, freedom of information, intelligence collection, centralized data banks, electronic surveillance, and government information classification systems (Benjamin, 1982).

Executive privilege has a long history in the United States and in common law, but only with Watergate was its importance renewed. As a communication problem, the issue is clear. Congress needs information to carry out its constitutional duties, the president seeks not to present information provided to him in confidence. Although the rationale behind a presidential decision to invoke executive privilege may vary from preserving the symbolic independence of the president to hiding illegal activities, the end result is an impass with congress over rights to information.

General secrecy in government has been accepted under conditions of military conflict, but military secrecy has been expanded to include sensitive nonmilitary matters, including legislative hearings. In Phillips's (1974) description of the history and dimensions of classification, he notes that despite efforts to minimize the proliferation of secrecy, it expanded beyond the Defense Department to include the Departments of State and Commerce. Congressional oversight responsibilities compounded the problems. Transmission of classified documents is more cumbersome than transmitting unclassified material. Even locating such documents in the absence of indexes limits their availability. Despite repeated reforms and orders to limit classification, no incentives for limiting classification exist. Penalties are assessed on those who leak information, not on those who needlessly classify.

Many of the issues of secrecy and openness in government have increased in intensity since the Freedom of Information Act and various sunshine laws were enacted. These statutes have entitled citizens or media to attend meetings of public bodies, subject to certain limits, and to gain access to certain "identifiable" documents. Immediately after the enactment of these laws, however, numerous problems arose. Deliberative bodies conducted more of their business in closed, executive sessions. Documents opened for public scrutiny were unindexed and unidentifiable. And most requests for information under the Freedom of Information Acts have come from business users rather than interest groups or private citizens (Wellford, 1974).

Organizational issues in politics and communication have extended beyond communication policy problems of the executive branch, although political researchers have observed the tendency toward executive rather than legislative or shared government. In part, this shift is a function of the communications revolution of the twentieth century. Technological developments in communication have been argued to be partially responsible for the transformation of power in government from Congress to a strong executive. Early use of the radio and a recognition of the institutional needs of journalists by Roosevelt (Halberstam, 1979) focused attention on the executive branch of government, an emphasis which continues today (Blanchard, 1974; Graber, 1982).

Nonetheless, studies of Congress have implicitly and explicitly looked at communication flows. As Frantzich recently pointed out (Frantzich, 1982, p. 88) "Congress sits at the vortex of three discrete communications flows: it is the target, sender, and subject matter of communications." Some studies have shown that members of Congress pride themselves on being able to keep in touch and understand their constituencies by keeping open channels of communication. Other research has focused specifically on the patterns of communication within the organization. Hattery and Hofheimer (1954) in one early study queried 14 Senators and 13 Representatives about the usefulness of their sources of information. In each body, committee hearings, staff and personal reading and consultations were the most important sources, whereas the political party and legislative counsel's office were least useful. There was little reported use of executive agencies, and floor debate was considered important only when little information concerning committee hearing results was available. The study focused only on expert information and therefore is more limited in scope than others considering all communications interactions.

Kovenock (1973) considered all interactions and information exposure for each legislator in the study. Using a communications audit, six Representatives were observed for seven full days. In general, Koenvock found influence through communication to be minimal despite proclaimed norms of openness; most had made up their minds on legislative decisions before the interactions. But the methods made it impossible to chart the flow of influence on decision making *before* the legislator's mind was made up. On those few occasions where influence attempts succeeded, the communicators were staff or Senators, (not Representatives), rather than lobbyists or media. Even with this comprehensive picture of communication patterns, observations of home, social, and other interpersonal communication were limited.

Kovenock's work failed to find interaction with constituents as a source of information, yet there are many possible channels of communication, including letters from constituents and lobbyists, editorials from hometown newspapers, polls, face-to-face contact with constituents and lobbyists, and campaigning. Most of these channels have been explicitly analyzed. Studies of Congressional polls (Brody and Tufte, 1964), and constituent mail (Dexter, 1956), for example, reveal a marked similarity of viewpoints between constituents and congressmen, but also reveal limited interactions. The importance of the letter writer was the best predictor of attention paid, according to Dexter. More recent work by Fenno (1978) underscores the importance of some constituents. Milbrath's work on lobbying (1960) reveals frequent interactions, but only a few channels where there are any opportunities for successful influence.

Much of the new research on Congress has shifted the locus of communication study from the search for patterns of influence on legislators, to the ability of Congress to collect and process information. Not only are there budgets and staffs to provide information (80% of the requests for information from the Congressional Research Service are answered within an hour); there are new resources to communicate with constituents (Robinson, 1981). The personalization of mass mailings to constituents simultaneously enhances the myth of personal communication and access while increasing the distance between the representative and the constitutent.

Organizational perspectives on communication were influential in the debate as to whether or not to broadcast the sessions of Congress. Although the Cable Satellite Public Affairs Network (C-SPAN) has been cablecasting House Sessions since 1979 with no revolutionary consequences, sessions of the Senate were not televised until 1986, in part because of the assumed effects on that body. Claims of the potential increase in grandstanding, and fears of decreased respect for the legislative process from overexposure to routine activities have not materialized as yet, but they governed Senate decisions to approach broadcasting warily. Perhaps most uncertain are the possible changes in the legislative institutions themselves. As currently structured, most legislative work occurs in committees, but with potential increased exposure from floor activities, the committees might wither away. The effects of broadcasting on legislatures in other countries already have been studied (Wilson, 1970; Colin-Ure, 1974).

Some government organizations have been created solely for the purpose of communicating. The International Communications Agency (formerly the United States Information Agency) has as its goal the presentation of a favorable image of the United States. Within many government agencies, public relations officers exist to promote departmental interests. These officers have responsibilities ranging from preparing press releases, to making final decisions on the availability of military equipment for assisting commercial makers of war films in finding suitable military equipment. The controversy over the *Selling of the Pentagon* illustrates the dimensions of government information departments as well as the defensiveness surrounding such bureaus.

In yet another area, political scientists have teamed with computer researchers to explore the implications of the introduction of computer technology in governance (Dutton, 1982, Danziger, Dutton, Kling, & Kraemer, 1982). Not only are there hints that the introduction of these technologies reinforce dominant elites, there also is some suggestion that the increased sophistication of these technologies has shifted some power from the hands of elected officials into the hands of expert bureaucrats comfortable with the technology.

The final areas of research on government communications policy have been on international communication policy (Fisher, 1979) and domestic regulation of communications through the Federal Communications Commission and emerging telecommunications policy (D. Schiller, 1982). Research by Cole and Oettinger (1978), Mosco (1979) and Kransow, Longley, and Terry (1982) has outlined the operation of the F.C.C., and the interactions among the Commission, industry, citizen groups, courts, White House, and Congress. But there is little evidence to suggest that the F.C.C. acts differently than any other Federal regulatory agency with respect to the key questions of capture by special interests, staff–commissioner interactions, relations with oversight committees in Congress, and so forth. Given the changing communications environment (partially the creation of the F.C.C.), however, in all likelihood the F.C.C. and other policy-making organizations will remain a focus for research for some time to come (Pool, 1982).

Internationally, there have been an increasing number of research studies on the implications of new communications technology. Research on the allocations of spectrum space (Howkins, 1979; Smith, 1980), domination of the international communication services by Western nations and the effect of the phenomenon on national sovereignty (Nordenstreng & Schiller, 1979), and the implications of the technology gap for information and ultimately economic control (H. Schiller, 1982) has made a convincing case that international communication policy and organizations have been established largely for the continuing economic and political benefit of Western economies. More than any other area, international communications has proven fruitful for critical researchers (Tunstall, 1977, *Journal of Communication,* 1983).

Outside of government, organizational perspectives have explained the mobilization of citizen participants. Each of the participatory activities cited by Milbrath and Goel (1977), including voting, lobbying, campaigning, and protesting have developed around communication processes. Indeed secondary associations and political parties have been referred to as communication aggregators created to send messages effectively to government elites. Although parties have been said to be on the decline (Crotty and Jacobson, 1980) for some time, due partially to the growth of electronic media (Polsby, 1980), other researchers are predicting a resurgence of parties as they innovate by capturing the new technologies (Everson, 1982). The recent successes of the Republican National Committee at raising funds through computer mailings, as well as anectodal evidence of the effects of party mailing on absentee balloting offers some indication that parties may find new roles in providing technical support through new communication technologies. Thus, for individual voters, parties may be less relevant, but for candidates, their innovations with technologies may make political parties more relevant (see Saloma & Sontag, 1972).

Institutional studies of news organizations and their relationship with government news organizations continue to make up most of the remainder of organizational research in politics and communication. However, more and more researchers have recognized that not only news plays a role in politics. Scholars are increasingly attending to the role that popular cultural media play in political socialization.

Rivers, Miller, and Gandy (1975) in their literature review of a decade ago cite four broad areas of inquiry: the setting in which news media operate, how news media function, the characteristics of journalists, and the nature of news content. Since their review, little in the study of news has changed (Martin, 1981). The only significant transformation in thinking about the relationship between government and news media has been the decreased emphasis on the adversary and "watchdog" roles of news media. Hachten (1963), for example, argues that the activities of government are observed to provide control over abuse of power. More recent observers have concluded that news media rarely act as watchdogs, but more as companion pets of government largely because relations between governments and news media are symbiotic rather than adversarial. Both governments and news organizations have a concern, according to this literature, for maintaining the social status quo. And although there might be episodic confrontations and occasional hostilities, on balance, the relations between the press and public officials are quite cordial.

Studies of news gathering and news disseminating processes are the most common topic. Gans (1983) attributes much of the research concern for news to the rise of television news, and a disjuncture between social science and journalistic perspectives on the role and practices of journalism. Historical overviews by Schudson (1978) and more recently by D. Schiller (1980) trace the rise of "objective" journalism, and Rubin (1981) explores the decline of partisanship in the press. The historical research concludes, among other explanations, that a combination of market factors, increased literacy, changing economic realities, and changing technology led to mass consumption of news media and ultimately to a transformation of news and news organizations.

There has been considerable convergence of findings concerning news gathering organizations. News institutions are shown consistently to have economic interests constraining the presentation of news (Halberstam, 1979, Jackson-Beeck & Kraus, 1980). Within those institutions, reporters feel constraints on the news that can be gathered or presented, while editors disseminate their world views (Gans, 1979). Although few have been able to demonstrate that partisan political biases emerge from these constraints (Hofstetter, 1976; Frank, 1973), other researchers (Gitlin, 1980) have found system- and regime-oriented ideological biases.

In part, these biases arise from the processes by which news appears. The titles alone of the book-length studies reveal the major perception of news held by scholarly researchers. Altheide (1976) writes of *Creating* Reality, Epstein (1973) of News from *Nowhere,* Fishman (1980) *Manufacturing* the News, Gans (1979) *Deciding* What's News, Schudson (1978) *Discovering* the News, Tuchman (1978) *Making* News, and Westin (1982) Newswatch: How TV *Decides* the News. Clearly these authors believe that news is a creation of journalists.

The need for information is most often met by going to where news is available. Thus the "beat" system arises to assure editors that reporters will return with stories. Government bureaus routinely provide "news" in the form of press releases to be consumed by reporters (Nimmo, 1964; Hess, 1981). And even if reporters do not admit that they use press releases (Glick, 1966; Hale, 1978), other evidence (Kaid, 1976) suggests they do. Sigal (1973) documents throughout his book not only the importance of the beat system, but the symbiotic relationship that exists between reporters and officials to meet their needs. In more recent research focused exclusively on the White House, Grossman and Kumar (1981) arrive at the same conclusion. Thus from these exchange models (Blumler and Gurevitch, 1981) it would seem that the power to define news resides in the hands of the government officials who limit access or make journalists compete, as much as it does in hands of the journalists who literally have the last word.

Other elements besides convenience have been shown to be important in the collection of news. Altheide (1976) documents the importance of aesthetic and time constraints in the production of local news. Taking a broader view, Tuchman (1978) writes of news as a creation of reality under a code that is forced to consider the relatively uniform professional, aesthetic, and personal values of journalists and their editors. To some extent, the uniformity of cultural backgrounds demonstrated by Johnstone, Slawski, and Bowman (1976) explains this. And Crouse (1973), covering journalists along the campaign trail, has indicated that there are few creative journalists, since most follow in a "rat pack" the lead of a few prestigious journalists.

Finally, research on the organization of the culture industries, notably television, has begun to suggest the impossibility of separating news from fiction in the analysis of politics and communication. Critics from the right (Stein, 1979) as well as from the left (Gitlin, 1983) argue that our understanding of the social and political world are guided by dramatic television programming and other popular cultural forms. Marxist critics in particular (Adorno & Horkheimer, 1972; Gouldner, 1976; Kellner, 1979, 1981) have noted the relationship between the structure of the culture industries and the presentation of system-supportive messages that ultimately reinforce dominant patterns of social control.

The reasons for this increasing concern with the culture producing organizations have been that there are empirically observed effects of exposure. Controversial evidence gathered over the years by George Gerbner and his associates (Gerbner, Gross, Signorielli, Morgan, & Jackson-Beeck, 1979; Gerbner, Gross, Morgan, & Signorielli, 1980, 1981; Hirsch, 1980, 1981) has suggested that differential exposure to dramatic television fare provides citizens with different views of the political world, and has pushed us towards a mainstream culture. And Robinson (1977) has argued it has created a tension between liberal social attitudes and conservative politics. Even if the linkages to political behaviors are indirect, however, the context for reception of political messages from news, candidates, or public officials is set by the popular cultural forms created by organizations with identifiable interests in maintaining the political order.

VII.   THEORIES OF POLITICS AND COMMUNICATION

In reviewing the events-based and organizational perspectives (more than the symbolic and linguistic perspective) on politics and communication, it is clear that an enormous number of approaches linking politics and communication have been offered. Some have identified political problems and issues raised by communications policies and practices. Some have sought to consider effects of information exposure. Other efforts are descriptive of the creating institutions themselves. But what most characterizes our knowledge is that the diversity of findings and the constant specification of contingent conditions have led researchers to operate largely without theory. Indeed most of the politics and communication literature has been descriptive rather than theoretical. Yet a few theories have emerged that explain consistent findings, and from time to time, theoretical issues have even driven empirical inquiries. The major theories include the two-step flow of communications, agenda-setting, uses and gratifications, and public opinion processes and information theories.

Explanations for the failure of Lazarsfeld and his associates to demonstrate direct media effects in their election studies led to the formulation of the two-step flow theory of communications. Derived from work at Columbia University's Bureau of Applied Social Research on community influence and the acceptance of innovation, this concept suggested an important relationship between mass and interpersonal communication. In their political research, Lazarsfeld and his colleagues (Lazarsfeld et al., 1948) found that there were two tiers to the flow of influence. Ideas might originate in the mass media, to which some influentials would attend. These individuals in turn dispersed what they heard to inattentive or nonexposed individuals. In general, the former group served as "opinion leaders", while the latter group were followers. Additional early work by Merton (1949), Katz and Lazarsfeld (1955), and Lipset, Trow, and Coleman (1956) supported the concept. Generlizations about the identities of the opinion leaders emerged. The research continued to explain the important political roles of school teachers and priests in rural Greek villages (Stycos, 1952), religious leaders in Turkey (Stycos, 1964), and rural Egyptian community leaders (Harik, 1971).

Yet slowly, the potency of the two-step flow and its dependence on opinion leaders began to unravel. Troldhal (1966) found that for certain types of learning, there was a one-step flow, directly from media. Other studies (Troldhal & Van Dam, 1965, Ostlund, 1973, J. Robinson, 1976) suggested that the two-step flow was an artifact of its times, and that media use has become so pervasive that now all are directly exposed. As was the case with many of the approaches cited earlier in this chapter, so many contingencies were specified to explain the conditions under which the two-step flow operated, that it no longer was a viable theory for explaining any communications and political behavior. At the same time, the ideological underpinnings of opinion leadership research began to come under considerable criticism (Gitlin, 1978).

Politics and communication research through most of the 1970s had as its foundation agenda-setting theories. Derived from the foreign policy work of Cohen, (1963), the concept was applied to political communication events and organizational research by McCombs and Shaw (1972). In its most basic form, the theory states that mass media are not so successful in telling us what to think, but are notoriously successful in telling us about what to think. Mass media selectively attend to certain issues, heightening their significance to audiences. The public, as a result of repeated exposure to these items, develops beliefs and attitudes toward these issues, and considers them worthy of civic attention. Hundreds of studies based on this simple formulation have emerged in the past decade.

The development of agenda-setting has led it to cover everything from agenda-setting in election campaigns to explaining the social organization of newsrooms. In the first compendium on agenda-setting, Shaw and McCombs (1977) outline nearly a dozen crucial variables in agenda setting, including events and issues, news choice and values, types of media, type of story, degree of emphasis, access to press, access to citizens, need for orientation, interest, social knowledge, and social behavior. Over the years, each of these has been studied, with more or less success (Weaver, Graber, McCombs, & Eyal, 1981).

Part of the appeal to political scientists of agenda-setting research has been that it fits neatly with aspects of power. Control of political agendas has defined power for several researchers. Bachrach and Baratz (1970), Lowi (1963), Mills (1956), and other believers in elite theory have argued that control of the agenda — putting things on as well as keeping them off — are the results of power distributions. A more comprehensive study of agendas by Cobb and Elder (1983) elaborates on the dynamics of agenda building.

As with the other theories, contingency specification has been the rule rather than the exception, so much so that exceptions now prevent generalizations. With respect to agenda-setting, Winter (1981) sadly noted that replication has been replaced with a quest for innovation, leaving each new investigator with a unique operationalization, and unique findings. The nature of issues, the characteristics of audiences in terms of exposure, discussion, demographics, and other variables now enhance or minimize the agenda-setting effects (McCombs, 1981). Perhaps the best critique has come from Becker (1982). After a review of some of the methodological and concept specification problems of agenda-setting research, Becker suggests that agenda-setting, like most other explanatory concepts, is not a concept of universal truth. Instead, it varies with individual needs, interpersonal discussion, and social situations. In other words, like all good social theories, the answer to whether or not there is agenda-setting is "it depends" (see McLeod, Becker, & Byrnes, 1974; Erbring, Goldenberg, & Miller, 1980; Weaver, Graber, McCombs, & Eyal, 1981).

Uses and gratifications research (Blumler & Katz, 1974; McLeod & Becker, 1981) has been another "theory" employed in politics and communication research. Basically, researchers have been concerned with how audiences use media, and in specifying what gratifications there are from media use. It assumes a more active audience than that posited by researchers of the 1960s, an audience with needs, real or imagined, that can be met by media. At the same time, as Noelle-Neumann (1983) points out, it shifted the question raised by critical researchers from what the media do with people, to what people do with the media.

Audience motives for seeking political information may include vote guidance and reinforcement, surveillance of the political environment, excitement, or functional utility. Derived from studies of the British electorate (Blumler & McQuail, 1969, Blumler & McLeod, 1974, Blumler & Fox, 1980), only recently have researchers applied this theory to explain political communication behavior elsewhere. Even then, a number of critics have suggested that the theory explains little that could not be intuited. With the exception of habit, there is no other reason to use media than to derive some unspecified pleasure. Moreover, it has been argued that the theory offers little beyond the functional approaches of the 1950s (Wright, 1975), and has little predictive value. With such criticisms, the problem for uses and gratifications theories has not been that too many studies have come to disparate results. Instead, it has proven a catch-all for findings unable to be explained by other, more rigorous theories. Researchers following the prescription of McCleod and Becker (1981), however, might well expand the utility of this concept into a coherent theory. But undoubtedly they would be struggling with an issue increasingly in the forefront of debates on the significance of finding media effects: to focus research questions on audiences absolves media institutions from confronting their potentially significant effects on society (Katz, 1978).

The two-step flow, agenda-setting, and uses and gratifications theories underlying much of the empirical work in politics and communication have shifted their emphasis between an underlying theory of media power with a passive audience (agenda-setting), and individual power with a passive media (uses and gratifications). Recent conceptual approaches offering more explanatory power for politics and communication have evolved around public opinion processes and information processing theories where both media and audiences are active. In particular, these approaches move away from simple "effects" research and simple correlational studies that have characterized much agenda-setting research.

Beginning with the work of Noelle-Neumann (1974), researchers have posited that media effects in the political arena are best found in public opinion processes by creating perceptions of the social environment. Recent work by Lang and Lang (1981, 1983), suggests that there are threshold conditions that must be met before any political issue or event has meaning. Thus, the Langs move away from simple measures like frequency of coverage or time lag between exposure to political information and ability to recall issues. Instead, they present a theory which takes into account individual needs and experience and combines these with system provided information (symbols, language, socialization) before predicting behavioral consequences. In the case of Watergate, for example, the Langs suggest that Watergate was a high threshold issue, impossible of achieving significance until presented by mass media in a way that conflicted with preexisting conceptions of important symbols such as the presidency. Lower threshold items, including those part of everyday experience, such as inflation or unemployment, offer less of an opportunity for media influence. In their conceptualization, an active media meets with an active human information processor before political behavioral consequences can be determined.

Lang and Lang's threshold notion is consistent with newer findings on political socialization where psychological development and critical periods are linked to individual information processing capability (Meadow, 1976, 1980a). Simply stated, this research suggests that the effects of media depend on ability to process information (Atkin, 1981). When individuals have reached specified levels of political maturity, they are in a critical period of readiness and susceptible to political learning. When this capacity has been attained, political information reaching them becomes meaningful.

Finally, Graber's recent work (1984) is another indicator of steps toward an information process oriented theory. Her research concentrates on the conditions required for coping with and processing political information, shifting the implications of information exposure to the individual and away from media institutions. What is becoming clear is that developmental concepts are emerging as important in understanding politics and communication. Empirical work using developmental, information and opinion process perspective theory is still thin (see Chaffee & Tims, 1982), but additional research will determine the ultimate strength of this new theoretical approach.

VIII.   FUTURE RESEARCH IN POLITICS AND COMMUNICATION

Having reviewed but a fragment of the voluminous literature on media and politics, and categorized some of the major research traditions and theories, two major questions remain: (a) Where have we come? and (b) Where is politics and communication research headed?

The answer to the first question is simple. Some researchers have come a long way, and others have not. Paradigms and findings of 40 years ago remain conventional wisdom in some texts. More than a handful of researchers insist on making careers out of specifying new contingencies to modify existing theories. Yet as we have shown, some have been bold innovators.

As for the second question, the answer is as complicated as we researchers make it. As I suggested at the conclusion of the last section, there surely will be more opinion process research. And if trends of the last decade continue, there will be considerably more critical research focused on the global political implications of the Western dominance of communication technologies.

More attention will also be focused on the culture industries, and the relationship between mainstream culture and political domination. Methods of research surely will change as well. No doubt survey research and content analysis will continue to dominate politics and communication research, but there will be further qualitative inquiry and increased semiotic analysis of communication processes.

Perhaps more than anything else, technological innovation will be at the core of politics and communication research. Computers per se will not be the basis of inquiry, but the interaction of people with computers and with each other will likely increase in importance (Rogers & Chaffee, 1983). And there will be whole new research questions that will emerge from the applications of new technologies and the social transformations that accompany their introduction. Some of these questions will be global in scale, as communication technologies continue to separate the more from the less prosperous nations, and as the predictions of many critical researchers of the early 1980s are tested. Other questions will arise from changing communications regulatory policies. Still other questions will enable researchers to return to the electoral arena in which much politics and communication research had its origins. As an extended example of the directions in which this research can go, let us consider research questions which might arise as researchers consider the application of new communication technologies in electoral politics.

IX.   POLITICS, COMMUNICATION, AND
THE NEW TECHNOLOGY

It is ironic that even in the mid-1980s, researchers still refer to television as the new technology which has had implications for political behavior during election campaigns. But there has been political advertising on television for over 30 years. Televised campaign debates have a 25-year history. But there are other, newer technologies that are used in political campaigns that have not undergone research scrutiny.

Certainly the new political campaign technologies are not developing in a theoretical or methodological vaccuum. Political communication research findings on the effects of exposure to news or political advertising no doubt underlie some of the applications of new campaign tactics. Notwithstanding the revision or even the death of the two-step flow paradigm in political learning, political practitioners have taken into account the importance of interpersonal communication as an important intervention mechanism in what otherwise could become, with automated dialing equipment, a highly automated, technology-intensive operation (such as developing a telephone bank). Findings concerning the importance of group affiliations and secondary associations have had a significant impact on the development of computer-generated, modern direct political mail. But the translation of findings derived from interpersonal communication research to the political world requires several leaps of faith.

Overall, then, when we speak of research on the new technology of politics, we are talking not only of applying old theories to the development of computer models of the electorate or narrow cablecasting of specific messages to targeted households. We are speaking as well of the honing of political campaigning through the accumulation of scientific understanding of political communication phenomena.

In the past few years, there has been an increased professionalism of political campaigning (Sabato, 1981). More and more political professionals are turning to the social sciences in their efforts to understand voting behavior. But social scientists have yet to develop answers to questions that are unasked of them. There are a number of questions that can be part of the research agenda for politics and communication (Meadow, 1985). What, for example, is the interaction between interpersonal communication and receptivity to targeted political mailings? Even the most basic questions on the effectiveness of various voter communications such as advertising, direct mail, and direct contact still have no answers. And what will be voter's use of interactive information retrieval or interactive, at-home voting systems during campaigns?

Although these questions raised by the new technologies are applied, and the answers in the short run are not likely to lead to theory building, they do remove politics and communication questions from the same, event-based, effects-of-television- news-on-attitudes research that has characterized inquiry for too long. There are many nonnews, nontelevision questions to be pursued. Some are policy oriented and global in scope and importance.

Other questions are rooted in new technologies with implications for politics. Direct-targeted electronic messages through cable systems are already a reality. Videotex and information bank services may make at-home issues or social research — for some — a possibility. Interactive systems may make it possible in campaigns to send individual responses to individual queries. It seems to me that now is the time to study these developments, before our research questions stagnate.

In the absence of firm commitments to the kinds of research outlined in this chapter, politics and communication researchers will yield inquiries on the impact of communication on politics as well as the impact of politics on communication to market researchers. But it seems to me that politics is too important, too special to be left to researchers from the private sector. In the coming years, the emerging new technologies, as well as the imaginative use of the older ones will offer a chance for new research efforts in politics and communication, perhaps even unhampered by the old paradigms.

REFERENCES

Adams, W.C. (1981). *Television coverage of the Middle East.* Norwood, NJ: Ablex.

Adams, W.C. (1982). *Television coverage of international affairs.* Norwood, NJ: Ablex.

Adams, W.C. (1983). *Television coverage of the 1980 presidential campaign.* Norwood, NJ: Ablex.

Adams, W.C., & Schreibman, F. (1978). *Television network news: Issues in content research.* Washington, DC: School of Public and International Affairs, George Washington University.

Adorno, T.W., & Horkheimer, M. (1972). *Dialectic of enlightenment.* New York, Seabury Press.

Almond, G., & Powell, G.B. (1966). *Comparative politics: A developmental approach.* Princeton, Princeton University Press.

Almond, G., & Verba, S. (1963). *The civic culture.* Boston: Little, Brown.

Altheide, D. (1976). *Creating reality: How tv news distorts events.* Beverly Hills, CA: Sage.

Andreoli, V., & Worchel, S. (1978). Effects of media, communicator and message position on attitude change. *Public Opinion Quarterly, 42,* 59–70.

Atkin, C.K. (1981). Communication and political socialization. In D. Nimmo & K. Sanders (Eds.), *Handbook of political communication.* Beverly Hills, CA: Sage.

Bachrach, P., & Baratz, M. (1970). *Power and poverty.* New York: Oxford University Press.

Barber, J.D. (Ed.). (1978). *Race for the presidency.* Englewood Cliffs, NJ: Prentice-Hall.

Becker, L.B. (1982). The mass media and citizen assessment of issue importance: A reflection on agenda-setting research. In D.C. Whitney, W. Wartella, & S. Windahl (Eds.), *Mass communication review yearbook III.* Beverly Hills, CA: Sage.

Bell, D. (1975). *Power, influence and authority.* New York: Oxford University.

Benjamin, G. (Ed.). (1982). *The communications revolution in politics.* New York: Academy of Political Science.

Berelson, B., Lazarsfeld, P.F., & McPhee, W.N. (1954). *Voting.* Chicago: University of Chicago Press.

Berger, R. (1974). *Executive privilege.* Cambridge, MA: Harvard University Press.

Bernstein, B. (1962). Social class, linguistic codes and grammatical elements. *Language and Speech, 5,* 221–233.

Bishop, G.F., Meadow, R.G., & Jackson-Beeck, M. (Eds.). (1978). *The presidential debates: media, electoral and policy perspectives.* New York: Praeger.

Blanchard, R.O. (Ed.). (1974). *Congress and the news media.* New York: Hastings House.

Blumler, J.G., & Fox, A.D. (1980). The involvement of voters in the European elections of 1979: Its extent and sources. *European Journal of Political Research, 8,* 359–385.

Blumler, J.G., & Gurevitch, M. (1981). Politicians and the press: An essay on role relationships. In D. Nimmo & K. Sanders (Eds.), *Handbook of political communication.* Beverly Hills, CA: Sage.

Blumler, J.G., & Katz, E. (Eds.). (1974). *The uses of mass communication.* Beverly Hills, CA: Sage.

Blumler, J.G., & McLeod, J.M. (1974). Communication and voter turnout in Britain. In T. Leggatt (Ed.), *Sociological theory and survey research.* Beverly Hills, CA: Sage.

Blumler, J.G., & McQuail, D. (1969). *Television in politics.* Chicago: University of Chicago Press.

Brody, R.A., & Tufte, E.R. (1964). Constituent congressional communciation of fallout shelters: The congressional polls. *Journal of Communication, 14,* 34–49.

Burke, K.A. (1945). *A grammar of motives.* New York: Prentice-Hall.

Burke, K.A. (1950). *A rhetoric of motives.* New York: Prentice-Hall.

Campbell, A., Converse, P., Miller, W., & Stokes, D. (1960). *The American voter*. New York: Wiley.

Campbell, A., Gurin, G., & Miller, W. (1954). *The voter decides*. Evanston, IL: Row, Peterson.

Chaffee, S.H., & Tims, A.R. (1982). News media use in adolescence. In M. Burgoon (Ed.), *Communication yearbook 6*. Beverly Hills, CA: Sage.

Clarke, P., & Evans, S.H. (1983). *Covering campaigns: Journalism in congressional elections*. Palo Alto, CA: Stanford University Press.

Cobb, R.W., & Elder, C.D. (1983). *Participation in American politics: The dynamics of agenda-building*. Baltimore: Johns Hopkins.

Cohen, B. (1963). *The press and foreign policy*. Princeton: Princeton University Press.

Cole, B., & Oettinger, M. (1978). *The reluctant regulators: The FCC and the broadcast audience*. Reading, MA: Addison-Wesley.

Colin-Ure, S. (1974). *The political impact of mass media*. Beverly, Hills, CA: Sage.

Combs, J.E. (1980). *Dimensions of political drama*. Santa Monica: Goodyear.

Crotty, W.J., & Jacobson, G.C. (1980). *American political parties in decline*. Boston: Little, Brown.

Crouse, T. (1973). *The boys on the bus*. New York: Random House.

Dangerfield, L., McCartney, H.P., & Starcher, A.T. (1975). How did mass communication, as sentry, perform in the gasoline crunch? *Journalism Quarterly, 52,* 316–320.

Danziger, J., Dutton, W.H., Kling, R., & Kraemer, K. (1982). *Computers and politics*. New York: Columbia University Press.

Deutsch, K.W. (1953). *Nationalism and social communication*. Cambridge: MIT Press.

Deutsch, K.W. (1963). *The nerves of government*. New York: Free Press.

DeVries, W., & Tarrance, V.L. (1972). *The ticket splitter*. Grand Rapids, MI: Eerdmans.

Dexter, L.A. (1956). What do congressmen hear: The mails. *Public Opinion Quarterly, 20,* 16–27.

Dorsen, N., & Gillers, S. (Eds.). (1974). *None of your business: government secrecy in America*. New York: Penguin Books.

Dorsen, N., & Shattuck, J. (1974). Executive privilege: the president won't tell. In D. Dorsen & S. Gillers (Eds.), *None of your business: government secrecy in America*. New York: Penguin Books.

Dubois, P.L. (1983). Election night projections and voter turnout in the west: A note on the hazards of aggregate data analysis. *American Politics Quarterly, 11,* 349–364.

Duncan, H.D. (1968). *Symbols and society*. New York: Oxford University Press.

Dutton, W.H. (1982). Technology and the federal system. In G. Benjamin, (Ed.). *The communications revolution in politics*. New York: Academy of Political Science.

Edelman, M. (1964). *Symbolic uses of politics*. Urbana: University of Illinois Press.

Edelman, M. (1971). *Politics as symbolic action*. Chicago: Markham.

Edelman, M. (1977). *Political language: words that succeed, policies that fail*. New York: Academic Press.

Efron, E. (1972). *The news twisters*. Los Angeles: Nash.

Elder, C., & Cobb, R. (1983). *The political uses of symbols*. New York: Longman.

Ellsworth, J.T. (1965). Rationality and campaigning: A content analysis of the 1960 presidential campaign debates. *Western Political Quarterly, 18,* 794–802.

Epstein, E. (1973). *News from nowhere: television and the news*. New York: Random House.

Epstein, L.K., & Strom, G. (1981). Election night forecasts projections and West Coast turnout. *American Politics Quarterly, 9,* 479–491.

Erbring, L., Goldenberg, E., & Miller, A. (1980). Front page news and real-world cues: another look at agenda-setting by the media. *American Journal of Political Science, 24,* 16–49.

Everson, D.H. (1982). The decline of political parties. In G. Benjamin (Ed.), *The communications revolution in politics*. New York: Academy of Political Science.

Fagen, R.R. (1966). *Politics and communication*. Boston: Little, Brown.

Fenno, R.F. (1978). *Home style: House members in their districts*. Boston: Little, Brown.

Fisher, G. (1979). *American communication in a global society*. Norwood, NJ: Ablex.

Fishman, M. (1980). *Manufacturing the news*. Austin: University of Texas Press.

Frank, R.S. (1972). *Shifts in symbolic communication as a result of international crisis*. Unpublished doctoral dissertation, University of Pennsylvania.

Frank, R.S. (1973). *Message dimensions of television news*. Lexington, MA: Lexington Books.

Frantzich, S. (1982). Communication in congress. In G. Benjamin (Ed.), *The communications revolution in politics*. New York: Academy of Political Science.

Fuchs, D.A. (1965). Election day newscasts and their effect on western voter turnout. *Journalism Quarterly, 42*, 22–28.

Fuchs, D.A. (1966). Election day radio-television and western voting. *Public Opinion Quarterly, 30*, 226–236.

Gans, H. (1979). *Deciding what's news: A study of the CBS Evening News, NBC Nightly News, Newsweek and Time*. New York: Pantheon.

Gans, H. (1983). News media, news policy, and democracy: Research for the future. *Journal of Communication, 83*, 174–184.

Garramone, G. (1983). Issues vs. image orientation and effects of political advertising. *Communication Research, 10*, 59–76.

Gerbner, G., Gross, L., Morgan, M., & Signorielli, N. (1980). The mainstreaming of America: Violence profile no. 11. *Journal of Communication, 30*, 10–29.

Gerbner, G., Gross, L., Morgan, M., & Signorielli, N. (1981). A curious journey into the scary world of Paul Hirsch. *Communication Research, 8*, 39–72.

Gerbner, G., Gross, L., Morgan, M., Signorielli, N., & Jackson-Beeck, M. (1979). The demonstration of power: violence profile no. 10. *Journal of Communciation, 29*, 177–196.

Gitlin, T. (1978). Media sociology: The dominant paradigm. *Theory and Society, 6*, 205–253.

Gitlin, T. (1980). *The whole world is watching*. Berkeley: University of California Press.

Gitlin, T. (1983). *Prime time television* New York: Basic Books.

Glick, E.M. (1966). Press government relationships: State and H.E.W. departments. *Journalism Quarterly, 43*, 49–56.

Gouldner, A.W. (1976). *The dialectic of ideology and technology*. New York: Seabury Press.

Graber, D. (1971). Press coverage patterns of campaign news. *Journalism Quarterly, 48*, 502–512.

Graber, D. (1976). *Verbal behavior and politics*. Urbana: University of Illinois Press.

Graber, D. (1980). *Mass media and American politics*. Washington, DC: Congressional Quarterly Press.

Graber, D. (1982). Executive decision-making. In G. Benjamin (Ed.), *The communications revolution in politics*. New York: Academy of Political Science.

Graber, D. (1984). *Processing the news: How people tame the information tide*. New York: Longman.

Grossman, M., & Kumar, J. (1981). *Portraying the president: the White House and the news media*. Baltimore: Johns Hopkins University Press.

Gusfield, J. (1963). *Symbolic crusade*. Urbana: University of Illinois Press.

Hachten, W.A. (1963). The press as reporter and critic of government. *Journalism Quarterly, 40*, 12–18.

Halberstam, D. (1979). *The powers that be*. New York: Knopf.

Hale, F.D. (1978). Press releases vs. newspaper coverage of California supreme court decisions. *Journalism Quarterly, 55*, 696–702, 710.

Harik, I. (1971). Opinion leaders and mass media in rural Egypt: A reconsideration of the two-step flow of communications hypothesis. *American Political Science Review, 65*, 731–741.

Hattery, L.H., & Hofheimer, S. (1954). The legislator's source of expert opinion. *Public Opinion Quarterly, 18,* 300–303.

Hess, S. (1981). *The Washington reporters.* Washington, DC: Brookings Institute.

Hirsch, P.M. (1980). The 'scary world' of the nonviewer and other anomolies. *Communication Research, 7,* 403–456.

Hirsch, P.M. (1981). Distinguishing good speculation from bad theory. *Communication Research, 8,* 73–95.

Hofstetter, C.R. (1969). Political disengagement and the death of Martin Luther King. *Public Opinion Quarterly, 33,* 174–179.

Hofstetter, C.R. (1976). *Bias in the news.* Columbus: Ohio State University Press.

Hofstetter, C.R., & Buss, T.F. (1980). Politics and last minute television. *Western Political Quarterly, 33,* 24–37.

Hovland, C.I., Janis, I., & Kelley, H.H. (1953). *Communication and persuasion.* New Haven: Yale University Press.

Hovland, C.I., Lumsdaine, A.A., & Sheffield, F.D. (1949). *Experiments on mass communication.* Princeton: Princeton University Press.

Howkins, J. (1979). What is the world administrative radio conference? *Journal of Communication, 29,* 144–149.

Jackson-Beeck, M., & Kraus, S. (1981). Political communication theory and research: An overview 1978–1979. In D. Nimmo (Ed.), *Communication Yearbook 4.* New Brunswick, NJ: Transaction Books.

Johnson, L.B. (1971). *The vantage point: Perspectives on the presidency.* New York: Harper & Row.

Johnstone, J., Slawski, E., & Bowman, W. (1976). *The news people: A sociological portrait of American journalists and their work.* Urbana: University of Illinois Press.

Journal of Communication (1983). *Ferment in the field* (Special edition), *33.*

Kaid, L.L. (1976). Newspaper treatment of a candidate's news releases. *Journalism Quarterly, 53,* 135–137.

Kaid, L.L. (1981). Political advertising. In D. Nimmo & K. Sanders (Eds.), *Handbook of political communication.* Beverly Hills, CA: Sage.

Kaid, L.L., & Sanders, K.R. (1978). Political television commercials: An experimental study of type and length. *Communication Research, 5,* 57–70.

Katz, E. (1978). Concepts of media effects research. Presentation at the 8th Flemish Conference of Communication Research. Brussels, Belgium.

Katz, E., & Feldman, J.J. (1962). The debates in light of research: A survey of surveys. In S. Kraus (Ed.), *The great debates.* Bloomington: Indiana University Press.

Katz, E., & Lazarsfeld, P.F. (1955). *Personal influence.* New York: Free Press.

Kellner, D. (1979). TV, ideology and empancipatory popular culture. *Socialist Review, 45,* 13–53.

Kellner, D. (1981). Network television and American society. *Theory and Society, 10,* 31–62.

Klapper, J. (1960). *The effects of mass communication.* Glencoe: Free Press.

Klein, M.W., & Maccoby, N. (1954). Newspaper objectivity in the 1952 campaign. *Journalism Quarterly, 31,* 285–296.

Kovenock, D. (1973). Influence in the U.S. House of Representatives: A statistical analysis of communication. *American Politics Quarterly, 1,* 402–464.

Kransnow, E.G., Longley, L.D., & Terry, H. (1982). *The politics of broadcast regulation.* New York: St. Martins.

Kraus, S. (Ed.). (1962). *The great debates.* Bloomington: Indiana University Press.

Kraus, S. (Ed.). (1979). *The great debates: Carter vs. Ford, 1976.* Bloomington: Indiana University Press.

Kraus, S., & Davis, D. (1976). *The effects of mass communication on political behavior.* State

College: Pennsylvania State University Press.

Laitin, D. (1977). *Politics, language and thought.* Chicago: University of Chicago Press.

Lakoff, R. (1974). *Language and woman's place.* New York: Harper.

Lang, G.E., & Lang, K. (1978). The formation of public opinion: Direct and mediated effects of the first debate. In G. Bishop, R.G. Meadow, & M. Jackson-Beeck (Eds.), *The presidential debates: media, electoral and policy perspectives.* New York: Praeger.

Lang, G.E., & Lang, K. (1981). Watergate: An exploration of the agenda-building process. In G.C. Wilhoit & H. de Bock (Eds.), *Mass communication yearbook II.* Beverly Hills, CA: Sage.

Lang, G.E., & Lang, K. (1983). *The battle for public opinion: The president, the press and the polls during Watergate.* New York: Columbia University Press.

Lang, K., & Lang, G.E. (1968). *Voting and non-voting: implications of broadcasting returns before polls are closed.* Waltham, MA: Blaisdell.

Larson, C.U., & Weigele, T.C. (1979). Political communication theory and research. In D. Nimmo (Ed.), *Communication Yearbook 3,* New Brunswick, NJ: Transaction Books.

Lasswell, H.D. (1927). *Propaganda technique in the world war.* New York: Peter Smith.

Lasswell, H.D. (1935). *World politics and personal insecurity.* New York: McGraw Hill.

Lasswell, H.D. (1948). The structure and function of communication in society. In L. Bryson (Ed.), *The communication of ideas.* New York: Harper.

Lazarsfeld, P.F., Berelson, B., & Gaudet, H. (1948). *The people's choice.* New York: Columbia University Press.

Lerner, D. (1959). *The passing of traditional society.* New York: Free Press.

Lever, H. (1969). The Johannesburg station explosion and ethnic attitudes. *Public Opinion Quarterly, 33,* 180–189.

Lieberson, S. (1970). *Language and ethnic relations in Canada.* New York: Wiley.

Lippmann, W. (1925). *The phantom public.* New York: Harcourt, Brace.

Lipset, S.M., Trow, M., & Coleman, J.S. (1956). *Union democracy.* Glencoe: Free Press.

Lowi, T.J. (1963). American business, public policy, case studies and political theory. *World Politics, 16,* 667–715.

Mackey, W.F., (1979). Language policy and language planning. *Journal of Communication, 29,* 48–53.

Mansfield, M., & Weaver, R.A. (1981). Political communication theory and research: an overview. In M. Burgoon (Ed.), *Communication yearbook 5.* New Brunswick, NJ: Transaction Books.

Martin, L.J. (1981). Government and news media. In D. Nimmo & K. Sanders (Eds.), *Handbook of political communication.* Beverly Hills, CA: Sage.

McCombs, M.E. (1981). The agenda-setting approach. In D. Nimmo & K. Sanders (Eds.), *Handbook of political communication.* Beverly Hills, CA: Sage.

McCombs, M.E., & Shaw, D.L. (1972). The agenda-setting function of mass media. *Public Opinion Quarterly, 36,* 176–187.

McLeod, J.M., & Becker, L.B. (1981). The uses and gratifications approach. In D. Nimmo & K. Sanders (Eds.), *Handbook of political communication.* Beverly Hills, CA: Sage.

McLeod, J.M., Becker, L.B., & Byrnes, J.E. (1974). Another look at the agenda-setting function of the press. *Communication Research, 1,* 131–166.

McLeod, J.M., Brown, J.D., Becker, L.B., & Ziemke, D.A. (1977). Decline and fall at the White House: A longitudinal analysis of communication effects. *Communication Research, 4,* 3–22.

Meadow, R.G. (1973). Cross-media comparison of coverage of the 1972 presidential campaign. *Journalism Quarterly, 50,* 482–488.

Meadow, R.G. (1976). *Information and maturation in the political socialization process.* Unpublished doctoral dissertation, University of Pennsylvania.

Meadow, R.G. (1980a). Information processing and political socialization. *International Journal of Political Education, 3,* 351–371.

Meadow, R.G. (1980b). *Politics as communication.* Norwood, NJ: Ablex.

Meadow, R.G. (1985). Political campaigns, new technology, and political communication research. In L.L. Kaid, D. Nimmo, & K. Sanders (Eds.), *Political communication yearbook, 1984.* Carbondale: Southern Illinois Press.

Meadow, R.G., & Sigelman, L. (1982). Some effects and non-effects of campaign commercials. *Political Behavior, 4,* 163–175.

Mendelsohn, H., & Crespi, I. (1970). *Polls, television and the new politics.* Scranton, PA: Chandler.

Merton, R.K. (1949). Patterns of influence. In P.F. Lazarsfeld & F.N. Stanton (Eds.), *Communication research, 1948–1949.* New York: Harper.

Meyer, T.P., & Donohue, T.P. (1973). Perceptions and misperceptions of political advertising. *Journal of Business Communication, 10,* 29–40.

Milbrath, L. (1960). Lobbying as a communications process. *Public Opinion Quarterly, 24,* 32–54.

Milbrath, L., & Goel, M.L. (1977). *Political participation.* Chicago: Rand McNally.

Miller, R.E., and Richey, W.M. (1980). The effects of a campaign brochure "drop" in a county level race for State's Attorney. In D. Nimmo *Communications Yearbook 4.* New Brunswick, NJ: Transaction.

Mills, C.W. (1956). *The power elite.* New York: Harcourt, Brace.

Mosco, V. (1979). *Broadcasting in the United States.* Norwood, NJ: Ablex.

Mueller, C. (1975). *The politics of communication.* New York: Oxford University Press.

Neusdadt, R. (1976). *Presidential power.* New York: Wiley.

Nie, N., Verba, S., & Petrocik, J. (1976). *The changing American voter.* Cambridge, MA: Harvard University Press.

Nimmo, D. (1964). *Newsgathering in Washington.* New York: Atherton.

Nimmo, D. (1977). Political communication theory and research: an overview. In B. Reuben (Ed.), *Communication yearbook 1.* New Brunswick, NJ: Transaction Books.

Nimmo, D. (1981). Mass communication and politics. In S. Long (Ed.), *Handbook of political behavior* (Vol. 4), New York: Plenum.

Nimmo, D., & Combs, J.E. (1980). *Subliminal politics: myths and mythmakers in America.* Englewood Cliffs, NJ: Prentice-Hall.

Nimmo, D., & Sanders, K. (Eds.). (1981). *Handbook of political communication.* Beverly Hills, CA: Sage.

Noelle-Neumann, E. (1974). The spiral of silence: A theory of public opinion. *Journal of Communication, 24,* 43–51.

Noelle-Neumann, E. (1983). The effect of media on media effects research. *Journal of Communication, 33,* 157–166.

Nordenstreng, K., & Schiller, H. (Eds.) (1979). *National sovreignty and international communication.* Norwood, NJ: Ablex.

O'Keefe, G., & Atwood, L.E. (1981). Communication and election campaigns. In D. Nimmo & K. Sanders (Eds.), *Handbook of political communication.* Beverly Hills, CA: Sage.

O'Keefe, G., & Sheinkopf, K.G. (1972). The voter decides: Candidate image or campaign issue. *Journal of Broadcasting, 18,* 403–411.

Ostlund, L.E. (1973). Interpersonal communication following McGovern's Eagleton decision. *Public Opinion Quarterly, 37,* 601–610.

Paletz, D., & Entman, R.M. (1981). *Media power politics.* New York: Free Press.

Patterson, T.E. (1980). *The mass media election.* New York: Praeger.

Patterson, T.E., & McClure, R.D. (1976). *The unseeing eye.* New York: Putnam.

Phillips, W.G. (1974). The government's classification system. In N. Dorsen & S. Gillers (Eds.), *None of your business: government secrecy in America.* New York: Penguin.

Polsby, N.W. (1980). The news media as an alternative to party in the presidential selection process. In R.A. Goldwin (Ed.), *Political parties in the Eighties*. Washington, DC: American Enterprise Institute.

Pool, I de Sola (1982). Government regulation in the communication system. In G. Benjamin (Ed.), *The communications revolution in politics*. New York: Academy of Political Science.

Prothro, J.W., & Grigg, C.M. (1960). Fundamental principles of democracy: Bases of agreement and disagreement. *Journal of Politics, 22,* 276–294.

Ranney, A. (1979). *The past, present and future of presidential debates*. Washington, D.C.: American Enterprise Institute.

Ranney, A. (1983). *Channels of power: the impact of television on American politics*. New York: Basic Books.

Rather, D., & Gates, G.P. (1974) *The palace guard*. New York: Harper & Row.

Ritter, K.W. (1981). The 1980 presidential debates. *Speaker and Gavel*. (Special Edition), *18.*

Rivers, W.L., Miller, S.H., & Gandy, O. (1975). Government and the media. In S.H. Chaffee (Ed.), *Political communication: Issues and strategies for research*. Beverly Hills, CA: Sage.

Robinson, J.P. (1976). Interpersonal influence in election campaigns: The two-step flow hypothesis. *Public Opinion Quarterly, 40,* 304–339.

Robinson, M.J. (1974). The impact of the televised Watergate hearings. *Journal of Communication, 24,* 17–30.

Robinson, M.J. (1976). Public affairs television and the growth of political malaise: the case of The Selling of the Pentagon. *American Political Science Review, 70,* 409–432.

Robinson, M.J. (1977). Television and American politics, 1956–1976. *The Public Interest, 48,* 3–19.

Robinson, M.J. (1981). Three faces of congressional media. In T. Mann & N. Ornstein (Eds.), *The new congress*. Washington, DC: American Enterprise Institute.

Robinson, M.J., & Sheehan, M.A. (1983). *Over the wire and on TV: CBS and UPI in campaign '80*. New York: Basic Books.

Rogers, E.M., & Chaffee, S.H. (1983). Communication as an academic discipline: A dialogue. *Journal of Communication, 33,* 18–30.

Rothschild, M.L. (1978). Political advertising: A neglected policy issue in marketing. *Journal of Marketing Research, 15,* 58–71.

Rubin, R. (1981). *Press, party and presidency*. New York: Norton.

Sabato, L. (1981). *The rise of political consultants*. New York: Basic Books.

Saldich, A. (1979). *Electronic democracy: television's impact on the American political process*. New York: Praeger.

Saloma, J.S., & Sontag, F.H. (1972). *Parties* New York: Knopf.

Sanders, K., & Kaid, L.L. (1978). Political communication theory and research: an overview, 1976–1977. In B. Reuben (Ed.), *Communication yearbook 2*. New Brunswick, NJ: Transaction Books.

Sapir, E. (1983). Symbolism. In *Encyclopedia of the Social Sciences*. New York: MacMillan.

Savard, J.G. (1975). *Multilingual political systems*. Quebec: Les Presses de l'university Laval.

Schattschneider, E.F. (1960) *The semi-sovereign people*. New York: Holt, Rinehart & Winston.

Schiller, D. (1980). *Objectivity in the news*. Philadelphia: University of Pennsylvania Press.

Schiller, D. (1982). *Telematics and government*. Norwood, NJ: Ablex.

Schiller, H. (1982). *Who knows: Information in the age of the Fortune 500*. Norwood, NJ: Ablex.

Schudson, M. (1978). *Discovering the news*. New York: Basic Books.

Sears, D.O., & Chaffee, S.H. (1979). Uses and effects of the 1976 debates: an overview of empirical studies. In S. Kraus (Ed.), *The great debates: Carter vs. Ford, 1976*. Bloomington: Indiana University Press.

Shapiro, M.J. (1981). *Language and political understanding: politics of discursive practice.* New Haven, Yale University Press.

Shaw, D.L., & McCombs, M.E. (1977). *The emergence of American political issues.* St. Paul, MN: West.

Sigal, L.V. (1973). *Reporters and officials.* Lexington, MA: D.C. Heath.

Singer, B.D. (1970). Mass media and communication processes in the Detroit riots of 1967. *Public Opinion Quarterly, 34,* 236–245.

Smith, A. *The geopolitics of information.* New York: Oxford.

Smith, B.L., Lasswell, H.D., & Casey, R.D. (1946). *Propaganda, communication and public opinion.* Princeton: Princeton University Press.

Steeper, F.T. (1978). Public response to Gerald Ford's statements on Eastern Europe in the second debate. In G.F. Bishop, R.G. Meadow, & M. Jackson-Beeck (Eds.), *The presidential debates: media, electoral and policy perspectives.* New York: Praeger.

Stein, B. (1979). *The view from Sunset boulevard.* New York: Basic.

Stempel, G.H. III (1961). The prestige press covers the 1960 presidential campaign. *Journalism Quarterly, 38,* 157–163.

Stempel, G.H. III (1965). The prestige press in two presidential elections. *Journalism Quarterly, 42,* 15–21.

Stempel, G.H. III (1969). The prestige press meets the third party challenge. *Journalism Quarterly, 46,* 699–706.

Stinchcombe, A.L. (1968). *Constructing social theories.* New York: Harcourt, Brace & World.

Stycos, J.M. (1952). Patterns of communication in rural Greek village. *Public Opinion Quarterly, 16,* 59–70.

Stycos, J.M. (1965). The potential role of Turkish village people leaders in programs of family planning. *Public Opinion Quarterly, 29,* 124–125.

Tannenbaum, P., & Kostrich, L. (1983). *Turned on television, turned off voters: policy options for election projections.* Beverly Hills, CA: Sage.

Tonkin, H. (1979). Equalizing language. *Journal of Communication, 29,* 124–133.

Trent, J. (1975). A synthesis of methodologies used in studying political communication. *Central States Speech Journal, 26,* 278–297.

Troldhal, V.C. (1966). A field test of a modified two-step flow of communication models. *Public Opinion Quarterly, 30,* 609–623.

Troldhal, V.C., & Van Dam, R. (1965). Face to face communication about major topics in the news. *Public Opinion Quarterly, 29,* 626–632.

Tuchman, G. (1978). *Making news: a study in the construction of reality.* New York: Free Press.

Tunstall, J. (1977). *The media are American.* New York: Columbia University Press.

Weaver, D., Graber D., McCombs, M.E., & Eyal, C. (1981). *Media agenda-setting in a presidential election: Issues, images, interest.* New York: Praeger.

Weinstein, B. (1982). *The civic tongue: political consequences of language choice.* New York: Longman.

Wellford, H. (1974). Rights of people: The Freedom of Information Act. In N. Dorsen & S. Gillers (Eds.), *None of your business: government secrecy in America.* New York: Penguin.

Westin, A. (1982). *Newswatch: how TV decides the news.* New York: Simon and Schuster.

Wilson, C. (Ed.) (1970). *Parliaments, people and mass media.* London: Cassell for the Inter-Parlimentary Union.

Winter, J.P. (1981). Contingent conditions in the agenda-setting process. In G.C. Wilhoit & H. de Bock (Eds.), *Mass communication review yearbook II.* Beverly Hills, CA: Sage.

Wirsing, R. (1973). Political power and information: A cross cultural study. *American Anthropologist, 75,* 153–170.

Wolfinger, R., & Linquitti, P. (1981). Tuning in and turning out. *Public Opinion, 56–60.*

Wright, C.R. (1975). *Mass communications: a sociological perspective.* New York: Random House.

Chapter 7

Political Sociology: An Overview of the Field for the 1980s

Betty A. Dobratz

Department of Sociology & Anthropology
Iowa State University

George A. Kourvetaris

Department of Sociology
Northern Illinois University

I. INTRODUCTION

In this review we will provide an overview and assessment of the field of political sociology during the last ten years or so.[1] Lipset, the major protagonist of political sociology, laid its groundwork more than 25 years ago in his first edition of *Political Man* (1960). Since that classic book was published, political sociology has come of age. During the last 20 years, more than two dozen textbooks and readers have been published on political sociology, with much of these having come during the last ten years.

In spite of the various textbooks, readers, journals, and the recent establishment of a political sociology section of the American Sociological Association, one develops the feeling that the field is not doing as well as in the 1960s and early 1970s. The field, traditionally considered a liberal one, has suffered from the more conservative tenor in American politics and society. One has the impression that we are returning to the cold war politics of the 1950s. Also reflecting this pessimistic attitude is the view that political sociology has contributed little toward the improvement of political conditions in the world, or even worse, that it has become part of establishment sociology and a willing tool of oppression (Lehman, 1977). One political sociologist felt frustrated with the development of the field and concluded that "Once a more or less radical perspective is developed — then what? Power elite rules — not much can be done about it."

We feel political sociology should be more than the study of the social base of politics. Political sociologists should ask who runs things and who gains and loses. It should inject a skeptical dimension into the political process or a concern about the propriety of what occurs behind the scenes in the world of politics. One cannot talk about political sociology without dealing with the concepts of the state, class, elites, inequality, power, conflict, and control of resources.

In this review we will focus on certain competing theoretical perspectives, their controversial themes, and the unsettled empirical issues. We will emphasize studies of the various levels of power and conventional means of obtaining power during the last ten years. Our central thrust will be on the relationships among class, power, the state, and politics.

---

[1] This paper is an extended and revised version of two of our articles: (a) Kourvetaris and Dobratz (1982), which considered power and the conventional political participation aspects of political sociology, and (b) Dobratz and Kourvetaris (1983). Other discussions of the state of political sociology include Lipset (1959), Bendix and Lipset (1966), Greer and Orleans (1964), Braungart (1981), Alford and Friedland (1975), Niemi and Sobieszek (1977), Flacks and Turkel (1978), Hamilton and Wright (1975), Hall (1981), Kourvetaris and Dobratz (1980a). Annual research compilations related to political sociology are the *Handbook of Political Behavior,* edited by S. Long (New York: Plenum); *Political Power and Social Theory,* edited by M. Zeitlin (Greenwich, CT: JAI Press); *Social Movements, Conflict, and Change,* edited by L. Kriesberg (Greenwich, CT: JAI Press 1978 and 1979); and *Political Economy,* edited by P. Zarembka (Greenwich, CT: JAI Press).

II. DOMINANT AND CONFLICTING PARADIGMS

Our task here is to identify and comment on the major theoretical frameworks operating within political sociology in the late 1970s and early 1980s. The most recurrent and dominant conceptual frameworks used in the literature are functionalist, pluralist, elitist, Marxist/class and conflict. For our extensive elaboration of these perspectives, see Kourvetaris and Dobratz (1980a, 1980b).

The antiestablishment movement of radical sociology in the 1960s split political sociology into different schools. The mainline or establishment political sociologists of the consensus, pluralist, and functional–structural schools were under attack by the elitists, neo-Marxists, and radical sociologists, who challenged the very values upon which the political consensus was based. The publication of *Power Elite* by C. W. Mills in 1956 gave impetus to the new radical movement of the early 1960s.

In the 1960s the debate in political sociology was basically between elitists and pluralists. The study of elites in the United States and other countries was extensive. There are two versions of elite analysis — the conservative and the radical elite approaches. The former draws from the writings of classical elite theorists (Pareto, Mosca, and Michels) and is more likely to be represented by political scientists than sociologists, while the radical is inspired by the conflict school of sociology (Hunter, Mills). Contrary to the elitist perspective is the pluralist (Dahl, Polsby) framework, which does not see one cohesive elite making society-wide decisions. The pluralists believe that American society is not ruled by one elite but by different elites and there is competition among these elites.

Both the elitist and pluralist perspectives have dominated political sociology in the past, resulting in neglect of other perspectives. The elitist–pluralist dichotomy has reached a stalemate. Despite the fact that there has been an increase of empirical studies using the elite perspective, this school is somewhat ahistorical and atheoretical. While we find the use of class/Marxist and elitist perspectives on the rise, the pluralist and functionalist perspectives are declining. In particular the pluralist suffers from a lack of recent empirical support.

In order to rectify the neglect of other perspectives within political sociology, Alford (1975) selects certain issues or concepts related to state and society and proposes a synthesis or a combination of the pluralist, elitist, and class paradigms. The core function of the state is viewed differently by each paradigm: "consensus" by the pluralists, "domination" by the elitist view, and reproduction and management of existing class relations by the Marxists. In terms of what forces shape the state, Alford suggests individuals and groups (pluralist view), bureaucracy (elitist view), and social class (the class view). He also distinguishes a utopian from a pathological version of each of the three paradigms. While Alford made a genuine effort of "model building" in political sociology, his discussion of paradigms must be expanded in order to more fully evaluate the possibility of a synthetic–analytic paradigm and be able to operationalize it.

Domhoff (1978a) is critical of Marxist, pluralist, and elitist perspectives, but in general he supports the "class-hegemony" paradigm that views social classes as the focal point in the analysis of power. Domhoff draws on elitist and Marxist perspectives in his work. He stresses the primacy of the ruling class in the capitalist system.

Other efforts have been made to construct typologies or paradigms for political analysis. Effrat (1972) focuses on the major points of theoretical and ideological dispute among the paradigms. Braungart (1974) proposes four models for studying the interrelationships between social and political phenomena. The first three models deal with the effects of society on politics and vice versa. The fourth model attempts to construct a macro-sociopolitical theory of society and politics. By using multivariate analysis, Braungart provides indicators or parameter estimates that define these relationships through time. He makes a genuine effort to fill the gap of theory construction, a much needed task in political sociology.

While most of the perspectives operating within political sociology have been in decline or are growing only at a moderate rate, there is a definite resurgence of various neo-Marxist approaches. In particular, the contributions of the neo-Marxist analyses of the capitalist state and the ruling class have become the focus in the late 1970s and in the early 1980s.[2] In addition, the neo-Marxist ascent was facilitated by the rediscovery of political economy that traditionally has enjoyed greater legitimacy and respectability in European academic circles. Political economy,[3] an older discipline, has made inroads into political sociology.

A.   The Neo-Marxist[4] Theoretical Perspectives of the State
Despite the diversity of neo-Marxist perspectives, for the purpose of our review we will discuss the structuralist and instrumentalist approaches and certain extensions of the neo-Marxist framework. These neo-Marxist perspec-

---

[2] Flacks & Turkel (1978) provide further evidence of the Marxist inroads in sociology and political sociology. The authors trace the origin and development, as well as the contributions of radical sociology, from the 1950s to the late 1970s. They make the point that contrary to what many sociologists think most radical sociology is not negative but substantive (see also Jessop (1982) for a discussion of Marxist theory and method).

[3] Concerning the reemergence of political economy, see Kourvetaris and Dobratz (1980b, p. 31–32) and McNall (1981).

[4] The Marxist and neo-Marxist core ideas are related to the school of critical theory and its intellectual progenitor, "The Frankfurt School" of 1923. For an excellent review of the nature of critical theory and its development, see Robert J. Antonio (1983). Also consult the critical theory journal *Telos* for similar articles.

tives use a nation-state framework, while the world system approach and the dependency school go beyond the nation-state framework. In general, we may say that neo-Marxist perspectives are efforts to interpret the role of the capitalist state and its relationship to the capitalist ruling class. The state in capitalist society is viewed by the neo-Marxists as serving the interests of the capitalist class. The neo-Marxists attempt to answer two complementary questions. One: Why does the state serve the interests of the capitalist class? And two: How does the state operate to maintain and indeed expand the capitalist system? (See Gold, Lo, & Wright, 1973, pp. 31, 32.)

1. **Structuralist versus Instrumentalist.** One view of neo-Marxism draws from the writings of Poulantzas (1973) and is called "structuralist" and the other one draws primarily from the work of Miliband and is known as "instrumentalist" (see Gold et al., 1975; Domhoff, 1980; Knoke, 1981). The major thesis of the structuralist view of the state is that the functions of the state are determined by the structures of society rather than by those who occupy state positions. Poulantzas (1973), for example, argues that what is important between the state and the ruling class is not so much the direct participation of the ruling class in management of the state but whether the interests of the dominant class coincide with what the state does.

Two additional works of the structuralist framework of the state are those by Therborn (1978) and E. O. Wright (1978). Therborn (1978) provides a systematic way to understand the class nature of the state and its effects on society. State power "is a relation between social class forces expressed in the content of state policies" (Therborn, 1978, p. 34, 35). In greater depth than Poulantzas, he shows how the state produces and reproduces its class interests.

E. O. Wright (1978) examines the relationships between class and state particularly in advanced capitalism. In his own words, he links Marxist theory and fact while engaging in a debate with mainstream sociology. Wright provides a significant discussion of the meaning and importance of structural causality by introducing six basic modes of determination (structural limitation, selection, reproduction/nonreproduction, limits of functional compatibility, transformation, and mediation). An important contribution of Wright's is his concrete suggestions of ways in which the Marxist concepts of class and state can be tested empirically.

Wright also analyzes the historical transformations of the accumulation process and the internal structures of the capitalist state, particularly bureaucracy. He considers how historically specific contradictions of advanced capitalism can affect the development of socialism and how socialists could use the capitalist state as a vehicle for socialist transformation. Most recently, Wright (1983) presents the conceptual framework for specifying possible forms of nonsocialist futures to capitalism. Giddens

(1979), who has a different theoretical approach, criticizes Wright for being too structurally deterministic and overly functionalist.

The instrumentalist view of the state sees the government as an instrument manipulated by the capitalist ruling class. Miliband (1977) argues that the state is controlled by people who occupy strategic positions either directly through the manipulation of state policies or indirectly through the exercise of pressure on the state. The emphasis is on the linkages between the ruling class, the state policies, and class interests. Domhoff's work is an example of the instrumentalist view of the state.

In general, the instrumentalists believe that the capitalists rule indirectly by manipulating or influencing political officials and dominant institutions including the state. The class interests of the capitalist class are maintained through lobbying, conspiracy, influence of mass media, and the like (Marger, 1981, p. 104). While the instrumentalists stress the instrumental manipulation of the government by the capitalist ruling class, they lack in-depth analyses of the strategies and actions used by ruling class groups. Furthermore, not all the government initiated programs and policies including cultural activities are manipulated by the capitalist class.

2.   **Extensions of the Neo-Marxist Approaches**   To overcome some of the deficiencies of structuralist and instrumentalist perspectives of the capitalist state, a number of Marxist political economists have suggested new approaches (Gold et al. 1975). One such approach is offered by Claus Offe (1975), who attempts to transcend the structuralist and instrumentalist limitations by looking at the internal structure of the capitalist state. A second is a theory of fiscal crisis suggested by O'Connor (1973), and a third one is a theory offered by Wolfe (1974, 1977), who attempts to make the Hegelian–Marxist view of the state more concrete by formulating a Marxist theory of politics. In short, all three theorists make an effort to reformulate and extend the Marxist theories of the capitalist state. All three attempt to analyze the internal mechanisms of the state, and each in his own way tries to develop a neo-Marxian dialectic of the capitalist state.

B.   Transnational Neo-Marxist Conceptual Frameworks

Thus far we have examined the contributions of the neo-Marxist theories in the analysis of the capitalist state within a national political economy framework. Using a transnational or world political economy approach, we will briefly discuss the world-system perspective and the dependency school.

1.   **The World-System Perspective.**[5]   The work of Wallerstein (1974, 1979), which draws from the work of Braudel, builds on the Marxist

---

[5] For a detailed review and critique of world-system theory, see Chirot and Hall (1982).

paradigm and the world political economy approach. Wallerstein traces the origin of the capitalist "world system" back to the sixteenth century. His work can be characterized as political economy, but it is also related to political sociology. Wallerstein sees the modern world capitalist system as basically a global system of division of labor of core, periphery, and semiperiphery countries. The core countries are the United States, Western Europe, and Japan. The core economically dominates both the periphery and semiperiphery. Using historical analysis, Wallerstein attempts to explain the structure and function of the world capitalist system that emerged out of the feudalist system. Wallerstein's aim is to provide us with an alternative paradigm to the theories of modernization and development.

The unit of analysis is the world system[6] rather than the society. The concepts of development and underdevelopment are now reconceptualized as different positions of core, periphery, and semiperiphery in a singular world division of labor. The core capitalist countries manufacture goods, while the countries in the periphery (Third World) produce the raw material. More recently, Wallerstein (1979) incorporates the criticisms of his previous work and broadens his perspective of world system. Unlike his previous work, this volume uses a political sociology as well as a political economy framework. He links world commerce with such ideas as state formation, geopolitics, productive organization, and stratification.

2. The Dependency School. Related to the world-system perspective is the theory of economic growth and dependency. This perspective has challenged the modernization theories and argues that dependency prevents economic development and modernization in general. Szymanski (1976) has suggested two conflicting interpretations of the dependency school within the Marxist tradition of social science. One interpretation sees imperialism as producing a net capital flow into the less developed (peripheral and semi-peripheral) countries, which results in their relative economic growth. This is a traditional Marxist position and has been promulgated by Lenin, Luxemburg, and more recently by Warren (1973). The other more radical interpretation maintains that dependency produces a real flow of capital and resources away from the less developed to the more developed countries. This phenomenon is carried out by multinationals of the industrialized core nations. Indeed, this revised radical version has been more dominant within the dependency school, especially as it applies to Latin America and other Third World countries. For example, Frank (1981) examines Third World economies during the present worldwide economic and political crisis.

---

[6] Works with similar themes are Chirot (1977), Anderson (1974a, 1974b) and Kaplan (1978). For critical reviews of Wallerstein, see Janowitz (1977), Skocpol (1977), and Thirsk (1977); of both Wallerstein and Anderson, see Hechter (1977); and of Chirot, see Skocpol (1979b). For a systematic comparison of world-systems theory and classical Leninst theory of imperialism, see Szymanski (1981).

III. THE STUDY OF POWER

We suggest that the study of power really provides the lifeblood of political sociology. In general we view power as the ability or capacity to obtain a specified outcome in a conflictual asymmetrical social relationship. Power relations reflect the inequality and struggle in society. We will first consider recent conceptualizations and frameworks of power[7] and then examine research on power relations at the community, national, and transnational levels.

A. General Approaches to the Study of Power

The major debate between elitists and pluralists has subsided and other frameworks, particularly neo-Marxists ones, have been advanced. Domhoff (1980) believes that power structure research started with Floyd Hunter, a radical structural functionalist who stressed the power of the economic elite. Later C. W. Mills, a radical Weberian, used the term power elite to characterize the interdependence of economic, political and military elites. The work of Hunter and Mills laid the foundation for the current conflict between the neo-Marxists (who suggest a *ruling class*) and the power structure researchers (who concentrate on the *elite* who occupy formal positions of power). The differences between Hunter and Mills may also have helped foster the internal Marxist debate between instrumentalists and structuralists.

Lukes (1974), Therborn (1976), and Manley (1983) support neo-Marxist approaches to the study of power. Lukes (1974) presents a three-dimensional model of power which goes beyond the one-dimensional pluralism and the two-dimensional model (decisions and nondecisions) of Bachrach and Baratz. Power can be exercised through manipulated consensus or thought control so that "Men's wants may themselves be a product of a system which works against their interests" (Lukes, 1974, p. 34).

Manley (1983) compares Marxist class analysis with pluralism I and pluralism II. Pluralism II refers to the revisions in pluralism I and in light of occurrences such as Vietnam, Watergate, and enduring economic and political inequality (see Dahl & Lindblom, 1976 and Dahl, 1982 for examples of neopluralism). Even this revised theory is characterized by tension between the underlying values and the performance of American polyarchy. Class analysis has greater explanatory power in explaining the gross inequality under capitalism.

Therborn (1976) identifies three approaches that try to answer different

---

[7] For detailed discussions and/or typologies of power, see Burt (1977), Bottomore (1979), Wrong (1979), and Luckenbill (1979). For information on the diverse conceptualizations of power within particular theories of politics, see Kourvetaris and Dobratz (1980b, pp. 20–25, 69–73). See Mintz, Freitag, Hendricks, and Schwartz, (1975) for a critique of the methodological approaches to power structure research.

questions about power. The first, the subjectivist, involves the debate between pluralist and elite theorists. In the second approach, the economic or functionalist, power is viewed as nonconflictual with the ideas of dominance, subordination, and change deemphasized. The major question becomes how much power rather than who has power. The third framework Therborn (1976) calls structural-processual or dialectical materialism. This Marxist perspective asks the questions: Power to do what? Power over whom?

Knoke (1981) offers a somewhat different conceptualization, which consists of the following five analytic models of power structures: (a) radical democracy, which requires participation in decision-making by all citizens; (b) democratic pluralism or the traditional pluralist approach; (c) power elite; (d) class conflict; and (e) multiple elites. Knoke supports the multiple-elite model, which is a variant of the democratic pluralism one. This model recognizes greater hierarchy and elite autonomy than the pluralist framework but does not support the idea of elite cohesion which the power elite model suggests. The state is neither a neutral political broker nor a captive of other institutional elites.

B. Breakdown–Deprivation, Solidarity–Mobilization, Corporatism, and Related Theories

Now we will briefly review some of the theoretical frameworks on power obtained through social movements and revolutions.[8] It should be stressed that the purpose of all forms of politics is to obtain power, but participants in unconventional politics usually hope to make major changes in their societies through somewhat unorthodox means.

Much of the early work on social movements examined sociopsychological characteristics of individuals, including status inconsistency, deprivation, rising expectations, and isolation thesis. These frameworks that view participants of movements as disorganized aggregates of people have been considered part of the mass society framework (Halebsky, 1976), the collective behavior paradigm (Gamson, 1975), or breakdown theories (Tilly, Tilly, & Tilly, 1975). Social movements express reactions of disorganized groups of people suffering from various strains and/or frustrations, including urbanization and industrialization. In mass society individuals are viewed as isolated, since they do not belong to groups that link them to society. This isolation results in extremist activity. Halebsky (1976) questions both whether intermediate groups have declined and whether they offer that much personal security. To him the individual is more rational than the mass politics model suggests.

---

[8] Space does not allow us here to examine the studies on unconventional politics. See Oberschall (1978), Lo (1982), Jenkins (1983), and Dobratz and Kourvetaris (1983, pp. 115–122) for discussions of some of the recent work on unconventional politics, especially social movements.

The more recent work that focuses on the organizational context is referred to as the group conflict perspective, resource management model (Orum, 1983; Gamson, 1975), or solidarity theory (Tilly et al., 1975). According to this perspective, movements are viewed as common occurrences and their explanations rest upon the same kind of forces and motivations that go into everyday behavior (Oberschall, 1973, pp. 27–29). Violence grows out of the struggles for power by well-defined organized groups strongly integrated into society (Tilly et al., 1975). Tilly (1978) tries to link the macrostructural changes (state-making, expansion of capitalism, urbanization, industrialization, and electoral politics) with the collective behavior of the common man (strikes, protests, etc.). In his *polity* model of interaction among groups the challengers try to enter the polity. Changes in the resources available affect the chances of gaining access to the system. Collective violence is due to the shifting alignments of classes and groups inside and outside the system. The *mobilization* model focuses on the behavior of a single contending group including the group's interests, organization, mobilization, collective action, and opportunity. McCarthy and Zald (1977) develop a resource mobilization model with a partial theory that draws upon political sociological and economic theories.

Oberschall (1978) reviews both breakdown–frustration and mobilization-solidarity approaches. He notes two unresolved methodological issues (group versus individual level of analysis and behavior assumptions of rational choice versus a more complicated psychology of the actor). Oberschall (1978, p. 314) concludes that neither of the two approaches has been successful in "providing a dynamic analysis of conflict as a process."

Lo (1982) surveys the recent literature on conservatives (though not right-wing extremist) movements and examines status preservativism, status symbolism, and status discrepancy theories. He briefly considers right-to-life, stop-ERA, and antibusing movements as well as conservative Protestantism, fundamentalism, Christian anticommunism, revivalism, and moral reform. He argues that status-politics theory, which pictures social movements as coming from societal breakdown and irrational behavior, is not very relevant. Rather there should be some combination of resource mobilization theory (which places conservative movements in the context of competing movements and the overall historical process of change) *with* the collective behavior tradition (which considers the interaction between movement and countermovement and the development of goals).

Wilson (1983) critiques various social movement frameworks and tries to explain the new "professional social movement." The resource mobilization model is flawed because it uses the movement organization as the unit of analysis, thus making it difficult to see the larger picture of the political and economic structure. This framework also ignores the role of the state vis-a-vis organizations. The elitist (modified pluralist) model allows one to examine the political structure in which movements take place; it also recognizes that the state is not a neutral force and certain organizations clearly have more resources and power than other organizations. This model does not, however, thoroughly recognize the influence of the state. It treats various interests as given and does not question how and why these interests exist.

Unlike the elitist model, a corporatist model tries to present a theory of the state and recognize the significance of class and the distinct interests of the state, capital, and organized labor. Decision-making has shifted away from the legislature and toward the executive. Political parties have lost much of their policy formation role. Wilson argues that one of the advantages of the corporatism model is that it closely examines the specific characteristics of capitalism, including how the interests of capital define the "public" interest. The corporatist model has mainly been applied to Western European societies; its applicability to the United States has been questioned because the corporatist agreements between labor, capital, and the state have been temporary and fragile. Wilson argues that a type of quasi-corporatism has developed in the United States with some agreement between labor, capital, and the state. Limits are placed on what are regarded legitimate claims on the state. The worker is committed to national reform including an equitable distribution of opportunity but is not interested in controlling the means of production.

Jenkins (1983), in his review of resource mobilization theory, stresses the role of resources, organizations, and political opportunities as well as traditional discontent. He argues that polity theory should be extended to deal with more than liberal democratic states and regimes, including the development of neocorporatism. A more advanced social psychology of mobilization is also needed.

Skocpol (1979) identifies four major groups of theories of revolution — Marxist, aggregate-psychological, systems/value consensus, and political conflict. She criticizes all four of them for the following reasons: (a) they have voluntarist images of how revolutions occur; (b) they focus primarily on intranational conflicts and processes of modernization; and (c) they either collapse state and society or reduce politics and the state to representations of socioeconomic factors. Skocpol (1974, p. 14) offers a nonvoluntarist structural framework that refers to transnational relations systematically and views states as administrative and coercive organizations that are potentially autonomous.

C.   Community Power Research

It was at the community power level that the debate between pluralists and elitists had been the most intense. Recently two cities which had been prominent in that debate have been restudied (Domhoff, 1978b, Hunter, 1980). Domhoff challenges Dahl's pluralist study of New Haven by providing a new methodological framework and linking the local elite to the national power structure and corporate business community. Domhoff stresses the need to incorporate the systemic, the structural, and the situational levels of power into one's study. The study falls somewhat short in providing a complete theoretical framework for the study of community power, however.

More recently, Domhoff (1983) has provided a broad theoretical framework by drawing on Molotch's conception of city power structures as growth machines that concentrate on land ownership. In order to create favorable conditions for outside capital investment (in Molotch's terms "prepare ground for capital"), the power structure tries to implement low business taxes, good municipal services, effective law enforcement, a willing and docile labor force, and few business regulations. The concept of the growth machine seems quite appropriate for New Haven and Atlanta, especially on the major issue of urban renewal.

Floyd Hunter (1980) revisited Atlanta to determine if the power structure had changed. He finds that the steeply pyramided structure of community decision-making that favors economic interests remains. The corporations exercise control over state politics by holding key positions in the various factions of the major political parties in Georgia. Hunter also stresses the need to link Atlanta to the state and national power structures.

Trounstine and Christensen's (1982) study of community power in San Jose also supports the elite model of power in the sunbelt. Ratcliff and Pennick (1983) analyze the property tax assessment appeal system in St. Louis to see who used it and who benefitted from this aspect of economic redistribution. Rather than the appeal decisions helping defuse citizen discontent, they provide tax concessions to the wealthy and powerful. This follows the general pattern of urban redevelopment policies that give tax breaks to the affluent. Katznelson (1981) uses the case study of Washington Heights–Inwood to discuss urban politics in the "city trenches." He maintains that a dual system has been created in which people operate on the basis of class and solidarity in the workplace, but at home in the community they function on the basis of ethnic and territorial solidarity.

Polsby (1980), who supports pluralist theory, critiques various prominent nonpluralist studies of community power. Stone stresses the need to develop stratification theory that considers the effects of systemic power on community decision-making. The effect of socioeconomic inequalities on the behavior of elected officials (the "class imprint on policy decisions") needs to be recognized in order to have a complete picture of community power. Walton (1976) suggests that the new field of political economy will supersede both the elitist and pluralist approaches in the study of urban politics. This framework is grounded in Marxist theory and is concerned with the origins of group and class struggles and their outcomes. Walton (1977), Tabb and Sawers (1978), and Lyon, Felice, and Perryman (1980) use the political economy approach for the study of the urban metropolis.

In testing the relevance of pluralist, elitist, and Marxist models, both Greer (1979) and Whitt (1979, 1982) generally support the Marxist paradigm. Whitt uses an historical, multiple-decisional approach to study issues surrounding the California public transportation systems. The elitist framework is better than the pluralist, because it allows one to consider behind-the-scenes manipulation, although it does not adequately consider the complexity of the situation. The class dialectical model is most appropriate for the community level, because it considers the issues of hegemony versus legitimacy and competition versus cohesiveness in the dominant class. Monopoly capitalism characterizes contemporary American cities and shapes both class structures and basic social contradictions. Whitt (1980) finds greater support for the instrumentalist view than the structuralist, because the capitalist ruling class maintains an effective political unity.

Liebert and Imershein (1977, p. 6) identify three different emergent research paradigms. The first approach is structuralist[9] and emphasizes various macrolevels of social organization and systemic power. Unfortunately, at times the selection of structural characteristics does not have much theoretical relevance. The second approach focuses on the microlevel relations and thus is more interested in the development of interpersonal power. The third approach supposedly "welded together the old elitist andd pluralist approaches" by using an exchange approach that involves analysis of elite networks. Laumann and associates have developed an extended network conception of community leadership within an interorganization perspective (Laumann & Pappi, 1976; Laumann, Galaskiewicz, & Marsden; 1978, Laumann & Marsden, 1979). One problem with this approach is its inability to consider how issues and decisions develop over time. One could argue that a large basis of community power depends on who controls the agenda for decision-making (Granovetter 1978, p. 1542).

We believe that studies of interorganizational networks may make more significant contributions to organizational literature and urban society than political sociology per se, because there seems to be little consideration of who benefits and loses in the asymmetrical power relationship. The most important recent contributions to community power research may well be those using the neo-Marxist framework. At the same time, however, these might be criticized for reducing political sociology to political economy.

D. State or National Power

Research on power at the national level often examines elites, particularly their social origins, the degree of cohesiveness, and their political input. Other research considers the ruling class vis-a-vis the working class and the role of the state. Dye's (1979, 1983) work supports both the pluralist and

---

[9] See Lincoln (1976) for an ecological model and Grimes, Bonjean, Lyon, and Lineberry (1976) for a critique of this approach.

elitist approaches while Domhoff (1978a, 1983), Simon and Eitzen (1982), and Parenti (1983) draw upon elements of both the class and elitist perspectives.

More specifically, Dye (1979, 1983) considers those with power during the Carter and Reagan years. He identifies 7,314 positions which are occupied by three major types of institutional elites – the corporate, government, and public interest sectors. The concentration of resources among a few corporations has been slowly increasing over time. The power of stockholders is labeled a "legal fiction," although there has been a decrease in family-and-individual-dominated corporations. Dye (1983, p. 6) stresses the necessity of elites and concludes "there cannot be large institutions without great power being concentrated within the hands of the few at the top of these institutions." He disagrees with the radical elite theorists who believe that the elitist character of society is due to capitalist exploitation, political conspiracy, or any specific malfunctions of democracy. Dye suggests that while profit is a major goal of corporate elites, most elites have a sense of corporate responsibility and social consciousness and want industry to help society.

Simon and Eitzen (1982) strongly disagree with Dye about the social consciousness and morality of elites. They see a systematic corruption of elites that has become an institutionalized part of elite power in America. They are concerned by the decline in public confidence that has been caused by reports of elite wrongdoing and economic crises. Both the international and national dimensions of economic and political deviance are documented, including America's support of repressive regimes and disregard for human rights, price gouging, business–government collusions, corporate bribery of foreign governments, the sale of known hazards by multinationals, monopolies, price fixing, and deceptive advertising.

Parenti (1983) recognizes two faces of the state. While the state is the most important force that corporate America can utilize, it also resists particular corporate interests and becomes the location where liberal and conservative ruling-class factions struggle over how best to maintain the system. The state is placed in a contradictory position because of the conflict between the "egalitarian expectations of democracy and the dominating thievery of capitalism" Parenti, 1983, p. 344). The struggle for democracy is part of the class struggle. The ruling class exploits people as *workers* because they receive only part of the value their labor creates, as *consumers* because they pay high prices to monopolies, as *taxpayers* because business does not pay their fair share in taxes, and as *citizens* because they get less government services than they pay for.

Domhoff is perhaps the most prolific writer on the ruling class. In *The Powers That Be* (Domhoff, 1978a, pp. 12–13), the ruling class is defined as a "clearly demarcated social class which has 'power' over the government (state apparatus) and the underlying population within a given nation (state)" while the power elite is "the leadership group or operating arm of the ruling class." Domhoff concentrates on four general processes (special interest process, the policy formation process, the candidate selection process, and the ideology process) through which the ruling class dominates government and subordinates other social classes. He is critical of many Marxists who have not recognized the primacy of the ruling class because they want the working class to replace capitalism with socialism.

Most recently Domhoff (1983) has attempted to synthesize his views in *Who Rules America Now?* He uses three types of power indicators: (a) Who benefits? (b) Who governs? and (c) Who wins? A key concept is domination, which is the ability to set the terms under which other groups and classes operate. The upper class comprises only 0.5% of the population. The upper class, corporate community, and the policy planning network are pictured as three intersecting circles with the corporate community being the common sector. The upper class sustains itself as ruling class due to its ability to influence the government as well as its status power, economic power, and expertise.

Moore (1979) and Useem (1979) both empirically examine the cohesiveness of United States elite networks. Moore suggests that the structure of the major central circle is broad and inclusive so that issues can be discussed and possible conflict resolved. The inner group M. Useem (1979) identifies consists of the primary owners or top managers of several major corporations who can mobilize great corporate resources and are involved in a common transcorporate social network. Useem tentatively suggests that the core business people who share in governance represent some degree of reconciliation of the conflicting and contradictory interests within the capitalist class.

Mintz and Schwartz (1982) tend to support the findings of Moore (1979) and Useem (1979). They use data on interlocking directorates to test and challenge the relevance of managerial, finance capital, and coalition theory for the study of modern corporations. The large corporation is not an autonomous and independent unit as managerial theory would suggest. The larger corporations are more likely to be involved in intercorporate relationships. The firms do not form flexible interorganizational alliances based on industry coalitions that pursue their mutual needs. Also the interlock network of the 1960s is not based on a number of relatively discrete coordinated interest groups of member firms as posited by traditional finance capital theory. Rather there is an integrated national network that is dominated by New York banks and insurance companies; this tends to support modified finance capital theory, which suggests a centralized structure of intercorporate relationships. Since power is not dispersed, there is some sense of unity with large companies being involved in each other's concerns. Such a process should minimize corporate conflict and result in "coordinated economic decision-making and united political action" (Mintz & Schwartz, 1981, p. 866).

As already noted, the relations between classes and the role of the state are important concerns of neo-Marxists (e.g., Therborn, 1978; Wright, 1978). Wright tries to suggest ways in which the Marxist concepts of class and state can be tested empirically. The issue of redistribution of wealth to the poor through government expenditure and taxation policies has been identified as a class issue by Hicks, Friedland, and Johnson (1978). They argue that national corporations and labor unions provide organized bases for opposing class interests and for class conflict. Large business corporations negatively affect governmental redistribution while labor unions positively influence it.

Garner (1977) and Piven and Cloward (1977) both use class and Marxist analysis in their studies of social movements in America. According to Garner (1977), one of the most important developments in class societies is the rise of the state. Behavior and ideas that threaten the political system are defined as nonlegitimate. Movements are ultimately produced by transformations of the material base in society. In examining poor people's movements, Piven and Cloward (1977) believe "those who control the means of physical coercion, and those who control the means of producing wealth, have power over those who do not." Rather than stressing organization and shared social goals, Piven and Cloward (1977) separate movements from formalized organizations and emphasize collective defiance as the major characteristic of a protest.

Isaac and Kelly (1981) identify two general theories on insurgency, the state, and welfare expansion. In the orthodox developmental/modernization perspective the state is viewed as an impartial mediator of various interests and insurgency is irrational. According to the political conflict/struggle model, disruptive insurgent movements may lead to greater welfare expenditure. The state is linked to the capitalist class and tries to legitimize the status quo. Conventional politics is not seen as an affective means for the relatively powerless. Isaac and Kelly conclude that the state, rather than being primarily concerned with the plight of the poor, is most interested in regulating the threat of the poor and legitimating the capitalist system.

Skocpol (1980) examines evidence from the New Deal to evaluate neo-Marxist theories of the state. She is critical of those theorists who believe political events are largely shaped by the farsighted capitalist ruling class. She does not believe that the neo-Marxists have seriously considered the impact of state structure and party organization upon society.

It is our contention that discussions of power at the national level need to focus on the key role of the state. What makes political sociology a major field of analysis is that the state is not simply one type of complex organization but a particular and peculiar one because of its monopolistic control of the legitimate organized means of violence. Unlike the functionalists, who tend to assume the state will represent the goals and values of the people, or the pluralists, who believe the people can make their will known through organized groups, we suggest that issues of autonomy of the state, who the state represents and doesn't represent, and how and why it represents certain elements need to be empirically investigated.

E.   Transnational Power

The study of multinational or transnational power and international power relations has been a recent phenomenon. In this literature one finds debates about the relative importance of each nation-state, the multinational corporation, and the position of nations in the world system. World-system theory has been proposed as an alternative to modernization theory, which had rejected the idea that structural factors could prevent economic progress and that the international context might be an obstacle to economic growth. The issue of class conflict was changed to international conflict (Chirot & Hall, 1982). According to world-systems theory, the capitalist world economy is divided into core, semiperiphery, and periphery nations. A country's position in the world economy vis-a-vis other nations shapes a wide variety of economic and political properties. Multinational corporations (MNCs) and nation-states are involved in a global power struggle over world resources, international alliances, and competing ideologies (Braungart & Braungart, 1979). While the headquarters of MNCs are usually located in developed countries, Wilczynski (1976) notes their rise in socialist countries and Kumar and McLeod (1981) discuss their growth in developing countries.

In *Dynamics of Global Crisis,* Amin, Arrighi, Frank, and Wallerstein (1982) discuss the origins and possible outcomes of the crisis in the world. All the authors agree that the crisis is rooted in systemic problems. Three of the authors believe the crisis is part of a transition from a capitalist economy to a socialist mode of production. Frank, on the other hand, believes the crisis serves as a means to reconstruct global accumulation.

There are four broad frameworks that consider the issue of who has power (see Bergsten, Horst, & Moran, 1978; Kumar, 1979; Kourvetaris & Dobratz, 1980b for greater detail). Two of the frameworks see the multinationals as junior partners with the home nation states. The *neoimperialist* framework suggests the capitalist class plays the dominant role while the *neomercantilist* emphasizes the home nation-state. The other two frameworks see the MNC as an important independent source of power. According to the *sovereignty-at-bay* (Vernon, 1971, 1977) or *liberal diffusionist interpretation* (Kumar, 1979), the MNCs work to the benefit of both the home and host countries. In strong opposition to this is the *Global Reach* or "*dependencia*" perspective which maintains that MNCs dominate, but they do so at the expense of the nation states.

Barnet (1980) examines the historical changes in world power, including the rise of MNCs, the increased dependence on important raw materials, and higher military expenditures. He advocates democratically planned public control of resources because "Whoever controls the world resources controls the world in a way mere occupation of territory cannot match" (Barnet, 1980).

Hawley and Noble (1982) argue that the internationalization of capital has resulted in the development of the transnational corporation (TNC) which has strongly influenced the ability of the nation-state to manage domestic economies. Nation-states have found it difficult to control TNCs and domestic economies because the TNCs are global and are diversified across industrial sectors creating an internal market. Prior to the 1970s the international system had been ordered around the hegemony of the United States. Since then there has been a process of disordering. State managers may be starting to consider the interests of the state as separate from the interests of capital. TNCs are caught in the contradiction between the dependency of transnational capital on its state (TNCs rely on one state and cooperate with it vis-a-vis other TNCs and other states) and its desire to be free of control from the state. According to Hawley and Noble (1982) TNCs do not seem to be a cohesive force that is able to stabilize the international system.

In their case study of the Trilateral Commission (TC), Kowalewski and Leitko (1983) examine the relationship between TNCs and intergovernmental organizations. They test three different hypotheses and find support for establishmentism which suggests that those corporations that dominate the international and national economic scenes will translate their power into the political realm as well. There appears to be a transnationalized "old-boy network" which engages in global political management in order to prevent harmful economic competition in the world market. The TC plays an important role in integrating the global market for the powerful TNCs. The smaller more dependent corporations are, however, left in a more competitive free-market situation. A global elite alliance has been created and dominated by the superelite of the world's elites.

Kumar (1980) and Sklar (1980) also discuss the impact of the transnational corporation on the world. Sklar (1980) shows how the upper class, through its control of global corporations, shapes national policy. She stresses the negative socioeconomic effects of transnational trilateralism on people in developing countries and advanced capitalist countries. Kumar (1980) argues that the effects of transnational enterprises on Third World countries are mixed but have often resulted in growing economic inequalities and consumption patterns of questionable social utility. The power of the TNCs is quite concentrated with fewer than 200 TNCs controlling half of the total direct foreign investment in the world.

Using data on the relationship of Latin America to the U.S. from 1960 to 1972, Szymanski (1976) tests two competing Marxist theories of dependency and recommends a synthesis of the two. Foreign capital seems to produce industrialization in the less developed countries, although not as rapidly as for core countries. Somewhat similarly, Delacroix and Ragin (1981) find that the negative effects of dependency on development are present only in the advanced periphery.

Diamond (1979) criticizes dependency theory for its lack of awareness of the substantial variation across relationships (e.g., between MNCs and host countries) and supports the idea of the "continuing preeminent importance of the nation." Braungart and Braungart (1981) also stress the role of nation states and nationalism as important forces in global development and power.

Several studies provide empirical cross-national support for the world-systems approach (Chase-Dunn, 1975; Rubinson, 1976; Thomas, Ramirez, Meyer, & Gobalet, 1979; Portes, 1979; & Snyder & Kick, 1979). Snyder and Kick (1979) combine the world-systems framework with block-model analysis, an empirically grounded theory of social structure. The block-model of the world system is based on four types of international networks: diplomatic relations, conjoint treaty memberships, trade flows, and military interventions. It provides strong support for the advantage of being located in the core. Kick (1983) also finds support for the world-systems framework with cross-national data on internal mass political and transnational military conflicts. Countries' structural positions in the world system are related to military intervention–internal war linkages. Using advanced statistical techniques (a polynominal control for development), Nolan (1983) finds a relationship between income inequality and position in the world system.

However, other studies (Delacroix, 1977; Delacroix & Ragin, 1978; Braungart and Braungart, 1979, 1980; and Hannan and Carroll, 1981) do not consistently support the world-system/dependency arguments. Delacroix (1977), for example, reports the limited or inclusive effect of a world-system variable (the extent of specialization in the export of raw materials) and the greater influences of internal processes on economic growth.

Thus research on world systems, multinationals, and nation-states show inconsistent and sometimes contradictory support for the various frameworks proposed. We may need to more carefully develop measurements that are consistent with the theory, and at other times we may need to specify the theory in greater detail. Additional comparative studies of countries within the core or within the semiperiphery as well as studies of countries in different world positions may help advance our knowledge. Braungart (1978a, p. 130) suggests that we need to study multinational elite structures and how they evolve out of the traditional forms of community power. This would include analysis of the decision-making process that influences corporate policy. We want to be able to explain under what conditions the nation's position in the world system is most important in explaining phenomena and under what conditions the nation state itself or the MNC has the greatest explanatory power. It is essential that the explanations consider both the possibilities of change and the dynamics of the relationships.

IV. POLITICAL PARTICIPATION

In the last two decades we have witnessed a tremendous rise and awareness of citizen participation in all aspects of domestic and international politics. The literature on political participation in both conceptualization and practice is extensive. The issues of political participation or nonparticipation reached prominence in Europe with the advent of liberal democracy which gave way to the extension of suffrage and ideally brought the masses of people into the political process. Citizens participation was seen by many as a form of sharing or influence in the exercise of political power.

Theoretically, every citizen has the right to participate in and influence the political process and share in the exercise of political power. In reality, however, there is an unequal degree of political participation and influence. While participation plays an important role in modern democratic polities, in more authoritarian regimes citizen participation is either limited or nonexistent. Alford and Friedland (1975) believe that participation without power is more characteristic of the poor and the working classes, while power with or without participation is characteristic of the rich and upper classes. For many, participation is seen as a civic duty and good citizenship. It varies, however, according to one's sociodemographic, economic, psychohistoric, situational, and social psychological perception of politics.

In earlier studies, the focus on political participation was on *psephology* or the scientific study of electoral behavior. Studies of participation became studies of conventional electoral politics. However, since the 1960s the rise of political sociology has contributed not only to the study of conventional but unconventional forms of political participation as well.

A number of scholars (Milbrath & Goel, 1977, p. 2; Verba & Nie, 1972, p. 2) define political participation as "all those activities by private citizens that seek to influence or to support the government and politics including the selection of governmental personnel and/or actions they take." Booth and Seligson (1978) define it in terms of "behavior influencing the distribution of public goods." Verba and Pye (1978) list four empirical indicators of participation: (a) actions, not attitudes or feelings; (b) voluntary not coercive activities; (c) activities for the selection of the rulers and the making of public policies; and (d) efforts to oppose the policies of government as a matter of right not privilege. Dahl (1971), on the other hand, lists eight requisites of political participation: freedom to join and form organizations; (b) freedom of expression; (c) right to vote; (d) eligibility for public office; (e) right for political leaders to compete for support; (f) access to alternative sources of information; (g) free and fair elections; and (h) institutions that tie public policies to voters and other expressions of preferences.

For the purpose of this review, we will be concerned with four basic questions of conventional politics:

1. Who participates or the social correlates of politics?
2. How do we learn our political attitudes?
3. What are some changes and trends in American electoral politics?
4. What are the conditions for a viable democracy?

A. Who Participates in Politics

The social basis of political participation is the most researched area in political sociology. In this section we will examine the following socio-demographic correlates of conventional electoral politics: age, sex, and generation; SES and class; and ethnicity and race.

1. Age, Sex, and Generation.   Middle-aged men are more active in voluntary associations, labor unions, political parties, and pressure groups than women, young men, and old men (Asher, 1976; Bone & Ranney, 1976; Ladd & Hadley, 1973, 1975; Milbrath & Goel, 1977; Braungart, 1981). Although women didn't participate in politics as much as men, they now have similar participation rates to those of white men except in the Deep South (Pomper 1975; Braungart 1978b, p. 269). Aging produces a net shift away from the Democratic Party. In the 1980 election the young split evenly between Reagan and Carter. Overall their political identification is shifting toward the Republicans (Clymer & Frankovic, 1981, p. 44).

2. SES and Class.   Surveys of socioeconomic class in many countries show the higher the SES the greater is the tendency to participate in politics and to vote for the more conservative party. A number of researchers have attempted to explain various types of political participation. Knoke (1979), for example, has found that education, occupation, and age are the main influences on social problem liberalism. Income and race have the main effects on economic conservatism. Race, age, and education are the main influence on racial policy preferences. Higher income leads to greater economic conservatism, while higher education fosters liberalism in social issues (Knoke, 1979; Weiner & Eckland, 1979).

Several authors have suggested that in the last quarter of the century there has been a steady decline in class politics (Ladd & Hadley, 1975; Abramson, 1978; Pomper, 1975). Ladd and Hadley (1975), for example, think the decline in class voting is due to the "embourgeoisement" of the American society and that the working class whites no longer vote as a politically conscious class. In the United States, class voting rose in 1976 but fell in 1980. Republican victories are associated with declines in class voting. Lipset (1981) argues that the decline in class voting is also true among other advanced industrial countries as well. While Lipset believes that the politics of postindustrial society is increasingly concerned with noneconomic issues, Reaganomics is less concerned with noneconomic or social issues.

In spite of the class decline, there is still a moderate relationship between political attitudes and social class (Verba & Nie, 1972; Nie, Verba, & Petrocik, 1979; Knoke, 1976; Lipset, 1981; Curtis & Jackson, 1977). While the more privileged whites supported Reagan in the 1980 election, the less privileged and minorities supported Carter. Pomper (1975) found that class voting is greater among persons with consistent subjective and objective class identification. There is now class polarization in the South. Perceptions on parties' positions on class relevant issues are strongly related to voting choice (independent of social class). An emerging voter alliance of highest and lowest education and occupational status within the Democratic party is in the offing.

While many studies use measures of status or prestige instead of economic class or occupation, Vanneman and Pampel (1977) find that the manual-nonmanual labor dichotomy predicts political attitudes better than the traditional measures of prestige. Robinson and Kelly (1979) develop indicators based on the ideas of Marx and Dahrendorf. They find these indicators help predict political attitudes beyond the traditional Duncan and Blau indicators. They conclude there is a significant but not dramatic link between class and political attitudes.

3. Ethnicity and Race. Ethnoreligious and racial background have been considered meaningful predictors of political participation in the United States. Jewish-Americans are slightly more active in politics than Catholics who in turn are slightly more active than Protestants (Braungart, 1981; Knoke, 1976). Overall, ethnic and racial group members are more likely to vote for the Democratic than the Republican party. Protestants are more Republican than they used to be and Catholics less Democratic (Clymer & Frankovic, 1981). Knoke (1976) finds that religion tends to have a stronger effect than SES on party identification. Frequent church attendance increases the propensity of Protestants to support Republicans and Catholics to support Democrats (Knoke, 1976).

Pomper (1975) suggests that racial differences in political participation have largely disappeared. However, Kuo (1977), using national data over time, finds whites are still more likely than blacks to register and vote. A broad racial division between blacks and whites has developed regarding most political attitudes (partisanship, vote, issues, candidate evaluations).

While, traditionally, Jews have been described as liberal, the recent developments in Israel, the Lebanese invasion by Israeli forces, and the massacre of Palestinians have divided American Jews. The issue of ethnoreligious identity seems to have precedence over liberalism. Blacks, traditionally liberal, have become even more liberal due to ethnic consciousness, community and racial interests, and Reaganomics, while Catholics have become less liberal, and lower and middle status Protestants more conservative. Black-

Americans, especially in the South, overwhelmingly voted for Carter. The mayoral victory of Washington in Chicago politics has given Blacks greater political confidence as they attempt to move into the spotlight of national politics. For example, a number of black leaders have endorsed Jesse Jackson as a president *or* have delayed the endorsement of any democratic candidate. Guterbock and London (1983) have tested the ethnic community hypothesis along Marxist, class, and conflict perspectives and have found that ethnic consciousness and class/radical interests increase political activities.

White upper-class Protestants outside of the South have become divided (Nie et al., 1979). In the 1970s, higher-status Northern white Protestants more often identified with the Democratic Party than they did in the 1950s. Those identifying with the Republican Party are tending to be less upper status (Nie, Verba, & Petrocik, 1976, p. 240).

B.   How Do We Learn Our Political Attitudes?

Political socialization is an important aspect of political culture and electoral politics. We learn our political attitudes and values the same way we learn to choose our friends. Orum, Cohen, Grasmuck, and Orum (1974) note three major perspectives of political socialization: the *political socialization,* the *situational,* and the *structural* approaches. The political socialization thesis emphasizes the formation of political attitudes in early childhood. Early studies stressed the political socialization model of children's attitudes and supported high rates of transmission of political culture through the family, especially the father. Children looked at Presidents and policemen as benevolent and idealized extensions of father figures. Children's early political images related to authority, leadership, and government were positive, although not uniform. There seemed to be a high degree of agreement between parents' and children's political attitudes. Childhood views of political authority were viewed as an important source of stability in the American political system.

More recent studies suggest less idealization of authority now than a decade earlier (Sears, 1975). Other literature shows mothers playing an important role in political socialization (Jennings & Niemi, 1974). The similarity between parents and their children is not as strong for general political orientations as it is for partisanship and voting (Niemi & Sobieszek, 1977). Niemi and Sobieszek (1977, p. 218) suggest that children may be reflections of their parents but are often pale reflections. While the literature on schools is inconclusive, Niemi and Sobieszek (1977) support the idea that the influence of college is greater in political socialization than that of high school (except for the peer group influence) and primary schools.

The other two models of political socialization do not stress early socialization but rather argue that political socialization is a life-long process in which the individual internalizes the attitudes, values, norms, and stereotypes of the community and culture he belongs to. The emphasis has shifted to the adult life span, life cycle, and generalizational effects and to events and the environment as major sources of situational and structural processes of political socialization. More recently, the socialization theory has been characterized by two major orientations (Wentworth, 1980). One is known as "conformity," a more functionalist view of an oversocialized individual in which the socialization process was looked upon as a passive process of internalization of cultural, social, and political norms. Socialization was synonymous with the role learning process through internalization. The second framework is called "creativity," an interactionist view of undersocialized individuals in which the human aspects of the individual are important. It is more psychological than sociological.

C.   Electoral Politics: Trends and Changes

Recently a number of scholarly books and articles on electoral politics (Nie et al., 1979; Niemi & Weisberg, 1976; Schlozman & Verba, 1979; Hart, Breglio, Penn, & Tarrance, 1980; Janowitz, 1978; Knoke, 1976; Converse, 1976; J. Wright, 1976; Guterbock, 1980; Lipset, 1979; Tufte, 1978; Ladd, 1978, 1980a; Verba, Nie, & Kim, 1978; Clymer & Frankovic, 1981) examine the changing character of electoral politics in the United States.[10] More recently, Ladd (1982) contends that for the last 15 years there is a gradual decline of political parties and a decline of public confidence in political parties, congress, courts, business, religion, and education. Parties in particular have lost the ability to compete, represent, and organize. Since space is limited, we will group some of these works by certain themes or major concepts.

Most of these studies deal with the decline of party identification, political participation, the changing American voter, the decline in political trust, the importance of issue voting, partisan realignment or dealignment, and societal change and politics in general. More specifically, we will identify six major trends and changes in American electoral politics.

1.   There has been a *decline in partisanship* and a rise in the *importance of mass media* in electoral politics (Nie et al., 1976, 1979; Ladd, 1978, 1980b; Hart et al., 1980; Guterbock, 1980; Budge, Crewe, & Farlie, 1976; Converse, 1976; Knoke, 1976; Hill & Luttbeg, 1983). Abramson and Aldrich (1982) assess the decline of electoral participation and show how political attitudes relate to the decline. Their main concern is with the formation of political attitudes and how these attitudes are formed and changed through presidential elections. They show the attitude formation of party identification, political efficacy, and government responsiveness.

---

[10] See especially a survey essay on "Changing Electoral Politics in America," by R. Braungart (1978b), who reviews about a dozen or so new books on American electoral politics.

2. *Realignment versus dealignment.* A number of scholars (Converse, 1976; Wright, 1976; Knoke, 1976; Clymer & Frankovic, 1981; Scannon & Wattenberg, 1980) have suggested a process of realignment, while others (Ladd, 1980b; Niemi & Weisberg, 1976; Norpoth & Rusk, 1982) see a trend of dealignment. Knoke (1976) lists three factors as evidence for realignment—the growth of independents, increase in split ticket voting, and weaker impact of party identification on congressional elections. Norpoth and Rusk (1982) offer four reasons for the partisan dealignment in the American electorate since 1964. They include the changing age composition of the electorate, the entry of new voters into the electorate, the party desertion of voters, and the suppression of age gains in partisanship.

3. *Emerging coalitions of the electorate.* The basic coalitions which made up the basis of support for each party have changed. The Democratic Party is more black, has more upper and upper middle class, and is less Southern than previously. The Republican Party tends to be more Southern, less black, less Catholic, less well-to-do and Protestant than it was in the 1950s (Nie et al., 1979).

4. There is a rise in issue voting and *issue consistency*, conditions which originally were present during the New Deal, declined in the 1950s, and reemerged in the 1960s. More voters are taking consistent left or right positions on different types of issues (social welfare, school integration, size of government, foreign policy, and the like). There is an increase in single *issue politics,* especially by what is called the new moral majority, which is supported by fundamentalist and evangelical religious groups. Many of these groups have allied with the traditional radical right to defeat liberal politicians.

5. *Ideological politics and political polarization.* New voters tend to be more utopian and idealistic than previous generations of voters, which results in ideological and polarized politics (Niemi & Weisberg, 1976; Braungart, 1978b). They tend to be more educated and less concerned with the accommodationist and partisan politics.

6. The country is moving toward a more conservative mood, although a number of commentators believe that the American electorate voted for Reagan in the 1980 election because they wanted change and because the Democratic Party was unable to stop inflation. At the same time the election of Reagan has created a climate for a revolt against modernity[11] and the rise of reactionary politics including the rise of Ku Klux Klan, moral religious advocates, the Aryan Nations, and other far-right political groups. Even a

---

[11] See, for example, Horowitz "The New Fundamentalism," Lipset "Failures of Extremism," Whalen "America's Identity Crisis," and Berger "Secular Branches, Religious Roots," in *Society,* Vol. 20, No. 1 (Nov./Dec), 1982, pp. 40–66.

number of professed liberals of the 1960s and early 1970s have become neoconservatives (see, e.g., Steinfels, 1979).

D. Prospects of Democracy

Modern democratic systems grew out of constitutional government and electoral politics. Lipset (1960, 1981) identifies six conditions that facilitate democracy: open class system, economic wealth, equalitarian value system, capitalist economy, literacy, and high participation in voluntary organizations. Shils has singled out three qualities of political democracy — civilian rule, representative institutions, and public liberties (quoted in Wasburn, 1982, p. 271). Braungart (1981) lists seven characteristics of democratic political systems: representative rule, universal suffrage, political participation, a high degree of individual autonomy, equal rights and privileges, a diffuse power base, and temporary control of constitutional government through elections.

If we look at the United Nations roster of 150 plus nations and apply the aforementioned characteristics, one is struck by the fact that only a handful of these nations can be genuinely characterized as democratic political systems. Indeed, the oldest and the most common form of government the world over is an authoritarian political regime in which power and authority are concentrated in the hands of the few. Frequently, military elites alone or in collaboration with civilian bureaucratic elites have become the leaders of authoritarian civil–military regimes in most countries of the Third World.

Two of the perennial problems of modern democratic political systems are the issues of stability and inequality, which were main themes in Lipset's *Political Man*. Linz and Stepan (1979) propose a typology that links efficacy, effectiveness, legitimacy, and stability/performance of political regimes. Both examine the causes of the breakdown of democratic regimes in Europe (Mediterranean countries) and Latin America. They compare the instability of democracy in various countries by means of the typology based on the concepts of legitimacy, efficacy, and effectiveness. Ineffectiveness weakens authority and legitimacy. The two party system contributes to stability but does not prevent breakdown. Of 18 countries with extreme multiparty systems, 7 experienced breakdown. The process of breakdown means the end of democracy. We might note that in the last several years we have seen the breakdown of dictatorships in Spain, Greece, and Portugal and the emergence of socialist political parties. All 3 countries are in the semiperiphery of the world capitalist system.

J. Wright (1976) explores the relationship between democracy and pluralism and argues the consensus model is not necessary to explain democratic stability. Wright develops a typology of three categories of citizens — the *consent* (about one-half of the population), the *assent* (those who go along with the system but see it as irrelevant to their immediate needs — close to one-half of the population), and the *dissent* (a very inconsequential group because of difficulties of mobilizing support). Olsen (1982), using data from Sweden and the United States, examines how it is possible to expand the democratic political process to maximize citizen's input in government policies. He examines the social content of political mobilization and participatory pluralism.

Tufte (1978) deals with the "political control of the economy." He attempts to develop a political theory of economic policy and shows how citizens of democratic countries can affect economic outcomes through the political process. The author makes four major points: (a) politicians believe that voters reward incumbents for prosperity and punish them for recession; (b) office holders act on this belief by increasing citizen's incomes just prior to elections; (c) Democrats and Republicans differ ideologically so that voters have a meaningful choice between policies, and (d) people vote largely on the basis of economic conditions. In other words, politicians respond to voters desires and voters respond to political control of the economy. Tufte underestimates the importance of the many agencies of the federal government, agencies whose actions can enhance the reelection chances of incumbents, and he overemphasizes the role of economic variables.

Parenti (1983) maintains that American democracy serves the interests of the privileged few. Parties, elections, and the right to speak are ineffective means or measures to check corporate wealth. The laws advance the interests of the haves at the expense of the have-nots. The author believes "democracy for the few" is a reflection of how the resources of power are distributed within the society. Parenti makes a plea for a humane democratic socialism in which the undemocratic features of a state-supported capitalism must be changed. He argues that people favor change but do not believe it is possible. However, objective conditions in the Third World and the recent failures of capitalist society are in the long run unfavorable indicators for capitalism.

Books by Janowitz (1978) and Lipset (1979) have direct bearing on American politics, democracy, and societal change. Janowitz attempts to assess the deficiencies of society in the last half-century by advancing the social control perspective as perscriptions for the improvement of American society. Janowitz believes that in order to achieve self-regulation and social control we need first to learn how to control ourselves and understand sociodynamic principles. Janowitz's use of concepts of social organization and control may reflect his preoccupation with military and organizational sociology. He writes like a diagnostician, but his diagnosis might not provide for the appropriate treatment for society. One's perspective obviously shapes the diagnosis and prescription.

Lipset (1979) tries to predict the future of postindustrial American society. He notes that social scientists are rarely able to predict the future. According to him, abundance is believed to be a prerequisite for democracy. One might add here, however, that abundance does not necessarily lead to democracy; it may still result in an unequal distribution of wealth and power. He also believes that the lack of economic growth leads to class conflict or despotism and should be avoided. He argues that political and institutional deficiencies rather than environmental factors could limit growth. However, environmental factors should not be discounted, especially for poor countries.

V. SUMMARY AND CONCLUSION

We made an effort to review the field of political sociology in the last ten years or so. Due to space limitations, we focused on major theoretical frameworks, power, and conventional politics. We had to be selective and concentrated on major publications which in our judgement had important political sociological relevance. The concept of power is at the heart of political sociology. There is a need for more in depth longitudinal and comparative studies of power. Political power tends to be linked to interest groups, organizations, classes, and those who occupy certain key positions in society. Studies of the state should be tied to international stratification and power. The community, national, and transnational levels of power cannot be understood independently of each other. At present the neo-Marxist frameworks seem to be best able to integrate various levels of analysis.

While studies of conventional political participation implicitly draw on the pluralist and functionalist perspectives, most studies in this area tend to be atheoretical and thus contribute little to the development of theory. Conventional political theory assumes there should be equal political participation among various groups, but in reality there are differences in rates of participation and even greater differences in the ability to influence the actual decision-making process. This is, of course, one aspect of the larger problem of social equality. The trend seems to be to learn politics through the mass media which engages in impression management so that we tend to associate our images of politics with celebrity political elites. The substantive issues of power and politics, including how resources are distributed and who gains or loses may be deemphasized or lost.

A blurring of traditional boundaries between political science and political sociology and some shift from political sociology to political economy has occurred. There has also been a rise in the Marxist perspective in political sociology. The class/Marxist model should be incorporated at all levels of empirical and theoretical analyses. Additional theory construction is needed at both the macro and micro levels.

Political sociology should especially concentrate on middle-range theories of power and class structure, which are major explanatory concepts of the larger sociopolitical system. The field should not be a potpourri of sociology and political science, but rather it should be redirected toward more systematic and intersystemic analyses of fundamental political processes and issues. Its special focus should be on certain unit ideas (e.g., power, class, state, participation, resource mobilization, group conflict, consensus, inequality, and ideology) and the relationships among them and to the overall political system.

Political sociology should draw on the developments in other related areas of sociology as they impinge on politics. The intersecting of organizational studies with political sociology (particularly in the subareas of movements and community power) has been beneficial, although we should not ignore the enormous impact of political power and its dynamics as they affect the lives of the average citizen, the nation-state, and the world.

In addition to examining politics and economy, we more broadly suggest an integration of common concepts in stratification and political sociology. We need to study systems of stratification and their impact on politics and vice versa. We should ask the crucial question of how the nation's and the world's resources are and will be distributed. Also the study of the military should be part of political sociology, because the military helps legitimate the position of those who rule, and occasionally, it is itself the ruler. The study of the military, stratification and inequality, and politics should be considered the major areas of concern for political sociologists.

Political sociology should not only monitor what is happening in the world of politics, but it should also maintain a critical and humane posture. It should be value-explicit, concerned with the many, the welfare of society, and the world as a whole. People in power should be accountable to the citizens who elect them. We suggest an integrated, independent, critical approach to the study of society and politics.

REFERENCES

Abramson, P.R. Class voting in the 1976 presidential election. *Journal of Politics, 40,* 1066–1072.

Abramson, P.R., & Aldrich, J.H. (1982). The decline of electoral participation in America. *American Political Science Review, 76,* 502–521.

Alford, R. (1975). Paradigms of relations between state and society. In L. Lindberg, R. Alford, C. Crouch, & C. Offe (Eds.), *Stress and contradiction in modern capitalism,* Lexington: D.C. Heath.

Alford, R., & Friedland, R. (1975). Political participation and public policy. *Annual Review of Sociology, 1,* 429–479.

Amin, S., Arrighi, G., Frank, A.G., & Wallerstein, I. (1982). *Dynamics of global crisis.* New York: Monthly Review Press.

Anderson, P. (1974a). *Passages from antiquity to feudalism.* London: New Left Books.

Anderson, P. (1974b). Lineages of the absolutist state. London: New Left Books.

Antonio, J.R. (1983). The origin, development, and contemporary status of critical theory. *Sociological Quarterly, 24,* 325–351.

Asher, H. (1976). *Presidential elections and American politics.* Homewood, IL: Dorsey Press.

Barnet, R. (1980). *The lean years.* New York: Simon and Schuster.

Bendix, R., & Lipset, S.M. (1966). The field of political sociology. In Lewis Coser (Ed.), *Political sociology.* New York: Harper and Row.

Bergsten, C., Horst, T., & Moran, T. (1978). *American multinationals and American interests.* Washington, DC: Brookings Institution.

Bone, H., & Ranney, A. (1976). *Politics and voters* (4th edition). New York: McGraw Hill.

Booth, J.A., & Seligson, M. (Eds.). (1978). *Political participation in Latin America.* New York: Holmes and Meier.

Bottomore, T. (1979). *Political sociology.* New York: Harper and Row.

Braungart, R. (1974). Political sociology: a proposed agendum for theory construction. *Journal of Political and Military Sociology, 2,* 1-19.

Braungart, R. (1978a). MNCs: new dimensions in community power. *Sociological Symposium, 24,* 117-135.

Braungart, R. (1978b). Changing electoral politics in America. *Journal of Political and Military Sociology, 6,* 261-269.

Braungart, R. (1981). Political sociology: history and scope. In S. Long (Ed.), *Handbook of political behavior* (Vol. 3). New York: Plenum Press.

Braungart, R., & Braungart, M. (1979). Axes of world structure and conflict. *Humboldt Journal of Social Relations, 6,* 4-45.

Braungart, R., & Braungart, M. (1980). Multinational corporate expansion and nation-state development. In L. Kriesberg (Ed.), *Research in social movements, conflicts, and change* (Vol. 3). Greenwich, CT: JAI Press.

Braungart, R., & Braungart, M. (1981). Nation state development, multinational corporate growth and citizenship: a theoretical comparison. *Humboldt Journal of Social Relations, 8,* 48-79.

Budge, I., Crewe, I., & Farlie, D. (1976). *Party identification and beyond.* New York: John Wiley & Sons.

Burt, R. (1977). Power in a social typology. *Social Science Research, 6,* 1-38.

Chase-Dunn, C. (1975). The effects of international economic dependence on development and inequality. *American Sociological Review, 40,* 720-38.

Chirot, D. (1977). *Social changes in the 20th century.* New York: Harcourt, Brace, Jovanovich.

Chirot, D., & Hall, T.D. (1982). World-system theory. *Annual Review of Sociology, 8,* 81-106.

Clymer, A., & Frankovic, K. (1981). The realities of realignment. *Public Opinion, 4,* 42-47.

Converse, P. (1976). *The dynamics of party support.* Beverly Hills, CA: Sage.

Curtis, R., & Jackson, E. (1977). *Inequality in American communities.* New York: Academic Press.

Dahl, R.A. (1971). *Polyarchy: participation and opposition.* New Haven, CT: Yale University Press.

Dahl, R.A. (1982). *Dilemmas of pluralist democracy.* New Haven, CT: Yale University Press.

Dahl, R.A., & Lindblom, C. (1976). *Politics, economics, and welfare.* Chicago: University of Chicago Press.

Delacroix, J. (1977). The export of raw materials and economic growth. *American Sociological Review, 42,* 795-808.

Delacroix, J., & Ragin, C. (1978). Modernizing institutions, mobilization, and third world development. *American Journal of Sociology, 84,* 123-150.

Delacroix, J., & Ragin, C. (1981). Structural blockage. *American Journal of Sociology, 86,* 1311-1347.

Diamond, L. (1979). Power-dependence relations in the world system. In L. Kriesberg (Ed.), *Research in social movements conflicts and change,* (Vol 2.). Greenwich, CT: JAI Press.

Dobratz, B., & Kourvetaris, G. (1983). An analysis and assessment of political sociology. *Micropolitics,* 1983, *3,* 89-133.

Domhoff, G. (1978a). *The powers that be.* New York: Random House.

Domhoff, G. (1978b). *Who really rules?* Santa Monica, CA: Goodyear.

Domhoff, G. (Ed.). (1980). *Power structure research.* Beverly Hills, CA: Sage.

Domhoff, G.W. (1983). *Who rules America now? a view for the '80s.* Englewood Cliffs, NJ: Prentice-Hall.

Dye, T.R. (1979). *Who's running America? the Carter years* (2nd ed.). Englewood Cliffs, NJ: Prentice-Hall.

Dye, T.R. (1983). *Who's running America? the Reagan years* (3rd ed.). Englewood Cliffs, NJ: Prentice-Hall, Inc.

Effrat, A. (Ed.) (1972). *Perspectives in political sociology.* New York: Bobbs-Merrill.

Flacks, R., & Turkel, G. (1978). Radical sociology: the emergence of neo-Marxian perspectives in U.S. sociology. *Annual Review of Sociology, 4,* 193–238.

Frank, A. (1981). *Crisis: in the Third World.* New York: Holmes and Meier.

Gamson, W. (1975). *The strategy of social protest.* Homewood, IL: Dorsey Press.

Garner, R. (1977). *Social movements in America.* Chicago: Rand McNally.

Giddens, A. (1979). Review of *Class, crisis and the state. American Journal of Sociology, 85,* 442–444.

Gold, D., Lo, C., & Wright, E. (1975). Recent developments in Marxist theories of the capitalist state. *Monthly Review, 27,* (Part I) (Oct), 29–43, and (Part II) (Nov), 36–51.

Granovetter, M. (1978). Review of *Networks of collective action* by E. Laumann and F. Pappi. *American Journal of Sociology, 83,* 1538–1542.

Greer, E. (1979). *Big steel.* New York: Monthly Review Press.

Greer, S., & Orleans, P. (1964). Political Sociology. In R. Faris (Ed.), *Handbook of modern sociology.* Chicago: Rand McNally.

Grimes, M., Bonjean, C., Lyon, J., & Lineberry, R. (1976). Community structure and leadership arrangements. *American Sociological Review, 41,* 706–725.

Guterbock, T. (1980). The unchanging party system. *Contemporary Sociology, 9,* 657–659.

Guterbock, T., & London, B. (1983). Race, political orientation, and participation. *American Sociological Review, 48,* 439–453.

Halebsky, S. (1976). *Mass society and political conflict.* London: Cambridge Press.

Hall, P. (1981). Political sociology. In S. McNall & G.N. Howe (Eds.), *Current perspectives in social theory* (Vol. 2). Greenwich, CT: JAI Press.

Hamilton, R., & Wright, J. (1975). *New directions in political sociology.* Indianapolis, IN: Bobbs-Merrill.

Hannan, M., & Carroll, G. (1981). Dynamics of formal political structure and event history analysis. *American Sociological Review, 46,* 19–35.

Hart, P., Breglio, V., Penn, M., & Tarrance, L. (1980). The uncertain mood of the American electorate. *Public Opinion, 3,* 46–49.

Hawley, J.P., & Noble, C. (1982). Internationalization of capital and the limits of the interventionist state. *Journal of Political and Military Sociology, 10,* 103–120.

Hechter, M. (1977). Lineages of the capitalist state. *American Journal of Sociology, 82,* 1057–1074.

Hicks, A., Friedland, R., & Johnson, E. (1978). Class power and state policy. *American Sociological Review, 43,* 302–315.

Hill, D., & Luttbeg, N. (1983). *Trends in American electoral behavior* (2nd ed.). Itasca, IL: F.E. Peacock.

Hunter, F. (1980). *Community power succession: Atlanta's policy makers revisited.* Chapel Hill: University of North Carolina Press.

Isaac, L., & Kelly, W. (1981). Racial insurgency, the state, and welfare expansion. *American Journal of Sociology, 86,* 1348–1386.

Janowitz, M. (1977). Sociological perspective on Wallerstein. *American Journal of Sociology, 82,* 1090–1097.

Janowitz, M. (1978). *The last half century: societal changes in politics in America.* Chicago, IL: University of Chicago Press.

Jenkins, J.C. (1983). Resource mobilization theory and the study of social movements. *Annual Review of Sociology, 9,* 527–553.

Jennings, K.M., & Niemi, R.G. (1974). *The political character of adolescence: the influence of families and schools.* Princeton, NJ: Princeton University Press.

Jessop, B. (1982). *The capitalist state.* New York: New York University Press.

Kaplan, B. (Ed.). (1978). *Social change in the capitalist world economy.* Beverly Hills, CA: Sage Publications.

Katznelson, I. (1981). *City trenches: urban politics and the patterning of class in the U.S.* New York: Pantheon Books.

Kick, E.L. (1983). World-system properties and military intervention-internal war linkages. *Journal of Political and Military Sociology, 11,* 185–208.

Knoke, D. (1976). *Change and continuity in American politics.* Baltimore: Johns Hopkins University Press.

Knoke, D. (1979). Stratification and dimensions of American political orientation. *American Journal of Political Science, 23,* 772–791.

Knoke, D. (1981). Power structures. In S. Long (Ed.), *Handbook of political behavior,* (Vol. 3). New York: Plenum Press.

Kourvetaris, G.A., & Dobratz, B.A. (1980a). *Political sociology: readings in research and theory.* N. Brunswick, NJ: Transaction Books.

Kourvetaris, G.A., & Dobratz, B.A. (1980b). *Society and politics: an overview and reappraisal of political sociology.* Dubuque, IA: Kendall/Hunt.

Kourvetaris, G.A., & Dobratz, B.A. (1982). Political power and conventional political participation. *Annual Review of Sociology, 8,* 289–317.

Kowalewski, D., & Leitko, T.A. (1983). Transnational corporations and intergovernmental organizations: the trilateral commission case. *Journal of Political and Military Sociology, 11,* 93–107.

Kumar, K. (1979). Multinational corporation and transnational relations. *Journal of Political and Military Sociology, 7,* 291–304.

Kumar, K. (ed.), (1980). *Transnational enterprises: their impact on Third World societies and cultures.* Boulder: Westview Press.

Kumar, K., & M. McLeod (Eds.) (1981). *Multinationals from Developing Countries.* Lexington, MA: Heath.

Kuo, W. (1977). Black political participation. *Journal of Political and Military Sociology, 5,* 1–16.

Ladd, E. (1978). *Where have all the voters gone?* (1st ed.). New York: W.W. Norton.

Ladd, E. (1980a). A Rebuttal: realignment? no dealignment? yes. *Public Opinion, 3,* 13–20, 56.

Ladd, E. (1980b). Symposium. A confusing search for clarity. *Contemporary Sociology, 9,* 607–608.

Ladd, E. (1982). *Where have all the voters gone?* (2nd ed.). New York: W.W. Norton.

Ladd, E., & Hadley, C. (1973). *Political parties and political issues.* Beverly Hills, CA: Sage.

Ladd, E., & Hadley, C. (1975). *Transformations of the American party system.* New York: W.W. Norton.

Laumann, E.O., Galaskiewicz, J., & Marsden, P. (1978). Community structure as interorganizational linkages. *Annual Review of Sociology, 4,* 455–484.

Laumann, E., & Marsden, P. (1979). The analysis of oppositional structures in political elites. *American Sociological Review, 44,* 713–732.

Laumann, E., & Pappi, F. (1976). *Networks of collective action.* New York: Academic Press.

Lehman, E. (1977). *Political society: a macrosociology of politics.* New York: Columbia University Press.

Liebert, R., & Imershein, A. (1977). *Power paradigms and community research.* Beverly Hills, CA: Sage.

Lincoln, J. (1976). Power and mobilization in the urban community. *American Sociological Review, 41,* 1–15.

Linz, J., & Stepan, A. (1979). *The breakdown of democratic regimes.* Baltimore, MD: Johns Hopkins University Press.

Lipset, S.M. (1959). Political sociology. In R. Merton, L. Broom, & L. Cottrell, Jr. (Eds.), *Sociology Today.* New York: Harper and Row.

Lipset, S.M. (1960). *Political man: the social bases of politics.* Garden City: Doubleday.

Lipset, S.M. (Ed.). (1979). *The third century.* Stanford: Hoover Institution Press.

Lipset, S.M. (1981). *Political man* (expanded edition). Baltimore, MD: Johns Hopkins University Press.

Lo, C.Y.H. (1982). Countermovements and conservative movements in the contemporary U.S. *Annual Review of Sociology, 8,* 107–134.

Luckenbill, D. (1979). Power. *Symbolic interaction, 2,* 97–114.

Lukes, S. (1974). *Power.* Atlantic Highlands, NJ: Humanities Press.

Lyon, L., Felice, L., & Perryman, M. (1980). Community power and population: an empirical test of the growth machine model. *American Journal of Sociology, 86,* 1387–1400.

Manley, J.F. (1983). Neo-Pluralism: A class analysis of pluralism I and pluralism II. *American Political Science Review, 77,* 368–389.

Marger, M.M. (1981). *Elites and masses: an introduction to political sociology.* New York: D. Van Nostrand.

McCarthy, J., & Zald, M. (1977). Resource mobilization and social movements. *American Journal of Sociology, 82,* 1212–1241.

McNall, S. (1981). *Political economy.* Glenview, IL: Scott Foresman.

Milbrath, W., & Goel, M. (1977). *Political participation* (2nd ed.). Chicago: Rand McNally.

Miliband, R. (1977). *Marxism and politics.* London: Oxford University Press.

Mills, C.W. (1956). *The power elite.* New York: Oxford University Press.

Mintz, B., Freitag, P., Hendricks, C., & Schwartz, M. (1975). Problems of proof in elite research. *Social Problems, 23,* 314–324.

Mintz, B., & Schwartz, M. (1981). Interlocking directorates and interest group formation. *American Sociological Review, 46,* 851–869.

Moore, G. (1979). The Structure of the national elite network. *American Sociological Review, 44,* 673–692.

Nie, N., Verba, S., & Petrocik, J. (1976). *The changing American voter.* Cambridge, MA: Harvard University Press.

Nie, N., Verba, S., & Petrocik, J. (1979). *The changing American voter* (2nd ed.). Cambridge, MA: Harvard University Press.

Niemi, R., & Sobieszek, B. (1977). Political socialization. *Annual Review of Sociology, 3,* 209–233.

Niemi, R., & Weisberg, H. (1976). *Controversies in American voting behavior.* San Francisco: W.H. Freeman.

Nolan, P. (1983). Status in the world system, income inequality, and economic growth. *American Journal of Sociology, 89,* 410–419.

Norpoth, H., & Rusk, J.G. (1972). Partisan dealignment in the American electorate: itemizing the deductions since 1964. *American Political Science Review, 76,* 522–537.

Oberschall, A. (1978). Theories of social conflict. *Annual Review of Sociology, 4,* 291–315.

O'Connor, J. (1973). *The fiscal crisis of the state.* New York: St. Martin's Press.

Offe, C. (1975). The Theory of the Capitalist State and the Problem of Policy Formation. In L. Lindberg, R. Alford, C. Crouch, & C. Offe, (Eds.), *Stress and contradiction in modern capitalism.* Lexington: D.C. Heath.

Olsen, M. (1982). Linkages between socioeconomic modernization and national political development. *Journal of Political and Military Sociology, 10,* 41–69.

Orum, A. (1983). *Introduction to political sociology.* Englewood Cliffs: Prentice-Hall.

Orum, A., Cohen, R., Grasmuck, S., & Orum, Amy (1974). Sex, socialization and politics. *American Sociological Review, 39,* 197–209.

Parenti, M. (1983). *Democracy for the few* (4th ed.). New York: St. Martin's Press.

Piven, F., & Cloward, R. (1977). *Poor people's movements.* New York: Vintage Books.

Polsby, N. (1980). *Community power and political theory* (2nd ed.). New Haven: Yale University Press.

Pomper, G. (1975). *Voters' choice: varieties of American electoral behavior.* New York: Dodd, Mead.

Portes, A. (1979). Illegal immigration and the international system, lessons from recent Mexican immigrants to the U.S. *Social Problems, 26,* 425–438.

Poulantzas, N. (1973). *Political power and social classes.* London: NLB and S&W.

Ratcliff, R.E., & Pennick, P. (1983). Property tax appeals and the distribution of the tax burden: an analysis of a losing battle in the citizens' 'tax revolt'. *Journal of Political and Military Sociology, 2,* 69–91.

Robinson, R., & Kelly, J. (1979). Class as conceived by Marx and Dahrendorf. *American Sociological Review, 44,* 38–58.

Rubinson, R. (1976). The world-economy and the distribution of income within states. *American Sociological Review, 41,* 638–59.

Scannon, R., & Wattenberg, B. (1980). Is it the end of an era? *Public Opinion, 3,* 2–12.

Schlozman, K., & Verba, S. (1979). *Injury to insult.* Cambridge, MA: Harvard University Press.

Sears, D. (1975). Political Socialization. In F. Greenstein and N. Polsby (Eds.), *Handbook of political science (Vol. II): micropolitical theory.* Reading, MA: Addison-Wesley.

Simon, D.R., & Eitzen, D.S. (1982). *Elite deviance.* Boston: Allyn and Bacon.

Sklar, H. (Ed.), (1980). *The trilateral commission and elite planning for world management.* Boston: South End Press.

Skocpol, T. (1977). Wallerstein's world capitalist system. *American Journal of Sociology, 82,* 1075–1090.

Skocpol, T. (1979). *States and social revolutions.* New York: Cambridge University Press.

Skocpol, T. (1980). Political response to 'capitalist crisis:' Neo-Marxist theories of the state and the case of the New Deal. *Politics and Society, 10,* 155–201.

Snyder, D., & Kick, E. (1979). Structural position in the world system and economic growth, 1955–1970. *American Journal of Sociology, 84,* 1096–1126.

Steinfels, P. (1979). *The Neoconservatives.* New York: Simon and Schuster.

Szymanski, A. (1976). Dependence, exploitation and economic growth. *Journal of Political and Military Sociology, 4,* 53–65.

Szymanski, A. (1981). *The logic of imperialism.* New York: Praeger.

Tabb, W., & Sawers, L. (Eds.) (1978). *Marxism and metropolis.* New York: Oxford University Press.

Therborn, G. (1976). What does the ruling class do when it rules? *The Insurgent Sociologist, 6,* 3–16.

Therborn, G. (1978). *What does the ruling class do when it rules.* New York: Shocken Books.

Thirsk, J. (1977). Economic and social development on a European-world scale. *American Journal of Sociology, 82,* 1097–1102.

Thomas, G., Ramirez, F., Meyer, J., & Gobalet, J. (1979). Maintaining national boundaries in the world system. In J. Meyer & M. Hannan (Eds.), *National development and the world system.* Chicago: University of Chicago Press.

Tilly, C. (1978). *From mobilization to revolution.* Reading, MA: Addison-Wesley.

Tilly, C., Tilly, L., & Tilly, R. (1975). *The rebellious century 1830–1930.* Cambridge: Harvard University Press.

Trounstine, J., & Christensen, T. (1982). *Movers and shakers: the study of community power.* New York: St. Martin's Press.

Tufte, E. (1978). *Political control of the economy*. Princeton, NJ: Princeton University Press.

Useem, M. (1979). Social organization of the American business elite and participation of corporation directors in the governance of American institutions. *American Sociological Review, 44,* 553–572.

Vanneman, R., & Pampel, F. (1977). The American perception of class and status. *American Sociological Review, 42,* 422–437.

Verba, S., & Nie, N. (1972). *Participation in America*. New York: Harper and Row.

Verba, S., Nie, N., & Kim, J. (1978). *Participation and political equality*. New York: Cambridge University Press.

Verba, S., & Pye, L. (Eds.). (1978). *The citizens and politics*. Stamford, CT: Greylock.

Vernon, R. (1971). *Sovereignty at bay*. New York: Basic Books.

Vernon, R. (1977). *Storm over the multinationals*. Cambridge: Harvard University Press.

Wallerstein, I. (1974). *The modern world system*. New York: Academic Press.

Wallerstein, I. (1979). *The capitalist world economy manual*. New York: Cambridge University Press.

Walton, J. (1976). Community power and the retreat from politics: full circle after twenty years? *Social Problems, 23,* 292–303.

Walton, J. (1977). *Elites in economic development*. Austin, Texas: University of Texas Institute of Latin American Studies.

Warren, B. (1973). Imperialism and capitalist industrialization. *New Left Review, 8,* 3–44.

Wasburn, P. (1982). *Political sociology: approach, concepts, hypotheses*. Englewood Cliffs, NJ: Prentice-Hall.

Weiner, T., & Eckland, B. (1979). Education and political party. *American Journal of Sociology, 84,* 911–928.

Wentworth, W. (1980). *Context and understanding: an inquiry into socialization theory*. New York: Elsevier.

Whitt, J.A. (1979). Towards a class-dialectical model of power. *American Sociological Review, 44,* 81–100.

Whitt, J.A. (1980). Can capitalists organize themselves. In G.W. Domhoff (Ed.), *Power structure research*. Beverly Hills, CA: Sage.

Whitt, J.A. (1982). *Urban elites and mass transportation: the dialectics of power*. Princeton, NJ: Princeton University Press.

Wilczynski, J. (1976). *The multinationals and East–West relations*. Boulder: Westview Press.

Wilson, J. (1983). Corporatism and the professionalization of reform. *Journal of Political and Military Sociology, 11,* 53–68.

Wolfe, A. (1974). New Directions in the Marxist theory of politics. *Politics and Society, 4,* 131–159.

Wolfe, A. (1977). *The limits of legitimacy*. NY: Free Press.

Wright, E.O. (1978). *Class, crisis and the state*. New York: Schocken.

Wright, E.O. (1983). Capitalism's future. *Socialist Review, 13,* 77–126.

Wright, J. (1976). *Dissent of the Governed: alienation and democracy in America*. New York: Academic Press.

Wrong, D. (1979). *Power*. New York: Harper and Row.

Author Index

Subject Index